AF691911

International Political Economy

The book gathers together a set of lively, provocative essays by leading voices in International Political Economy to debate the evolution of the field, its current state and its future directions.

Prompted by recent commentaries on the existence of a 'transatlantic divide' in IPE between an 'American school' and a 'British school', the essays provide a wide-ranging discussion of whether it is useful to think of the field in these terms, what the 'American' and 'British' schools look like, what their achievements and shortcomings are, and what are the desirable future directions for IPE scholarship. The diverse responses to these questions reflect the ongoing vibrancy and diversity of the field of IPE, and open up an imaginative and engaging discussion about where we need to go from here.

Featuring contributions from the most influential scholars in the field from North America, Europe and Australia, this book is essential reading for anyone interested in the cutting edge debates in contemporary international political economy.

Nicola Phillips is Professor of Political Economy and Director of the Political Economy Institute at the University of Manchester, and editor-in-chief of the journal *New Political Economy* (Routledge). Her most recent books are *Development* (co-authored with Anthony Payne, Polity Press, 2010), *The Southern Cone Model: The Political Economy of Regional Capitalist Development in Latin America* (Routledge, 2004) and, as editor, *Globalizing International Political Economy* (Palgrave, 2005).

Catherine E. Weaver is Associate Professor at the LBJ School of Public Affairs and Distinguished Scholar and Research Coordinator at the Robert S. Strauss Center for International Security and Law at the University of Texas at Austin. She is co-editor of the journal *Review of International Political Economy* (Routledge). Her most recent book is *Hypocrisy Trap: The World Bank and the Poverty of Reform* (Princeton University Press, 2008).

'This book captures the best contributions to the absorbing conversation that IPE has had with itself over the past few years about its origins, achievements and identity. It is essential reading for everybody interested in this important and growing part of the intellectual landscape of the contemporary social sciences.'

Anthony Payne, *University of Sheffield, UK*

'This is an excellent book, edited by Phillips and Weaver, two of the field's rising stars and increasingly prominent voices of measured, productive debate. Phillips and Weaver have framed the controversy over the transatlantic divide in IPE with a smart, thoughtful introduction and brought together an outstanding collection of essays on the state of IPE. The editors have produced a volume of required reading for the next several generations of students and scholars.'

Rawi Abdelal, *Harvard Business School, USA*

'What is the current state of the study of international political economy? Why are scholars so divided in their views on the appropriate methods to study IPE? With papers from many of the leading scholars in the field, this important volume addresses these questions and suggests how the study of IPE should best be pursued in the future.'

John Ravenhill, *The Australian National University, Australia*

'This collection will be an invaluable resource for those scholars and students interested in understanding the recent debates around geographical and theoretical divides in IPE – as well as for those who seek to question them.'

Jacqueline Best, *University of Ottawa, Canada*

GEORGE MASON UNIVERSITY
UNIVERSITY LIBRARIES

International Political Economy

Debating the past, present and future

Edited by Nicola Phillips and Catherine E. Weaver

Routledge
Taylor & Francis Group
LONDON AND NEW YORK

First published 2011
by Routledge
2 Park Square, Milton Park, Abingdon, Oxon OX14 4RN

Simultaneously published in the USA and Canada
by Routledge
270 Madison Avenue, New York, NY 10016

Routledge is an imprint of the Taylor & Francis Group, an informa business

© 2011 Selection and editorial matter, Nicola Phillips and Catherine E. Weaver; individual chapters, the contributors

Typeset in Times by Wearset Ltd, Boldon, Tyne and Wear
Printed and bound in Great Britain by TJ International Ltd, Padstow, Cornwall

All rights reserved. No part of this book may be reprinted or reproduced or utilized in any form or by any electronic, mechanical, or other means, now known or hereafter invented, including photocopying and recording, or in any information storage or retrieval system, without permission in writing from the publishers.

British Library Cataloguing in Publication Data
A catalogue record for this book is available from the British Library

Library of Congress Cataloging in Publication Data
International political economy : debating the past, present, and future / edited by Nicola Phillips and Catherine E. Weaver.
p. cm.
1. International economic relations. 2. Economics–History.
I. Phillips, Nicola. II. Weaver, Catherine, 1971–
HF1359.I584 2010
337–dc22 2010012337

ISBN: 978-0-415-78056-8 (hbk)
ISBN: 978-0-415-78057-5 (pbk)
ISBN: 978-0-203-84250-8 (ebk)

Contents

HF
1359
.I584
2011

Notes on contributors

Mark Blyth is a Professor of International Political Economy and Faculty Fellow at the Watson Institute, Brown University, USA.

Ian Bruff is a Lecturer in International Political Economy at the University of Manchester, United Kingdom.

Benjamin J. Cohen is Louis G. Lancaster Professor of International Political Economy at the University of California, Santa Barbara, USA.

Robert Cox is Professor Emeritus of Political Science at York University, Canada.

Henry Farrell is Associate Professor of Political Science and International Affairs at George Washington University, USA.

Martha Finnemore is Professor of Political Science at International Affairs at George Washington University, USA.

Randall D. Germain is Professor of Political Science at Carleton University, Canada.

Eric Helleiner is a Professor and holds the CIGI Chair in International Governance at the University of Waterloo, Canada.

Helge Hveem is a Professor in the Department of Political Science, University of Oslo, Norway.

Peter J. Katzenstein is the Walter S. Carpenter, Jr. Professor of International Studies at Cornell University, USA.

Robert O. Keohane is Professor of International Affairs at the Woodrow Wilson School, Princeton University, USA.

Jonathan Kirshner is a Professor in the Department of Government at Cornell University, USA.

David A. Lake is the Jeri-Ann and Gary E. Jacobs Professor of Social Sciences and Distinguished Professor of Political Science at the University of California, San Diego, USA.

Kathleen R. McNamara is an Associate Professor of Government and Foreign Service at Georgetown University, USA.

Daniel Maliniak is a doctoral student in the Department of Political Science at the University of California, San Diego, USA.

Layna Mosley is an Associate Professor in the Department of Political Science, University of North Carolina at Chapel Hill, USA.

Craig N. Murphy is M. Margaret Ball Professor of International Relations at Wellesley College, USA.

Ronen Palan is a Professor of International Political Economy at the University of Birmingham, United Kingdom.

Louis W. Pauly is Professor of Political Science and Director of the Centre for International Studies, University of Toronto, Canada.

Nicola Phillips is Professor of Political Economy and Director of the Political Economy Institute at the University of Manchester, United Kingdom.

Magnus Ryner is Professor in International Relations at Oxford Brookes University, United Kingdom.

J.C. Sharman is a Professor at the Centre for Governance and Public Policy, Griffith University, Australia.

David A. Singer is an Associate Professor of Political Science at the Massachusetts Institute of Technology (MIT), USA.

Michael J. Tierney is Weingartner Associate Professor of Government and Director of the Institute for the Theory and Practice of International Relations at the College of William and Mary, USA.

Geoffrey R.D. Underhill holds the Chair of International Governance at the University of Amsterdam, Netherlands.

Bastiaan van Apeldoorn is a Reader in International Relations at the University of Amsterdam, Netherlands.

Robert Wade is a Professor of Political Economy and Development at the London School of Economics and Political Science, United Kingdom.

Catherine E. Weaver is Associate Professor at the Lyndon B. Johnson School of Public Affairs, University of Texas at Austin, USA.

Introduction

Debating the divide – reflections on the past, present and future of international political economy

Nicola Phillips and Catherine E. Weaver

Intellectual reflection can be a sordid endeavor. In the past few years, many scholars of international political economy (IPE) have engrossed themselves in debate over the state of our discipline. At heart of this discussion is a concern that our field of inquiry, once depicted by Susan Strange (1984: ix) as an 'open range', is starting to splinter. Fences have been erected, flags have been planted, and distinct approaches or schools of thought labeled and championed. Worse yet, many scholars fear a growing dialogue of the deaf between silo communities of IPE who doggedly pursue chosen paradigms, epistemologies, and methodologies with little regard to alternative world views. Rather than the end of history, we have realized a clash of intellectual civilizations (Murphy and Nelson 2001; Dickens 2006; Blyth 2009b). Or, then again, perhaps we are imagining communities and constructing divides in our minds that do not exist in reality.

We thus begin this book with a note of caution. Reflecting on academic disciplines can easily devolve into narcissistic distractions or political stock-taking exercises. Worse yet, such reflection can be misinterpreted as a malicious effort by some to tally the score and declare a victor with respect to who has the 'right' or 'superior' approach to inquiry in the IPE discipline. We must not fall prey to such paranoia. As Albert Camus wrote, an intellectual is someone whose mind watches itself. We are inherently wired as an intellectual community to be introspective and self-critical. As much as we hate the poking, prodding, and occasional drawing of blood, we also know that a thorough diagnosis is the best way to determine the health of the discipline and to make sure we are on the most productive path to the accumulation of knowledge. So what has happened recently that makes us pause and turn our focus inwards? Why do we think that we have perhaps gone astray?

If we were to try to pinpoint the catalyst for the current wave of self-contemplation, it would be Benjamin Cohen's recent description of the transatlantic divide in IPE (Cohen 2007, 2008a). In Cohen's (2008) intellectual history, IPE at its founding nearly 40 years ago was a truly pluralist endeavor, initiated by a dynamic group of young scholars, driven by an unfettered curiosity about the nature and dynamics of the world economy, and willing to use whatever disciplinary and methodological tools proved most adept at asking and answering the big questions (Keohane 2009). Today, he argues, IPE – at least in the Anglo-American world – looks very different.

Cohen argues that IPE has split along two tracks: an 'American' school, bound by a tripartite allegiance to liberalism, positivism, and quantitative methods, and a 'British' school that is more epistemologically agnostic and drawn to normative or critical lines of inquiry. Cohen's intent in constructing these schools of thought was benign. He meant these to be parsimonious devices to describe the world of IPE and to frame his intellectual history. Yet, much to his surprise, scholars reacted quickly with varying degrees of shock, assent, and ire. To many, Cohen had drawn a proverbial line in the sand. Some took issue with his categorization and labels. Others strongly agreed with his assessment, and sought to explain why we had reached this disjuncture. A nerve had been struck (Cohen 2009: 136).

This book seeks first to capture and reflect upon the lively debate in IPE that has elicited such an emotional response over the past several years. Our goal is to sum up some of the commentary that has been offered on the state of the discipline and the perceived transatlantic divide. Indeed, the discussions have been replete with evocative language: the Magnificent Seven, a knife's sharp edge, monocultures, torn lovers, split brains, manifest destinies, Moog synthesizers.... How do such creative and cathartic images come together to describe IPE today? How are they used to explain how we have reached this state of affairs, and what the consequences are for the future of IPE?

Our second objective in this book is to look forward. We propose ways in which we might mend the transatlantic divide or, at a minimum, get past the debate to pursue research agendas that capture the diversity of intellectual questions and approaches in the field. Quite appropriately, this is coordinated by editors from two IPE journals, one of which is managed in the United States (*Review of International Political Economy* (*RIPE*)), and the other which is housed in the United Kingdom (*New Political Economy* (*NPE*)). This book is thus more than just another forum for talking about how we *should* bridge the transatlantic divide. It represents an initial effort to *do* so.

IPE, past and present

The origins of this book lay in a series of events that started in May 2007, when *RIPE* published an essay by Benjamin Cohen entitled 'The Transatlantic Divide: Why Are American and British IPE So Different?' (Cohen 2007). *RIPE* was immediately flooded with requests to respond to Cohen's depiction of the IPE field and his arguments regarding the implications of the divide (see, e.g. Ravenhill 2008; Higgott and Watson 2008; Patomaki 2009; Leander 2009). Then, in November 2007, at the second annual meeting of the International Political Economy Society at Stanford University, Daniel Maliniak and Michael Tierney presented their research on the American school of IPE. Their paper tested Cohen's characterization of the American school using original survey results from international relations faculty in the United States and Canada as well as data gathered from the 12 leading international relations journals on the paradigms, epistemologies, methodologies, and other characteristics of IPE work from 1980 to 2006. Their findings strongly supported Cohen's portrayal of the field.

The reaction of the packed audience at the International Political Economy Society meeting ranged from muted celebration to great concern. *RIPE* quickly moved to assemble a special issue to comment on Maliniak and Tierney's findings and to speculate on the causes and consequences of American IPE's current state of affairs. The resulting essays, reprinted here in Part I, were written by some of the most prominent scholars in the field, representing a variety of paradigmatic, epistemological, and methodological perspectives as well as geographical and demographical positions. They tackled four key questions. First, are the depictions of the American school of IPE accurate, as offered by Cohen (2008) and Maliniak and Tierney (2009)? In other words, as Peter Katzenstein, Henry Farrell and Martha Finnemore, Katheleen McNamara, and others suggest, have we missed a large part of the field by focusing on what has been published in the mainstream journals and forgoing other publication venues, such as books? Have we conflated the American school with something else, such as the Open Economy Politics (OEP) approach as described by David Lake, or the Harvard school, as described by Randall Germain? Or, as Nicola Phillips, Robert Wade, and Germain propose, does the 'shackling' of IPE to the discipline of international relations in the United States lead us to an anemic depiction of the American school that obscures the diversity that still thrives in our field?

Second, if the prevailing depictions of the American school are correct, how did we get here? Lake argues, and Robert Keohane largely agrees, that the current prominence of OEP in the United States simply reflects a consensus on OEP's ability to provide more rigorous and persuasive explanations of social phenomena than approaches that adopt contrary epistemologies. Others suggest instead that the American school as we see it is the product of social processes or the exercise of professional power. For example, Phillips and Germain both argue (and Katzenstein disputes) that the character of the American school is to some extent the result of editorial control over the leading journals. McNamara, Finnemore, and Farrell (and later Cox, Underhill, and Weaver in the *NPE* special issue) emphasize that this has deeper roots in graduate school training and professional incentive structures in the job market and tenure processes.

Third, what are the consequences of the current state of affairs for the health of the IPE discipline in the United States (and anywhere else that emulates the American-school model)? Not all agree that the divide is *ipso facto* a bad outcome, as long as it avoids the fate of becoming intellectual monopolies (Lake) or monocultures (McNamara). At the same time, IPE scholars in the United States should temper their eagerness to emulate the discipline of economics. As Wade warns, American IPE is in danger of suffering the same fate as the neoclassical economic orthodoxy, whose obsession with formalization and quantification made it insular, static, and increasingly disconnected from the 'real economy'.

Finally, what is the future of the American school of IPE? Nearly all of the contributors to the *RIPE* special issue (and later the *NPE* issue) call for greater methodological, epistemological, and paradigmatic pluralism within the American school, as well as more effort to bridge the divide. Likewise, they call for such pluralism and bridge-building to be broached via greater pragmatism, analytical eclecticism, and a focus on more problem-driven research.

In September 2009, *NPE* published a parallel issue on the British school, reprinted in Part II of this volume. The first objective of the *NPE* special issue was to expand the discussion started in *RIPE* by taking the so-called 'British school' as the point of departure. This seemed especially fitting not only as a way to balance *RIPE*'s attention to the American school, but also because Cohen's characterization of British-school IPE has so far provoked some of the most indignant critiques of his *Intellectual History*. The *NPE* special issue assembled people associated (or who associate themselves) with what might be called a 'British school', as well as scholars who stand further outside it. Like the *RIPE* issue, the collection of essays on the British school aimed in this way to reflect the diversity of perspective and opinion that currently exists within our field, and foster a constructive and instructive engagement between often quite stridently divergent positions in the debate.

Echoing the remit of the *RIPE* special issue, the *NPE* issue addressed four central themes. First, is there such a thing as a 'British school', as identified by Cohen, and is this a useful device for thinking about how our field is currently organized? Is there, as suggested by Mark Blyth, Catherine Weaver, and others, a very clear divide which operates largely along the axis identified by Cohen, especially in terms of methodological approach? Or is such a characterization distinctly Anglo-American-centric, to the extent that the field of IPE and scholarship within something called the 'British school' are misrepresented? Robert W. Cox, Craig Murphy, Helge Hveem, and others all worry about the voices that are excluded as a result of this categorization of a 'British school', as well as a 'transatlantic divide', and argue for the much greater future incorporation of scholarship from outside the narrow world of Anglo-American scholarship. Geoffrey Underhill argues that the European origins of both the American and British schools, as conceived by Cohen, are underplayed and obscured, to the extent that the notion of a 'transatlantic divide' misrepresents the genesis of the field and its primary influences. But many are willing to accept *as a starting point* the contention that there is something that can be called a 'British school', and reflect critically on the field, its accomplishments, and its future challenges, even while there is lively disagreement about what the field looks like and how it should be understood.

Second, if it is accepted, is Cohen's characterization of the 'British school' accurate? Again, the essays reflect a real divergence of perspective. Murphy, supported by others, takes issue with the accuracy of Cohen's depiction of the pioneering influences on the field in his questions about the 'left out', and Eric Helleiner and Hveem both find it difficult to recognize the field depicted by Cohen from their vantage points in, respectively, Canada and continental Europe. Underhill and Blyth are the most trenchant in their critique of the British school, both emphasizing what they see as its penchant for 'template theorizing', in Underhill's words, but at the same time engaging equally critically with the tendencies of American-school scholarship. Ronen Palan is keen to stress the achievements of the 'British-school' approach, especially in understanding the global financial crisis of the late 2000s: the proof of the pudding, he argues, is in the eating, and at that moment the British school emerges triumphant. Later, in Part III, Apeldoorn *et al.* echo some of these sentiments in their defense of the body of 'critical IPE' which is often taken to be emblematic of the 'British school'.

Third, what is the relationship of British- and American-school IPE? Aside from objections to the Anglo-American-centrism of this categorization, not all agree that the divide is quite as deep as many suspect. Helleiner, Blyth, Underhill, Weaver, and others all struggle either to see such a clear separation, including in their own intellectual outlook, or to agree with the notion that there is such a thing as a homogeneous 'British school' or 'American school' which can be constructed against one another. Many, such as Palan, also take the cue to think about how a more constructive form of engagement – perhaps even bridge-building – might be undertaken.

Finally, what is its likely future trajectory? Where are the key advantages of and difficulties with the 'British-school' approach? What, if anything, does it have to gain from an exercise in 'bridge-building', especially with American-school scholarship? Nearly all of the contributors see the need for a greater level of interest and curiosity about different approaches in the field, many emphasizing in a constructive sense what each can learn from the other, and offering different perspectives on what these lessons might be. But many also point directly to the advantages for IPE as a whole of being more open to voices outside the Anglo-American context and thereby developing a more globally inclusive field of study.

The future of IPE

For Part III of this book, we solicited new essays from five prominent IPE scholars to comment on the future of the IPE beyond the transatlantic divide debate. As a set, these essays warn against becoming too deeply entrenched in disciplinary reflection. In turn, they offer suggestions on how we might progress both in terms of bridge-building between the American and British school as well as substantive agendas for research within these schools.

Jason Sharman, speaking from an Australian perspective, begins with a cautionary note: as an intellectual community, we need to be more careful in our call for greater dialogue and bridge-building, lest the 'repeated public protestations of the desire to bridge the gap between the American and British school IPE scholars might not amount to much'. Moving past the inward-looking debate and closing the divide, he suggests, requires clear benchmarks through which we hold ourselves to account. But more importantly, we also need to recognize the pragmatic constraints to establishing dialogue given the profound differences between pedagogical and professional foundations of the IPE disciplines across different countries. For example, Sharman argues, if we want British IPE and its 'Antipodean intellectual offshoots' to pay more attention to American IPE and vice versa, we need to recognize that one barrier is methodological training. In other words, it may be lack of math requirements at both undergraduate and graduate levels that inhibits young British-school scholars from attaining the statistical fluency to read the bulk of IPE in the United States. Likewise, a lack of philosophical and qualitative training that may impede third-generation American IPE scholars from understanding British-school scholarship. That said, we are already seeing progress on both shores. The United Kingdom is moving toward a Canadian model for compulsory methods training and the United States is becoming more pluralist through the Perestroika movement and the establishment of new training forums such as the Institute for Qualitative Research Methods (IQRM).

Jonathan Kirshner, a US-based IPE scholar, takes a more direct swing at the American school and what it bodes for the future of IPE. The central problem, he argues, is that American scholarship has recently turned from IPE to IpE. In other words, the problem is the disappearance of politics and a current obsession with quantitative methods as the ends, rather than the means, of intellectual inquiry. The immediate task for IPE in the United States, he argues, is to abandon its rigid adherence to 'Hyper-rationalism, Individualism, and Materialism [HIM]'. Like Sharman and others in this volume, Kirshner argues that this requires a return to a truly interdisciplinary approach in the professional training and socialization of graduate students in the United States (and elsewhere) that embraces not just economics, but also sociology, history, and cultural studies.

Louis Pauly, a Canadian IPE scholar and current co-editor of *International Organization*, takes a more optimistic tone. The transatlantic divide, he argues, is more imagined than real, the current state of the discipline is not as unhealthy and monocultural as some might claim, and we should not be so easily alarmed by a perceived hegemonic bid by the American school or third-generation of US IPE scholars. Nonetheless, like others in this volume, Pauly advocates ontological and epistemological pluralism and analytic eclecticism. He argues that a healthy future for IPE requires a return to past – specifically the 'magnificent seven' of Susan Strange's tenets for studying and producing scholarship in IPE. To do this, one step we could take is to facilitate scholarship outside of the United States and United Kingdom to integrate non-Anglo-American voices into the lead journals and book presses. We also need to increase dialogue and collaboration via funding for international research partnerships and provide more travel grants and post-doctoral research opportunities outside the Anglosphere.

The last two essays in Part III comment more on substantive agendas for future IPE research. Bastiaan van Apeldoorn, Ian Bruff, and Magnus Ryner start by reminding us that there is in fact a 'third way' in IPE. This is the critical theoretical approach that is distinct from what is widely seen as an 'American' rational-institutional approach and a 'British' constructivist-institutionalist perspective. They view critical IPE, too often conflated with the British school (especially by American audiences), as oriented around the interpretation of social reality and well positioned to ask the big, normative questions called for by Cohen, Keohane, Palan, and others. More importantly, the critical theory approach is already inclusive of non-Anglo-American voices. Thus, the future of IPE in their minds need not be wedded to notions of dialogue or analytical eclecticism; instead we need to recognize and appreciate alternatives to the American and British schools of thought that have been regrettably neglected in the current disciplinary debate.

Layna Mosley and David Singer, both US scholars mainly working in the American-school tradition, offer a set of prospective research questions. Like Palan in Part II, Mosley and Singer argue that IPE specifically needs to focus on three issues that have become more salient since the recent global financial crisis: (1) the complex determinants of cross-national variation in financial regulation; (2) the rise of new forums of economic decision-making and governance, such as G20, G7, and the Financial Stability Forum (FSF), and the role of emerging market countries in them; and (3) the interplay between individual firms-as-political-actors and public policy outcomes. Whereas Kirshner argues that the discipline's ability to address contemporary problems requires a renewal of the 'P' in IPE and Keohane (in Part I) calls for a return to the 'I' (more attention to international or structural processes underpinning political economy), Mosley and Singer argue that the future of IPE requires more emphasis on the 'C'. Namely, they claim, scholars need to be more willing to blur the lines between comparative and international political economy. Epistemologically and methodologically, their prescription is much like others' support for pluralism and eclecticism, with more tolerance for empirical research driven by problems rather than methodological agendas.

At the end of the day, we claim neither a representative sampling nor a definitive end to the discussions on the past, present, and future of IPE. Rather, our modest goal in this volume is to raise a provocative set of questions and arguments that will help us to reflect on how we have thus far approached our field of inquiry and how we might proceed in the near future.

It thus seems fitting to give the last word to Benjamin Cohen, who started us down this path with his prescient *Intellectual History*. Cohen aptly sums it all up by suggesting that perhaps, finally, we have worked our way through the four key stages of 'grief' and reached a point of acceptance. What we have 'accepted' is not any kind of consensus on what our field actually looks like, how we got there, or where we should be going, but rather the notion that greater inclusiveness, openness, and dialogue should be part of our collective endeavor and can open up imaginative new directions in the future of IPE.

Part I

Perspectives on the 'American school' of IPE

1 The American school of IPE

Daniel Maliniak and Michael J. Tierney

D. Maliniak and M.J. Tierney (2009) 'The American school of IPE', *Review of International Political Economy* 16(1): 6–33, published by Taylor & Francis Ltd, http://www.informaworld.com. Permission has been granted by the publisher.

In a keynote speech to the inaugural meeting of the International Political Economy Society (IPES) at Princeton University in November 2006, Benjamin Cohen argued that there were at least two distinct schools of thought that have adopted the moniker 'IPE' (international political economy) – the 'British school' and the 'American' school.[1] According to Cohen, the intellectual evolution of the IPE field has produced an American school characterized by 'the twin principles of positivism and empiricism' and a British school driven by a more explicit normative, interpretive, and 'ambitious' agenda (Cohen, 2007: 198–200). These schools diverge in the ontologies, epistemologies and normative stances that each employs to study the same subject – 'the complex linkages between economic and political activity at the level of international affairs' (Cohen, 2007: 197). In Cohen's view, IPE is increasingly fractured along conceptual and geographical lines, yet the American and British schools remain complementary. As such, he ends his reflection on IPE's transatlantic divide by calling for mutual respect, learning and a 'meeting of the minds' (Cohen, 2007: 216–17).

Cohen's speech, subsequent article in this journal (Cohen, 2007), and book (Cohen, 2008) have sparked a vibrant and contentious debate on the origins, character, and even desirability of a transatlantic IPE divide.[2] Our reaction was less visceral than most. Nonetheless, we were provoked by Cohen's depiction of the field and inspired to treat his characterizations of each school, based upon his interpretive intellectual history, as hypotheses that merit further testing. This interest coincided with our ongoing project on Teaching, Research, and International Policy (TRIP): a multi-year study of the international relations field in the United States and Canada. In the TRIP project, we employ data gathered from two extensive surveys of international relations (IR) scholars and a new journal article database that codes all the articles in the 12 leading political science journals that publish articles in the subfield of IR. Our journal article database covers the years between 1980 and 2006 (see below for note on methodology). While the TRIP project was not designed to provide the definitive test of Cohen's thesis, it does provide us with some leverage on his claims. More importantly, since the TRIP project utilizes distinctive data collection, coding, and analysis methods – compared to Cohen's methods – it provides a potentially powerful cross-check on Cohen's findings about the nature of the IPE subfield and its purported divide.

Thus, the purpose of this article is to use the TRIP data to investigate the American IPE school upon which much of Cohen's argument is premised and from which the lively discussion surrounding the American versus British school has sprung. Ultimately, unlike Cohen, we do not seek to persuade others of the existence of stark differences between IPE scholarship in the United States and Europe. Indeed, our data are limited to IPE scholars in the United States and Canada and to the top journals in the field of IR (as determined by their Garand and Giles impact scores).[3] Thus we consciously refrain from making assertions about the nature of the British IPE and the existence or nature of any transatlantic divide.[4] Moreover, we remain agnostic about the prospects or desire for transatlantic bridge building within IPE (we leave this debate to others, including those who are contributing to this special issue of *RIPE*). Yet we are convinced that good bridges require solid foundations; and solid foundations require a clear understanding of the shores on which the foundations are built. Using the TRIP data, we can at least say something systematic about the American shore.

We have two specific objectives in this article. The first is to 'test' specific hypotheses derived from Cohen's argument. If Cohen's depiction of the American IPE school is consistent with the results of our survey and patterns of journal article publications, then his broader thesis about the IPE subfield are further validated and the implications of his argument merit the animated debate that we have already witnessed. If Cohen's depictions are not consistent with our findings, we should question his underlying assumptions and direct further research into the 'myth' of the divide – questioning why some perceive a divide that is non-existent or quite small.

Our second objective is to use the TRIP data to assess prominent trends in American – and to a lesser extent Canadian – IPE. The TRIP project is well equipped to do this, insofar as it is quite broad in scope. The survey questions and variables coded in the journal article database capture the essential human and institutional 'demography' of the IR field, as well as the paradigmatic, theoretical, methodological, and epistemological orientation of that field. We can parse out variables most relevant to the American IPE subfield. In doing so, we reveal some remarkable and sometimes surprising findings that raise numerous questions directly relevant to understanding the state of IPE in the United States and its place within the broader IR discipline. In this paper, we take particular note of four trends in American IPE: its institutional and human demography, its 'paradigmatic personality', the growing methodological homogeneity, and the surprising absence of any 'ideational turn' which is so prominent in the other subfields of IR.

We expect this paper to generate more questions than answers. While some of our data is formatted so that it directly speaks to extant hypotheses, much of what follows simply describes patterns of behavior, publication, or the aggregated opinion of IPE scholars in the United States and Canada. We were quite surprised by some of our findings and expect them to provoke a variety of explanations, reflections on the past, and consequences for the future of the discipline.

Brief note on project methodology

In order to describe the American school of IPE we utilize the Teaching and Research in International Policy (TRIP) project's databases.[5] First, we employ results from two surveys: one of American IR scholars from 2004 and one of American and Canadian scholars surveyed in 2006 in order to describe the research practices of IPE scholars in those institutions.[6] We also report United States IPE scholars' views on the broader IR discipline and on some pressing foreign policy issues. In order to distinguish IPE scholars from the broader IR community, we often compare the responses of these two groups. Second, we use the TRIP journal article database, which covers the top 12 journals in political science that publish research on international relations. The time series spans 1980–2007 (Maliniak *et al.*, 2007a).[7] Since publication in these journals is not limited to American IPE, this data source – unlike the survey – can help to describe both the American and British schools of IPE.[8] The article database reveals which of the top 12 journals publish the most (and most cited) articles within the IPE subfield. This database also allows us to identify trends in the substantive focus of IPE research, the rise and fall of paradigms in the IPE literature, the methods employed most frequently, direct comparisons between the IPE literature and the broader IR literature, and whether IPE generates theory and methods that diffuse into the rest of the IR literature or vice versa.

In addition to a description of the American IPE subfield, we employ the TRIP journal article database in order to provide some preliminary tests of Cohen's comparative hypotheses. Are non-American IPE scholars publishing work that is substantially different from their American IPE cousins? Is American work more positivist, quantitative and formal, while British and European IPE is more non-positivist, normative, and qualitative? If these claims are true on average, how large are the differences between American and British styles of IPE and are these differences growing or shrinking? While Canada is not in Europe, some preliminary research suggests that it may be somewhere between United States and Britain in terms of the sensibilities of scholars located there and in terms of the research they produce. The 2006 TRIP Survey included IR and IPE scholars at Canadian universities and they appear to fit more comfortably in Cohen's 'British school' than in the American one right next door.

The journals in the TRIP database are dominated by scholars at American institutions. One bit of evidence suggesting that there are two distinct IPE communities is the pattern of publication displayed in Figure 1.1. When we compare

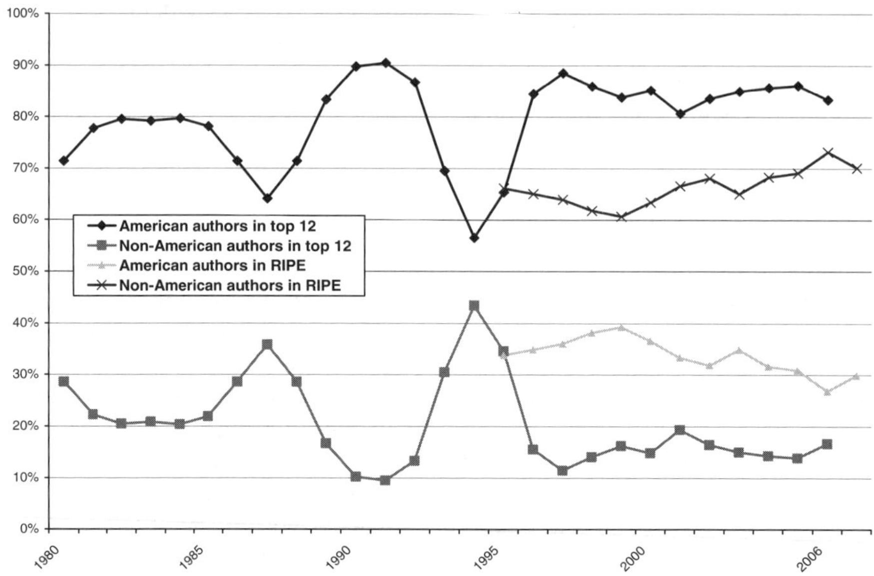

Figure 1.1 Percent of US/non-US authors publishing in top 12 journals versus *RIPE*.

Note
For ease of presentation, all time series data in this paper are reported using three year rolling averages.

the percent of authors at non-US institutions in our sample to those publishing in *RIPE*, we see a dramatic difference. For every year over the past decade we observe less than 20% of non-US authors publishing IPE articles in the top 12 journals. This differs dramatically from the distribution of articles at *RIPE*, where we never observe less than 60% of non-US authors. Over the past ten years the percentage of US-based authors publishing in *RIPE* has dropped from around 40% to just 30%. So, if we accept the Murphy and Nelson characterization of *RIPE* as the flagship journal of British style IPE, then we have some evidence for a large and growing gap between British IPE and IPE published in the other leading journals.

The field: what does American IPE look like?

The demography of American IPE

How do IPE scholars differ from the rest of the field of international relations within the United States? Using answers to the TRIP surveys allows us to measure specific characteristics of the individuals who make up the IPE subfield. In some respects scholars who claim IPE as their primary or secondary issue area differ from the broader population of IR scholars, but in other ways they are indistinguishable. IPE scholars are trained at different schools, they use different methods, they study different regions of the world, and they come from different regions of the world (specifically, they are far more international than their other IR colleagues at United States institutions). However, in other respects where we might expect variation across areas of study, we see very little. The percent of men and women studying IPE as IR is basically the same; IPE scholars are the same age on average as their IR counterparts, and they rank journals, PhD programs, and threats to United States national security about the same as the broader IR community. Overall, 30% of IR scholars in the United States do work in IPE.[9]

Specific schools have reputations for being particularly strong in IPE (Harvard, Berkeley, Princeton, UCSD, and UCLA often get mentioned at the American Political Science Association (APSA) bar), but the conventional names today are not always the same programs that have produced the largest number of IPE scholars in the United States over the past 40 years. At minimum, this variation suggests that comparative advantages within the top PhD programs change over time.

Table 1.1 Departments training the most IPE scholars

Rank	*University*	*Percent*
1	Yale University	5
2	Columbia University	4
2	Cornell University	4
4	Harvard University	4
4	University of California, Berkeley	4
4	University of California, Los Angeles	4
4	University of Wisconsin	4
8	University of Michigan	3
9	MIT	3
9	Princeton University	3
9	Stanford University	3
9	UNC Chapel Hill	3

Table 1.2 Departments training the most IR scholars

Rank	*University*	*Percent*
1	Columbia University	5
2	Harvard University	5
3	University of Michigan	4
4	University of California, Berkeley	3
5	Cornell University	3
6	University of Virginia	3
7	Ohio State University	3
8	Stanford University	3
9	MIT	3
10	University of Chicago	2

Table 1.3 Number of IPE articles produced since 1980

Rank	*University*	*Percent*
1	Harvard University	5
2	Columbia University	3
3	Stanford University	3
3	University of Colorado	3
5	University of Chicago	3
6	Princeton University	2
6	University of California, Los Angeles	2
6	Yale University	2
9	Duke University	2
10	New York University	2
10	Ohio State University	2

Although only 2% of all IR scholars received their doctoral training from Yale University, more IPE scholars (5%) trained at Yale than any other program. In addition to Yale, several other institutions have produced proportionately more IPE scholars than IR scholars studying in other issue areas. For example, University of Wisconsin at Madison ranks fourth for IPE but only 13th overall, Princeton University is tied for tenth with University of North Carolina, but these two schools rank 15th and 26th in terms of the total number of IR scholars produced.

In addition to what universities are training the next generation of graduate students, the article database reveals which programs produce the most IPE articles in the top 12 journals. We code the home department of authors upon publication of their article, and find that Harvard tops the list, with its scholars having penned 5% of all the IPE articles in the top journals since 1980. The top three schools for IPE are the same programs in order as IR generally. Strikingly, University of Colorado is tied for third in IPE articles, yet is 11th for the broader IR category.[10]

IPE scholars at United States institutions are neither younger, nor more diverse in terms of their gender than other IR scholars. On average, IPE scholars received their PhD two years later (1992) than the broader group of IR scholars. This is somewhat surprising, since both groups have the same average age, which implies that IPE scholars either start graduate programs at a later age or they take longer to obtain their degree than other IR scholars. However, the late start or extended stay in graduate school may pay off later as IPE scholars are more likely to hold the position of full professor (37%) than those studying in other subfields (33%).

Similarly, we find no evidence of a gender distinction within IPE that is different than the general IR population.[11] While the percentage of women in IR as a whole is 23%, the percent who study IPE is only 22%. Research on publication rates in political science and IR demonstrate that women publish less than their male colleagues and IPE provides no exception to this trend. Since the year 2000 only 14% of all authors of IPE articles published in the leading journals were women. Despite this fact, there is strong evidence from the TRIP survey that IPE scholars value the research of women to a greater extent than other IR scholars do. More women appear in the various top 25 lists for greatest impact on the field (3), most interesting work (6) and most influential on your own research (4). In all three of these categories IPE scholars are more likely to list women than are IR scholars who study other issue areas.[12]

Where is IPE research published?

Within the IR literature, articles with an IPE focus make up only 13% of those published since 1980 (despite 30% of IR scholars in the United States reporting their first or second field as IPE). Over this period, IPE's share of articles in the top 12 journals has ranged from a high of 20% in 1984 and 1985, to a low of 5% in 1994. Within the journals analyzed there is significant variation. Thirty-seven percent of IPE articles since 1980 are found in the pages of *International Organization* (*IO*), with *International Studies Quarterly* (*ISQ*) and *World Politics* containing 22% and 10%, respectively. Perhaps not surprisingly then, IPE scholars rank *IO* and *ISQ* as two of the journals they read most often in their area of expertise, with 53% and 34%, respectively, and *World Politics* sixth, with 15%.[13] *American Political Science Review* (*APSR*) and *International Security* (*IS*) both rank in the top five despite accounting for only 4% and 1% of IPE literature, respectively. For the *APSR*, this is somewhat unsurprising given the limited space devoted to IR in general. Within *APSR*, IPE articles account for 15% of published IR articles. The same cannot be said for *IS*, whose sole mission is publishing IR articles with a security focus. Over a 26-year period, less than 1% of the articles published by *IS* fit into the IPE category. In contrast, 18% of *IO*'s articles deal with issues of international security.

In addition to looking at the number and percentage of IPE articles published in various journals, we also used citation counts in order to determine which journals publish IPE articles that have the greatest impact on the way other scholars think about their work. Despite *IS*'s exclusion of IPE-focused articles,

Table 1.4 Number of IR articles produced since 1980

Rank	*University*	*Percent*
1	Harvard University	6
2	Columbia University	3
3	Stanford University	3
4	Ohio State University	2
5	University of Michigan	2
6	Princeton University	2
7	Yale University	2
8	University of Illinois	2
9	University of Chicago	2
10	University of California, Los Angeles	2

since 1990, they hold the highest average number of cites per IPE article, 57.[14] However, this is a result of the one IPE article that *International Security* published in the sample we coded, Michael Mastanduno's 'Do Relative Gains Matter? America's Response to Japanese Industrial Policy'. For the other journals, IPE articles are cited less frequently (on average) than other IR articles in the same journals. The lone exception is the other security-focused journal, *Security Studies*, whose four IPE articles are cited an average of once more than all other articles in the journal. Not surprisingly, the three journals that publish the most IPE are also the three journals with largest number of aggregate citations of their IPE work. *International Organization* accounts for 49% of all the citations of IPE articles over the past 17 years, *World Politics* accounts for 15% and *ISQ* for 10%. The main outlier here seems to be ISQ, which publishes 22% of the IPE literature, yet only accounts for 10% of the citations. This may be a good proximate measure for the overall impact of the IPE work being published in a given venue. Therefore, the third best outlet of highly cited IPE work is *APSR*, which publishes 4% of the IPE literature but accounts for 9% of the total citations of IPE articles.

Paradigmatic personality of American IPE

In 1991, Susan Strange argued that the study of IPE should be 'an open range, like the old Wild West, accessible … to literate people of all walks of life, from all professions, and all political proclivities' (Strange, 1995: 33). We are pretty sure that Strange would not be happy with the state of the field today. In stark contrast to the broader field of IR, work in the area of IPE often falls within one of the four major paradigms identified in the TRIP article database (realism, liberalism, Marxism, or constructivism).[15] In fact, only 45% of the broader IR literature comfortably fits into any of the major paradigms, while 73% of IPE articles are either realist, liberal, Marxist, or constructivist. This is not terribly surprising as many scholars have traditionally divided theories of IPE into three of these categories (Frieden and Lake, 1999; Gilpin, 1987; Katzenstein *et al.*, 1998; Lake, 2006). IPE is, overall, more oriented around paradigmatic debates than the general field of IR.

The paradigms preoccupying IPE work have changed quite dramatically over time. Historically, Marxism played an important role in the inception of modern IPE. However, today it is clear that arguments rooted in the Marxist paradigm almost never appear in the top 12 journals.[16] Although the timeframe of our study does not cover the pre-1980 era, evidence of Marxism's previous importance is visible at the beginning of our time series. As seen in Figure 1.2, articles in the Marxist tradition represent the largest proportion of the IPE literature in the early 1980s, but fall from their height of 39% in 1980 to 11% by 1986. This decline pre-dates the fall of the Soviet Union, suggesting that epistemic factors (rather than political ones) were driving the decline. David Lake (2006) suggests, Marxist political economy models simply were not doing a very good job accounting for trade patterns, aid flows, persistent underdevelopment in Africa,

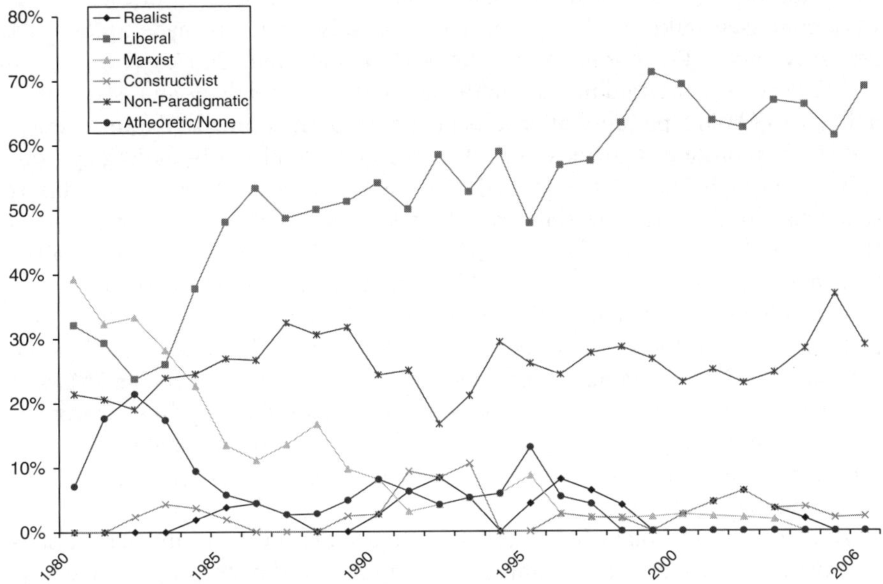

Figure 1.2 Paradigms employed within IPE, 1980–2006.

or the other substantive issues that IPE scholarship attempts to address. Moreover, according to Lake, Marxist approaches 'failed to develop a unified, logically consistent, and empirically robust theory of under-development, or at least one that could compete in rigor and explanatory power with neoclassical economic theories of growth and development' (Lake, 2006: 760). Since 1990 Marxist IPE has never represented more than 10% of the overall IPE literature and in recent years we observe no Marxist IPE articles being published in any of the leading journals.

So what has replaced Marxism as the paradigm of choice? With the exception of period from 1980 to 1983, liberal research has been the most utilized paradigm by scholars publishing work on IPE. From 1988 to 1994 and 1996 to the present the majority of articles published in IPE employed a theory that fit within the liberal paradigm. This rise and dominance of liberal work comes at the expense of the atheoretic and Marxist literature, both of which have seen significant declines over the period we analyze. The fall of atheoretic work in IPE closely mirrors that of the IR field in general (Maliniak *et al.*, 2007a); however, IPE has always been the most theoretically oriented of all the subfields. While we observe declines in atheoretic work across the board, there have been no atheoretic IPE articles published in the leading journals over the past nine years! This is not true for security, environment, human rights, international organization, international law, or other subfields within IR.

The other two major paradigms, constructivism and realism, are dwarfed in comparison to liberalism and do not reach over 11% in any given year since

1980, and not over 6% in any of the past ten years. The overall picture of IPE work contrasts starkly to the IR field more broadly, which is made up of work primarily outside the four major paradigms (Maliniak *et al.*, 2007a).

While two of the traditional paradigms of IPE – liberalism and Marxism – individually hold a plurality of articles published for a portion of the time series, realism is represented in very little IPE research. Realist IPE is largely non-existent through the 1980s and peaks in 1992 and 1996 at just 8%.[17] This is somewhat ironic since the standard IPE textbooks used in graduate seminars (Frieden and Lake, 1999; Gilpin, 1987) present realism as if it were one of the three main paradigms in the study of IPE. One explanation for this situation may be that although few Realist IPE scholars exist, the ideas of certain realists, such as Robert Gilpin, Stephen Krasner, and Joseph Grieco, have been used as the counter arguments, framing devices, and straw-men for many liberal and Marxist accounts. Below we provide some indirect evidence in support of this interpretation. A different way of getting at the impact of various paradigmatic ideas is to survey scholars about the individuals and the journals that have the biggest impact on their thinking.

Among those scholars listed as having the most profound impact on self-identified IPE scholars, the top three reflect a great deal of theoretical diversity: Robert Keohane (19%), Robert Gilpin (12%) and Alexander Wendt (8%) all represent distinct paradigmatic commitments. Further inspection of Table 1.5 illustrates the diversity of individuals 'having the most profound impact' on IPE scholars (Maliniak *et al.*, 2007c). Citation data provide further evidence for the claim that realism in IPE represents more of a straw-man than a research program. Realist IPE articles on average are cited more times than any other category – paradigmatic, non-paradigmatic or atheoretic articles. This finding is consistent with the hypothesis that many authors frame counterarguments in a traditional paradigmatic manner. Having a relative dearth of realist IPE articles from which to choose, authors find it necessary to continue trashing the same realist articles. In addition, the realist IPE literature is more frequently cited (20.5) than the rest of the realist literature (17.3) in IR by roughly three cites per article. Non-paradigmatic IPE articles also are more cited in IPE than in the IR literature generally, but that is only by just under one cite per article (0.8). Being true for both Marxist and liberals (2.5 and 5.7 fewer cites per IPE article, respectively), this suggests that paradigmatic work outside of an issue area in which it is traditionally strong may be a key to receiving more citations; however, they may all be negative citations that take the form, 'Can you believe how dumb professor Smith is?'

Moreover, the data on the variable 'alternative paradigms taken seriously'[18] in an article suggest that citations are more likely cursory mentions and not the result of authors engaging alternative paradigmatic positions. With this strict definition, we do not just code those articles that include a citation of work from another paradigm; rather the author must take theoretical implications of the other paradigm seriously, not just using it as a straw-man. It turns out that realism is taken seriously less often in IPE articles (13%) than in non-IPE

Table 1.5 Most profound impact on your own research

Rank	*Scholar*	*Percent*
1	Robert Keohane	19
2	Robert Gilpin	12
3	Alexander Wendt	8
4	Joseph Nye	7
4	Peter Katzenstein	7
6	Robert Cox	6
7	Jeffrey Frieden	6
7	John Ruggie	6
7	Kenneth Waltz	6
10	Stephen Krasner	5
11	David Lake	5
11	G. John Ikenberry	5
11	James Fearon	5
14	Bruce Bueno De Mesquita	4
14	Ernst Haas	4
14	Samuel Huntington	4
14	Susan Strange	4
18	Helen Milner	4
18	Immanuel Wallerstein	4
18	Ronald Rogowski	4
21	Andrew Moravcsik	3
22	Beth Simmons	3
23	Hans Morgenthau	3
24	Hayward Alker	3
25	Martha Finnemore	3

Note
The question said: 'List up to four scholars who have had the most profound impact on your own research and the way that you think about IR.' These are responses of scholars in the United States who indicated IPE as their primary or secondary field. For the Canadian list see Lipson *et al.* 2007.

articles (17%).[19] Overall, just as in the general IR literature, a majority of IPE articles, 64%, do not take seriously any paradigm other than the paradigm they are advancing.

The 'mismatch' between how the field is traditionally divided in text books and graduate syllabi versus the characteristics of published articles carries over into the description of IPE scholars as well. Of the 269 scholars who responded that their primary or secondary field was IPE in the 2006 survey, realists and constructivists accounted for 17% and 13%, respectively. This is greatly out of proportion to the number of articles published since 2000, in which only 3% are realist and 3% are constructivist. Although only 37% of IPE scholars described their paradigm as liberal or neo-liberal, liberal articles account for 66% of the IPE literature since 2000. This finding begs the question: Why is there such a preponderance of the liberal paradigm in IPE journal articles?

Six percent of scholars in the 2004 and 2006 surveys describe their work as falling under the Marxist paradigm, while less than 1% of the IPE work published in the top 12 journals is Marxist since 2000. With very few scholars and a limited body of work, we are left to wonder why the field's theoretical debates continue to be framed such that Marxism is still advanced as one of the three paradigmatic pillars upon which IPE stands.

Methodology in 'American style' IPE

For most political scientists in the United States, political economy is not conceived as a field, but rather as 'the methodology of economics applied to the analysis of political behavior and institutions' (Weingast and Wittman, 2006: 3). While David Lake defines IPE as 'a substantive topic of enquiry, rather than a methodology in which economic models are applied to political phenomena', IPE's association with economics in the United States make it an obvious place to bring the tools of economics to bear on issues of political behavior and institutions. However, Lake also notes, 'Where IPE was originally constrained to case

Table 1.6 Greatest impact on the field of IR

Rank	*Scholar*	*Percent*
1	Robert Keohane	64
2	Kenneth Waltz	41
3	Alexander Wendt	28
4	Joseph Nye	16
5	Robert Gilpin	16
6	John Mearsheimer	12
7	James Fearon	11
8	John Ruggie	11
9	Samuel Huntington	11
10	Stephen Krasner	11
11	Bruce Bueno de Mesquita	10
12	Robert Jervis	8
13	Peter Katzenstein	7
14	Robert Cox	6
15	Helen Milner	5
16	Jeffry Frieden	5
17	Bruce Russett	4
18	Hans Morgenthau	4
19	Michael Doyle	4
20	Susan Strange	4
21	Immanuel Wallerstein	3
22	J. Ann Tickner	3
23	James Rosenau	3
24	Mancur Olson	3
25	Peter Gourevitch	3

Note

The question said: 'List up to four scholars who have had the greatest impact on the field of international relations over the past 20 years.' These are the responses of IPE scholars about the broader field.

studies or, at best, statistical tests based on very limited data, some of the best new research employs very large time series data-sets and powerful econometric tools' (Lake, 2006: 772). If Lake is correct, we should see a substantial increase in quantitative work being published in IPE compared to past patterns. In fact, as illustrated in Figure 1.3, this is precisely the pattern we observe and the increase in quantitative work is dramatic.

As illustrated in Figure 1.3, for most of the 1980s and 1990s qualitative methods were the most frequently used empirical tools in the IPE journal literature. A cursory glance at the data suggests that the methods used within IPE are similar to those used in the field overall, with qualitative as the mildly dominant method for most of the time period and quantitative methods ascending and taking the top spot more recently. However, the overall amount of quantitative work and its increasing use in recent years is much more pronounced within IPE than in the rest of IR (compare Figure 1.3 to Figure 1.4). This is all the more surprising if one considers the historical positions of qualitative versus quantitative work in the IPE subfield versus all of IR. In the 1980s and early 1990s, qualitative methods were much more prevalent in IPE articles than in IR in general. Yet over the past five years, this relationship has reversed itself at a remarkable rate. By 2006, fully 90% of all IPE articles in our sample employed quantitative methods. Why has there been such a precipitous decline in qualitative IPE research in favor of quantitative work in the leading journals?

While conventional wisdom suggests an increase in quantitative research, the rate of increase in quantitative work merits a more detailed discussion. If we look

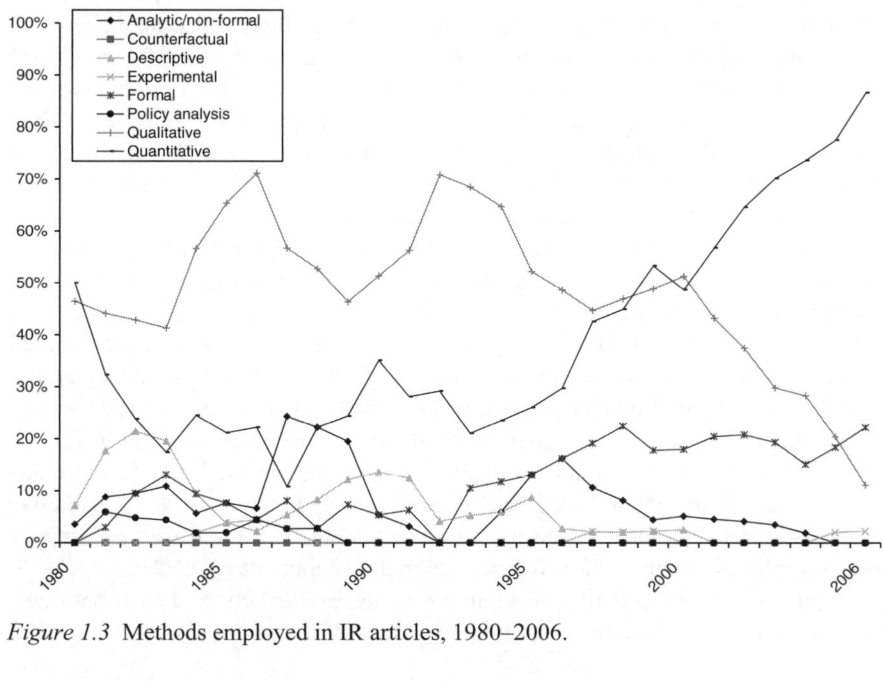

Figure 1.3 Methods employed in IR articles, 1980–2006.

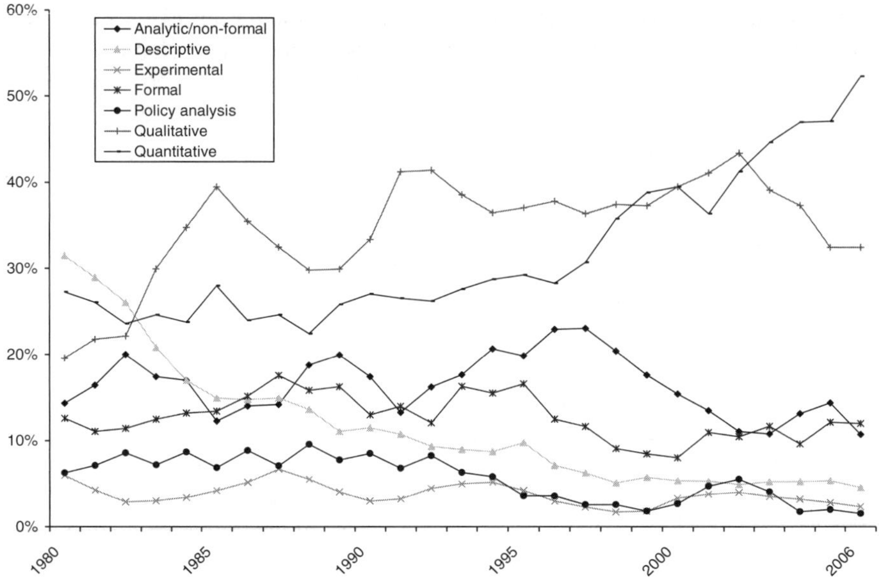

Figure 1.4 The Material Turn in IPE.

at the entire population of IR articles in the literature (see Figure 1.4), qualitative methods are never used in more than 43% of the articles in any given year, and only represent an average of 35% over the entire time period. Within the IPE literature, qualitative research peaks twice at 71% of the articles published in a given year and over the entire time period is used in an average of 48% of IPE articles. The real story here is that IPE literature employs both qualitative and quantitative methods at higher rates and at earlier points in the time series than the rest of the IR field. Apparently, IPE is a disciplinary leader in terms of the methods used – increases in these methods throughout the IR field lag about ten years behind their widespread adoption within IPE.

When Jeffrey Frieden and Lisa Martin (2002) wrote that IPE had approached a 'consensus on methods', they were referring to methodology in a broader sense – consensus on substantive questions, the relevance of institutions, and the utility of rationalist approaches to empirical questions. However, at this same time the field was approaching a consensus on methodology in narrower terms as well. Quantitative methods are now (by far) the most utilized method in IPE articles. The increase in quantitative work – while evident in all of IR – is particularly strong in IPE. In the ten years from 1993 to 2003, quantitative methods are used in 49% more articles (a jump from 21% to 70%). This increase comes at the expense of qualitative methods, which over the same period fell from 71% to 30%, on its way to currently being employed in only 11% of IPE articles in the 12 journals we coded.

While the use of quantitative methods is not exclusively tied to economics, the prevalence of econometric techniques in the IPE literature suggests that Lake

(2006) was correct in claiming that the methods of economics are the standard tool of IPE scholars publishing in the top journals. Further evidence of economic methods breaking into IPE can be seen in the increased use of formal models. From 1992, when there were virtually no formal methods used in IPE research, their prevalence has increased sharply to 22% of the IPE literature in 1998, and since has consistently hovered around 20%. As with quantitative work, this is substantially higher than the amount of formal work being done in other subfields of IR. In 2006 formal was the second most highly used method at 22%, 11% higher than qualitative work. Formal methods do not enjoy the same popularity in the IR literature as whole, and declined from 17% in 1995 to 12% in 2006. Given the methods employed in the IPE literature, it is unsurprising that a larger percentage of IPE scholars report using quantitative and formal methods in their research than other IR scholars do. The years of qualitative prominence prior to the rather sudden methodological shift in IPE are also reflected in the 90% of IPE scholars who continue to consider qualitative as their primary (65%) or secondary (25%) method. However, this seems to be the result of a generational gap. For those who received (or will receive) their doctorate in 2000 or later, 36% consider quantitative methods as their primary approach. IPE scholars who received their PhD in the 1990s rely less on quantitative methods (27%), and those who received their PhDs in the 1980s or earlier utilize quantitative methods even less (18%). This trend holds for the rest of IR scholars as well, but the differences are much starker within IPE. Twenty-three percent of non-IPE scholars who received (or will receive) their PhD after 1999 consider quantitative methods as their primary tool, with those who received their PhDs in the 1990s (20%) and those who received theirs in the 1980s or earlier (15%) each having progressively less reliance on quantitative methods.

IPE also seems to exhibit two distinct periods of theoretically focused work. These 'theory bumps' of analytic/non-formal work (see Figure 1.3) feature articles devoted to analytic or theoretical issues without reference to significant empirical evidence or a formal model.[20] These surges in theoretical articles occur once before the end of the Cold War, peaking in 1987 at 24%, only to fall away and represent

Table 1.7 Survey results on primary and secondary methods for IPE versus IR

Method	*Primary method*		*Secondary method*		*Total*	
	IPE (%)	*Non-IPE (%)*	*IPE (%)*	*Non-IPE (%)*	*IPE (%)*	*Non-IPE (%)*
Quantitative	27	19	31	29	58	48
Qualitative	65	70	25	22	90	92
Formal modeling	2	2	15	11	17	12
Experimental	1	1	3	8	5	9
Counterfactual analysis	1	1	25	24	26	25
Pure theory	2	2	20	17	22	19
Legal/ethical analysis	2	4	19	21	20	25

little to none of the IPE literature from 1991 to 1994.[21] The purely theoretic work again rises to prominence in 1996 at 16%, and steadily declines from that point to the present day. These theoretic works of the mid-1990s may be the result of the oft-lamented 'paradigm wars' in the IR literature. Regardless of their source, the following period sees a dramatic increase in quantitative, qualitative and formal IPE. One interpretation of these trends suggests that many of these theoretical debates provided fertile ground for empirical investigation, especially for quantitative researchers. Data on the citations of analytic/non-formal articles are suggestive, as the average number of citations is 30 per article, compared to formal, qualitative and quantitative research, which average eight, 15 and nine citations per article. The big ideas in analytic/non-formal articles may shape the research agendas in the subsequent periods that look more like Kuhnian 'normal science'.

What regions of the world do IPE scholars study?

In this issue, Robert Keohane laments the fact that contemporary IPE scholars are not asking the 'big questions' about issues that are 'important in the real world' and are instead too focused on creating/testing extant theories or finding questions that could be addressed with sophisticated methodologies. One of the four 'big questions' that Keohane discusses is the rise of China. While we do not have a direct measure of the number of IPE scholars working on this question, we do have evidence on what IR and IPE scholars believe are the big questions and we have evidence on whether IPE scholars are publishing more on East Asia than their IR colleagues are.

The TRIP survey indicates that IPE scholars in the United States are more likely to believe that East Asia is strategically important today compared to non-IPE people, 23% to 17%, while 6% fewer IPE scholars believe that the Middle East is the most strategically important region today. However, the two groups converge on the choice of which region will be strategically important in 20 years, 67% for IPE and 65% for non-IPE agree it will be East Asia. IPE scholars are only slightly less likely to think that the rise of China is one of the three most important foreign policy issues that will face the United States in the next ten years, 40% compared to 41% of all IR scholars.

The regional focus of IPE is, perhaps not surprisingly, tied to economically developed countries. Thirty-five percent of IPE articles contain data or cases drawn from the United States, and, with obviously some overlap, 35% consider data and cases from Canada and Western Europe. The third largest region gaining attention in IPE is East Asia with 29%, followed closely by Global work, or those papers use data and cases covering every country or region in the world.

Ideational turn in IR . . . but not IPE

Much has been made of the 'ideational turn' in IR over the past few decades, with many now considering constructivism to have overcome its subaltern status and achieved paradigmatic popularity on par with realism or liberalism (Checkel,

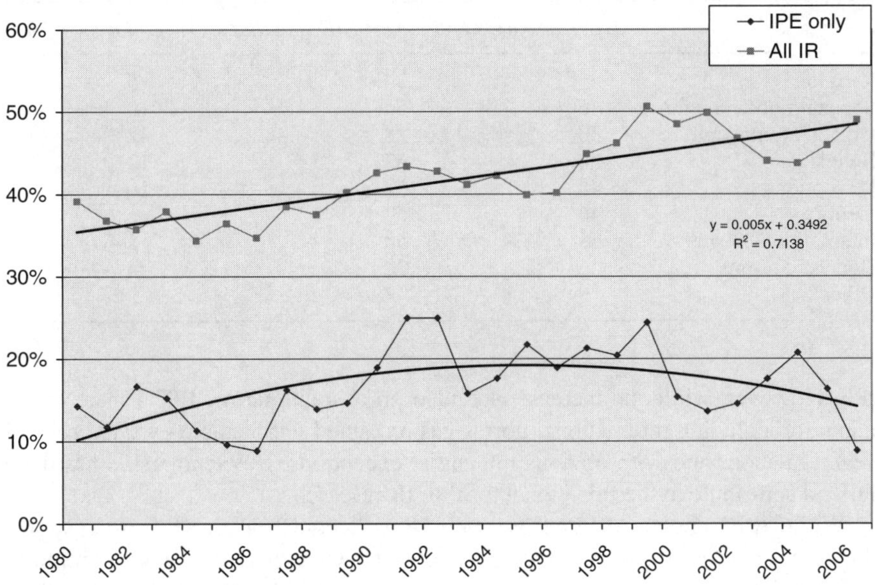

Figure 1.5 The Material Turn in IPE.

1998). As illustrated by Figure 1.5, however, this turn appears to be almost nowhere evident in IPE articles published in the top journals, and, if evident at all, seems to be turning in the opposite direction.[22] While at least 34% of the journal articles we coded contained ideational factors for every year since 1980, in the IPE articles this number never reaches above 25%, and for the majority of our time period it is below 20%. Even beyond the absolute differences between the two groups, the trends they display are markedly different. The overall IR literature displays a near linear increase (*r* 2 = 0.7138) over the time period, while the trend in IPE appears parabolic, falling off after 1995.

In 2004, we asked IR scholars whether they emphasized the role of ideational factors in their research, and if so, which factors they emphasized. Overall, IPE scholars were 19% less likely than scholars in other subfields to report a focus on ideational factors in their research. However, the majority, 64%, do emphasize ideational factors, compared to the 83% of non-IPE scholars who employ ideational factors in their analyses. Not only do they employ ideational factors at different rates, but IPE and non-IPE scholars focus on different ideational variables in their work as well. As seen in Table 1.8, IPE scholars who do study ideational variables are more likely to focus on societal/political culture, international norms, domestic norms, and organizational culture, by ten, five, four and 2%, respectively.[23] In our article database, we only code for one of these variables specifically: international norms. Analysis of this variable, as seen in Figure 1.6, shows that there is in fact an increase in the number of articles including discussion of international norms in

Table 1.8 Types of ideational variables used in IPE verses IR

	IPE scholars (%)	*Non-IPE scholars (%)*	*Difference (%)*
Religion	25	30	−5
Societal/political culture	66	56	10
Organizational culture	30	28	2
Beliefs	50	62	−12
Perceptions	48	57	−10
Identity	46	52	−6
International norms	55	50	5
Domestic norms	36	32	4
Other	10	7	2

IPE. However, while the increase is evident in absolute terms, IPE's share of the literature including international norms has remained fairly stable over the past 27 years. In short, and with obvious influential exceptions, IPE scholarship has done little to contribute to the 'ideational turn' in IR research.

While IPE scholars differ from their IR colleagues on these two questions, they are remarkably similar in their response to whether or not their attention to ideational factors has changed over time; 53% of IPE scholars say that their attention has increased as compared to 51% of non-IPE scholars. Nevertheless, this increased attention does not seem to make its way into the articles in our database.

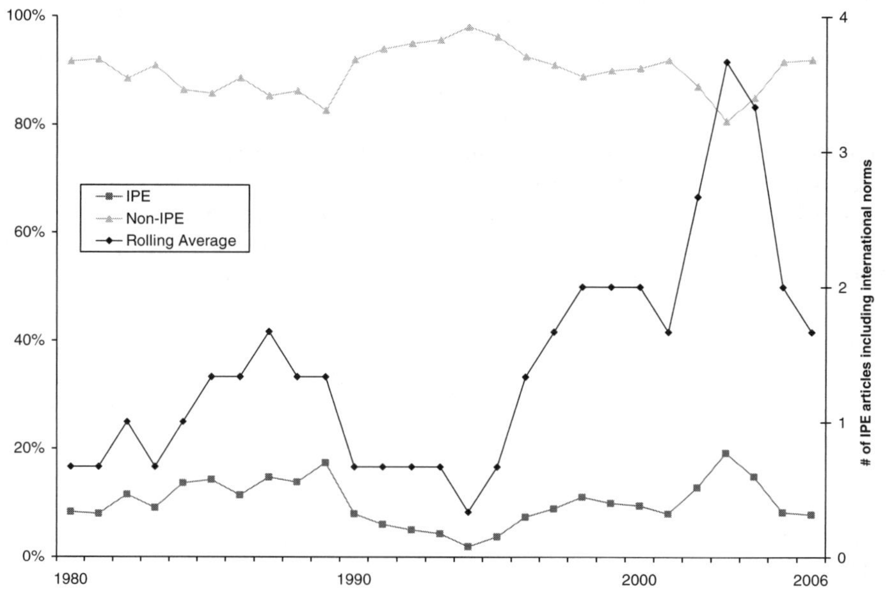

Figure 1.6 Articles including international norms, IPE and non-IPE compared.

Perhaps not surprisingly given these results on ideational questions, IPE also exhibits an epistemological trend that is much more positivist than the rest of the IR literature (although both are becoming more positivist over time). What is quite apparent on this front is the relatively drastic and absolute change in IPE epistemology, consistent with the quantitative methodology trends we have already discussed. As shown in Figure 1.7, IPE went from a low of 67% positivist articles in 1983 to 98% just three years later. This drastic change is far from an outlier, as positivist articles make up no less than 91% for the rest of the time period.

IPE: an American enterprise?

Many prominent scholars argue that IR is a 'not so international discipline',[24] and is instead dominated by United States scholarship (Hoffman, 1977; Waever, 1998). Similar claims about IPE have focused on both American hegemony, but also on bipolarity, namely the split between the American school – based on or around the journal *IO* – and the British school – known also as critical IPE and centered around *RIPE* and *New Political Economy* (Murphy and Nelson, 2001: 394). Among the differences between these two poles, as claimed by Murphy and Nelson (2001), are methodological and epistemological pluralities on the British side contrasted with a narrower view of science and obsession with broader theoretical debates on the American side – claims that mirror the comments of Cohen (2007). Admittedly, we do not have data on British IPE.

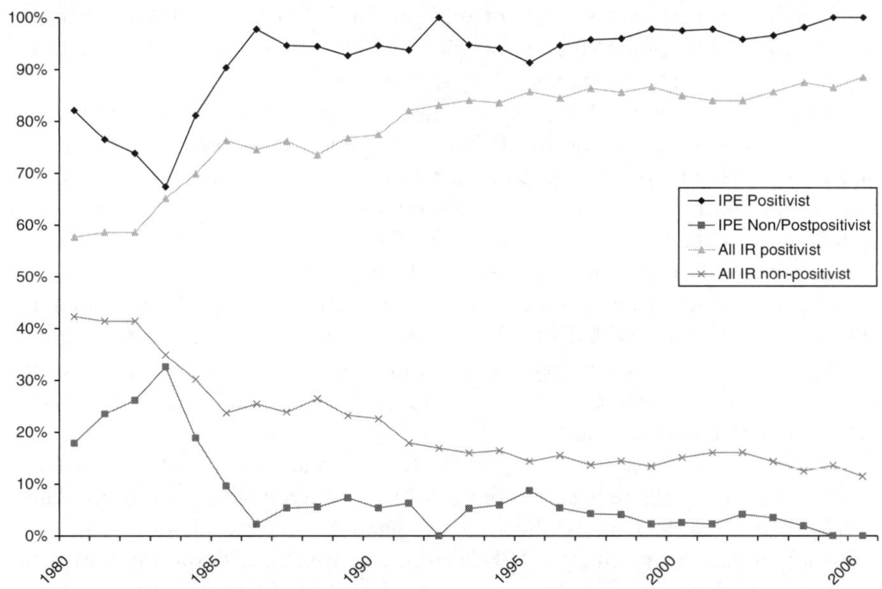

Figure 1.7 Epistemology in IPE and IR compared.

However, we can help to confirm or refute claims about the American field with more specificity.

Murphy and Nelson (2001: 397) argue 'the *IO* school is more concerned with set debates about ways to study international relations', albeit using little more than anecdotal evidence and a restatement of terminology coined in previous issues of *IO*. The amount of literature that fits within one of the four major paradigms (73%) helps to confirm this claim. In addition, Murphy and Nelson claim that neither the American nor the British schools adheres to the norms of science. The two norms they identify as characterizing a 'scientific' approach are the systematic collection and analysis of data and systematic theory building – or, essentially quantitative, empirical work and formal theory. They claim that political science and the sub-field of IR have indeed adopted a systematic empirical orientation, and that a cursory glance at any *APSR* is proof of this claim. But IPE is a laggard, according to Murphy and Nelson. This claim is not true today, if it ever was. Our data clearly demonstrate that American IPE is now more quantitative and more formalized than any other area of IR. Moreover, this happened while retaining a commitment to theoretical traditions despite the claim that this was a major barrier (Murphy and Nelson, 2001: 403).

Conclusion

Cohen (2007, 2008) describes the field of IPE as one that is extremely divided in terms of theory, method, normative commitments, and epistemology. He believes that both sides of the transatlantic divide have a great deal to learn from each other and at various points he advocates dialogue, bridge building, and synthesis between these two schools of thought. Both Waever (1999) and Murphy and Nelson (2001) perceive a similar divide, but both are pessimistic about the prospects for dialogue, bridge building, or theoretical synthesis.

The picture we paint of IPE in the United States is one of a community distinct from both American IR and British style IPE. The picture is not complete, and we still have more work to do in order to have comparable measures for the UK or Europe. In future research, we could include analysis of data we have collected on Canadian IPE. As the home of Robert Cox and other IPE scholars whose work may more aptly be described as non-American IPE, Canada may offer the bridge that Cohen wants us to walk across. Alternatively, Canadian IR/IPE may simply be divided into European and American camps with equally large gulfs between their respective communities. In other work (Lipson *et al.*, 2007), we suggest that Canada sits in the scholarly middle ground between American and European traditions.

Because we only are able to depict the American shore, our data do not allow us to make strong inferences on the probability of overcoming the transatlantic divide in the future. It does allow us to conclude that the picture that Cohen paints of an American school of IPE is largely consistent with our findings. And, given many of the characteristics on which the divide is based, it does seem as though the divide has grown in recent years. When we analyze the responses of

IPE scholars to the survey questions we conclude that the consensus in the American school seems increasingly robust on a range of factors that are addressed by Cohen – epistemology, methods, and theory. More strikingly, the analysis of published articles in the top 12 journals provides even stronger evidence that is consistent with Cohen's story. A complete test would require data on non-American IR/IPE that are similar in quality and form to the data we have presented in this paper. Unfortunately, we currently have very little systematic evidence from surveys or book/journal article analysis on IPE outside the United States.

In the summer/fall of 2008 we will field a survey of IR scholars from the UK, Ireland, Canada, Israel, South Africa, New Zealand, Hong Kong, and Singapore. Further we will initiate a journal coding project that will include the next five IR journals that are more closely associated with European IR (beyond *EJIR, JPR*, and *BJPS*, which we have already coded). After these data collection efforts we will be able to provide multiple measures for the size of the transatlantic divide and the degree to which it has grown or shrunk over time. We will also be able to ascertain the specific areas in which the divide is large and those where a relatively short bridge would help to realize Cohen's goal of constructing a more coherent subfield of IPE.

Acknowledgements

We would like to thank Kate Weaver for convincing us to write this paper and then corralling an array of diverse scholars to engage the broader questions that we address briefly herein. For comments, inspiration, and tough questions (many of which remain unanswered), we thank Mark Blyth, Phil Cerny, Benjamin Cohen, Marty Finnemore, Judy Goldstein, Robert Keohane, and David Lake.

Notes

1 The lecture was later revised and published in *Review of International Political Economy* in May 2007. All future citations will refer to Cohen (2007).

2 See, for example, the responses by John Ravenhill and by Richard Higgot and Matthew Watson in the February 2008 issue of *Review of International Political Economy*. Cohen's arguments contradicted prior claims that the field of IPE had by the late 1990s more or less reached a consensus on theories, methods, and questions (Frieden and Martin, 2002), while reifying previous assertions of a schism between an American discipline and a British one (Murphy and Nelson, 2001).

3 The original source for the TRIP journal article database was Garand and Giles ranking from 2003. See Garand and Giles (2003).

4 With the data we have at this time, we cannot effectively determine whether or not Cohen's depiction of the British school is more or less accurate and can offer only limited evidence on the general trends in British or European IPE scholarship (by seeing what European scholars have published in the top IR journals). However, the TRIP project is in the process of preparing a survey of British IR scholars that will be conducted in September and October 2008. A European-wide survey will follow in 2010. Moreover, we plan to expand the journal article database to include the next

five leading journals that publish IR articles. These include journals that disproportionately publish work by European scholars and include: *Review of International Political Economy*, *Global Governance*, *Millennium*, *Review of International Studies*, and *Journal of Common Market Studies*.

5 For more information on the TRIP project and related databases see Maliniak *et al.* (2007a, 2007b, 2007c, 2008); Peterson *et al.* (2005a, 2005b); Lipson *et al.* (2007); and the TRIP website at www.wm.edu/irtheoryandpractice/ trip/.

6 For the 2006 survey conducted in the United States we used a list compiled by *U.S. News and World Report (USNWR)* to identify all four-year colleges and universities in 2005–2006. There were 1,199 such institutions. We also included the Monterey Institute and seven military schools that were not rated by *USNWR* but have a relatively large number of political science faculty who teach courses on international relations. We then found the IR faculty members teaching at these schools through an extensive series of web searches, email contacts, and phone calls to department chairs, secretaries, and individual scholars. We identified a total of 2,838 individuals who appeared to research and/or teach IR at these institutions. A total of 133 respondents or their agents informed us that they did not belong in the sample because either they had been misidentified and neither taught nor did research in the field of IR, or they had died, changed jobs, or retired. These individuals were not included in our calculation of the response rate. In all, 1,112 scholars responded to the United States version of the survey, either online or through the mail. Certainly, there are additional individuals who were misidentified by our selection process but who never informed us. Hence, our response rate of over 41% is a conservative estimate.

7 For the TRIP journal article database we include data from articles in the 12 leading journals in the field, selected according to their Garand and Giles (2003) 'impact' ratings. The journals include *American Political Science Review*, *American Journal of Political Science*, *British Journal of Political Science*, *European Journal of International Relations*, *International Organization*, *International Security*, *International Studies Quarterly*, *Journal of Conflict Resolution*, *Journal of Peace Research*, *Journal of Politics*, *Security Studies*, and *World Politics*. Although *Foreign Affairs* and *Foreign Policy* were ranked higher than some of the journals on our list, we did not include them because neither is peer-reviewed. In the IR-specific journals – *European Journal of International Relations*, *International Organization*, *International Security*, *International Studies Quarterly*, *Journal of Conflict Resolution*, *Journal of Peace Research*, *Journal of Politics*, *Security Studies*, and *World Politics* – we code every article in every issue for every year of their publication between 1980 and 2007. In the general political science journals – *American Political Science Review*, *American Journal of Political Science*, *British Journal of Political Science* – we only code those articles that fall within the IR subfield (broadly defined). For this paper we drew a sample of articles for the 26-year time series by coding every article in issue #1 and #3 for every year. This means that our sample is roughly half the size of the entire population of articles. The total number of articles in our sample for this paper was 1806. For more precise rules that were followed see the TRIP codebook that is posted online at: http://mjtier.people.wm.edu/TRIP.pdf

8 Our list of journals may not capture the journals that are perceived as most influential among European scholars. To identify these journals would require a survey. Instead, we rely upon the Garand and Giles (2003) impact ratings, which combine measures of citations per article, familiarity, and strength of evaluation. Murphy and Nelson argue that the two IPEs – British and American – are centered on the two journals: *International Organization* for the American school, and *Review of International Political Economy* for the British. Since the TRIP journal article database regrettably does not cover *RIPE* (it was number 76 on the Garand and Giles rankings in 2003, but by 2007 was ranked 33) this significantly constrains our comparative

analysis. However, our data do contain all the articles from the *British Journal of Political Science*, *Journal of Peace Research*, and the *European Journal of International Relations*, which tend to publish proportionately more work from scholars at non-American institutions.

9 This number represents those who answered that their primary or secondary area of study/substantive focus was IPE. In 2004 36% of respondents reported IPE as either a primary or secondary area of study. We are surprised and have no explanation for the six point drop from 2004 to 2006.

10 The finding on University of Colorado could be called the 'Leblang effect', since David Leblang has published so many IPE articles in the leading journals over the past few years. When we analyze only articles published after 2000, we find that Pennsylvania State University and Stanford are the top producers. Also making it into the top ten are LSE (fifth), University of Pennsylvania (fifth), University of California, San Diego (ninth), and University of Illinois, Urbana–Champaign (ninth). Note: there is a five-way tie for ninth.

11 For a detailed analysis of women in the IR discipline and what issue areas they tend to study see Maliniak *et al.* (2008).

12 Further, many of the women who get named on these three lists have made substantial contributions to research in IPE (Beth Simmons, Helen Milner, Martha Finnemore, and Susan Strange). For the complete lists see Maliniak *et al.* (2007c).

13 Question reads, 'List the four journals you read most regularly or otherwise rely on for the best research in your area of expertise'.

14 All citation data come from the Social Science Citation Index. Due to access problems, we collected data only for articles published in or after 1990. The values were recorded in August 2007.

15 For detailed definitions and coding rules for these paradigms see TRIP codebook variable #10. The codebook can be found here: http://mjtier. people.wm.edu/TRIP.pdf.

16 Based on what we know about other IR journals in the field, we expect that if we expanded our sample of journals to include the next 12 journals on the Garand and Giles list we might get different results. Similarly, if we coded books as part of the IPE literature, this would also likely change our findings. However, the labor intensive nature of the coding project, limited time and funds has thus far precluded such analyses.

17 While few commentators would expect realism to dominate the study of IPE, most do assert that it dominates the broader discipline of IR (Doyle, 1997; Vasquez, 1998). While this may have been true at some point in the pre-1980 era, it has never been true since then. For startling evidence of realism's relatively small proportion of the IR literature see Maliniak *et al.* (2007a).

18 This variable captures which paradigms are discussed in a serious way – that is, treated as alternative explanations, used to derive testable hypotheses or used to frame the research question. A simple 'straw-man' depiction of an alternative paradigm does not qualify as 'taken seriously'. Instead, the reader needs to learn something about the utility, internal logic, or scope conditions of the alternative paradigm (or a specific model following from some alternative paradigm), in order to be categorized as 'taken seriously'. The fact that a particular model or theory has implications for a given paradigm does not mean that the article takes that paradigm seriously. With one exception, we DO NOT allow the same value to be entered for 'paradigms taken seriously by author' as for 'paradigm advanced/advocated by author or used to guide analysis'. For example, if an author is advancing a 'defensive realist' approach and he/she tests an alternative 'offensive realist' approach, then the coder would enter 'realist' for 'paradigm advanced/advocated by author or used to guide analysis' but not for 'paradigms taken seriously by author'.

19 This finding is even more striking because there are proportionally fewer realist articles in IPE, and 'paradigm taken seriously' can only take on a value other than the

paradigm of the article. Therefore, since only 3% of the IPE literature is realist, 97% of the articles are eligible to have realism as an alternative paradigm taken seriously. Whereas liberal articles represent 66% of the IPE literature, and only 34% of the remaining IPE literature can include liberalism as an alternative paradigm taken seriously. In short, Lipson (1984) may be right, in practice scholars employ liberal theories to explain IPE and they employ realist theories to explain security affairs.

20 Wendt (1987), Dessler (1989), and Waltz (1979) are all examples of analytical/non-formal conceptual articles. We do not code an article this way if it employs any of the empirical methods (Quantitative, Qualitative, Formal Modeling, Counterfactual, Descriptive, Policy Analysis, or Experimental methods). This means that articles with a significant non-formal theoretical component DO NOT get coded as 'Analytic/Non-formal' even if they make a significant theoretical contribution (for example, Lake, 2006).

21 Due to the use of rolling averages, the values of zero in 1992 and 1993 imply that 1991 and 1994 also were years in which no Analytic/non-formal articles were published.

22 For interesting and striking recent exceptions see a variety of books that articulate the importance of ideational factors in explaining IPE outcomes (Abdelal, 2001, 2007; Abdelal *et al.*, forthcoming; Best, 2005; Blythe, 2002; Germain, 1997; Hall, 1999; McNamara, 1998; Parsons, 2003; Rupert, 2000; Seabrooke, 2006; Sharman, 2006; Sinclair, 2005; Weaver, 2008). The fact that such research is appearing in books rather than the top 12 journals may result from editorial board screening by an entrenched American IPE mainstream. Alternatively, scholars with ideational arguments may not submit to these journals because they have either stopped reading them or believe their work won't get a fair hearing. Alternatively, this pattern may follow from the nature of ideational work where book length manuscripts are a more effective format for the kind of qualitative work that is often associated with ideational arguments. Of course, this last possibility would not explain the large increase in ideational arguments published in these same journals outside the IPE subfield. Finally, it may simply be that the 12 journals we coded do not include existing and new journals that tend to attract qualitative work (foremost *Review of International Political Economy* and *New Political Economy*). The creation of *RIPE* in the mid-1990s may have reduced the number of ideational submissions to these other journals.

23 This does not necessarily imply that they are incorporating these into their work in IPE, since they very well may only include these variables in other (non-IPE) projects.

24 Susan Strange (1995: 290) famously argued that IPE was not only dominated by the American school, but that Americans 'are deaf and blind to anything that's not published in the USA'.

2 The old IPE and the new

Robert O. Keohane

R.O. Keohane (2009) 'The old IPE and the new', *Review of International Political Economy* 16(1): 34–46, published by Taylor & Francis Ltd, http://www.informaworld.com. Permission has been granted by the publisher.

The fascinating documentation of changes in American IPE (international political economy) by Maliniak and Tierney, and Benjamin Cohen's work on the transatlantic divide in the field – published in RIPE in 2007 and as part of his 2008 book (Cohen, 2007, 2008) – provide an appropriate occasion for reflection on the history of the IPE field and where it stands now. My reflections are highly personal, since I was 'present at the creation' of the field in its present form, and since in recent years my work has addressed broader questions of international relations and has diverged from mainstream IPE. In comparing the old and the new IPE, I comment on what seems to be missing from contemporary work and on what I regard as promising directions for future scholarship.

The old IPE

When Susan Strange, Joseph Nye, Peter Katzenstein, Stephen Krasner, John Ruggie, and I started to explore IPE – Susan in the 1960s, Joe and Steve and I around 1970, Peter and John a few years later – there was no field. Very little research was being done. Most economists were ignoring politics, and international relations specialists saw political economy as 'low politics', minor, boring, and incomprehensible. So our task – and opportunity – was first one of identification, then of broad interpretation. In his RIPE paper and his book, Professor Cohen provides an account that closely corresponds to my memory of these early days.[1] Identification of IPE as a proper subject of study was inaugurated in the United Kingdom by Strange's 1970 article in *International Affairs*, 'International Economics and International Relations: A Case of Mutual Neglect' (Strange, 1970), followed by her book, *Sterling and British Policy* (Strange, 1971), which traced connections between politics and economically historically. The key markers in the United States were three special issues of *International Organization* during the 1970s – on transnational relations (Keohane and Nye,

1972), politics and economics (Bergsten and Krause, 1975), and foreign economic policies of advanced industrialized states (Katzenstein, 1978).[2]

It would be misleading to give the impression that these new formulations were entirely original. Indeed, we responded in part to what Richard Cooper, in *The Economics of Interdependence*, defined as the central problem of international economic cooperation: how to maintain openness while enabling states to retain sufficient autonomy to pursue legitimate objectives (Cooper, 1968: 5). In 1970 Charles Kindleberger edited a volume on the multinational corporation that contained an essay by Kenneth Waltz on the 'myth' of interdependence that presented an important challenge for Nye and me, and in 1973 Kindleberger published *The World in Depression*, which made a great impact on all of us (Kindleberger, 1970, 1973). In 1971 Raymond Vernon, who was at the Center for International Affairs at Harvard, published his book on multinational corporations, *Sovereignty at Bay*, as the culmination of years of work on this subject (Vernon, 1971). Finally, Nye's work, and mine, were influenced by the contributions of Ernst B. Haas, particularly to the study of regional integration (Haas, 1958). Nye and I contrasted what we called the 'politics of interdependence' with then-dominant statist and security-oriented conceptions of international relations. We sketched out broad concepts – such as transnational relations, transgovernmental relations, and connections between asymmetrical interdependence and power. We characterized what Realists viewed as 'reality' in world politics as an ideal type, and contrasted it with another ideal type, that of 'complex interdependence'. In situations of complex interdependence, we argued, there were multiple actors (rather than just states), multiple issues that were not necessarily hierarchically ordered, and force and the threat of force were not valuable tools of policy. In our view, neither the Realist model nor complex interdependence fully described world politics; but regional politics, and issue areas, varied in how close they were to one pole or the other.

Nye and I also elaborated a concept first brought to the IPE literature in another special issue of *International Organization* by Ruggie (Ruggie, 1975: 570–3): that of *international regimes*. In *Power and Interdependence* (Keohane and Nye, 1977) we sought to describe and explain regime change, not merely theoretically but also with systematic empirical work on the politics of money and oceans, and on US relations with Australia and Canada.[3] In his edited volume on foreign economic policies, which also appeared in 1977, Katzenstein demonstrated that our international relations analysis of what was now called 'international political economy', or IPE, was too one-dimensional. Genuinely comparative analysis was required, since there was no single template of state responses to interdependence. Peter Gourevitch brilliantly pursued a related theme in his notable 1978 article on 'the second image reversed' (Gourevitch, 1978), and Ruggie followed several years later with his creative concept of 'embedded liberalism' (Ruggie, 1982). During the 1970s this cluster of challenges to Realism was itself challenged most cogently by Robert Gilpin, most notably in his 1975 book on *U.S. Power and the Multinational Corporation*

(Gilpin, 1975); and by Krasner, in a major article on 'State Power and the Structure of International Trade' (Krasner, 1976).

We were young, exuberant, and friends with one another, neither expecting nor wanting general agreement.[4] In her brilliant paper in this symposium, Kathleen McNamara captures well the richness – I would say, 'joyous contestation' – of these debates. To us, the under-explored area of political economy offered irresistible territory for intellectual adventure and, one might say, conquest. To paraphrase the words of a famous Tammany Hall boss, 'we seen our chance and we "tuk" it'. But in the context of contemporary political science, our empiricism was loose and sketchy, and we did not engage in sophisticated causal inference to support our grand theories.

IPE and OEP: increasing rigor and the price that was paid

As Cohen (2008) argues, the dominant norms and incentive structures of American social science then took over, bringing with them reductionism, epistemic rigor, and the models of economics. In many ways, the results are impressive. We have much more comprehensive and precise descriptive mappings of how the world political economy works, in multiple dimensions. In some areas scholars have made some progress toward valid causal inferences, although as Martha Finnemore and Henry Farrell, and David Lake argue, such inferences are very difficult to make. Certainly the quantity of data brought to bear on IPE problems has expanded, and the field is much more sophisticated about methodological problems such as selection bias and endogeneity. Lake's paper lucidly describes this progress, from the 'inside', so to speak, as the elaboration of an open economy politics (OEP) frameworks model. As he says, 'OEP begins with sets of individuals that can be reasonably assumed to share (nearly) identical interests', defined as preferences over alternative outcomes, measurable in material terms. Since interests are deduced from economic theory, OEP can build on the edifice of contemporary economics. The resulting structure has an impressive coherence, quite different from the 'cacophony' of the early years. This is the intellectual foundation on which the International Political Economy Society, co-founded by Lake and Helen Milner, has been constructed. As Maliniak and Tierney show, its commitment to liberalism, and to quantification, have swept into dominance in the field, as measured by publications in high-prestige journals.

I was not one of the people who formulated OEP, although Helen Milner, one of its leading advocates, was both an undergraduate student and PhD advisee of mine, and is one of my closest friends. Much of the OEP work has direct links to my rationalist argument in *After Hegemony* (1984), and it is also consistent with the methodological program laid out in *Designing Social Inquiry* (King *et al.*, 1994), works that almost bracket my own years at Harvard (1985–1996). It would be understandable, therefore, for me to identify with Randall Germain's social construction of the 'Harvard School', and to see OEP as a natural continuation of my earlier work that should properly dominate the IPE field. Yet despite my sympathy with many aspects of the OEP model, and my great respect for its leading proponents, I view it with a gnawing sense of dissatisfaction.[5]

On the positive side of the ledger, many of the disputes of the 1970s and 1980s are no longer salient because they have actually been resolved. Politics and economics are inextricably linked – and the politics of international and transnational economic relations are not 'low politics', unimportant and inferior. Transnational relations are important aspects of world politics, linked in multiple ways to states and interstate politics. What we called complex interdependence is now conceptualized in much more sophisticated ways in terms of networks. There is general acceptance that both differential state and non-state power, and multilateral institutions, are important factors affecting policy outcomes. Under different conditions, states may seek to promote other states' interests, hinder them, or be indifferent to their fate. In other words, many of the earlier controversies have faded because consensus on the answers to them developed, and they became mere background characteristics for more focused and rigorous analysis. To me, this shift represents progress, and is gratifying.

Also on the positive side of the ledger, on the whole, is that fact that during the last 20 years, IPE has been increasingly difficult to distinguish from comparative political economy, or CPE. The original and challenging insights of Gourevitch and Katzenstein have become conventional wisdom. The brightest students in graduate school in the 1980s also recognized that it was not adequate to assume 'state interests', and then to vary systemic conditions such as power structures and institutions. In their own work, they vigorously unpacked the black box of the state (Milner, 1988, 1997; Moravcsik, 1998; Simmons, 1994). A cohort of scholars has demonstrated, in a variety of areas, the importance of domestic conditions. Recent work on coordinated and liberal market economies by Peter Hall and David Soskice (2001) represents a continuation of this line of thought – with a direct line, in my view, back to Katzenstein's special issue of *International Organization* on 'power and plenty' in 1977.

One of the great virtues of the open economy politics model described by Lake is that it integrates IPE and CPE into a common framework. In some respects, therefore, the OEP model is an advance over the old IPE. It highlights the fact that the most important explanatory variables in the field often reflect variation in domestic politics, reflecting different factor endowments and structures of industrial production, which as Albert Hirschman and Peter Gourevitch have emphasized, are partly endogenous to the world political economy itself.

Yet as Peter Katzenstein argues in more detail, a price has been paid. In particular, there is too little emphasis on how 'interests' are constructed – how the ideas that people have in their heads, and that they share collectively, affect their preferences. OEP is, to my mind, too materialistic and much of it is too inclined to identify rationality with egoism – an analytical mistake, since altruists, and suicide bombers, can act quite rationally.[6] As long ago as 1988 Judith Goldstein and I began discussions of the role of ideas leading to our edited 1993 volume, *Ideas and Foreign Policy*. We cast our argument in a rationalist framework, but in many ways it was closer to what has come to be called Constructivism than to the materialistic rationalism of the OEP orthodoxy. In our more individualistic formulation, interests are in a symbiotic relationship with ideas: material interests (as Marx argued) indeed affect the ideas people hold, but ideas are not just 'hooks' for interests: they have independent impact. That volume contains major papers by, among other scholars now known as Constructivists, Peter Katzenstein and Kathryn Sikkink; and an important paper on sovereignty by Stephen Krasner, whose work is unclassifiable in paradigmatic terms since it represents an original synthesis of Realist, Institutionalist, and Constructivist elements.

One price not emphasized by Katzenstein is the assumption in much work that, as Beth Simmons and her colleagues say in a recent issue of *IO*, 'processes of policy change can adequately be understood by conceiving of national governments as making decisions independently of each other' (Simmons *et al.*, 2006: 787). If this null hypothesis were correct, IPE, as opposed to CPE, would essentially be relegated to the study of contextual background factors. We could dismiss IPE in the words Trotsky used in discussing a socialist foreign ministry: we could 'issue a few proclamations and shut up the joint'.

I have been disheartened by this suppression of the 'I' in IPE, but I take heart not just from the symposium in the fall 2006 issue of *IO* but from the emphasis on networks, diffusion, convergence, and strategic interaction in a number of recent papers. As Simmons and increasing numbers of other scholars now argue, the null hypothesis that national governments make decisions independently is not sufficient to explain the spread of liberalism or of convergence in certain sectors. Competitive pressures seem to play a major role, and there is some evidence, less clear, that coercion, learning and emulation also are significant factors. In other words, the distinctively international and transnational processes studied by IPE have to be brought back into the picture.

This 2006 *IO* symposium seems to me to present some of the best of the new IPE. Yet there is still something missing. One thing that is missing, as McNamara and other contributors to this symposium argue, is sustained attention to issues of structural power, as they affect the processes of international political-economic interaction and negotiation. In the 1970s, Marxists and Realists raised these issues and forced the rest of us to grapple with them. Surely similar issues are now being raised by the major shifts in power – toward Asia – taking place in the world political economy, and exemplified by the July 2008 breakdown of the WTO Doha Round negotiations. As structural changes occur, it will become apparent that we have taken for granted certain power structures that are in fact changeable, and the theoretically rich and historically comprehensive style of work, best represented in the previous generation by Gilpin, and now by Katzenstein – discussed so well in this symposium by McNamara – will become increasingly important.

The discussion of causal realism and pragmatism by Finnemore and Farrell, in this issue, provides a way for me to clarify my epistemological stance, which may suggest some differences with some of the ways in which some practitioners of OEP have recently taken the field. I am a very American Mid-Westerner, pragmatic to the core. I have always hesitated to label myself in terms of the philosophy of science, since I am not trained in that field; but my sympathies are much closer to scientific realism, or what Finnemore and Farrell, following Daniel Little, call 'causal realism', than to strict positivism. Finnemore and Farrell contrast these two views by saying that 'causation is important, but also ... causal mechanisms exist independently of directly measurable relationships between variables'. In *Designing Social Inquiry*, King, Verba and I cite Little's 1991 book in saying much the same thing: 'any coherent account of causality needs to specify how the effects are exerted' (King *et al.*, 1994: 85). My commitment to qualitative analysis as an intrinsic part of good social science does not reject sophisticated quantitative analysis in the least, but does reflect a view that causal mechanisms are best elucidated with case studies and narratives, conducted in an analytically rigorous way.[7]

Substantively, what is missing for me in contemporary IPE is the *synthetic interpretation of change*. Nye, Strange, and I saw huge changes taking place before our eyes and we tried – in intuitive and not very scientific ways – to interpret them. Scholars now have a much harder task because the volume of work is so much greater and our knowledge of the complexity of these systems is so much richer. Nevertheless, those of us who are not in the field of IPE – scholars, policy-makers, or citizens – need to know what the best research says about the big questions. One of them, the diffusion question, is now getting the attention it deserves. But there are others.

Five big questions about change

Suppose we asked, as Nye, Strange and I did in 1970: what are the big changes going on in the world political economy? Surely one could make a longer list, including such issues as outsourcing and migration, but I will mention five major changes:

1 *For the first time in human history, genuine economic development is taking place for much of the world's population.* East Asia (excluding China) led the way with four decades of high sustained growth, and growth has for over two decades been rapid in India and extremely fast in China. In more recent years, there have been indications that sustained rates of high growth may be emerging in parts of Latin America, although the situation in most of sub-Saharan Africa remains bleak (Rodrik, 2007: 14). Our theories of IPE were constructed in a very different world: of 'developed' and 'developing' countries – the latter identified mostly by the fact that they were *not* developing. Indeed, for this reason perhaps, Gourevitch, Katzenstein, Nye, and I paid most of our attention to developed countries (Krasner, 1985 is a notable exception). Dependency theory, of course, emphasized – and it now seems, exaggerated – the structural differences between countries in the center and in the periphery. It is perhaps less obvious that the assumption of political as well as economic hierarchy between rich and poor is also deeply embedded

in the theories of asymmetrical interdependence that Nye and I, and others developed, and in realist or quasi-realist theories of American hegemony and western dominance such as those of Krasner. I expect that our implicit hegemonic assumptions will continue to hamper our vision until scholars from Brazil, India and China, and other emerging great powers, become more prominent in the field.[8]

2 *China in particular has become a huge player in international trade and finance*, as the manufacturing center of the world for a huge number of products in ordinary life. China was the largest economic power for centuries, before the industrial revolution, although in those times economic interdependence was much lower than now. China's re-entry into the world political economy since 1978 has been a huge shock to the system – it would seem to be at least comparable to the opening up of the North Atlantic grain trade in the 1870s so memorably studied by Gourevitch. An appropriate metaphor is that of a elephant jumping into a small pond. The effects are already evident in trade, and will increasingly be apparent on financial issues, since China's foreign reserves of well over $1 trillion constitute a political as well as an economic resource.[9] In the West, scholars have been slow to take China sufficiently into account, although there are signs of change. Without China, we would be staging *Hamlet* without the Prince.

3 *Volatility in financial and energy markets has been extreme*. Kindleberger (1978) long ago emphasized the tendency of capitalism toward 'manias, panics, and crashes', and his insight was borne out again in 2008. At the same time, oil price shifts have again been driving shifts in power and asymmetrical interdependence. The sharp rise in oil prices up until mid-2008 contributed to policy changes such as the resistance of oil producers, from Venezuela to Russia and even to Saudi Arabia, to American demands; Brazil's leadership in ethanol production and technologies to use ethanol in automobiles; and China's drive for energy resources in Africa, which is undercutting 'good governance' initiatives, and the influence of the international organizations like the World Bank, on that continent. In the 1970s, rising oil prices, and greater leverage for producers, had major effects on world politics, reflected in the creation and persistence of OPEC and the Arab oil embargo of 1973, which led to the creation of the International Energy Agency, associated with the OECD. But OPEC turned out to be ineffective and prices declined sharply in the mid-1980s and stayed well below late 1970s prices, in real terms, throughout the twentieth century. What will happen to them now is a great unknown. There is some discussion now of how oil affects democracy (Ross, 2001), civil conflict, and aggressive foreign policy, but the demand for analysis of the causes and consequences of oil price fluctuations surely exceeds by far the supply of serious scholarship on the subject.

4 *Truly global actors are now important in world politics.* Global corporations and NGOs such as Human Rights Watch, Oxfam, or Greenpeace are exemplary. As John Ruggie comments, 'This isn't "IPE" any more, and it certainly

isn't "CPE". Global actors demand global rules.'[10] There is some work on this aspect of globalization, but we still have relatively little systematic knowledge about the implications of global civil society for political outcomes. Law faculties have paid attention: one of the most important research programs on this topic focuses on the new field of 'global administrative law' (Kingsbury and Krisch, 2006; Kingsbury *et al*., 2005). Anne-Marie Slaughter (2004) has written about a 'new world order', in which the state is disaggregated and networks of governmental sub-units, NGOs, private corporations, and a variety of regulatory and coordinating bodies become prominent participants in rule-making. John Ruggie has played an important policy role in this emerging global society and has also commented on the politics that ensues (Ruggie, 2004). It would be good if some IPE scholars could turn their attention, and their analytical tools, toward what might be called 'GPE', or 'Global Political Economy'.

5 *Electronic technologies have become the basis for global communications.* We are aware of how such technologies have affected commerce, finance, and investment, but what about their effects on political power? To exercise influence, sets of individuals with common values or interests need to be able to communicate with one another, to form groups, and to act collectively. Indeed, Hannah Arendt once defined power as 'the ability to act in common'. Historically, such communication has been very difficult except through formal organizations, including the state, and all but impossible across state boundaries except with the aid of states. This formerly constant reality has been changing with incredible speed during the last two decades, but we have hardly begun to understand the implications of this momentous fact. One implication may be that collective action on a global scale, for good or ill, is easier than it has ever been before. In this sense, there is *more power* in the system than in the past. Since variations in power are crucial to world politics, the changes in electronic technology have to be important, but I have not seen recent work addressing these issues of communication and power.[11]

In discussing these big questions, innovative scholars may discover rigorous and quantitative methods that can illuminate them. If so, more power to them. But we cannot afford to wait to address these questions for such methods, if they are not available now. As Finnemore and Farrell, and McNamara argue, more attention needs to be paid in graduate programs to rigorous qualitative methods, which have undergone a renaissance during the last 15 years; and as Katzenstein argues, more problem-oriented research is needed to maintain a focus on really important questions. I would urge scholars now active in the IPE field to spend more of their time pondering the big questions about change, and asking not only what the best existing research tells us about them, but what interpretive leaps may be necessary to point the way to more profound and relevant scholarship. I offer this admonition particularly to those scholars who have attained reputations for science and can therefore afford to let the wings of imagination spread.

Study major changes in world politics using a diverse portfolio of methods: this is the message of my brief essay. The best insights of the British school and contemporary American IPE are both valuable – so are contributions from historical and economic sociology, and from the 'ideational turn' in much international relations scholarship. Our standards should be high; but a monoculture, as McNamara implies, depletes the soil from which it grows.

Normatively, I value the critical spirit of British IPE, and of Susan Strange and Robert Cox, because, like them, I am unwilling to accept the contemporary political-economic system as either natural or good. Injustice and inequality are endemic to IPE. But I also value the discipline of social science, as reflected in American IPE, which seeks to separate value judgments from positive analysis. I believe that in the long run, social scientists can have a more positive impact on the human condition through rigorous, persuasive analysis than through subjective criticism. But for us to help improve the human condition, we need to reflect on the big questions.

Acknowledgements

I wish to thank Michael Tierney for urging me to contribute to this symposium at a point when I was reluctant to do so, and Peter Gourevitch, Peter J. Katzenstein, Stephen D. Krasner, Joseph S. Nye, and John Gerard Ruggie for comments on an earlier version of this paper. I am especially grateful to Peter Katzenstein for pressing me to keep going further in explicating my themes. Kate Weaver provided especially thorough and perceptive comments on the penultimate version of this paper, helping me to link it to other papers in this symposium.

Notes

1 Some of the arguments in this paper were originally put forward in a commentary on an earlier version of Professor Cohen's paper, 'The Transatlantic Divide: Why are American and British IPE so Different', at the first meeting of the International Political Economy Society, Princeton University, 17 November 2006. In my view, Professor Cohen's original paper on the transatlantic divide, as published in RIPE in 2007, is excellent – well-researched, thoughtful, sensitive to historical context, and respectful of both American and British international political economy, or IPE. Perhaps it is not surprising that I think so, since we are of the same generation – indeed, we were both on the Board of Editors of *IO* in 1970, along with Susan Strange.

2 Citations are to the published volumes. The transnational relations issue of *International Organization* appeared in the summer of 1971 and the foreign economic policies issue in the fall of 1977. It should be noted that C. Fred Bergsten, among young policy-oriented economists, was a leader in fostering connections between economics and politics, and that all of this work was indebted to Shonfield (1965).

3 It is interesting, and sobering, to note that in our field, people keep reading the conceptual and theoretical 'promissory notes', but the empirical work that follows – in many ways harder to do and certainly more time-consuming – disappears from citations and reading lists. I see many references to Chapters 2 and 3 of *Power and*

Interdependence, and still receive requests to reprint them; but I almost never see any references to the empirical material in Chapters 4–7.

4 Robert Gilpin was a referee for Princeton University Press of *After Hegemony*, and I was a referee for the same press of *The Political Economy of International Relations*. Both reviews were enthusiastic, although as is well known, Gilpin and I differed on many issues.

5 As Peter Katzenstein notes, although many of the founders of IPE received their PhDs from Harvard and started thinking about political economy issues around the lunch-table at the Center for International Affairs, few of us really identified with Harvard (for example, I was on leave at Harvard in 1972 from Swarthmore). The Harvard label also obscures the great influence of Ernst Haas, at Berkeley (the teacher of John Ruggie), and Robert Gilpin, at Princeton. And several of us who received our PhDs at Harvard were based elsewhere while doing our most important work: this is true of Gourevitch, Katzenstein, Krasner, and myself. But the most serious problem with the 'Harvard School' label, as Katzenstein points out, is that few of us who launched contemporary IPE are in sympathy with the 'monocultural turn' in IPE documented by Maliniak and Tierney. Indeed, Randall Germain may be surprised to learn that I agree with much of what he says about the dangers of 'acute scholarly autism' in contemporary IPE. If contemporary IPE were really dominated by the 'Harvard School' as he characterizes it, I would also count myself an 'outsider'.

6 For my most recent and careful discussion of egoism and rationality, see Keohane (2001: 1–13). This essay is reprinted in my *Power and Governance in a Partially Globalized World* (Routledge, 2002), where the relevant passages appear on pp. 255–7 in a section entitled, 'The Limits of Rational Egotism'.

7 The 'state of the art' in this vein is, in my judgment, by an economist. See Greif (2006).

8 The reader may note, in this passage (written for the first draft of this paper in May 2008), another point of agreement between myself and Randall Germain.

9 Clearly, this interdependence is not entirely one-sided, since China would also lose from a collapse of the dollar. It would be good to see the complexities of Chinese–US economic interdependence more thoroughly explored by scholars with intimate knowledge of China, the United States, and IPE.

10 Personal communication, May 2008.

11 One could speculate further. In particular, *our conceptions of time may be changing*, prompted by the internet and the cell-phone. Blogs and the 24-hour news cycle have had a major impact on American politics. Economically, as the saying goes in the internet era, 'if you stop to eat lunch, you are lunch'. In personal relationships, many people are available by cell-phone virtually continuously, and people commonly apologize for not replying even to routine emails within a day or two. But most people in the world still want to stop to eat lunch, to spend time with their families and friends, to relax. It would be interesting to inquire about the implications for world politics of the speeding up of time, and perhaps its fragmentation as continual interruptions and multi-tasking become accepted aspects of modern life.

3 TRIPs across the Atlantic

Theory and epistemology in IPE

David A. Lake

D.A. Lake (2009) 'TRIPs across the Atlantic: theory and epistemology in IPE', *Review of International Political Economy* 16(1): 47–57, published by Taylor & Francis Ltd, http://www.informaworld.com. Permission has been granted by the publisher.

Scholarship is a collective enterprise. What constitutes a valid explanation or even a fact is determined not by any individual but only by the community of scholars and other experts. Anyone can claim a new finding or denounce an old one, but knowledge can only be validated by the appropriate collective.

International political economy (IPE), and the larger field of international relations (IR) of which it is part, has been fraught with debates over paradigms and methods throughout its brief history. These debates are contests over what constitutes knowledge, facts, and valid explanations. In turn, our 'contributions' as scholars and our professional careers are deeply affected by the outcomes of these contests. Recognizing this helps us understand – and perhaps appreciate – the intensity of these 'academic' squabbles and their unfortunate tendency to become highly personalized and vitriolic.

I have relatively little patience for the Great Debates in IR and IPE. Accepting that my views have been shaped by the community of which I am part, and hoping that I have played some small role in shaping its knowledge in return, I often wish that scholars would stop contemplating *how* to do research and simply get on with the business of explaining, understanding, and possibly improving the world we inhabit and, in part, create. Thus, I approach with some skepticism the essay by Benjamin Cohen (2007), the surrounding debate (Cohen, 2008a; Higgott and Watson, 2008; Ravenhill, 2008), and the new essay by Daniel Maliniak and Michael Tierney (2009, this issue) which brings evidence from a survey of North American academics to bear on Cohen's description of the American school. Like Peter Katzenstein (2009: 123), I find that as contributions to the analysis of international relations, these articles have little value in and of themselves. They do not improve our understanding of, say, trade or exchange rate policy. Nor do they shed light on the causes of economic growth and development, income inequality, or effective governance. Yet, the essays do provide a window into what constitutes knowledge in different communities of IPE. It is worthwhile, occasionally, to reflect on the assumptions and standards that define a community of scholars. The value of such reflection – and interchange between communities – is that it may open up new, progressive lines of inquiry.

In this essay, I begin from the Teaching, Research, and International Politics (TRIP) survey as described by Maliniak and Tierney (2009, this issue). I proceed to outline what I see as the most important emerging paradigm in IPE, known as open economy politics (OEP). I see OEP as the core of what Cohen (2007) characterizes as the 'American' school, itself a contested and inappropriate appellation for reasons I shall explain. After providing what I believe is a more accurate depiction of the American school of IPE based upon an OEP approach, I then contrast its epistemology with that of the 'British' school of IPE, which is neither wholly British nor a single school. I argue that the transatlantic divide, such as it is, is really over what constitutes a valid or satisfying explanation of social phenomena, and that a more careful epistemological comparison can lay the groundwork for determining where and how a transatlantic bridge may (or should) be built.

The TRIP survey

Maliniak and Tierney (2009, this issue) report on a survey of IR scholars conducted in the United States (in 2004 and 2006) and Canada (2006 only).[1] The TRIP survey was developed for purposes other than adjudicating the debate begun by Cohen; limited to North American scholars of IR, it reflects only indirectly on whether or not a transatlantic divide exists in IPE and, if so, what its contours are. There is undoubtedly selection bias in who responded to the TRIP survey, but we cannot know its direction or magnitude.[2] The journals used for the article database are neither comprehensive nor randomly selected, and thus again we would expect some unknown selection bias. Nonetheless, the survey appears to be competently carried out given limits on time and resources and its origins in a study of IR scholars in general rather than IPE scholars in particular. Future improvements promise better and more comprehensive results, but I do not think it is terribly profitable to speculate on what scholars in other countries think or what coding additional journals will reveal until that research is actually completed. Thus, although some (like Randall Germain, 2009, this issue) may be tempted to quarrel with Maliniak and Tierney's results, their findings should be presumed to be a relatively accurate depiction of IR and IPE as it is now practiced in the United States and Canada.

The TRIP results also largely fit my own, more subjective assessment of the field of IPE in the United States. It is undeniable, for instance, that American scholars of IPE have moved increasingly toward formal models and statistical tests over the last decade. The weakness of the TRIP survey, however, is that by focusing on broad existing paradigms and methods for the entire discipline of international relations it channels scholars into established categories for identifying themselves and their work. As would any such survey, it lacks subtlety and focuses more on past than future research programs. The TRIP survey, for instance, does not even include OEP on its list of research programs – and thereby misses the emergence of the most important paradigm in American IPE scholarship.[3]

Open economy politics

As Robert Keohane (2009, this issue) describes in his essay, IPE included a broad array of differing theoretical approaches in its earliest years: dependency theory, hegemonic stability theory, endogenous tariff theory, domestic structures, and more. By the late 1980s, a new school of IPE known as OEP began to emerge from the cacophony. OEP is largely rationalist in orientation, assumes the interests of actors are derived from their position within the international division of labor, and examines how strategic interaction and institutions condition the pursuit of those interests.[4] As other approaches fell from popularity – some because they were falsified by events, others from sheer trendiness – OEP gained prominence. By the mid-1990s, OEP had dramatically reshaped the study of IPE in the United States and stimulated an ongoing period of Kuhnian normalcy aimed at elaborating its logic through formal models, testing its implications in large-scale, cross-national statistical analyses, and extending its scope from trade, where it began, to other issue areas.[5]

OEP is classically 'liberal', but most scholars of OEP do not, in my experience, think of themselves self-consciously in this way – even if they might have checked 'liberal' on the TRIP survey for want of a more accurate paradigmatic category.[6] Yet, its growth in American academia is, I suspect, driving the TRIP results on the disproportionately liberal nature of IPE scholars, the relative absence of the 'ideational turn' in IPE, and the burgeoning use of formal and quantitative methods (Maliniak and Tierney, 2009, this issue).

OEP begins with sets of individuals – firms, sectors, factors of production – that can be reasonably assumed to share (nearly) identical interests. Relevant units of analysis vary by technology, institutions, and other factors. Cohen's (2007: 199) characterization notwithstanding, units are not ontologically given nor are states the primary unit of analysis, although state policy is often the object to be explained.[7] OEP derives interests, defined as preferences over alternative outcomes, from the distributional implications of different economic policies, which in turn follow from how a unit is located relative to others in the international economy. Classes or factors of production in any country, for instance, are abundant or scarce relative to the world economy and, thus, prefer greater economic openness or closure, respectively.

Deducing interests from economic theory was the essential innovation of OEP. Rather than treating units simply by assumption or inferring them from the political actions we often want to explain, interests are derived from a prior, falsifiable, and empirically robust theory. The movement of OEP towards economics is not driven, in my view, by disciplinary envy but by the insights that economic theory provides for political interpretations of policy choice. Building on established theories and models of economics also promotes the use of formal models and existing economic data sets in IPE. Despite Robert Wade's fears (2009, this issue), drawing on economic theory does not necessarily lead to the narrowness or narcissism of economics as a discipline. To date, and hopefully into the future, IPE in general and OEP in particular has been disciplined by an intense concern for explaining real world phenomena. Nonetheless, through its link to economics and by focusing on the distributional implications of economic openness for individuals and groups, OEP has inherited a fundamentally materialist conception of interests – perhaps explaining why many American scholars of IPE missed the 'ideational' turn.

After specifying the interests of differing units, OEP turns to how these interests are aggregated through domestic political institutions. Institutions serve to define what political power means in a particular society, largely by setting the reversion point for policy in the absence of agreement between units. All institutions bias how group interests are combined into a national policy. Drawing on institutionalism theory in political science, OEP thus theorizes how interests get refracted through political institutions and then translated into policy.

With domestic interests specified and aggregated through varying sets of institutions, OEP then understands states as bargaining to influence one another's behavior and, in turn, the joint outcome of their interactions. In focusing on bargaining, OEP once again emphasizes institutions, but now at the international level. Just as institutions aggregate interests within states, international institutions can facilitate cooperation by providing information, thereby reducing bargaining failures, or codify redistributive bargains reached between states, which then 'lock in' gains for the winners.

Few scholars give equal weight to all three steps in the OEP approach. Most focus on only one step – for instance, how institutions aggregate societal interests – and treat others in 'reduced form', or as analytic simplifications that are unmodeled in the specific inquiry (see below). In principle, the shared assumptions of OEP allow the components to be connected together into a more complete whole. Originally formulated in the context of trade policy, OEP has been extended to monetary and financial relations (Berhard *et al.*, 2003; Frieden, 1988, 1991b), foreign direct investment (Jensen, 2006; Pinto and Pinto, 2008), immigration (Leblang *et al.*, 2007), foreign aid (Milner, 2006), regulation (Mattli and Woods, 2009; Richards, 1999), corporate governance (Gourevitch and Shinn, 2005), and global governance (Kahler and Lake, 2003).

OEP is also not the only approach accepted or used by American scholars of IPE. As the TRIP results show in the number of adherents to paradigms other than liberalism, not all international political economists in the United States identify even indirectly with OEP. There is, as Cohen's critics have pointed out, high within country variation (Ravenhill, 2008: 27). Nor is OEP confined to the United States. It informs the work of significant groups of scholars, often with training in Economics but strong interests in politics, in Argentina, Germany, Italy, the Nordic countries, and Switzerland – although it appears to have few direct adherents in Britain. In this way, it is inappropriate to refer to an 'American' school of IPE, as does Cohen. Rather, OEP represents an emergent *international* paradigm with, perhaps, a center of gravity in the United States.

Epistemology, not methodology

I leave to others whether there is a British equivalent to OEP. From an outsider's perspective, there appears to be greater variation in approaches to IPE in Britain and less agreement on how research should proceed both theoretically and empirically.[8] One key difference between OEP and most variants of British IPE is epistemology. What is a 'satisfying' explanation of any given phenomenon varies by school. This is one of the most important ways in which one paradigm differs from another. Resonating with the second Great Debate in international relations, which pitted Hedley Bull against several American interlocutors on the 'scientific' study of world politics, this epistemological difference appears to be of long standing (see Knorr and Rosenau, 1969).

Like much (but not all) of political science in the United States, OEP adopts a partial equilibrium or comparative statics approach to theory.[9] Research within OEP progresses by bracketing many obviously varying features of a political-economic environment and treating them as exogenous for purposes of isolating and studying a single causal effect.[10] One might, for instance, bracket where interests 'come from' and study how variable features of domestic institutions aggregate these interests in different ways. Employing the classic hypothetico-deductive method, testable hypotheses thus take the form of *all else held constant*, a change in X leads to a change in Y. In reality, of course, all else is not constant, and various research designs are employed to deal with problems of causal inference created by this background variation.

For scholars working within OEP, a satisfying explanation requires a rigorous and logically specified (but not necessarily mathematical) theory and an appropriately designed test that maximizes variation in the causal variable while controlling for possibly confounding effects. Few studies fully meet this standard, and thus research continues to refine the implications of the theory and explore alternative research designs. But in general, scholars sharing this epistemology are willing to sacrifice empirical richness and context for (1) more parsimonious, but therefore more fully specifiable theories, and (2) more narrow, but therefore more easily controlled empirical tests. A satisfying explanation in this tradition is one that 'knows' well specified causal relationships with some degree of certainty.

Recognizing again that I am an outsider to the British school, that there is great variation within the study of IPE in Britain, and that our own epistemologies may blind us to others, it seems fair to say that scholars of British IR and IPE prefer a more holistic approach to explanation. Less comfortable with partial equilibrium analyses, and impatient with the notion that all else can be held constant, adherents to a holistic epistemology seek to endogenize much of what those who use a partial equilibrium analysis treat as exogenous in any particular study.[11] To continue with the example above, even if one were interested in the effects of institutional variation on policy outcomes, a holistic explanation would not find it appropriate to bracket interests; rather, an essential part of the analysis would be to understand how interests and institutions co-evolve and perhaps constitute one another. This approach, in turn, explains through narratives that explicate the contexts of decisions and explore the plausible alternatives to those that were actually selected at key historical junctures. Accordingly, there is a tendency to emphasize the uniqueness of particular outcomes, rather than to generalize to classes of events. Of course, not every narrative can begin with the big bang or even the comparatively recent dawn of human civilization. Guided by theory, scholars make choices about where and when to begin any analysis, and what factors to include. Even holistic approaches are in some sense partial. Nonetheless, a satisfying holistic explanation is one that shows why the phenomenon under study had to turn out the way it did – and equally why it did not take some other possible path.

The difference between partial equilibrium and holistic epistemologies is not the same as that between positivist and post-positivist epistemologies or qualitative and quantitative methods – and thus is not well captured within the TRIP survey that necessarily focused on more readily discernible categories. For instance, most of my published work has been postpositivist (indeed, critical realist), qualitative and historical, but it clearly employs a partial equilibrium epistemology.[12] Conversely, holistic scholars sometimes employ statistical analyses in their work.[13] As Henry Farrell and Martha Finnemore (2009, this issue) suggest, the divide is less about whether one uses 'numbers' or not, but more about how and in what ways those numbers are used.

Although epistemologies are incommensurable on many dimensions, as Higgott and Watson (2008) fear, this particular difference may be bridgeable, as Cohen (2007) hopes. Scholars on either side of this divide typically do not find the explanations of the other entirely convincing; each is slightly dismissive of the other as 'just stories' or 'just numbers'. But partial equilibrium and holistic analyses do complement one another, if approached with an open mind and a willingness to consider the strengths of the other approach. Partial equilibrium analysts know many specific, narrowly drawn causal relationships well, and can accept or reject generalizable conclusions on these relationships with some measure of confidence. Holistic analyses capture feedback effects necessarily ignored by the partial equilibrium approach, and generate insights into historical contingencies – those dimensions of context that are unique to particular events. Each type of explanation generates important but complementary insights into political events that, taken together, are undoubtedly more insightful and complete than either alone.

Yet, it is unlikely that a large number of partial equilibrium analyses will ever sum to a holistic account, or that a holistic explanation can be broken down and tested as a series of comparative static propositions. Given the emphasis on feedback effects and contingency in holistic accounts, and their absence in partial equilibrium models, we have no reason to expect that either type of explanation scales up or down easily into the other. Thus, I am skeptical whether a seamless and sturdy bridge can be built across the epistemological divide identified by Cohen in transatlantic terms. But it certainly seems possible that a disjointed, irregular bridge with inevitable bumps and gaps can be constructed so that we can visit the other shore on an occasional basis. The scholars on the other side may use concepts and terms that require translation but by crossing over we learn to appreciate better both the 'foreign' community of scholars and our own.

Conclusion

The TRIP survey usefully documents important trends in IR and IPE in North America. Limited in its possible questions and categories of responses to those readily understood by all members of the profession, it is necessarily backwards looking and cannot capture emergent research programs or epistemological subtleties. It is a blunt but nonetheless useful tool, better at describing where we have been than in predicting we are going. The study of IPE in the United States has begun to coalesce around OEP. Like any community, by privileging some assumptions over others, OEP has its blind spots, lacunae, and topics that it cannot discuss without calling the collective enterprise itself into question.[14] Yet, it has proven to be a remarkably progressive approach, in the Lakatosian sense (Lakatos, 1978), that integrates diverse economic transactions under a common theoretical umbrella outlined above. Within the approach, there has been a real cumulation of knowledge.

The existence of a transatlantic divide, and variance on both sides, does not worry me. Indeed, perhaps disagreeing with Cohen on this score, I believe it should be encouraged. Research without guiding paradigms is aimless and fails to cumulate. We should not debate first principles without end, lest we as individual scholars advance the understanding of no one but ourselves. At the same time, while applauding the achievements of OEP, it would be wrong – indeed, it would be utterly without foundation – to declare that any one approach has proven superior to others. The accumulation of knowledge within OEP needs to be paired with a tolerance for pluralism or at least civil dialogue with other approaches, lest it suffer from the problems of monoculture identified by McNamara (2009, this issue) and Wade (2009, this issue). It is a mistake to limit competition between different approaches. Progress in a paradigm is something we should seek, but not at the cost of constructing intellectual monopolies. We all have our hunches, and have placed our bets accordingly. But we do not and cannot now know which current or future paradigm will eventually prove more useful in understanding the international political economy. For this reason, though I agree that trips across the Atlantic are useful and even necessary, I do not believe that the schools should be dissolved or integrated, especially if this occurs at the level of the lowest common denominator. We cannot make progress without paradigms to guide research. Yet, at this stage, we should not all live within the same one either.

Notes

1 See also Maliniak *et al.* (2007).
2 The response rate (41%) was relatively high, suggesting that the results are less biased that other, similar surveys of academic disciplines, but this is impossible to judge for sure. See Maliniak and Tierney (2009, this issue).
3 See questions 0028 and 0029 on the TRIP survey (Maliniak *et al.*, 2007). Reflecting the inherent problem of capturing any emergent research program, however, respondents to the survey might not even recognize OEP as a distinct school of IPE and, especially, IR.
4 On the early diversity in IPE and for a fuller account of OEP, see Lake (2006). The label OEP comes from Bates (1997). Foundational work was done by Frieden (1991a), Gourevitch (1977, 1986), Milner (1988), and Rogowski (1991). For an early manifesto, see Frieden and Rogowski (1996) in the equally important edited volume by Keohane and Milner (1996). OEP is a subset of the Strategic Choice approach in IR. See Lake and Powell (1999). As the citations in this note suggest, OEP originated not with the Magnificent Seven identified by Cohen (2008b) but with some of their perhaps underappreciated contemporaries and the first generation of graduate students they trained.
5 On normal science, see Kuhn (1970) and Lakatos (1978).
6 See question 0042 on the TRIP survey (Maliniak *et al.*, 2007).
7 On the endogenous nature of units, see Hiscox (2002).
8 Given the emphasis on critical theory in Britain, moreover, I suspect that many British readers will see this as an entirely good and proper thing.
9 Constructivism, which employs what I describe below as a more holistic approach, is the major exception to partial equilibrium analysis in the United States – confirming that there is considerable 'within country' variation.
10 Lake and Powell (1999) refer to this as a 'boxes-within-boxes' approach.
11 By holistic here, I do not mean approaches that emphasize structure over agency, as the phrase has sometimes been used. Rather, I mean to denote precisely the duality or recursive nature of structure and agency central to much of British IPE. An alternative label might be a general equilibrium approach, but this loses the dynamic connotations central to work in this tradition.
12 See Lake (1988, 1999). For years it surprised and annoyed me to be classified by others as a 'quantitative' scholar until I came to understand the common confusion described here between epistemology and methodology.
13 Although American-trained and, perhaps, not technically part of the British school, the best example here is the work of Jeffrey M. Chwieroth (now at the London School of Economics). See Chwieroth (2007a, 2007b).
14 I have indicated directions for future research in OEP in an earlier chapter (see Lake, 2006). A full explication of the limitations of OEP is a challenge left for a future essay.

4 Ontology, methodology, and causation in the American school of international political economy

Henry Farrell and Martha Finnemore

H. Farrell and M. Finnemore (2009) 'Ontology, methodology, and causation in the American school of international political economy', *Review of International Political Economy* 16(1): 58–71, published by Taylor & Francis Ltd, http://www.informaworld.com. Permission has been granted by the publisher.

Both Benjamin Cohen's (2007) original essay and Daniel Maliniak and Michael Tierney's response paper point to important – and for the most part underexplored – questions concerning the 'American school of international political economy' and its differences from the kinds of international political economy studied in the UK. Cohen identifies the relationship between ontology and epistemology as key to understanding the American approach to international political economy (and indeed its UK counterpart). In this short article, we examine a slightly different relationship – that between ontology and *methodology*. We argue that the relationship between the fundamental ontological assumptions of American scholarship on international political economy, and the methodologies that scholars use to test these assumptions is much messier than it might appear at first glance.

We explore disjunctures between ontology and methodology in the American school to better understand both the limits of this approach and ways we can counter its blind spots. Tierney and Maliniak's TRIP data point to a strong elective affinity between, on the one hand, rationalist/liberal ontological assumptions and quantitative methodologies, and on the other, constructivist assumptions and qualitative methodologies. As we argue later, this affinity is not as natural or obvious as it might seem at first glance. It also points to a deeper set of issues for the field. As a variety of philosophers of science have insisted, we need to do *much* better in thinking about the relationship between our underlying notions of causation and the methodological tools that we employ. By so doing, we will not only be able to better build social-scientific knowledge, but also better help bridge the empirical-normative gap that Cohen identifies. More broadly, we suggest that by combining a more thoughtful approach to causation with a broadly pragmatist approach to the philosophy of science we can both remedy some of the defects of the American school of international political economy, and provide some pointers to the British school too.

The relationship between ontology and methodology

In order better to understand the relationship between ontology and methodology in the study of international political economy, we would ideally like to examine the relationship between the ontological assumptions (that is, the basic understandings of how the world works) of the two main theoretical approaches to international political economy – rational choice and constructivism – and the methodological approaches and associated methodologies – statistical or qualitative – that proponents of each ontology use to investigate the world.[1]

While we do not have space to provide a complete account of these ontologies and methodologies, we note that constructivism and rational choice accounts start from quite different accounts of how the world operates. Typically, constructivists employ ontologies that invoke mutual constitution and transformation, while rationalists, whether materialist or ideationalist, work from models in which actors' understandings of the world are complete and fixed.[2]

On the basis of non-systematic observation, we suspected that there would be a strong and obvious relationship between ontology and methodology in IPE scholarship. IPE scholars adopting a rational choice (or, in our proxy, liberal – see below) ontology would be more likely to use quantitative methodology, and IPE scholars using a constructivist ontology would be more likely to use qualitative methodological techniques. The TRIP dataset, which covers a broad sampling of articles from the major journals in the field, does not provide us with precisely the data one would like to test this. There is no specific code for rational choice assumptions in the data. However, we suggest that liberalism provides a reasonable proxy for rational choice: while liberal scholarship need not be rational choice,[3] we believe that most liberal articles in the field of international political economy invoke either soft or hard rational choice assumptions.[4]

Our expectation of affinities between rational choice and quantitative methods and between constructivism and qualitative methods were amply confirmed. We had originally intended to use relative risk ratios to illustrate the changing relationship between liberal/constructivist ontologies and quantitative/qualitative methodologies over time. However, this proved impossible; there are *zero* constructivist international political economy articles that employ quantitative techniques in the TRIP dataset (given their sampling technique, this figure has a confidence interval of +/−4.5% at the 95% level).[5] Even if there are a couple of articles that the sample has missed, this suggests an even stronger relationship between constructivist ontology and qualitative/case study methodology than we had first anticipated.[6]

When we look in contrast at the dataset's evidence regarding liberal IPE scholars' use of quantitative and qualitative techniques, we find instead that not only is there a strong contemporary emphasis on quantitative work, but that this emphasis appears to have become dramatically more pronounced in the recent past. Here, 1997 appears to have been the cusp year in which there were as many liberal articles with quantitative methodology published as with qualitative methodology (using the three year average to smooth out noise). From this point on, we see a rapidly increasing dominance of quantitative articles, so that in the three year average for 2006 there are 11 times as many articles published with a liberal ontology and quantitative methodology as there are articles with a liberal ontology and qualitative methodology, almost exactly reversing the ratio seen in 1986.

Why is this relationship so strong?

We doubt that this finding comes as a complete surprise to many scholars in the American school of IPE, whether rational choice or constructivist: it confirms our everyday presuppositions about the relationship between ontology and methodology. Yet, as others in this special issue argue, we do not think this relationship is natural or inevitable. Economic sociologists share many common ontological assumptions with constructivist political scientists, yet they frequently carry out quantitative empirical work to assess claims based on these assumptions.[7] Nor is there any reason why quantitative techniques of the kind that are usually employed in international political economy (multiple regression and its cousins) should be especially appropriate to rationalist arguments. Indeed, one might plausibly suggest that the opposite is true. Peter Hall (2003) argues that multiple regression and its variants are in fact badly suited to investigating game theoretic claims, which frequently argue that possible outcomes off the equilibrium path of play are key to explaining those equilibria that are selected. Hall makes a plausible case that qualitative evidence and process tracing provide better purchase than commonly used quantitative techniques for elucidating the kinds of causal processes that game theoretic models point towards.

Thus, we cannot assume that the very striking relationship we see between ontology and methodology flows from some underlying affinity between assumptions and research techniques. Instead, as Kate McNamara and Nicola Phillips argue in this issue, we suggest that this relationship more plausibly has its origins in the sociology of the field, that is, the social processes through which scholars are trained, come to select their fields of study, construct their disciplinary identities and decide where to submit their work and how to frame it. While the TRIP dataset can illustrate intriguing correlations, it cannot really get at the causal mechanisms that underlie those correlations. We can reasonably speculate however, regarding two possible mechanisms that we strongly suspect are important.

The first of these has to do with training. We suspect that American doctoral programs in IR disproportionately emphasize training in quantitative methods. It would hardly be surprising, then, if American IR scholars disproportionately favor these methods in designing their research. To investigate, we asked what methods courses are (a) required and (b) offered at the top IR PhD programs

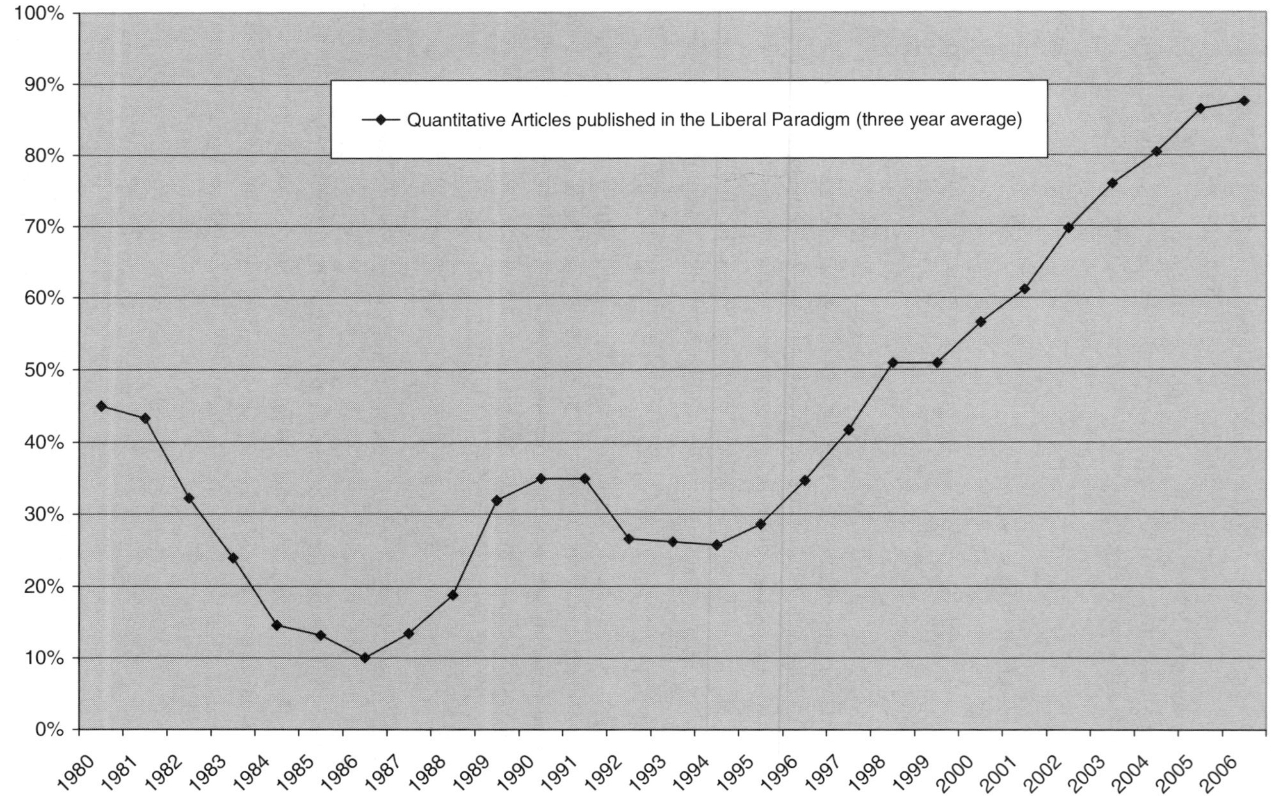

Figure 4.1 Quantitative articles published in the liberal paradigm of IPE as a percentage of the total of quantitative and qualitative articles (three year average).

listed by respondents in the TRIP survey (Q22).[8] Based on curricula and program requirements listed on their websites, all but seven of the top programs require at least one course in quantitative methods and six of them require at least two such courses. No program lists a qualitative methods course as required for their PhD. Requirements aside, quantitative methods offerings are much richer than offerings in qualitative methods. Quantitative offerings range from three to 12 distinct courses offered over a two year period (the usual duration of coursework for a doctoral student) at top departments, with an average of 7.5 different courses on offer; qualitative offerings range from zero to 1.5 different courses over a two year period with an average of 0.64 distinct qualitative courses offered in a two year period. Rough as they are, these data support our suspicion that quantitative methods are given pride of place in US training.

The second mechanism, as Nicola Phillips and Randy Germain also suggest, has to do with incentives for publication. Here, we have no data that would allow us to investigate the relevant causal processes, beyond occasional policy statements from editors and our assessment of the collective wisdom of the field from gossip and conversation with others. We suspect that both social processes and strategic incentives are important to explaining who submits articles where, and which articles get published. Scholars are likely to be strategic in where they submit articles and how they frame them. In particular, scholars in research-oriented departments who have not achieved tenure are highly motivated to adhere to the perceived implicit norms of major journals in order to get published, and hence improve their chances of tenure and promotion. They will be keenly interested in any information, however ambiguous, as to what criteria reviewers and editors for particular journals are likely to use in deciding whether to recommend acceptance or rejection.

This means that authors' decisions about whether to use, say, quantitative or qualitative methodology to investigate a particular research question is likely to be affected by their perceptions of how their choice of methodology might affect their chances of getting published in a particular journal or small subset of journals. If they believe that qualitative research exploring hypotheses derived from rational choice theory, or quantitative research exploring hypotheses derived from constructivism, is likely to be poorly received by reviewers and editors, they may decide not to write the article. Alternatively, where possible, they may rewrite it to change either research methodologies or ontological assumptions so that it accords better with the perceived preferences of reviewers and editors.

Authors' perceptions about what will and will not get published may thus be guided by assessments about the priorities of particular journals. They may also involve self-reinforcing information cascades. If a journal begins to publish more (or less) of a particular type of article than others, for purely random reasons, this may create a perception among potential authors that this journal is a good (or bad) venue to try to place articles of a particular kind. As more authors submit (or decline to submit) work of the relevant kind, this impression may become self-reinforcing, even if the editor and reviewers for that journal do not in fact particularly favor or disfavor articles of the relevant type. Without further data (and for obvious reasons data about the social aspects of the reviewing process are hard to come by), it is impossible to assess how accurate these assessments are. Nonetheless, the ubiquity of gossip among international scholars about which journal is publishing who and why and the potential impact of changes in editorial teams in major journals suggests (although it certainly does not prove) that these impressions are likely to be causally important in shaping scholars' publication strategies.

Why should we care?

What implications flow from the relationship between ontology and methodology in the American approach to international political economy? Or, to put it more bluntly, why should we care about abstruse questions of metatheory? The first and most obvious reason to care is that it suggests that there are important intellectual gains to be made from exploring the underutilized combinations of ontology and methodology – that is, from the combination of constructivist ontology and quantitative methodology on the one hand, and rational choice ontology and qualitative methodology on the other. The second and more subtle reason is that if we think more carefully about the relationship between methodology and ontology, we will in turn be more likely to be careful when we talk about causation.

If we are right that there is no a priori intellectual reason why a rationalist ontology should go together with quantitative methodologies, or why a constructivist ontology should be especially well suited to a qualitative methodology, several interesting implications follow. First, there are important gaps in our knowledge – it is highly likely that quantitative evidence will be helpful to constructivists in investigating and refining their arguments and qualitative information will similarly be helpful to rational choice scholars in investigating and refining theirs. Second, as a consequence, these gaps are remediable (and as we note, there are examples in related fields of inquiry which provide guidelines as to how these gaps might be filled). Third and finally, if these gaps are to be remedied quickly and properly, it will require not only effort on the part of individual scholars, but also collective changes in graduate student training and publication norms.

Carrying out the last of these steps is perhaps the hardest. Graduate programs need to incorporate rigorous training in qualitative methods of research. The necessary resources for, and interest in, such a change clearly exist. The American Political Science Association's (APSA's) Qualitative Methods organized section is now the Association's second largest (as of February 2008) and the number of students attending the Institute for Qualitative and Multi-Method Research (IQMR) has roughly tripled since 2002 (from 45 to 129) (Collier and Elman, 2008).[9] 'Mainstreaming' qualitative methods training into students' home departments as part of the standard curriculum is clearly the next step. Changing the perceived and actual norms of publication and submission is likely to be more difficult. As a plethora of research on organizations tells us, informal norms and perceptions such as those that shape the publication process in editorial boards and professional associations, are often deeply entrenched. Some efforts to reform these norms and perceptions in the past have been at least partially successful (e.g. the steps that were taken to make the *American Political Science Review* a more friendly-seeming journal to qualitative approaches following criticisms from the Perestroika movement). But changes of this sort involve serious investments of time and energy, and even then their success is chancy.

We do not provide specific proposals about how this change should take place. Instead, we suggest that we need to begin a frank and open-ended conversation about (a) how we train our graduate students, (b) how we submit articles on the one hand, as working academics, and assess them on the other, as editors and reviewers, and (c) what we are missing out on (or leaving out) of our analyses, using the very helpful data that Maliniak and Tierney provide as a starting point. The disconnect between the ways that scholars talk about graduate training and publication practices in private conversations, and the ways that they publicly present their own research or assess the research of others is sometimes rather startling. As professors in public debate, we often present the processes of training and publication as relatively neutral and efficient means of furthering the dissemination of knowledge. As professors in private conversation, we sometimes obsess about how 'our' perspective is faring against those of others in the academy, or how the publishing priorities of this or that journal are shaped by the editor's idiosyncrasies or perceived social connections.

The point is not that either the public or the private perspective has a monopoly on the truth: the field of international relations is both a means for gathering knowledge about the world, *and* a social institution, with all the power struggles and idiosyncrasies that we expect social institutions to have. Rather, the point is that we often forget (or want to forget) the ways in which the informal social understandings of our field shape our research, training and publishing agendas. But if we do not pay attention to these understandings – and think hard about what they blind us to as well as what they reveal – we're likely to miss out on much that is interesting and important in the modern international political economy.

Where we should be going

As our own initial contribution to this conversation, we would like to push scholars (a) to think more clearly about causation, and (b) to start thinking about both issues of causation and broader research agendas in a more *pragmatic* way. Our call has features in common with Peter Katzenstein's plea in this issue for more problem-driven research, but also appeals to a tradition of pragmatist claims about the purposes of social inquiry. We want to use pragmatist and causal realist arguments, to argue against *both* the casual positivism of many scholars in the American school of international political economy, *and* the post-positivist or mixed normative/positivist stance of many scholars in the British school.

Getting scholars of international political economy to think more carefully about causation is even more important than encouraging them to try out underexploited combinations of ontology and methodology. The lack of attention to how ontology and methodology relate goes together with a deeper disregard for problems of causation. On the one hand, 'mainstream' scholars in the American school often appear to carry out research on the basis of a not-very-well-thought-through positivism. That is, they directly or indirectly suggest that all we need to pay attention to are variables and relationships between them that are best explored either through statistical hypothesis-testing or through qualitative methods that seek to replicate the logic of statistical inquiry (King *et al.*, 1994). On the other, many scholars in the UK, Europe and (in smaller numbers) the United States, adopt explicitly post-positivist ontologies, in which they either do not try to arrive at causal or generalizable findings, or else mix together normative and positivist claims so that critique and empirical claims are impossible to separate from each other.

We differ from both, although we happily recognize that scholars using both sets of assumptions have made very substantial contributions indeed to our understanding of international politics. Instead, we are more convinced by social-scientific variants of scientific realism, which stress (in contrast to post-positivists) that causation is important, but also (in contrast to positivists) that causal mechanisms exist independently of directly measurable relationships between variables.

What Daniel Little calls 'causal realism' is fully compatible with each of the major methodological approaches to international relations (Little, 1998, n.d.). We can identify constructivist (Wendt, 1999), sociological (Little, n.d.), historical institutionalism (Mahoney, 2003) and rationalist (Johnson, 2006) variants of these arguments in the theoretical and empirical literature. These various authors likely disagree, either mildly or vigorously, about the *precise mechanisms* that are most helpful to social explanation, but all of them agree that we should pay proper attention to causal mechanisms, and that we should treat them as being distinct from the observed statistical or qualitative relationships from which we infer their existence. Social scientists trying to find mechanisms are rather like physicists trying to demonstrate the existence of new fundamental particles using data about collisions in accelerators – while we cannot observe the mechanisms themselves, just as the physicists cannot observe the particles, we can nonetheless make inferences about their existence and nature from the data that we have. We do not have space to do more than begin to sketch out what these views entail, but we do wish to point out, following James Johnson, that causal realism usefully complements a *pragmatist* account of the task of explanation in many respects (Johnson, 2006). That is, it goes hand-in-hand with accounts of scientific explanation that 'treat theory and methods as tools for solving problems, and so judge them instrumentally in terms of their consequences' (2006: 227). Rather than seeking necessarily to construct coherent bodies of law-like generalizations on the one hand, or to deny the usefulness of the scientific enterprise on the other, these accounts (in their social-scientific form) seek to identify relevant causal mechanisms, and arrive at useful, but often imperfect, judgments regarding the scope conditions under which these mechanisms are likely to apply. Useful causal explanations will invariably rest on unobservables (Mahoney,

2003). Articulating the relevant mechanisms is thus, at bottom, a theoretical enterprise, one that must be aided by the best possible empirical research, but that cannot be reduced to measurement and inference. Pragmatist accounts of how politics works are thus more modest in their scientific ambitions than many forms of positivism in not requiring law-like generalizations but also are explicitly committed to the refining, testing and re-testing of empirical knowledge. They are notably more ambitious than positivist accounts in that they aspire to *explanation* rather than simple correlation.

Finally, pragmatists are committed to the generation of *useful* knowledge. Again, this helps to throw into relief a set of issues that are partially obscured by existing debates. International political economy, in both its American and English variants, possesses no equivalent of *International Security* – that is, a highly prestigious journal which seeks to bridge the divide between scholars interested in theory, and practitioners interested in the generation of useful knowledge. This lacuna both reflects and reinforces a division between the generation of theory and the generation of practical knowledge. Interestingly, this division is less marked in other academic approaches to the same issues (including approaches that might seem, on the face of it, more abstract, such as economics). When practitioners want academics' advice on how to reform, for example, the International Monetary Fund or the Appellate Body of the WTO, they typically turn to economists or legal scholars rather than to scholars of international political economy.

From the perspectives of the existing schools, this is by no means necessarily a bad thing. Scholars of the American school (even while casting the occasional envious glance at their colleagues in the economics department) may reasonably prefer to engage in the scientific enterprise without having to fend off the dubious enticements of consultancy fees and influence over the policy process. Scholars of the British school for their part may identify (with some reason) engagement with the policy process in its current form as tantamount to selling out to the enablers of global capitalism.[10]

Even so, we suspect that the dearth of connective tissue between the study of international political economy and the processes through which decisions are actually made in that economy weakens both approaches. On the one hand, this disconnect leads to a certain degree of aridity in much of the bread-and-butter work of the American school of international political economy. While the outstanding contributions of that approach provide deeply important insights into how the international political economy actually works, much current research is neither scientifically cumulative in any very convincing way, nor especially interesting on its pragmatic merits to non-specialists.

On the other hand, while the best work in the British school weds together normative and empirical insights so that each reinforces the other, some of the less inspired contributions instead use normative arguments to try to patch over holes in their empirical evidence. Often, these weaker articles and monographs also fail in their own stated purpose as a result. They do not provide useful contributions to an overall critique of global capitalism that might prove helpful to those trying to change it.

Scholars of both approaches then might benefit from some deeper pragmatic consideration over the kinds of knowledge they are generating, and the ways in which this knowledge is likely to be useful. Furthermore, even though we do not for a moment believe that an infusion of pragmatism would dissolve the divisions between the two schools, we do suspect that it might recast the debate between them in some beneficial ways. It would also help IPE scholars move forward from the often sterile 'paradigm debates' discussed by Tierney and Maliniak to a more developed understanding of the specific contribution that different combinations of ontology and methodology have to offer to the understanding of the international economy. Finally, it would help international political economy to focus on some of the 'big questions' that Keohane identifies in his contribution to this volume. A subdiscipline which purports to understand the world economy, but which fails to address the major changes in train in that economy, will have only limited ability to generate useful knowledge.

As we have argued in this short article, both ontology and methodology are important. But very often, the ways in which they relate to each other are the contingent result of the sociology of the field (and individual and collective struggles for recognition and legitimacy) rather than independently rooted complementarities between assumptions and methods. Scholars may thus build hardened identities around specific ways of relating ontology and methodology that may be less solid than they appear at first.

Reorienting our scholarship so that it focuses on questions of usefulness is one good way of revisiting these identities. However, it also challenges the ways that these identities relate to each other, and (as Cohen suggests) partially constitute each other. If we move from asking the question of which ontological and methodological assumptions are 'better' in some absolute sense, to the more nuanced question of which assumptions are more useful for which purposes, we will have advanced debate. There would still be substantial room for disagreement, not only over the particular merits of specific combinations, but over the questions of *useful for what* and *useful to whom*. However, a debate over these issues is more likely, we think, to be useful than the extended stand-off that we have seen over the last 20 years.

Acknowledgements

We are grateful to Mike Tierney and Dan Maliniak for making their data available to us, and to Dan Maliniak for both data analysis and his extraordinary patience with repeated requests for more data. Amir Stepak provided valuable research assistance. We are also grateful to Jim Johnson, Daniel Nexon, Kate McNamara and Kate Weaver for very helpful comments.

Notes

1 As we discuss further below, the Tierney Maliniak dataset does not specifically code for rational choice.

2 Standard game theoretic models require that there are 'no surprises' – i.e. that actors have complete knowledge of the game tree, and all possible outcomes, even if they do not necessarily know which part of the game tree they are on. See further, e.g. Farrell (2003).

3 See Doyle (1983a, 1983b). For overviews of different varieties of liberalism see Zacher and Matthew (1995), Doyle (1997), and Moravcsik (1997).

4 For discussion of the coding rules for 'liberal' see Maliniak and Tierney's discussion of codings for variables 4 and 10 (Maliniak *et al.*, 2007: 33–8). The most obvious general exception is work on the democratic peace, which has a strong strain of work that is identifiably liberal, but descends either from idealist or classical republican thought. However, this body of literature rests outside international political economy.

5 More generally, of all 207 constructivist articles (international political economy and non-international political economy) coded in the dataset, only 19 use quantitative methods.

6 An anecdote in David Lake's contribution to this special issue neatly exemplifies how powerful this identification between quantitative methodology and liberal ontology has become; although most of Lake's work is qualitative and historical, he found himself identified to his chagrin as a 'quantitative' scholar because he adheres to a liberal and rational choice ontology (Lake, 2009, this issue).

7 See, for example, Fligstein (1985) and Davis *et al.* (1994). Work by sociologists in the 'world polity' tradition pioneered by John Meyer and others have relied heavily on quantitative methods from its earliest days. See *inter alia* Meyer and Hannan (1979) or more recently Drori *et al.* (2006).

8 For an earlier examination of these issues, see Bennett *et al.* (2003).

9 Summary statistics on IQMR supplied by Colin Elman, personal communication.

10 See Germain (2009, this issue) for relevant observations on this point.

5 Of intellectual monocultures and the study of IPE

Kathleen R. McNamara

K.R. McNamara (2009) 'Of intellectual monocultures and the study of IPE', *Review of International Political Economy* 16(1): 72–84, published by Taylor & Francis Ltd, http://www.informaworld.com. Permission has been granted by the publisher.

By its very nature, international political economy (IPE) involves the juxtaposition of opposing logics, and the interaction of complex dynamics across multiple national, subnational and international political arenas. Markets, whose actors are presumed to be driven by logics of efficiency in the pursuit of profits, intersect with politics, where actors are motivated in large part by logics of power. Both operate within a broader cultural and ideational context. Domestic interest groups, bureaucracies, civil society, political elites, and firms all play a role in creating foreign economic policy, in conjunction with states, international institutions and international markets. Understanding important contemporary IPE issues, like the geopolitical implications of China's economic rise, the interplay of forces bringing about the end of the Bretton Woods system, or the potential foreign policy implications of sovereign wealth funds, demands the ability to probe the tensions and interactions across a multitude of political, social and economic realms. Like a puzzle with many pieces, the study of IPE begs for diversity in theoretical approach, scholarly method, and empirical focus. Indeed, the phenomena under study would seem far too important and multifaceted to leave to one analytic or methodological perspective alone.

And yet, that seems to be where we have ended up in the American academy, according to the results of Daniel Maliniak and Michael J. Tierney reported in this special issue. Examining articles published in 12 top political science journals, they find that the field of IPE has largely converged around a single theoretical perspective, liberalism; a single ontological position, rationalism; and a single method, quantitative analysis. Their findings demonstrate that in the past decade or so, as measured in the mostly American journals on their list, IPE work has become distinct from trends in the larger international relations (IR) field. While there is paradigmatic, ontological, and methodological diversity in IR as a whole, IPE has strikingly departed from the broader field as well as its own history of pluralistic scholarship.

Monocultures, be they intellectual or agricultural, are never healthy. IPE, as now found in the American high status political science journals and as taught in the most prominent United State graduate programs, has overly narrowed to the point that too much work in our field has become academically arid and risks leaving unsolved the big, important real world puzzles. Fortunately, however, outside of this narrow monoculture there is a continued diversity of work to be found in the broader American IPE academy. This work is appearing in other fora from that surveyed in Maliniak and Tierney, primarily in book form and in alternative journals, as well as in cognate disciplines such as economic sociology. If political scientists want to remain relevant beyond a small circle of like-minded interlocutors, we need to focus less on purported schisms across our field and on protecting our own version of IPE truth. Despite professional incentives in some camps that exist for continue narrowing, countervailing real world forces will push for diversity in the study of the international political economy. To dismantle this intellectual monoculture, we need to reembrace diversity in IPE graduate training, publish a variety of perspectives and methods in mainstream high status journals, and reward those who seek out important real world puzzles and answer them effectively, regardless of their methods or ontologies.[1] After all, the current narrow definition of what constitutes quality work in IPE (liberal, rationalist and quantitative) is itself a socially constructed definition driven by a particular epistemic community with its own interests to protect. Recognizing this is a key first step to escaping the ills of intellectual monoculture.

The pluralist foundations of IPE[2]

For many of my generation of scholars, our first introduction to IPE grappled head on with its complexity, namely in the work of Robert Gilpin and his 'blue book', the magisterial synthesis of *The Political Economy of International Relations* (1987). The rich and nuanced interplay of human drives evident in IPE – for efficiency, for power, and for social status – was thoroughly explored by Gilpin, who although a realist, engaged deeply with alternative perspectives. In particular, three characteristics stood out in Gilpin's work and provide a striking contrast to much of today's scholarship. The first characteristic is a non-negotiable view of the economy as permeated by *politics and state power*. This may seem obvious, perhaps trivial, but if one reads current work in the field of IPE, one finds that power is strangely absent, and that economic motives often substitute for political ones. A second characteristic of Gilpin's, expressed so well in the blue book, is the profoundly *interdisciplinary nature* of his scholarship. He seemed in preparing that book to have read and thoroughly digested nearly everything written on the topic, in the last several centuries, by an astonishing range of political scientists, historians, economists and sociologists. Again, while the current vogue in IPE is to burrow into a narrow circle of like-minded academics, Gilpin cast a much bigger and more catholic intellectual net, and showed that one can catch a lot more by doing so. For example, in *War and Change in World*

Politics (1981), Gilpin's attention to power, legitimacy, and the rules of governance demonstrated his singular ability to engage both rational materialist and ideational arguments, and remains remarkable in a field riven with ontological cleavages. Finally, Gilpin's work, in the blue book and elsewhere has always had a deep *grounding in history*. Placing any given episode of currency crisis or trade openness or closure within a long historical context allowed Gilpin to shed light on the broader dynamics at work in producing change or continuity. I suspect that these three facets of Gilpin's work have contributed to his high ranking on the list of 'most influential' authors in Maliniak and Tierney's survey of IPE scholars. The question (and puzzle) is how much Gilpin's influence is actually visible in the prominent journal articles that are the focus of Maliniak and Tierney's survey, and to what degree Gilpin's model of pluralistic inquiry is still the norm.

In terms of graduate training more generally, doctoral seminars in IPE taught at top research universities a decade or two ago also ranged across a diverse group of authors. My firsthand experience with a doctoral seminar in IPE taught at a first rank research university reflected an astonishingly rich set of ideas and methods. The required reading included Douglass North's (1990) explanations of the rise and decline of nations as a function of the long history of their institutional arrangements, Peter Gourevitch's (1986) probing of the social and political sources of severe economic depressions, Fernand Braudel's (1992) stunning historical exploration of the role of exchange in transforming social and political relations, Stephen Krasner's (1976, 1983) analysis of the role of hegemony on trade openness, and Ronald Rogowski's (1990) path breaking work on political cleavages across factoral groups.

I doubt my experience with IPE training was unique: in the United State academy in the first half of the 1990s, theoretical and methodological pluralism reined. Markets and politics were examined through the theoretical lens of microeconomics, sociology, historical institutionalism, power politics, and investigated with the aid of both qualitative and quantitative tools. IPE was deeply intertwined with the field of IR as a whole, with key debates about American decline and hegemonic stability, regimes, absolute and relative gains, the role of institutions all arising from substantive IPE and crossing over to illuminate much broader dynamics of international politics. Volumes such as the *International Regimes* book and *Cooperation under Anarchy* (Oye, 1986) brought together scholars from security, IPE and international organization (IO), whether realist, liberal, or ideational, under broad conceptual frameworks. Syllabi of the era, the debates in the literature, and Maliniak and Tierney's data demonstrate the original character of IPE as diverse, and influenced by and influential beyond its subfield boundaries. The goal of doing high quality work on important questions, whatever the method, was what permeated much first rate graduate training.

Today's IPE monoculture?

So what would a graduate student learn today in a typical IPE class at a high status research university? Like Farrell and Finnemore, I suspect that many of the trends we observe in the American school of IPE are inextricably linked to changes in the processes of graduate training and professional socialization. Surveying current IPE doctoral classes at major research universities identified as those training the most IPE students in the Maliniak and Tierney article (2009, this issue: Table 1), I find that they would largely read a syllabus constructed around a more strikingly narrower view of IPE than in previous decades.[3] The works read would be almost entirely from a liberal perspective, with little to no discussion of the role of geopolitical power or social identity in shaping economic outcomes. The ontology is rationalistic, with no mention of the role of ideas, perceptions, or social institutions in shaping markets, economic policies, or outcomes in the international political economy. The works would be almost entirely formal or quantitative in method, with no qualitative work, historical process tracing, or discourse analysis.

Because of this narrowed focus, big chunks of scholarship, both old and new, on the workings of markets and politics are completely left off. For example, most IPE students at these top programs will read no scholarship from the historical institutionalism approach, which seeks to trace complex institutional and societal interactions over time. Thus, the varieties of capitalism approach, pioneered by Peter Katzenstein among others, is absent, despite being a major school of the scholarship explaining foreign economic policymaking for the past several decades. Dovetailing the findings of Maliniak and Tierney regarding journal articles, the syllabi likewise contain virtually no examples of any 'ideational turn' in IPE. The role of ideas, norms and culture, whether done by political scientists or sociologists, is not taught to IPE students in most of the high status IR departments – despite the presence of such theories in the main IR field seminars.

Most notable, perhaps, given the foundation that Gilpin laid down early on in the intellectual development of IPE, is that debates in the literature occur along quite circumscribed lines in today's syllabi. While it is surely a sign of intellectual progress that scholars can have fruitful debates about things like the measurement of data and coding, rather than the essential assumptions and causal models at work, it is hardly believable that such debates capture the extent of potential explanatory cleavages in IPE. Big debates across diverse perspectives would seem necessary in graduate training, if only to spark original and creative questions and approaches to the workings of the global political economy.

Finally, on these syllabi, it is striking that many of the works on these syllabi are written by scholars trained in economics, not political science. Unlike Albert Hirschman, Douglas North or Benjamin Cohen, all trained as economists but deeply interdisciplinary in their scholarly writing, the new IPE economists on these syllabi work solidly within the microeconomic rationalist traditions of their training. As will be discussed in a moment, and as highlighted by Robert Wade in his contribution to this special issue, this is particularly curious given the opening in the past decade of the discipline of economics itself to more heterodox approaches.

High status United State university graduate training, as evidenced by a sampling of current syllabi, thus matches the depiction of Maliniak and Tierney of our field as centering on the triptych of rationalism, liberalism, and quantitative analysis. It also lends supports to the US half of Jerry Cohen's depiction of the transatlantic divide in IPE (Cohen, 2007). However, it is necessary to realize that this intellectual monoculture is not inevitable or reflective of what is going on in the American IPE field outside those journals or top research schools. If we probe a little deeper, the picture changes substantially.

A parallel world?

The most striking empirical reality of American IPE today, but one not captured in my survey of selected graduate syllabi, or in Maliniak and Tierney's data, is the flourishing of diverse approaches in IPE within the broader academy. This is hinted at in the response from IPE scholars surveyed, of which 64% of IPE scholars report emphasizing ideational factors in their work, yet only 16% of the IPE articles in Maliniak and Tierney's database are coded as including ideas as a component part. The anomaly is explained by the observation that the most influential work from the constructivist and realist perspectives is being published not in the journals surveyed by Maliniak and Tierney, but in the top United States university presses. These prestigious university presses have lists filled with widely read and well reviewed books that take all manner of paradigmatic, ontological, epistemological and methodological approaches to IPE.

For example, Cornell University Press has published upwards of 25 books in the field of political economy since 2000, many in the 'Cornell Studies in Political Economy' and 'Cornell Studies in Money' series. Those books have included substantial contributions to the constructivist and historical institutional study of IPE approaches. Jacqueline Best's *The Limits of Transparency: Ambiguity and the History of International Finance* (2005) examines the positive role that ambiguity has played in stabilizing the international financial system, contra the conventional wisdom that more transparency is always better. In *Playing the Market: A Political Strategy for United Europe* (2006) Nicholas Jabko demonstrates how crafty political actors may use frames and ideas about 'the market' to move forward their own policy agendas, as they did in the European Union's remarkable creation of the European single market and the euro. Cornell also published numerous other books in IPE across a variety of academic perspectives, such as Patricia Goff's *Limits to Liberalization: Local Culture in a Global Marketplace* (2006) and Leonard Seabrooke's *The Social Sources of Financial Power* (2006). Princeton University Press, with a smaller list, has still published significant works in IPE that continue to represent the best of the pluralist foundations laid down by Gilpin and others. In particular, attention to the interplay between security considerations and economic interests is found in both Jonathan Kirshner's *Appeasing Bankers* (2007), which carefully traces out the aversion that financial interests historically have displayed to political conflict and war, and Stephen Brooks' *Producing Security* (2005), which creatively links the globalization of production to changes in the nature of security.

In addition to these monographs representing a variety of IPE approaches, the outpouring of empirically grounded, theoretically sophisticated work that makes an 'ideational turn' has now provided a basis for collaborative works that seek to map out the range of constructivist IPE. There are several edited volumes in progress by networks of United States based scholars that demonstrate the vitality and usefulness of sociologically informed approaches to markets and politics. For example, Mark Blyth, Craig Parsons and Rawi Abdelal, having all individually contributed key works in the field, have compiled a manuscript, *Constructing the World Economy* (2009), that lays out this research agenda. Jacqueline Best and Matthew Paterson's 'Cultural Political Economy' (n.d.) delineates the ways in which culture permeates all aspects of the political economy. Without culture, they argue, it is impossible to explain and understand key shifts in identity and behavior that shape today's IPE, such as consumerism, financialization, and neoliberalism.

It is therefore simply not true, as a colleague at another university recently told me when I asked why he had no ideational or social constructivist works on his IPE syllabus, that 'there is no constructivist IPE'. There is a world of scholarship beyond the liberal quantitative rationalist one, and several generations of recent IPE scholars have carved out successful careers, getting post-docs, tenure track jobs, and eventually, tenured positions at good universities while working in varied traditions – despite their lack of presence in many of the most highly ranked political science journals. This may explain Maliniak and Tierney's puzzling anomaly of quite high numbers of IPE scholars who identify themselves as other than liberal and/or quantitative in their approach, yet whose work is does not appear to exist when measured by the Maliniak and Tierney data. Maliniak and Tierney note that 'realists and constructivists accounted for 17% and 13%, respectively. This is greatly out of proportion to the number of articles published since, 2000, in which only 3% are realist and 3% are constructivist' (Maliniak and Tierney, 2009: 17, this issue). While it is possible that realists and constructivists are simply less smart and productive than liberals, it also is possible that the index used is simply not picking up the flourishing research community at work in books and alternative journals. Maliniak and Tierney are commendably beginning a new data collection project which will enlarge the index to book publications. In the meantime, it would be regrettable if the current index, in conjunction with all the other signals they are getting in their training, leads graduate students to believe that only one type of work will produce a successful career in IPE, further hardening a monocultural status quo.

Monocultures and polycultures

Monocultures, being all about specialization, are efficient, as every good IPE student worth her Adam Smith knows. Monocultures can produce a much higher level of productivity and output with the same resources than would occur without specialization. In agriculture, planting the same crops means cultivation needs are standardized and plants are not in competition from other species. There is less chance of loss, less unpredictability, and no need for trial and error cultivation. Intellectually, similar advantages to specialized, standardized research programs seem obvious. Progress surely can be made much faster if we don't have to spend time arguing about the 'isms', first principles, or the nature of human existence every time we sit down to write something. Broad agreement on the contours of what constitutes 'modern political science' or 'real' social science in IPE must surely allow us to move our research agenda forward.

However, monocultures in agriculture can be dysfunctional if they exhaust resources and leech out soil nutrients in their pursuit of uniform productivity. Polyculture, the planting of diverse crops and multiple uses, is required to enrich the fields rendered arid. Intellectual monocultures, where one theoretical perspective, ontological position, and method are used exclusively, may well result in a similar desiccation of the field of study. Although rarely stated in polite company, there are many in IR who believe that IPE has reached this point. Tierney and Maliniak's data show a curious dip in the number of people who define themselves as IPE scholars in their most recent survey. Anecdotally, based only on my experience in two graduate programs, there has been a decline in the number of IR students applying to PhD programs who state an interest in specializing in IPE, a decline in the number of IPE dissertations, and a decline of IPE applicants for junior professor slots when a general IR search is advertised.[4] Might the monoculture of IPE be partly to blame?

Another indicator of desiccation is the decline in the number of debates generated in IPE scholarship that engage scholars across the IR field. Hegemony, waning or waxing and its various guises and effects, took root in American IPE in the 1970s and 1980s and translated into a multiplicity of debates capturing the interest of IPE and non-IPE scholars alike. Debates over the role of absolute versus relative gains began in empirical discussions about the United States in economic negotiations, and spilled over to other areas of IR. Through the 1990s, neoliberal institutionalism more generally was part of a broader debate about the effects, if any, of institutionalization in international politics. These big 'research agenda setting' debates do not seem to have parallels today in IPE. For example, the fervent and ongoing debate about the meaning of unipolarity has occurred largely in the security field, with relatively few contributions examining how United States power today is shaping, or shaped by, international markets or economic institutions. Interesting debates are surely occurring within the liberal mainstream IPE crowd, and the more heterodox IPE scholars I have mentioned above, yet they are going on in separate rooms, and are not spreading out to the IR field as a whole. Cross-fertilization would surely allow for a better chance at probing these issues more fully and providing for better policy recommendations.

The particular IPE monoculture that has arisen in the top ranked schools and journals is not inevitable. Liberalism, rationalism, and quantitative methodology are all distinct approaches that have no necessary linkage, as Farrell and Finnemore argue in their contribution to this special issue. In fact, work in cognate fields outside the newly narrowed IPE canon demonstrates the benefits that may occur when these approaches are delinked. The two disciplines most closely related to IPE, economics and sociology, have seen a flourishing of heterodox perspectives on how markets work. Economics has moved into decision making, and unpacked and upended rationality, with Daniel Kahneman receiving a Nobel Prize for his path breaking scholarship with the late Amos Tversky. Economic sociologists have developed and applied very sophisticated quantitative techniques to their studies of the ways in which culture shapes markets and social institutions impact a variety of economic policy outcomes, demonstrating that one can study social constructivist outcomes using many different of methods. Indeed, over the past decade, economic sociology as a subfield has grown in membership, stature, and in the vibrancy of its debates. It is a major school of research, whose adherents often hold prestigious positions at places like Harvard, Princeton or Berkeley and publish in the top ranked sociology journals.

The different path political scientists have taken is itself, of course, the result of the fact that, as Farrell and Finnemore note in this issue, 'the field of international relations is both a means for gathering knowledge about the world, *and* a social institution, with all the power struggles and idiosyncrasies that we expect social institutions to have' (2009: 65). The various networks and incentives that structure our field have clearly mattered a great deal in the professional dominance of the liberal and rationalist approach, rather than being driven by functional necessary in any substantive intellectual sense.

The ultimate irony is that the scholars who shun the notion of social constructivism are successful in the field of IR in no small part because of their ability to navigate the very processes they discount. As they have an exclusive and narrow view of what the field *should* look like, in an evolutionary struggle for journal space, these approaches will win out over more pluralistic views.[5] An epistemic community of like-minded liberal quantitative thinkers who disdain other approaches is ideal for effectively structuring the discipline once they take up gatekeeping positions. The notion of what constitutes top flight scholarship then becomes a self-fulfilling prophecy, as only particular types of work will make it past the epistemic community of gatekeepers and get published in the top ranked journals. This outcome, which is portrayed as inevitable by several of the scholars quoted in Maliniak and Tierney's piece, is not the result of some abstract and objective criteria of evaluation, but rather stems from shared preferences and tastes on the part of like-minded scholars in the field. If you read closely, the process of social construction of the inevitable takeover of such work is evident in Maliniak and Tierney's own essay. In tracing out the development of the IPE field, they write:

> Lake also notes, 'Where IPE was originally constrained to case studies or, at best, statistical tests based on very limited data, some of the best new research employs very large time series data-sets and powerful econometric tools' (Lake, 2006: 772). If Lake is correct, we should see a substantial increase in quantitative work being published in IPE compared to past patterns. In fact, as illustrated in Figure 3, this is precisely the pattern we observe and the increase in quantitative work is dramatic.
>
> (Maliniak and Tierney, 2009: 19, this issue)

Referencing Lake, Maliniak and Tierney assume that the 'best' work will be published at a higher rate, and that the increase in quantitative work in the high status journals confirms Lake's views on the superiority of these methods. The problem is that the statements and beliefs of prominent IPE scholars, such as Lake, are themselves endogenous to the outcomes they are observing, as such disciplinary leaders obviously help shape our professional standards by their mentoring of junior scholars, manuscript reviews, conference organization, editorial board activities, and graduate student training. By setting up their analysis of the field of IPE and measuring prominence without attention to the role of social institutions in shaping the professional trajectory of the field, Maliniak and Tierney contribute to the naturalization of the very phenomena that they are attempting to study. Ironically, the social construction of the field through the anointment of econometric analysis as the 'best' type of work provides a powerful example of the role of ideas in shaping the academic IPE markets, as evidenced in Maliniak and Tierney's own data.[6]

The real world may rudely interrupt

Monocultures may strip the land of nutrients, but they have an even more dramatic downside potential. Because of their reliance on one standard crop, monocultures increase the possibility of catastrophic failure in the face of some newly emergent threat, such as disease or a change of climate. The Irish suffered the dire consequences of reliance on potatoes when faced with *Phytophthora infestans*, and European vineyards, and their communities, were devastated because of the lack of diversification when *Phylloxera* attacked their vines in the nineteenth century.

If the real world of IPE is overtaken by future challenges in the world economy, it is not clear that a top flight, highly productive American IPE academy that has rewarded a single narrow orthodoxy will be prepared to respond. Contemporary issues demanding attention include the collapse of the global financial regime, based on overextended credit systems in the United States, a fragile dollar but little in the way of clear substitute for a reserve currency, as well as the introduction of new actors into the system such as sovereign wealth funds. The grinding failure of the Doha Round and the deadlock between the North and South on trade liberalization, with traditional roles reversed on the need for freer trade, seems to be spelling an end to Bretton Woods regime. The rise of China and other explosively growing economies, in tandem with political systems that are not likely to take the same paths to democratic capitalism as the West, should be provoking serious and sustained consideration of the potentially changing nature of the international economic system. Ideas like the potential for a 'World Without the West', with international institutions designed to circumvent those of the last century, beg further analysis from IPE scholars. Energy issues and the rising price of oil also seem ripe to reorder the international political economy in ways that we as a field have not adequately analyzed.

The largely unforeseen collapse of the USSR made many in IR think that the field's commitment to neorealism may have left them blind to some of the empirical trends at work in prompting that change. Ten years from now, are we likely to look back at mainstream IPE and blame it for similar lack of scholarly attention in the face of profound change in the global political economy? If monocultures tend to suffer cataclysmic failure, perhaps our currently parallel debates will be reintegrated by the rude intrusion of the real world on IPE. If political scientists want to remain relevant beyond a small circle of like-minded interlocutors, we need to reembrace diversity alongside quality once again in IPE graduate training and publish a variety of perspectives and methods in mainstream journals. That would be a much more desirable path back to polyculture than waiting for catastrophic failure in the form of irrelevance.

Notes

1 I thank Roland Stephen for conversations on the drawbacks of intellectual monoculture.

2 My argument has much in common with Benjamin Cohen's observations about a transatlantic divide between a positivistic American school and a more normatively driven British school. The split I identify is not so much between Brits and Yanks, but rather between a view of IPE as enriched by diversity and one which assumes that there is only one correct way to study the interaction of markets and politics. Inasmuch as the so-called British school shuns diversity of thought and method, it will suffer the same ill effects of intellectual monoculturalism as its American cousin.

3 No better overview of the foundations of modern IPE can be found than Benjamin Cohen's latest book, *International Political Economy: An Intellectual History* (2008).

4 This summary is based on my survey of the last few year's of IPE doctoral syllabi, as available on the web, at major research universities identified as those training the most IPE students in the Maliniak and Tierney article. The sole highly ranked program that continues to offer a pluralistic IPE field seminar is Cornell University.

5 Interestingly, the decline in graduate student interest has not occurred at the undergraduate level, where IPE lectures classes are oversubscribed and students are clamoring to debate the direction of the global political economy. The breadth of topics and reverence to real world events demanded by an undergraduate IPE survey class is one way to keep scholars engaged with diverse topics of real world importance. However, as prominent scholars at the top rank universities have their teaching obligations dramatically reduced, and as introductory lecture classes are taught less and less by such faculty, scholars are less likely to have their narrower research foci challenged by the rigors of teaching undergraduates.

6 I thank Jonathan Kirshner for this point.

6 The slow death of pluralism

Nicola Phillips

N. Phillips (2009) 'The slow death of pluralism', *Review of International Political Economy* 16(1): 85–94, published by Taylor & Francis Ltd, http://www.informaworld.com. Permission has been granted by the publisher.

The lively recent discussions surrounding the transatlantic divide in international political economy (IPE) starkly illuminate how far the American school is from constituting the 'open range' that Susan Strange (1984) famously advocated for the field. It is, if anything, moving apace in the opposite direction. The reflections offered by Cohen (2007, 2008), the responses by Higgott and Watson (2008) and Ravenhill (2008), and the data presented by Maliniak and Tierney reveal clearly the bases of the contraction and demeaning of pluralism – an openness to a variety of theoretical perspectives, methodological approaches and empirical concerns – that many will recognize and accept as an accurate characterization of the contemporary American school. Liberalism is manifestly in the ascendant, Marxism has almost disappeared and there has been a sharp methodological homogenisation. Few of the more recent theoretical innovations, such as ideational and constructivist approaches, have found significant expression in IPE scholarship published in the leading American international relations (IR) journals which Maliniak and Tierney survey. It should be added that the profiles of these journals are also dominated by United States authors (over 80%), by people working in a fairly small handful of the most prestigious United States universities (29% of articles from 11 universities), and by men (86%).

What I wish to do in my contribution to this debate is to reflect briefly on these trends towards a contraction of pluralism in the American school – where they originate, what implications they carry and what they tell us about the divide between American-school and British-school IPE that some have identified (Cohen, 2008; Murphy and Nelson, 2001) – as well as to provide some direct reactions to Maliniak and Tierney's interesting discussion. While my own sympathies and affiliations lie with what has come to be called the 'British school', this is not intended to be yet another instance of lazy fist-waving at the American school from the safe shores of the 'other side'. Rather, it is an attempt to engage with the present debate concretely about the American school, emphasising what I see to be the troubling implications of the trends we are discussing here. My observations do not discount the parallel questions that need to be asked about the 'British-school' vision of IPE, and there will be another moment in this wider debate to reflect on those.[1]

IR-centrism and the problems of disciplinarity

Maliniak and Tierney (this issue) base their discussion on the '12 leading political science journals that publish articles in the sub-field of IR' (Maliniak and Tierney, 2009: 7, this issue). In so doing, they produce a set of interesting and provocative insights into the state of the field, which themselves suggest a stimulating array of questions and issues for future reflection. But they also, entirely unquestioningly, reinforce from the outset the strongly disciplinary association of IPE with IR. This is an association that is by no means universally accepted, particularly outside the American-school community. In my view, it is also highly problematic. IPE scholars publish in IR journals, they are telling us – sometimes also in more properly 'political science' journals, but the point is that we know where to find IPE scholarship, and in surveying these 12 journals we can uncover what we need to know about the state of the field. It would be hard to find a clearer assertion of what the field of IPE is and what it should be. Regrettably, it is one that perhaps the huge majority of IPE scholars in the American school would accept without hesitation.

The obsession with journal rankings and citation indices, which is spilling over increasingly into the ways in which academic life is organized outside the United States, mean also that the 'holy grail' for aspiring IPE scholars, and the natural homes for successful and eminent ones, are represented by the small handful of journals that Maliniak and Tierney identify in their survey. Most of them are what we would call 'generalist' IR and political science journals, which should, according to that definition, publish scholarship drawn from across the field to which they correspond. Yet, the point is that these 'generalist' journals are not in fact 'generalist' at all. The arresting narrowness of their remit, particularly in terms of the types of articles published is well documented by both Maliniak and Tierney and Cohen (2009, this issue). Over 80% of authors publishing in these journals are from or working in the United States, no articles employing a Marxist frame of reference have appeared in any of the 12 journals since 1990, close to 70% of all articles published in these outlets between 1980 and 2006 have worked within the liberal paradigm, and 90% of all IPE articles published in 2006 employed quantitative methods.

Cohen's (2008) book provides us with pertinent observations about the provenance of the intellectual trends that are reflected in these statistics. But we are missing a sustained focus on how the practice of editorial screening, or what some like to call 'gate keeping' – establishing and policing the remit and focus of journals, and deciding what is and is not appropriate and acceptable scholarship – is at least as important as wider intellectual trends, and indeed may well be a crucial *cause* of their emergence. Indeed, the impact of particular kinds of incentives and disincentives for publication is a preoccupation for several of the contributors to this special issue. In this regard, the more revealing clues about why IPE has moved in this direction in the American school would surely lie in data not on the nature of articles published in these journals, but rather on *submissions*, particularly in terms of how many and what kinds of articles are rejected on the grounds that they are not suitable in their theoretical or methodological approach, or even empirical focus, for the journal in question.

It would also be highly illuminating (although naturally a much more difficult undertaking) to consider the issue of 'non-submissions', as scholars are systematically deterred from approaching particular outlets for their work. Journals hostile to particular kinds of scholarship become known for their assiduous screening practices, to the extent that disincentives to submit to particular journals are continuously reinforced. Many scholars perceive that it is simply not worth the time and trouble even to have a shot. Anecdotal knowledge of the experiences of scholars not associated with the mainstream of the American school in submitting to the 'top' United States IR journals certainly indicates that such data on submissions (and insights into non-submissions) would be helpful in understanding the extent to which screening and gate-keeping practices contribute to the manner in which the field of IPE and its intellectual trends are consciously and cumulatively constructed. As John Ravenhill (2008: 26) points out, it is precisely for this reason that many will be watching with interest the direction taken by *International Organization* since its recent move to an editorial base in Canada and a new editorial team, in the expectation and hope that one of the results may be a decline in the number of articles based on formal modeling and a greater receptiveness to theoretical and methodological approaches other than those associated with liberalism and quantitative analysis.

Supposedly the great concession to a higher level of 'pluralism' in the dominant United States journals over the last couple of decades was, of course, the incorporation of constructivism and the so-called 'ideational turn' in IR. Indeed, the hallmark of the progressive IR journal became the inclusion of constructivism alongside the other well-worn paradigms, and much was made in the bars and corridors of IR conferences of the new receptiveness of journals such as *International Organization* and *International Studies Quarterly* to constructivist work. Maliniak and Tierney show us that this turn has been less well represented in IPE scholarship than IR scholarship, and indeed that IPE scholarship has made little discernible contribution to the relevant debates in IR, at least in the pages of the leading journals (see McNamara's paper in this issue). This is troubling, and the reasons for it invite much more reflection. Maliniak and Tierney's speculation in a footnote that the most influential constructivist scholarship is showing up in book form rather than as journal articles again prompts us to think about the role of journals in defining the contours of the field. But it also induces us to reflect on (and indeed doubt) the extent to which a survey of 'leading' journals can be effective in revealing the condition of the field of IPE or the substance of the scholarship pursued within it.

Even so, a concession to constructivism or ideational arguments does not go very far in representing the diversity of IPE scholarship even in the United States, let alone in the wider IPE community. One is struck by the absence of data on critical approaches such as feminism, for instance, which goes entirely unmentioned in the discussions of American-school IPE that have prompted the present debate, or indeed post-structuralism and other critical, non- and post-positivist approaches. Again, one suspects that these approaches may be comparable to those which emphasize ideational factors and have achieved less representation in IPE than in IR, although data that encompassed these kinds of scholarship would be valuable. Is it the case that we have been seeing a widening of IR scholarship over recent years and at least some movement towards a more pluralist definition of the subdiscipline, but a contraction in IPE of the kind of pluralism that was once heralded as precisely what the field stood for? And if IPE is so explicitly defined by its relationship to IR, why should this be the case?

The strongly disciplinary association of IPE with IR also, necessarily, has the effect of squeezing the space for interdisciplinary work, not only in the United States, but also, one fears, in non-US scholarship. A propensity to think of IPE as inherently an interdisciplinary enterprise has been associated strongly with the British school (Cohen, 2008: 4), and an interdisciplinary bent has long been what we have thought to be one of the defining features of what IPE does and should look like, as summed up in Susan Strange's invocation of the 'open range'. The most salient contributions to the development of British-school IPE have been self-consciously open to a variety of disciplinary and, indeed, theoretical perspectives, leading to the 'eclecticism' for which the work of scholars such as Robert Cox, among others, has been celebrated by many of British-school persuasions and variously ignored or scorned by many in the American school. Yet what we see is a dilemma, especially for ambitious younger international political economists on the promotion ladder or tenure track, between this intellectual commitment to interdisciplinary openness (and eclecticism, as suggested by Peter Katzenstein in this issue) and the creeping pressures to publish in what remain strongly discipline-based journals. We have seen a proliferation of league tables of journals disseminated to all colleagues and used increasingly as a proxy indicator of the quality of a person's research in selection and promotion committees. The same, supposedly 'generalist', political science and IR journals that appear in Maliniak and Tierney's (this issue) survey are strongly represented in these lists. The emphasis on citation indices as a similar indicator is also manifestly increasing, to the consternation of many, particularly given the widespread indifference of United States scholars to British-school scholarship (Cohen, 2008: 65). In this sense, despite the constant promotion of interdisciplinary research in universities and all the major funding bodies (Moran, 2006), we are in fact *returning to* a heavily disciplinary approach to matters of publications and indicators of recognition. This is very much in the style of United States academic practice and in keeping with the IR-centrism of the American school of IPE. If sustained, this may herald a rather more difficult time for British school IPE in its commitment to interdisciplinary openness.

Notwithstanding these worrying prospects for the future, the commitment to openness and pluralism does not appear immediately to be waning as the defining characteristic of the British school. In this sense, it is perhaps interesting to wonder whether taking Maliniak and Tierney's exercise across the Atlantic, as they suggest they will, has the capacity to reveal anything meaningful about the state of IPE outside the United States. Targeting what are perceived to be the top IR journals in search of their 'IPE' content would, it seems to me, be looking in entirely the wrong place. The best British-school IPE scholarship is instead scattered across journals identified variously with such fields as IR, politics, political economy, sociology, development studies and geography, with representation from those associated with such fields as anthropology and management and business studies, and found also in generalist social science journals, including those with particular theoretical inclinations. Given the much wider spread of regional interests in the British school, and the much greater attention to political economies outside the small handful of advanced industrialized countries, one is also obliged regularly to consult work published in journals with a specific regional or country focus and in those which identify more explicitly with the fields of comparative political economy and development studies. Focusing predominantly on IR journals would, in this sense, capture only a tiny part of what members of the British school would consider to be the totality of IPE scholarship.

In a related vein, a strongly discipline-based focus on scholars working in departments of politics and international relations, as in Maliniak and Tierney's survey of the American school, would exclude attention to an array of colleagues whose work is considered by many to be of considerable importance to the enterprise of IPE. With the same trepidation as John Ravenhill (2008: 24), when he lists some of the figures associated with the British school, I will offer merely a very small clutch of illustrative examples: Giovanni Arrighi, Saskia Sassen, Michael Mann or William I. Robinson, all professors of sociology, David Harvey, working as a geographer in an anthropology department, Neil Smith, also a professor of geography and anthropology, Robert Wade, working in a development studies department, trained as an anthropologist and economist, and Richard Whitley or Karel Williams, who work in a business school, not to mention a wide array of philosophers and economists. The work of these scholars and many such others – on capitalism, development, space, neoliberalism, globalisation, financialisation, business systems, firms, international organisations, East Asia, Latin America, poverty and inequality – is admired and cited extensively in British-school IPE. They make crucial contributions to the key debates in the field, but are not scholars who are identified with the disciplines of politics and international relations.

If IPE is defined by its strong association with IR, these people are, as it were, political economists rather than International Political Economists. However, if, like many in the British school, one thinks that IPE is a field rooted at least as much (or indeed should be rooted much more) in the traditions of political economy as in the field of IR (Gamble *et al.*, 1996; Phillips, 2005; Underhill, 2000; Watson, 2005), then the task for Maliniak and Tierney in discovering where to find 'International Political Economists' outside the United States becomes manifestly more challenging than a trawl through departments of politics and international relations. Similarly, an exercise like Cohen's of assembling the 'magnificent seven' of British-school IPE would immediately pose a huge number of problems in deciding who qualifies in this vision of the field as an international political economist. In short, a critical reaction to Maliniak and Tierney's proposal to replicate their exercise in the British-school context would have to be sceptical of the utility of basing it on the same strongly disciplinary, IR-centric view of IPE as that which prevails in the United States.

This may be considered yet another reflection – and not a flattering one – of the lack of boundaries and the excessive inclusiveness of British-school IPE. This may be a valid observation, and it is most certainly an issue which deserves sustained and critical debate. But my point here refers to the deficiencies and dangers of the continued shackling of IPE to IR and the prevailing IR-centric vision of what IPE is and should be – a vision which both produces and is reflected in the screening functions of the dominant journals. This demeans the worth of interdisciplinary openness and, furthermore, carries important consequences for the substantive value of IPE scholarship. I will make just a few comments on this latter point in the space that remains.

What is of interest in IPE?

Cohen (2008: 82–3) argues that the American school today is characterized by a 'loss of ambition' and a move to a much more 'micro' view of the world. These trends form the basis of Robert Keohane's (2009, this issue) criticism, in this issue and elsewhere, of IPE's growing inattention to the 'big questions' in the global political economy. The 'micro' view of the world is inevitably reflected in the ways in which the key questions for IPE are identified and formulated, as well as the theoretical and methodological apparatus that is constructed for the purpose of scholarly analysis.

In part, this narrowing of the remit of IPE is clearly the result of the growing dominance of quantitative methods, inasmuch as a preference for mathematical modeling and other forms of quantitative analysis plays a key part in defining what *can* be studied in IPE. Recall that by 2006, 90% of IPE articles published in the twelve journals employed quantitative methods – the clearest possible indication of what is now judged in the American school to constitute 'proper', 'rigorous', 'scientific' enquiry. As Robert Wade argues in his contribution to this issue, the deficiencies of such techniques in the discipline of economics have been increasingly recognized over many years now. Yet, the drift (or indeed lurch) towards a dominance of quantitative methods in American-school IPE has continued either regardless of or oblivious to these critical debates in the field from which these methods are drawn. The result is an array of restrictions not just on the inclination, but also on the *ability* of American-school IPE to address the 'big picture'. How can one subject to quantitative analysis questions of systemic transformation, for instance? How to deal with power in any convincing kind of way? How to think about the role of ideology and ideas in shaping the global order? The difficulties extend to a whole range of issues that are critical to the global political economy but less (or not at all) amenable to quantitative methods, such as, among many others, informal and illicit activity, the 'macro' questions about migration, the gendered dimensions of global political-economic processes, 'unfree' forms of labor and informal employment, and a whole range of questions about development and inequality. Equally, the regional scope of interests in the field of IPE is inevitably narrowed when the field is becoming more and more dependent on the availability of reliable data. Such data are often not available to students of developing economies, who are much more likely to pursue their work through systematic and extensive qualitative research, often in the form of field research. The result is an entrenchment of a narrow empirical focus on a small handful of advanced industrialized countries – predominantly the United States, but also Europe and Japan, and increasingly the major East-Asian economies (Phillips, 2005; see also remarks in Cohen, 2008: 145, 167).

Yet, this narrowing of the substantive scope of IPE is not only the result of trends in methodology. It is also directly the result of the IR-centric vision of IPE which prevails in the American school. Just as IR was constructed as a discipline both for and about the 'great powers', and an 'American social science' (Hoffman, 1977), so IPE has crystallized as a field in which the primary concerns and theoretical frameworks are both derived from the experiences of the advanced industrialized powers and built for the principal purpose of analyzing the particular political economy of advanced capitalism that knits them together and underpins their dominance. In other words, as Cohen's (2008) survey of the 'magnificent seven' reveals, American-school IPE developed in the United States as a means of addressing a set of questions of very particular relevance to the United States itself, namely the problem of hegemony and the position of the United States as the global hegemonic power. While this is not to say that everything was explicitly *about* the United States in a direct sense, nevertheless the ties to a set of core questions about the position and nature of United States power in the global political economy were central. As such, the American school in its origins was marked by an innate 'parochialism' in its concerns and its identified remit, to borrow the term Kalevi Holsti (1985) uses to describe the introspection and narcissism of United States IR. It is a narrowness that has not only persisted but also, as a result of the growing prioritisation of what can be quantified and modeled, been steadily reinforced.

Maliniak and Tierney (2009: 23, this issue) report that 67% of IPE scholars believe that East Asia will be the 'strategically important' region over the next 20 years, and implicitly suggest that this region will therefore feature prominently in the future agenda for IPE. It is indeed entirely correct that the growth of East Asia, particularly China, presents (and for some time has presented) students of IPE with a range of profoundly significant questions, including those of a 'big picture' nature concerning the manner in which the global political economy is being and will be restructured over the coming decades. Yet, three observations are warranted on this point. First, again, the agenda is being defined by what is 'strategically important' to the United States, reinforcing still further the excessively narrow focus on the advanced industrialized countries. Second, we have here clear evidence again of the IR-centrism of IPE in the 'international' focus on a particular region and its relationship to the United States. Maliniak and Tierney (2009: 23, this issue) go on in the same paragraph to frame the data in terms of the 'most important foreign policy issues that will face the United States in the next 10 years'. This can be interpreted as an indication that the agenda for IPE will be driven, as in the past, by these questions of strategic concern to the dominant power, particularly in terms of the regions from which the primary economic competition emanates. The parallels with the explosion of interest in Japan in the 1970s and 1980s, which was hugely influential in defining the field of IPE, are very clear. And third, the manner in which East Asia is studied in IPE is strongly tied to the staple IPE questions of trade, finance, competition, regulation and so on. It is much less tied to the relevance of the growth of East Asian economies to questions of global development, migration, poverty, labor standards, environment and climate change, and so on. It is consequently to be expected that it is the issues that are associated very directly with the 'strategic importance' of East Asia to the United States, rather than their wider global resonance, that will preoccupy the American school over the coming decades.

Concluding thoughts

If it is indeed the case that we are seeing the slow death of pluralism in the American school of IPE and if – a very big if – there is any consensus at all that this might not be a desirable thing, then collectively we face the question of what might be done. That is clearly not something that can be addressed in the context of a short response to recent interventions in this debate, and will be something that should preoccupy us for some time to come. But one conclusion that both Maliniak and Tierney's discussion and my comments here suggest is that the role of journals and their editorial boards is important. Collectively, there is a responsibility to reflect carefully on publishing strategies and to recognize that a greater pluralism carries with it an array of merits and benefits. The question of whether greater engagement is even possible between the so-called American and British schools, which some of the responses to Cohen (2007) have answer in the negative (e.g. Higgott and Watson, 2008; Ravenhill, 2008), is a rather different point, and not one there is space to address fully here. But, to state the obvious, without greater exposure to work being conducted in the other school – or, put more constructively, to work which starts from different theoretical paradigms, methodological approaches or empirical interests – there can be no prospect of any future engagement, and the dialog of the deaf will simply continue. As Robert Wade observes in his contribution to this special issue, the present, strikingly homogenous profile of articles in the most visible journals is not in itself an indicator of the health of the discipline – and, I would suggest, quite the contrary. Equally damaging is the continued shackling of IPE to the discipline of IR, which, in my view, is stunting the development of the field in deeply unfortunate ways. The benefit of greater pluralism, in all its guises, is something on which we could do well to reflect.

Note

1 A special issue of *New Political Economy* (forthcoming in late 2009) will continue this debate, concentrating on the 'British school' of IPE.

7 The 'American' school of IPE?

A dissenting view

Randall D. Germain

R.D. Germain (2009) 'The "American" school of IPE? A dissenting view', *Review of International Political Economy* 16(1): 95–105, published by Taylor & Francis Ltd, http://www.informaworld.com. Permission has been granted by the publisher.

What is at stake in a name? Plenty, apparently. Benjamin Cohen's (2008) depiction of the differences between what he calls the 'American' and 'British' schools of international political economy (IPE) seems to have provoked a mini bout of introspection over the disciplinary organization of IPE. This can only be helpful, if for no other reason than to make those who consider themselves to be IPE scholars more self-conscious about what it is they do and how they are organized to do it. The real value-added aspect of Cohen's work – in contrast to some recent attempts to chart the state of the discipline but which really are advancing a particular conception of IPE (Lake, 2006; see also Lake's contribution to this special issue) – is that he at least attempts to bring together research agendas that do not always speak to each other as clearly as they might. If this debate makes more of us aware of the richness and variety of IPE on offer, it will be a win–win debate for the field as a whole.

Many of the features of 'American' IPE described by Dan Maliniak and Michael Tierney in this volume clearly resonate with those of us who practice IPE outside of America. In this short contribution I focus on three aspects of this debate that strike me as particularly interesting. First, and most importantly, I do not think it is 'American' IPE that Maliniak and Tierney (and Cohen) describe; it is a truncated and rather introverted slice of IPE in the American academy that they mistakenly equate with 'American' IPE. Unpacking this mistake demonstrates the great care we need to take when manufacturing *data*, whether about the real world or the academy. Second, what I believe Maliniak and Tierney do reveal is the astonishing concentration of disciplinary power within an important segment of IPE in America. This concentration – where power and authority truly meet – is also part of the story that Cohen tells, although he seems peculiarly shy about commenting on its implications. I am not so shy. And finally, I argue that those of us who ply our trade outside of America need to engage more fulsomely with 'American' IPE, although we may take or leave (following our personal preferences) the version Maliniak and Tierney outline. The issues and problems that have generated an interest in IPE are serious affairs, and future generations would rightly chastise us were we to abandon this field of study to what I will call, following an earlier critique motivated by different concerns, the 'Harvard' school of IPE (Long, 1995).

Data, citations and fields: IPE and the 'dirty dozen'

In his determination to demonstrate the existence of important cleavages between the 'American' and 'British' schools, Cohen (2008) focuses on the use of systematic empirical data as a critical point of distinction between the two: one school engages in the systematic testing of hypotheses against evidence to accumulate knowledge, while the other is led by its critical normative stance to reflect on individual case studies that make it difficult to accumulate generalizable knowledge.[1] Maliniak and Tierney follow in the tradition of 'American' IPE by gathering data mined from the Teaching, Research, and International Policy (TRIP) survey in order to map its salient characteristics. Using this data they confirm many of Cohen's suppositions about the 'American' school.

But is the field that Maliniak and Tierney (and Cohen) map really the field of IPE *as it is actually constituted* in America? This is not an unimportant question, for if their map is deficient or distorted, the manner in which we outside of America engage with our colleagues within America becomes open for recalibration. I argue that because of the particular way in which they construe their data, what they purport to 'map' is a narrow slice of IPE that cannot be considered to be the field as a whole. Most critically, by relying on what respondents perceive to be good scholarship, rather than what they actually use or where they publish, we get a good picture of how some scholars would like to think of themselves, but a distorted picture of what they actually are and do. *Making* data in this way compromises the inferences that Maliniak and Tierney are able to draw, most importantly in terms of the theoretical axes of the field. To pursue this claim, which I can only do suggestively given the space provided, I focus on two parts of the TRIP survey: the choice of journals to constitute the 'field', and the coding of paradigms. Together, I argue that these data mislead us as to what is actually going on within IPE in America.

Following Garand and Giles (2003), Maliniak and Tierney choose what they describe as the 12 leading journals that publish IPE research to act as a proxy for the field; that is, for the purposes of this exercise these journals mark the field's boundaries. But this is problematic, not perhaps in terms of measuring the 'impact' that some journals reputedly possess – although as we will see this also may be contentious – but as a measure of the field's existence: for what this list 'measures' is desire rather than accomplishment. It is a list of journals compiled from a survey of scholars asking them both what journals they are familiar with and to which they would like to submit their work.[2] The critical point here – the point where data get *made* – is that this list privileges self-perception rather than actual practice.[3] Another way of phrasing this is to say that it does not measure actual material reality, which in this case is where scholars really do publish their work (and not just those scholars who respond to surveys). The material domain of the field of IPE can only be the actual sum total of its scholarly output and not the self-perception of where scholars would like to publish if given half a chance; this is perhaps better rendered as its *ideational* domain. If the field were mapped as it actually exists – that is to say, where the ideational and material are joined and fused organically – then the work published in these journals would be easily identified for what it is: a small part of the overall effort to accumulate knowledge through the publication of scholarly research. We can only turn the publications contained in these 12 journals – the 'dirty dozen' – into the 'American' school of IPE by simply ignoring in excess of 95% of the actual published work of IPE scholars, spread as it is among so many other journal outlets (not to mention other formats such as monographs, which might be, by some measures, the true 'research' anchors for the 'field').[4]

Yet, Maliniak and Tierney, along with Garand and Giles and tenure and promotion committees everywhere, are rightfully allowed to discriminate within the actual universe of published scholarship, and indeed they do so by considering the impact scores which journals now cultivate assiduously. However, here again we must be careful to consider how such data are *made*, for impact scores reflect not only the actual influence of particular journal articles in the accumulation of knowledge sweepstakes, but also (partly? mostly? entirely?) the desire to locate scholarship, broadcast pedigree and (if successful) ingratiate oneself into a particular school of scholarship.[5] And here the nature of *data* becomes crucial, for if citations are about allowing others to locate scholarship and trumpet pedigrees, then the inferences we make about citations – including their supposed impact – must be suspect. In the end, my hypothesis would be that the so-called 'top' IPE journals in the United States – *International Organization* (*IO*), *World Politics* and *International Studies Quarterly (ISQ)*, not to mention *American Political Science Review (APSR)* and *American Journal of Political Science (AJPS)* – are used heavily by scholars for tenure and promotion purposes, but rather less so for the mundane purposes associated with the actual accumulation of knowledge. My point here is not to denigrate these journals – I too put them at the top of my wish-list for where I would like to publish my 'best' work in the TRIP survey (and who wouldn't, since doing otherwise would contravene our most cherished self-perceptions) – but rather to suggest that data *made* in a certain way do not always reflect what we actually do as scholars. Acknowledging this of course begs the question of how in fact we are to portray our field. I would humbly suggest that our answer not include citation indices or very limited (and non-random) representations of journal universes. These may have their place in measuring the 'importance' of journals, but not in defining fields.

Such a pinched portrayal of IPE in America can also be seen at work in the way in which Maliniak and Tierney portray the weight of the field's main theoretical paradigms. One of their most interesting findings is that marxism and constructivism are poorly represented in 'American' IPE. I, along with McNamara and others in this special issue, also find this odd, as there are entire journals devoted to marxist and historical materialist themes, and one does not have to look too hard to uncover panels, conferences, entire research programs and even whole institutes open to and engaged with this form of scholarship.[6] Only when we mistakenly portray a field can such an abundance of scholarship be overlooked. The absence of an ideational turn, however, is more perplexing, since this is the most significant new development in 'American' IR since the advent of neo-realism. Authorities no less than Katzenstein *et al.* (1998: 683), after all, end their *IO* version of IPE's history with the claim that rationalism and constructivism now benchmark the field's most promising analytical orientations.

Again, it seems to me that we have a problem of data *construction*. For example, in order to map the weight of constructivism in IPE, Maliniak and Tierney scan their journal universe for the variable 'international norms' as the key indicator of a constructivist paradigm at work, and can barely discern its presence. Part of the explanation of course is the admittedly narrow database they use, which must raise questions about the robustness of their findings. For example, as McNamara suggests elsewhere in this volume, much of this research is now published in book form by major university presses. But also at work here are the catchwords they use as proxies to represent this type of research. Ideas and norms, for example, have long been a staple of much radical scholarship in political economy, but they have been rendered as 'ideology' or inter-subjective frameworks rather than as 'international norms': do a citation search for 'neo-liberalism' and you can read for years. But if we only look for the term 'international norms', we will miss much of the actual research on ideas and norms that has suffused the field for decades. Ruggie and Kratochwil (1986) warned us about such cognitive dissonance over 20 years ago, but their line of critique seems to have been conveniently forgotten amid the rush for social scientific refinement.

The problem of data construction also appears in the way in which the TRIP survey codes the paradigms that scholars use to frame their research. TRIP's codebook variable #10, which describes how paradigms are coded, stipulates that articles are read for their content and not for the self confessed theoretical predispositions of their authors. In other words, it is the coders rather than the authors who determine what kind of paradigm is being deployed; indeed, it is the coders who define the paradigms in advance of the coding (so that they can recognize the paradigms in the first place). Thus, Alex Wendt may be coded as a realist if he discusses the causes of war in terms of a distribution of power, or as a constructivist if he emphasizes the role of ideas. That Wendt could be coded as a realist and as a constructivist (or should that be scientific realist?) is certainly an interesting proposition.[7] More importantly, it means that the role of the 'coders' becomes crucial for determining the paradigmatic contours of the field: it is they rather than the research community more generally who outline the theoretical paradigms we use and develop, and they may well make erroneous or contentious judgments. For example, David Campbell will be very surprised to learn that he is now a 'British constructivist' (Cohen, 2008: 174). For my money, the most egregious claim is made on behalf of those who are clamoring to rearrange international relations (IR) into the contrasting camps of rationalism and constructivism: how can they insist that someone as fully engaged with historical materialism as Robert Cox now be considered a constructivist (Adler, 2002: 88)?[8] While I can appreciate the desire by some to make and remake *data* like this, I am unsure whether the rest of us should acquiesce so easily. Once again, how data are *made* becomes crucial, which I suppose means that there is in fact plenty at stake in the practice of naming.

Hierarchy and power

Even though I am unconvinced by Maliniak and Tierney's (as well as Cohen's) claim that there is an 'American' school of IPE, I am astonished and concerned at the high degree of hierarchy within IPE in America that their work reveals. Anyone in education of course is fully aware of the hierarchy at work in scholarship and academia, but that it should be exposed so baldly by the TRIP survey must give pause for thought. Moreover, if this survey were to be extended to enquire into the distribution of research funding in America, I suspect that even stronger inferences could be made about this hierarchy. What the TRIP survey does reveal is that nearly 45% of IPE scholars in America are trained at fewer than 12 institutions, which is about 1% of the higher education institutions in the country. And approximately 30% of published output in the 'dirty dozen' comes from faculty based more or less in the same institutions. I wonder what the Anti-Trust Division in the Department of Justice would say about the state of competition in such an 'industry'.

But in one important way it is even worse. Cohen's very readable and informative intellectual history of the field makes abundantly clear the central role played by the journal *IO* (cf. Katzenstein *et al.*, 1998; Murphy and Nelson, 2001; and indeed Keohane's contribution to this special issue). This is partly why it can lay claim to being the premier journal in the field. But it is astonishing how many of its editors are Harvard graduates; indeed, between 1972 and 2006, Harvard-trained scholars were at the editorial helm of *IO* for the entire period except for one four-year stint in the mid-1990s. Even Cohen's 'Magnificent Seven' – and they truly are magnificent, as much for their ambitions and leadership as for their scholarship – come disproportionately on the American side from Harvard. Only Kindleberger and Gilpin are non-Harvard graduates, and both came to be intimately involved in the scholarly network that grew around Harvard from the late 1960s onwards (as was true for Cohen himself). This is why I think even Murphy and Nelson (2001) mischaracterize the nature of the 'American' school when they call it the '*IO*' school. In reality, it appears much more to be a 'Harvard' school of IPE, dominated by Harvard graduates and teachers, radiating outwards to populate American universities and journals with its products and progeny.

Should we worry about this seeming concentration of academic influence within IPE in America? I think so, for at least two reasons. The first is that such a degree of concentration promotes group think and herd behaviour. Many of us have marveled at the frankly bizarre herding of a sizable chunk of our American colleagues into and out of debates that might fairly be described as narrow, myopic and almost narcissistic. Cohen sympathetically lays to rest the enormous literature on hegemonic stability and international regimes that was sprung on us by a very small band of Harvard-trained faculty, but which yielded so little fruit; my own personal favourite is the neo-institutional/neo-realist debate which threatened to derail energies and efforts for a decade, but which thankfully fizzled after only a few years. Why the rest of us should be held hostage to these finegrained and detailed internal debates between scholars who train together, organize workshops and debates together and of course publish together is beyond me. But then, I am outside the 'Harvard' school and thus have only my own common sense and intimations of rationality to guide me. Or rather, I have the rest of the world for solace and inspiration, which is rather a good thing given some of the debates promoted over the years by the 'Harvard' school.

However, there is another reason for worry, and it follows from the propensity of members of the 'Harvard' school to become involved with American government policy: both Joseph Nye Jr and Stephen Krasner, for example, have held relatively senior posts in recent American administrations. Now, while this may have salutary effects on American foreign policy – who after all would not have given up their first-born child to have had Joseph Nye Jr in the Bush Administration to at least put forward the case for a multilateral foreign policy? – I believe it has a malign effect on the constitution of the field, precisely because it too easily allows the 'Harvard' school to equate IPE with what Susan Strange (1988: 12) long ago identified as the politics of international economic relations (PIER). I do not believe that we can allow IPE to become only or even primarily about foreign economic policy, much less American foreign economic policy. Yet, this is exactly what the subtext of the 'Harvard' school implies: IPE is about understanding how the interests and preferences of individual actors support and/or constrain the global economy, and how optimal equilibria among these interests and preferences can be molded and directed.[9] And while I admire the normative stance of many 'Harvard' school scholars, this narrows the universe of questions so palpably that if you are not interested in the first instance in America and its stake in the contemporary global political economy, then IPE will not be your field of choice. When combined with the predilection towards tightly controlled internalized debates, such academic closure to the outside world needs to be resisted.

Resistance and engagement

And so we come finally to the nub of the issue: how to rescue the depiction of IPE in America as being constituted by the 'Harvard' school? My advice is to take two tracks. One is to press Maliniak and Tierney to include in their survey meaningful questions about what IPE scholars actually do – how they fund and conduct their research, where they actually publish, and crucially what research they genuinely use in their own work that adds to our common stock of knowledge. It would also be very interesting to learn what knowledge, if any, we as scholars think has been accumulated since the rebirth of IPE some 40 years ago. These kinds of questions would, I think, provide a more complete and accurate map of the universe of scholarship from which we could begin to make robust inferences about the state of the field. They may also wish to revisit how they code the paradigms researchers use to bring a greater degree of critical sensibility to their survey. I agree with them that we need good information on the boundaries and contours of our field, but I disagree that we get this by asking questions based on what scholars wish they could do (or be) rather than what they actually do (and therefore are). For the purposes of tenure and promotion – as well perhaps as somehow measuring scholarly reputations – we may always need to rely on citation indices and an informed profile of publication esteem indicators. However, where our purpose is to measure entire scholarly fields and ascertain their organizational, demographic and operational dynamics, we need to consider the whole 'universe' in which the production of knowledge takes place rather than just its most visible so-called 'top' tier. This is akin to measuring the mass of an iceberg based on the bit that sticks out of the water. Asking questions on the TRIP survey that plumb the depths of the field, along with a more refined coding framework, would I believe elicit a portrayal of IPE in America that is much richer, more variegated and above all more accurate than the truncated snapshot currently on offer. *This* field is truly worth engaging with.

The second track is for the rest of us to pick up on Cohen's exhortation to build bridges where possible by engaging with scholarship that crosses boundaries and is itself open to the critical interchange of claim and evidence. Higgott and Watson (2008), in a rather churlish rejoinder to Cohen in a previous issue of *Review of International Political Economy* (*RIPE*), correctly argue that IPE is not a field identified by its method; but neither is it, as they insist, a field defined by some kind of conceptual core. There is no standardized conceptual core to IPE, nor can there be, because IPE is a field of inquiry that spans very many competing and sometimes conflicting analytical traditions. This is why citation indices are not useful ways of gauging impact on the field *as a whole*: we read, respond and contribute to many kinds of debates organized around a myriad of competing problems located in very distinct analytical traditions. But this does not mean IPE is a non-field. Rather, it means that it can (should?) be defined by its subject matter, which in this case is an integrated global political economy that is now several centuries old and is organized around a myriad competing and cross-cutting political, economic, social and cultural frameworks. How to investigate that subject depends upon a number of factors, including the particular problem that marks the entry point of investigation, the conception of knowledge used to apprehend that problem, the ontological predispositions of the scholar and the analytical traditions he or she works within. None of these can be determined in advance, and none certainly can come to be defined by the field or agreed upon as a consensus, at least beyond a small and limited cohort such as that represented by the 'Harvard' school. Liberals, realists, rationalists, constructivists, marxists along with many others[10] all have their place within actually existing IPE in America (and beyond), precisely because they all have something to contribute to our knowledge about how this global political economy is historically and actually organized. And long may it continue to be the case.

Acknowledgments

I wish to thank Michael Williams, Herman Schwartz, Adam Morton and Craig Murphy for helpful comments on an initial draft, as well as the editors of *RIPE* both for the invitation to contribute to this issue and for their critical feedback. I of course bear full responsibility for the views expressed in this article.

Notes

1 Interestingly, this bifurcation parallels many of the distinctions between the IR disciplines as organized and practiced in Britain and the United States (cf. Schmidt, 2008).

2 As Giles and Garand (2007: 742) describe the process, they adapted earlier surveys of reputational indices and consulted colleagues as to the status of various journals, thereby arriving at an initial universe of 115 journals.

3 I will ignore for the purpose at hand the interesting question of impact. However, it is an open question as to the import of citation impact scores: if the average *IO* article is cited 6.24 times over a two-year period within a journal universe of 90 journals (Giles and Garand 2007: 742), what are we to make of the fact that it is, for the most part, ignored by the vast majority of publications in its domain? To put this another way, if just over six of the approximately 2000 articles published by these journals during this period cite an *IO* article, how exactly should we evaluate its 'impact'? And this of course ignores the practice of 'citation-pumping', in which authors (increasingly it seems encouraged by journal editors) cite articles in their journal of publication in order to purposely massage the citation impact scores.

4 This point is also made in a slightly different manner by McNamara *et al.* in this special issue. It would be an interesting exercise to map the universe of journals to which IPE scholars submit their work and in which they get published. Garand and Giles began their list (from which Maliniak and Tierney culled the 'dirty dozen') with 115 journals, but these were only journals in Political Science. As McNamara, Wade and Phillips correctly indicate, the journal universe for IPE is much larger and more variegated, precisely because IPE has not yet been sanctified as a stand-alone field. Its potential journal universe crosses disciplinary boundaries, and is quite possibly three or four times the size of Garand and Giles's initial list. Thus, my claim that the research published in the 'dirty dozen' represents at best 5% of IPE scholarship probably comes in at the top end; it is perhaps nearer to 1%.

5 I am reminded here of Robert Cox's (1996: 178–79) discussion of the sociology of groupies, gatekeepers and loners. For him, graduate school seems more or less designed to produce groupies who can perpetuate and extend the dominance of gatekeepers.

6 In America, journals such as *Monthly Review*, *Science and Society* and *Rethinking Marxism*, are dedicated to ongoing debates within Marxist or historical materialist scholarship, while institutes such as the Fernand Braudel Center at SUNY-Binghamton and the Institute for Research on World-Systems at UC Riverside are very open to historical materialist and Marxist-inspired research. The number of conferences devoted to themes that resonate with such scholarship is not trivial. With

respect to research programs connected to individual scholars, one need only point to the work of William Robinson, David Harvey and Mark Rupert for vibrant examples of this tradition of political economy at play today. And of course, Americans are frequent contributors to established left-inspired journals in Britain such as *New Left Review, Capital & Class,* and *Historical Materialism.*

7 Part of the reason for this seems to be the introductory textbook style of the paradigm-signifiers deployed by the coders. They are quite elementary, as of course they must be in order to accentuate the distinctions they are meant to uncover. Thus, again does data get *made*.

8 For Cox's own confessions as to his theoretical lineage, see Cox (1996: Chs. 2 and 6, esp. pp. 58 and 416).

9 This subtext comes through very clearly in the TRIP survey, where scholars are asked to comment on and rank important foreign policy issues in terms of their significance for the United States. As a Canadian answering this survey I felt distinctly queasy about this section, partly because I am not American but more critically because of the underlying assumption of how scholarship can or should be enlisted in the service of public policy. I can only hope that the questions in this section will be substantially revised for the European version.

10 'Other' theoretical traditions open to the aspirant IPE scholar include numerous feminist, post-modern and post-structural traditions, as well as several historical traditions of political economy – which is where I would locate my own work. Of course, they are not really 'other' traditions at all; rather, they are equal component parts of the organic tradition of political economy that comprises the theoretical universe out of which our knowledge of the world is fashioned.

8 Beware what you wish for

Lessons for international political economy from the transformation of economics

Robert Wade

R. Wade (2009) 'Beware what you wish for: lessons for international political economy from the transformation of economics', *Review of International Political Economy* 16(1): 106–121, published by Taylor & Francis Ltd, http://www.informaworld.com. Permission has been granted by the publisher.

Many American international political economy (IPE) scholars champion economics as the epistemological, methodological, theoretical, and normative model for IPE. Indeed, many see IPE as a handmaiden to economics, whose task is to take economists' conclusions about international economics as given and add more politics. They study the politics with much the same tools as economists use, and operate within the same kind of world view. They thus form part of one of the mega-trends in American academia – the application of economic analysis (especially neoclassical analysis) to traditionally noneconomic areas such as political science, international relations (IR), law and sociology; a trend which some critics have called, unkindly, 'economic imperialism'.

Maliniak and Tierney document the fast transformation of American IPE from pre-1985 pluralism to post-1990 quantitative-liberalism. This essay draws attention to parallels between the transformation of IPE and the earlier transformation of American economics from pluralism to neoclassicism. Understanding what happened in economics can alert us to possible *societal* forces shaping IPE, and caution against seeing the changes in IPE as simply the result of internally-driven evolution towards better theory and better explanations. It can also alert us to the costs of present IPE trends, as seen in what happened to economics in the postwar decades. Only in the last couple of decades or so has economics begun to rescue itself from the mess it got itself into, and the lesson for IPE is: don't hurry down that path because it takes a long time coming out. This history suggests that journal editors and reviewers should pay attention to the downsides of the increasingly robust consensus on epistemology, methods, theory and values within the American school of IPE, and act to protect diversity.

The transformation of American IPE

Maliniak and Tierney's (2009, this issue) findings in their Teaching, Research, and International Policy (TRIP) project suggest that a period of pluralism in American IPE before 1985 gave way in a remarkably short time to the now prevailing monoculture – what for lack of a better term could be called quantitative-liberalism (liberalism in a sense closer to the European meaning than the American meaning). In terms of methods, quantitative articles in the top twelve international relations journals rose from about 20% in 1985 to 90% in 2006; qualitative articles fell from about 70% in 1985 to 15% in 2006; and the share of articles using a formal model rose from 10% in 1985 to 20% in 2006. The bottom line is that almost all the IPE-related articles in Maliniak and Tierney's top 12 journals through the 2000s were 'quantitative'.

In terms of meta-theory, between 1980 and 1985 (and presumably before 1980 too) the top journals published a significant percentage of articles rooted in each of the 'liberal', 'realist', Marxist', and 'constructivist' paradigms, not to mention the residual category of 'no-paradigm'. By 1990 this variety had substantially shrunk and the liberal paradigm emerged as predominant. Between 1985 and 2006, the share of 'liberal' articles rose from 40% to 70%; the share of 'non-paradigmatic' articles remained at around 25–30%; and the share of articles rooted in other paradigms (realism, Marxism, etc.) fell from around 35% to less than 5%. Maliniak and Tierney do not code for 'rational choice', but as Farrell and Finnemore argue in this issue, one can presume a close affinity between 'liberalism' and 'rational choice'. In this case one can also say that US IPE has become dominated by the rational choice approach.[1]

The transformation of economics

The transformation of economics from pluralism to neoclassicism occurred between the interwar years and the postwar years, or roughly between 1920 and 1960.[2] In the first period several approaches to economics flourished in the United States at the same time. The most visible and arguably dominant grouping was the 'institutionalists' (including such leading figures as Thorstein Veblen, Wesley Mitchell, Walton Hamilton, John Commons, J.M. Clark, Rexford Tugwell). It was a broad and non-exclusive movement which cohered around a shared commitment to: (a) scientific investigation; (b) empirical research; (c) theory building (but not based on deduction from simple assumptions); (d) emphasis on the importance of institutions in determining economic outcomes; and in particular (e) the need for public policy and public regulation to offset the inadequacy of unregulated markets. Alongside these economists was a range of more neoclassical scholars, who shared a greater respect for marginal analysis, mathematics, and the market system. The major journals took articles from across the spectrum, and leading universities employed economists espousing a range of approaches, even if they were sometimes at each other's throats.

By 1960 the mainstream of American academic economics, as seen in journal articles, was defined by formalization, quantification, and neoclassical faith in self-adjusting free markets (the combination can be referred to as 'neoclassical economics' for short) (Backhouse, 1998).[3] Other approaches – including not only institutionalism but also Marxism – were relegated to the backwaters, where they remain, with odd exceptions. Keynesian economics still had its adherents, but 'being a follower of Keynes was a dubious label for American economists' (Morgan and Rutherford, 1998: 16). Paul Samuelson claimed to synthesize Keynesian economics with neoclassical economics to make the 'neoclassical synthesis'. But Samuelson's introductory textbook 'was widely vilified for the dangerous Keynesian ideas it contained', at the same time as it was widely adopted (Goodwin, 1998: 58).

More specifically, the mainstream by the 1960s was marked by the following features:

- a substantive commitment to the free market as the overarching institutional form;
- a methodological commitment to tool-kit economics;
- an increasing focus on issues that 'were primarily of concern only to academic economists. Economics was becoming more inward looking' (Backhouse, 1998: 106), even as its subjects of study expanded beyond material well-being to the non-traditionally economic;
- disdain for the qualitative, the normative, and for history, which is the converse of the rise of formalism; and
- an assertion that a valid macroeconomics (about aggregates) had to rest on strict microeconomic foundations, composed of propositions about rational individuals.

Evolution of the neoclassical monoculture

Most economists today believe that neoclassicism triumphed because of an internal evolutionary process: it provided better theory and better explanations than other species of economics, as judged by the criteria of science prevailing at the time, and therefore won out in the race to replicate itself.[4] This could be called the hypothesis of Whiggish progress, based on the idea of cumulative knowledge, which implies that the latest knowledge is by and large the best knowledge. The hypothesis provides the implicit justification for the absence from economics departments and syllabi of both the history of economic thought and the history of economics as a discipline, and the rarity with which economics papers more than 10 years old are cited. (See the papers by McNamara, and Farrell and Finnemore in this issue for parallels with IPE syllabi today.)

To assess the Whiggish progress hypothesis we have to distinguish between criteria of science prevailing at the time of the emergence of the new economics, and criteria prevailing today. It may (or may not) be that the case that neoclassical economics provides better theory and better explanations than more institutionalism, Keynesian or Marxist ones against *today's* criteria of science. But this is irrelevant to the causal hypothesis that the new economics triumphed because it provided better theory and explanations as judged by the criteria of science prevailing at the time. Since the criteria have changed, there are no stable internal criteria against which to measure progress. Without going into the issue further, it can be said that the Whiggish progress hypothesis is implausible as compared with hypotheses that emphasize changes outside economics, especially political ones. Here I emphasise external political contingencies which delegitimized non-neoclassical species, and had internal effects by changing the discipline's incentives and socialization.

The first hypothesis about external forces relates to the Cold War and the larger US strategy of opening the world economy to trade and investment. It says that the nationalism and climate of fear generated by the Cold War pushed US societal values towards an image opposite that which the same forces generated for the 'communist bloc'. The communist bloc was said to be based on the suppression of freedom, markets, competition, private property; and in response the US self-image gave maximum emphasis to all these. The in-between area of New Deal and war-time market 'intervention' became illegitimate. Also, the strategic objective of opening the non-communist world to trade and investment boosted the credibility of arguments which said that free markets were best for all. Hence the shift in US strategic objectives in the 1940s and 1950s conferred competitive advantage to neoclassicism, which had been but one species of the interwar pluralism. The spooky McCarthites intensified the process by targeting anyone who could be labelled a sympathizer of 'government intervention', including Keynesians. As Crauford Goodwin explains:

> Increasingly in the 1940s and 1950s, John Maynard Keynes and his American disciplines, led by Alvin Hansen, became favourite targets of cold-war witch-hunters. This was partly because Keynesian macroeconomic theory seemed to provide a persuasive rationale for a strong state. Wasn't this, after all, the Marxist prescription? But in addition, the name 'Keynes' was a convenient personification of economic heresy... There were no longer enough home-grown Marxists to make the name 'Marx' a credible threat on the home front.... Moreover Keynes was a foreigner, and an Englishman to boot, with a one-syllable name like the name 'Marx'... Even though Keynes's and Marx's ideas were as different as night and day, they were lumped together in this period by many a demagogue.
>
> (Goodwin, 1998: 58)[5]

The same politics drove the ascendancy of formalization and quantification, because these techniques conferred the protection of 'scientific objectivity' and allowed exponents to talk to each other in ways which zealots outside economics could not understand.

In response to this climate of fear, many established prewar nonneoclassical economists converted to neoclassicism and steered their graduate students in the same direction. But the shift was also driven from outside economics by patrons who wanted 'safe' teachers, and researchers who would reach 'acceptable' findings. The patrons included, above all, university administrators and leaders of higher education who could influence appointments in the direction of those who would minimize external criticism and maximize external funding. They included government officials who influenced university and research funding. And they included the business community and foundations such as the Ford Foundation. For example, a report of the Ford Foundation's Study Committee on Policy and Program in 1949 said that economists must re-examine 'basic theories' and 'subject them to the acid test of verification'; in effect saying that they must reject pluralism in favor of neoclassicism. The main author of the report explained in a memorandum to the head of the foundation that the foundation should concentrate its funds on economics (as distinct from other subjects), because the 'fundamental elements of the ideological appeal and international propaganda attack of communism are economic' (quoted in Goodwin, 1998: 77–8). US-style economics was an important weapon in the hands of non-communist nations, he said. To command consensus it had to be clear, coherent, rigorous, formal, and quantitative, because these were the hallmarks of objective science.

In short, the Cold War hypothesis says that the burst of US nationalism in the first decades of the Cold War shrank the range of legitimate beliefs and the legitimate ways of expressing them in economics. The beliefs narrowed to neoclassicism and the ways of expressing them narrowed to the ostensibly neutral and objective languages of mathematics and quantification.

A second 'external' explanation for the rise of the neoclassical monoculture is the 'changing criteria of scientific objectivity' hypothesis. It says that the transformation of economics was fuelled by a profound change in the notion of 'scientific objectivity' in science at large. In the interwar period scientific objectivity was conceived as something that depended on personal attributes of the researcher, like honesty and integrity. In the postwar period this gave way to the notion of objectivity as dependent on the use of a set of techniques or tools – mathematics for the theory and statistics for the empirics.

Practicing the strand of economics which most embraced mathematics and statistics, neoclassical economists claimed the warrant of objectivity not only for their techniques but also for their results and their policy advice (advice about, for example, 'efficiency' as distinct from value-laden 'equity'). Indeed, they claimed objectivity for the whole edifice of neoclassical theory – including the foundational belief that the free market, competition, and the primacy of the self-interested individual was the best arrangement for economic activity, because this belief was most consistent with ultimate truths about human nature. Economics came to be hailed – not only by economists but by university administrators, foundations, policy makers, politicians, many other social scientists, and sections of the general public – as the queen of the social sciences.

These two external drivers – Cold War politics and the changed notion of scientific objectivity – changed incentives and socialization within the profession. The high value attached to formalization in the postwar environment led to the promotion of economists committed to this project, who shaped the emerging agenda of the discipline. For them, the formalization of the theory of self-adjusting markets was more important than engagement with empirical phenomena. John Hicks' *Value and Capital* (1946), one of the seminal works in microeconomics, illustrates the trade-off. Hicks made an explicit defence of a priori reasoning on grounds that it was legitimate to build a theoretical edifice on the basis of certain assumptions about firms and consumers which were chosen (over alternative assumptions) *because* they were necessary for the development of tractable mathematical models with determinate solutions:

> [I]t has to be recognized that a general abandonment of the assumption of perfect competition … must have very destructive consequences for economic theory. Under monopoly [and oligopoly] the stability conditions become indeterminate; and the basis of which economic laws can be constructed is therefore shorn away … It is … only possible to save anything from this wreck – and … the threatened wreckage is that of the greater part of general equilibrium theory – if we can … suppose … that *marginal* costs do generally increase with output at the point of equilibrium [that is, increasing returns do not generally exist]. [T]hen the laws of an economic system working under perfect competition will not be appreciably varied in a system which contains widespread elements of monopoly. At least, this getaway seems well worth trying … I doubt if most of the problems we shall have to exclude for this reason are capable of much useful analysis by the methods of [neoclassical] economic theory.
>
> (Hicks, 1946: 84–5; emphasis in original)

Hicks said, in other words, that theory-building economists can legitimately ignore phenomena which might challenge the prior commitments to formalization and the virtues of competitive markets. It sounds like no more than an innocent application of Occam's Razor, but the argument had a profound effect on conclusions about the real world. It injected a bias in favor of the hypothesis that market failures are self-correcting and against the hypothesis that market failures are (often) self-reinforcing.

Also happening at about this time was the redefinition of economics away from its long-standing focus on the material well-being of individuals or nations and towards the 'choice process'. In Lionel Robbins' formulation, 'economics is the science which studies human behaviour as a relationship between ends and scarce means which have alternative uses'; on the basis of which Robbins claimed that economics should study any form of behaviour which is influenced by scarcity. 'There are no limitations on the subject-matter of Economic Science save this', he said (Robbins, 1932: 16). Nobel Memorial Prize winner Gary Becker became the champion of this approach to *homo economicus*. Explaining his method he said, 'The combined assumptions of maximizing behaviour, market equilibrium, and stable preferences, used relentlessly and unflinchingly, form the heart of the economic approach as I see it' (Becker, 1976: 5).

It was also the case that the modeling techniques themselves became increasingly complex. A high degree of mathematical ability became increasingly necessary to master them and attain competence, and graduate courses lengthened and became more intellectually demanding. This led to the increasingly held assumption that only the very brightest could become economists. And it led to an increasing recruitment into the profession of people who were less driven to try to explain how the world actually works or how policy could make it work more efficiently or more fairly, and more motivated to prove themselves members of an elite group of masters of an arcane craft.

The combination of formalization, quantification and neoclassicism gripped the discipline like a creed. Convinced there was only one true approach, economists gave little value to the intellectual equivalent of biodiversity. In department after department, neoclassicals, once having reached a critical mass, tended to gang up on non-neoclassicals and force them out or block their appointment. Patrons in the world of foundations and business reinforced their conviction; and the increased emphasis on ranking of journals and economists added another feedback loop.[6]

Alternative theoretical approaches (species) fared poorly in this environment. For example, institutionalism approaches (now sometime referred to as 'old institutional economics') suffered because they were typically harder than neoclassical economics to teach: they relied on detailed study of particular cases, knowledge of law as well as maths and economics (even sociology in the case of Veblen), and their results were less easy to transport from one jurisdiction (one city, county, state, country) to another. As graduate numbers swelled, teachers standardized their syllabi around neoclassical theory and models. And as the US population became more geographically mobile and universities competed for faculty, economists could expect to spiral around the whole country in the course of their careers. Both trends put institutionalism approaches at a competitive disadvantage in replicating themselves in the minds of graduate students. In contrast, neoclassical economics replicated itself more easily. It was based on maths and statistics, presented itself as founded on laws as universal as the laws of engineering, and was committed to the idea that markets self-adjust (and hence tended to treat politics as a source of impediments to self-adjustment). Whoever learned it would not be disadvantaged in moving from place to place.

Weaknesses of the neoclassical monoculture

It took the mainstream of American economics the best part of four postwar decades, until at least the mid 1980s, before it showed much sign of moving beyond the neoclassical creed. The Harvard economist and Nobel Memorial Prize winner Wassily Leontief characterized the state of US economics in 1982:

> Year after year economic theorists continue to produce scores of mathematical models and to explore in great detail their formal properties; and the econometricians fit algebraic functions of all possible shapes to essentially

> the same sets of data without being able to advance, in any perceptible way, a systematic understanding of the structure and the operations of a real economic system.
>
> (Leontief, 1982: 104, 107; see also Leontief, 1971: 1–7)

A survey of US graduate students in economics in the late 1980s confirmed Leontief's observation. Only 3% thought that 'having a thorough knowledge of the economy' was 'very important' for achieving success in the profession, and 68% thought it 'unimportant' (Colander and Klamer, 1987). Tim Besley, a distinguished economist of the 1990s–2000s, agrees that 'mainstream economics in the 1960s to 1980 had a tendency to be narrow, self-referential, theoretical, static, and sometimes lost its focus on real-world issues' (Besley, personal communication, 22 May 2008).[7]

But it was not just that economics turned away from the analysis of real world economic systems. The same syndrome of characteristics imparted substantive content by biasing conclusions about the real world in favor of self-adjusting markets and occluding arguments that would upset this way of seeing.

The strength of the commitment to free markets is captured in a survey of economists' opinions from the early 1980s. The survey elicited responses to 27 propositions about the economy from about 1000 economists in five industrialized countries, in terms of 'generally agree', 'agree with provisos', and 'generally disagree'. With respect to the proposition 'tariffs and import controls lower economic welfare', 79% of the American economists said 'generally agree', far more than economists of the other four (continental European) countries. At the other end, only 27% of the less neoclassically inclined French economists said 'generally agree'.[8]

The evidence adduced in support of the free trade proposition typically involves a regression between 'trade regime' and economic growth or other measure of performance. To effect the regression, all the information about each country's trade regime is collapsed to a single number on a scale of trade liberalization. The approach leads economists to focus on the regression and not on the actual operation of the trade regimes; and so to rely on official tariff levels and policy statements about non-tariff barriers as distinct from the experience of people who transact through the trade regime. In studying the East Asian capitalist countries, economists routinely overlooked strongly 'illiberal' features of the trade regimes (both overt and covert) in their desire to hold up these successful cases as proof of the virtues of freer trade, and the regression methodology made it easy for them to do so (Wade, 1992; Wade, 2004: Chs. 3 and 5).

Another example of disciplinary bias in favor of free markets is economists' predisposition to find the cause of relatively high unemployment in Europe in 'rigid' labor markets, and therefore to urge a curbing of trade union power, an expansion of employers' right to hire and fire, and wage flexibility downwards. They hardly consider pro-labor forms of flexibility like 'family friendly' work hours; or the hypothesis that high unemployment is due to the failure of budgetary and monetary policies to maintain demand for a prolonged period (Wade, 2007a).

This kind of economics too easily became an apologia for the pliant consensus of the ruling class, under the banner of 'objective' knowledge. One is reminded of Keynes' explanation of the popularity of Ricardo's theory of comparative advantage:

> That it could explain much social injustice and apparent cruelty as an inevitable incident in the scheme of progress, and the attempt to change such things as likely ... to do more harm than good, commended it to authority. That it afforded a measure of justification to the free activities of individual capitalists, attracted to it the support of the dominant social force behind authority.
>
> (Keynes, 1936: 33)

Neoclassical economics retained the support of the 'dominant social force behind authority' by turning its back on the analysis of economic and political power, whether Marxist or non-Marxist; which contributed to the Cold War task of suppressing awareness of class and class conflict in free market societies in order to blunt the appeal of communism. It continued to promote the model of perfect competition as the ideal social arrangement not only because the model yields determinate mathematical solutions but also because it is a social arrangement without power (the power of any one actor to influence market-wide outcomes). The *Palgrave Dictionary of Economics* published in the late 1980s had no entry for 'power' in its 4000 pages.

Economists also gave scant attention to inequality of income and wealth, reflecting an assumption either that 'objective' advice about efficiency could be delivered independently of effects on equity, or that the distribution of income and wealth which results from market competition ought to be accepted as just and efficient, with the arguable exception of absolute poverty. Willem Buiter, professor of European economics at the London School of Economics, recently declared, '[Absolute] poverty bothers me. Inequality does not [nor relative poverty] ... I simply don't care' (Buiter, 2007).[9] His insouciance is typical in the discipline, as seen in the scarcity of articles about income and wealth inequality in the top economics journals over the decades since the Second World War.

Underlying these several ideological commitments is a certain view of human nature, seen as self-seeking, prone to opportunism and shirking when the chances of detection are judged low enough and bare-knuckle competition not intense enough. This is the rational choice way of seeing, which presumes that laws of society must be derivable from universal laws about individual behaviour and about combinations of actions of individuals with different preferences. It is interesting to observe how, in specific cases, the assumption is protected from question. Economists analysing large Japanese companies, for example, have been puzzled by the low level of corruption, despite shareholders exercising only weak monitoring control (shareholder monitoring being regarded as key to efficiency in the neoclassical model). Since they *know* that nobody is honest and diligent unless subject to external control, they hunt for some other *external* control. Sure enough, they find a functional substitute for the external control of the stock market – namely, the 'main bank' system. Having identified this external substitute, their minds come to rest. They ignore the alternative hypothesis that the community nature of a Japanese firm – especially the fact that it is not run primarily for the benefit of shareholders – imposes peer-group moral constraints on those who are selected, after a lifetime of membership in the company, to be the company's top managers, or elders (Dore, 2000: 79). This possibility might question the bedrock rational choice assumption about human nature.[10]

'Moral constraints', like 'ruling class consensus', are as alien to economists' conceptual universe as 'water' is to the conceptual universe of fish. The assumptions embedded in the discipline make it hard to understand that people-in-general do seem to have deep instincts for fairness, empathy, and attachment; and that some societal arrangements bring out these instincts more than others, where the institutional arrangements themselves cannot be explained as the result of prior rounds of self maximizing.

The neoclassical world view protects not only the underlying assumptions about human nature and the virtues of the self-adjusting market but also the rightness of US leadership of the 'free world'. It has the same legitimacy-boosting effect, though through a different mechanism, as American accounts of the Second World War, which routinely write the Russians out of the story and cast the United States as the uniquely virtuous protagonist. To this day, American economists tend to frame the debate about public policy responses to globalization not in terms of how we get a good society, but in terms of what price we have to pay to keep the bastard voters and other countries on our side in globalizing the world – globalizing meaning to come as near as possible to the ideal world where any economic actor is able to invest, work and sell anywhere in the world, with national borders reduced to no more economic significance than the borders of US states (Summers, 2008a, 2008b;Wolf, 2004: 4).

However, in the past two decades or so economics, once a colonizing discipline, has become colonized around the edges by fields it had conquered. It is being challenged by psychology, sociology, and history, if not political science. Although this counter-colonization has not subverted the neoclassical core, the invasion by contiguous fields has made economics a much livelier and policy-relevant subject than it was. Indeed, the recent rise of a sub-branch of experimental or behavioral economics is even beginning to challenge some of the core axioms of neoclassicism, by re-splicing economics and psychology and showing how people often choose in conditions of confusion, myopia and herd following.

Warnings for IPE

If Maliniak and Tierney's findings are taken at face value, they suggest that a consensus on 'normal science' has emerged in American IPE, where this normal science is defined as (a) rooted in the liberal paradigm; (b) reliant on statistical techniques; and (c) codified in a mathematical model wherever possible (e.g., in mathematized versions of rational choice and game theory). To this extent the consensus mirrors neoclassical economics.

The history of economics from interwar pluralism to postwar neoclassicism should sound warning bells about helicoptering the model of neoclassical economics into IPE. The model biases conclusions towards:

- the virtues and prevalence of self-adjusting systems,
- an anodyne notion of power,
- a functionalist kind of explanation (for example, 'firms and international organizations exist because they lower transaction costs'),
- the virtues of American hegemony and the need to preserve it.

The model biases conclusions away from:

- inequalities of income and wealth,
- go-it-alone power, network power, and other forms of structural power (Grewal, 2008; Gruber, 2000),
- the advantages (in terms of power relations between states, preservation of cultural traditions, valued institutions, social solidarity, etc.) of states retaining power to shape internal arrangements within frontier controls.[11]

Further, IPE should be alert to the dangers of elevating formalization and quantification as primary criteria for the selection of research subjects. When the existence of a 'data set' suitable for rigorous analysis becomes an almost necessary condition for selection, big questions and propositions not amenable to 'rigor' get marginalized (as has happened in IPE, Keohane suggests in this symposium). It is like unraveling a colorful tapestry in order to end up with piles of different colored wools. It prompts the question, 'I see your bridle, but where is your horse?'

Equally, though, as Nicola Phillips also suggests in this issue, IPE should be alert to the dangers of its present tether to IR (as in, 'IPE is a better class of IR'). As an outsider – schooled in economics and anthropology and approaching IPE subjects from development studies rather than IR – I have been puzzled by the way that IPE textbooks and journal articles often begin by reference to a debate between the 'paradigms' of liberalism, realism, Marxism, and constructivism. It seems like a kind of Punch-and-Judy show, a mock war of the worlds. Indeed, Maliniak and Tierney find that while the percentage of IPE journal articles set within a realist or Marxist paradigm has fallen away to practically zero, the frequency of citation of a handful of realist or Marxist IPE articles remains high. But the citations are of a cursory kind, seemingly intended to signal the author's membership of the liberal community before getting down to serious business. The debate owes its continued existence mainly to a wistful wish for battle-lines to divide the virtuous from the wicked.

In the spirit of Susan Strange, let IPE be 'an open range … accessible to people of all walks of life, from all professions and all political proclivities'. The editors and reviewers for the top IR journals (Germain's 'dirty dozen') have a special responsibility to recognize that the present composition of journal articles – almost entirely quantitative and in large majority rooted in the liberal paradigm – is not an unambiguous sign of disciplinary health. They should draw lessons not only from the fate of economics for the best part of four decades after the war to the mid 1980s and beyond, but also from ecology: a healthy ecology depends on a substantial degree of biodiversity, and below a threshold the ecology degenerates by itself. Let editors and reviewers nurture a fecund and peaty diversity. For a start, it would help to jettison the IR-tethered name 'international political economy' and replace it with the more capacious 'global political economy'.

Acknowledgments

I thank Ron Dore, Radhika Desai, and Kate Weaver for their comments.

Notes

1 For purposes of this essay I take Maliniak and Tierney's findings at face value, ignoring the qualifications made by other contributors to this symposium.
2 Neoclassical economics is centered on general equilibrium analysis, which shows how the national economy operates as a *self-regulating* system of many interdependent activities. The general idea received its translation into calculus and algebra by Leon Walrus and Vilfredo Pareto, mathematically trained engineers, in the late nineteenth and early twentieth centuries. My potted history is indebted to Mary Morgan and Malcolm Rutherford (1998) and other essays in the same volume; and to years of participant-observation among the Economists.
3 Backhouse says it would be possible to classify articles by attitude to Keynes, but he did not do it.
4 David Lake (2009: 50, this issue) comes close to embracing the Whiggish hypothesis when he argues: The movement of OEP [open economy politics] towards economics is not driven ... by disciplinary envy but by the insights that economic theory provides for political interpretations of policy choice. The interesting question is how one would 'test' Lake's hypothesis, as against those emphasising 'envy' or the interests of patrons or other variables I emphasise in my account of the evolution of economics to neoclassical economics.
5 Goodwin (1998: 58) further says: John Kenneth Galbraith, who could wear both Institutionalist and Keynesian labels, was nearly dismissed for his convictions by the Harvard Corporation and was targeted by an alumni group called the Veritas Foundation.
6 The case of Paul Davidson, a leading American Keynesian economist, illustrates one of the mechanisms by which the antibodies extrude non-neoclassical ideas. Through much of the 1970s Davidson was chair of the Rutgers University Economics Department. The department contained nearly 80 economists, of whom only five were non-neoclassical. Davidson's friend, John Kenneth Galbraith, was a friend of the president of Rutgers. Galbraith urged the president to capitalize on the presence of a leading Keynesian and get some more Keynesians into the department. With the president's blessing Davidson specified that the next new appointment should give preference to a Keynesian economist. The majority neoclassicals were so angry that they sent a delegation to the president and provost to argue (in Davidson's words) that 'these types of non-mainstream economists would not be able to obtain lucrative government and foundation grants since the peer reviewers

were much more mainstream'. The delegation persuaded the president and provost to withdraw the Keynesian specification from the advertisement, and Davidson resigned the chairmanship. Later, in the early 1980s, a new editor took control at the *American Economic Review* and Davidson had all his subsequent submissions rejected, whereas previously he had built his reputation as a leading Keynesian by publishing several papers in the journal. He contacted the editor, who informed him that under his editorship the journal would not publish articles by Keynesians. The editor suggested that if he and his like-minded friends wanted to keep publishing they should start a specialist journal of Keynesian economics. Davidson and others went ahead and founded a journal to be called *Journal of Keynesian Economics* – until someone did the acronym and the title was changed to the clunky *Journal of Post-Keynesian Economics* (Davidson, personal communication, 25 May 2005).

7 Besley continued: But since then [1980s] we have had revolutions which bring information, psychology, imperfect markets and political economy back into the center of things. That is why 'alternative economics' no longer gets any traction, because the mainstream is now broad enough that Joe Stiglitz and Paul Krugman are squarely within it in their economics (as distinct from their politics).

8 See Frey *et al.* (1984). My guess is that trade policy cognoscenti would today be less inclined to tick 'generally agree' than at the time of Frey's survey; but their qualifications have not made much impression on the larger community of economists. Wade (forthcoming) asks 'Does trade liberalization promote economic progress?'.

9 Buiter also says that 'too much' of Europe is occupied by 'dirigiste, stultifying, anaemic societies'. For reasons why he and the discipline are wrong see Wade (2007b) and other chapters in the same volume.

10 The core argument of Dani Rodrik (2007) is vulnerable to the same objection.

11 There is also a chronic problem of statistical techniques appropriate for large samples being used on samples which are too small. Charles Ragin and collaborators have developed 'qualitative comparative analysis' specifically for moderate sized samples of the kind common in IPE research, too small for standard variable analysis and too big for case studies. See Ragin (2000), Ragin *et al.* (2003) and Wade and Goldstein (2003).

9 Mid-Atlantic

Sitting on the knife's sharp edge

Peter J. Katzenstein

P.J. Katzenstein (2009) 'Mid-Atlantic: sitting on the knife's sharp edge', *Review of International Political Economy* 16(1): 122–135, published by Taylor & Francis Ltd, http://www.informaworld.com. Permission has been granted by the publisher.

Not so long ago, Richard Nisbett (2003) published *The Geography of Thought: How Asians and Westerners Think Differently… and Why.* The book maps the geography of thought, as revealed in a set of experiments probing American, Asian and Asian-American cognitive styles. Nisbett reported some of the fascinating experimental results that researchers had found in the emerging field of cultural psychology. The central point I took from Nisbett's book was simple. Psychology was perhaps less of a universal social science than the cognitive turn of the last generation had made us believe. While the book spoke to me, it decidedly did not speak to Sherry Ortner (2003), an ethnographic anthropologist who reviewed it for the *New York Times*. Predictably and quite correctly, Ortner charged Nisbett with reifying his objects of study, creating impossibly large analytical categories (Asians and Westerners), and failing to theorize and test for differences within, rather than between, these categories. The geography of our thoughts, Ortner reminds us, is after all constructs, and in this case large and potentially pernicious ones.

Since the same thing can surely be said about the American and British schools of international political economy (IPE), this recollection resonates with my reaction to the *Review of International Political Economy* (*RIPE*) symposium. Journal editors have a well-honed nose for intellectual controversies that touch raw nerves as this one does. International relations theory has featured a number of such debates during the last two generations – between realism and idealism, realism and liberalism, neo-realism and neo-liberalism, constructivism and rationalism, and within and between variants of each of these schools of thought. I agree with David Lake (2009: 48, this issue) that such debates can become tiring if they are carried on too long, and if they are interfering unduly with the more urgent task of doing the research that actually may help us understand better developments in the world. But such debates have one undeniable virtue – they remind us of the foundations of the normal work we do in our research and teaching.

Before Benjamin Cohen published his article on the transatlantic divide between the American and the British schools, the study of international and comparative political economy had not been given much attention in these debates. Cohen's (2007) article, the two responses by John Ravenhill (2008) and Richard Higgott and Matthew Watson (2008), and Cohen's rejoinder (2008), all add up to a resounding victory for each of the authors' well crafted arguments. Unable to find a unified Anglosphere in this domain of scholarship, Cohen is right in pointing to two distinct styles of analysis, American and British, in international and comparative political economy. Ravenhill is also correct in pointing to a large body of empirical scholarship, his own surely included, that this binary distinction elides. Higgott and Watson uncover standards of normality in Cohen's argument that, despite and because of Cohen's evident sense of fairness and impartiality, inevitably marginalize contributions from the eastern shore of our imaginary Atlantic. Cohen's (2008) rejoinder graciously acknowledges the existence of different arguments, but refuses to give an inch on his central claim. Using extensive data gathered through surveys and a journal coding system, in this special issue Maliniak and Tierney's paper supports Cohen's depiction of IPE scholarship in the United States. Rather than adjudicating between these excellent statements, and parsing the truth in the manner of medieval scholasticism, I would like to reflect on what I think this forum can teach us about our scholarship and teaching: the importance of intellectual diversity, not formulaically acknowledged as a professional mantra but actually reflected in our daily practice as scholars and teachers.

Before I engage two important issues this symposium raises, I would like to make two prefatory remarks. In the interest of candor I feel compelled to acknowledge, with some embarrassment, that vanity got the better part of me. I was particularly drawn to the tables in Maliniak and Tierney's article which reported my and Cornell's (and in that order) standing in this domain of scholarship and for this Anglophone audience. The results are both gratifying and disturbing and in any case offer food for thought about the issues this symposium is debating.

First, Tables 5 and 6 in Maliniak and Tierney's (2009: 17, 18, this issue) article show that 7% of the respondents report that my work has had 'the most profound impact' on the respondent's research. And the same percentage thinks that my work had 'the greatest impact on the field of IR'. Even though I wished that the figure would be 93% higher, it strikes me as fundamentally correct that the two percentage figures are the same. My research has not had any effect on the paradigmatic debates, which have defined the field over the last several decades. In sharp contrast, the writings of the top three scholars on the list (Keohane, Waltz, and Wendt) have done a great deal to sharpen the paradigmatic debates in the field of IPE and international relations (IR). Contributing to paradigmatic debates (the data suggest and I agree within limits, as I argue later) is a very important and valued contribution of the scholarship we do, especially when it helps to broaden rather than narrow our debates.

Second, there is my interest in Cornell's standing. I was very pleased to see that Cornell ranked very high in the number of most IPE (rank 2) and IR (rank 5) graduate students trained during the last 40 years, especially since its Government Department is so much smaller than most of its peer institutions ranked either right above or below in Tables 1 and 2 of Maliniak and Tierney's (2009: 11, this issue) paper. Tables 3 and 4 on the other hand report that Cornell does not make the top 10 in either IPE or IR articles published since 1980 (2009: 12). This is certainly a disturbing finding. Are too few professors at Cornell training too many students so that the little time that remains outside of teaching must *per force* be given over to foraging for food and collecting firewood to survive the harsh winter in upstate New York? Although this is the story that we are, unsuccessfully, telling our Deans, the fact of the matter is different. Cornell is a 'book' not an 'article' department, reflected by the fact that Cornell University Press is issuing two well-known book series in IPE that are edited by two members of the Cornell Government Department. Regrettably, this clashes with the views of some undergraduates/younger scholars who believe that Wikipedia/journal articles have replaced books as sole conveyors of knowledge and learning. Although inadequate data are always better than no data, the questions that Germain, McNamara and Phillips raise in their contributions about the limitations of the data on which this symposium is based are in my opinion very much to the point. Our interpretations of the data must take account of inherent limitations, as Maliniak and Tierney (2009: 14, n. 16, this issue) do quite properly concede in their article, although, for my taste, a bit too late.

I would like to focus in the remainder of this paper on two issues that this symposium highlights – how to think about actor preferences and interest on the one hand and professional power on the other. David Lake's discussion of open economy politics (OEP) in this issue strikes Benjamin Cohen, in his concluding paper, as 'triumphalist' in tone. I thought of OEP as a serious intellectual contribution that will be cited prominently and approvingly should the empire strike back – perhaps in a symposium on the failings of the British school, issued by one of the US journals Maliniak and Tierney have sampled. OEP resonates in the US academy with sweet commonsense. On economic issues, actors who are price takers with clearly ordered preferences rank policies and outcomes based on how they affect their expected future incomes. OEP analysis seeks to make special adjustments for situations when one or several of these assumptions are not met. Economic interests clearly matter on questions of IPE. Lake's argument is thus both sensibly pragmatic in getting one's work done and at the same time, I shall argue, curiously uninterested in wanting to taste some of the grass growing on the other side of the fence.[1]

Actors and interests in American IPE: a critical reflection on open economy politics

The issue of how to deal with actor preferences and interests is, I believe, of fundamental importance and not only in the field of international political economy.

Robert Keohane's contribution to this special issue characterizes the developments in IPE pithily and accurately. He writes that since the 1980s important progress has been made in not simply assuming state preferences and interests but to unpack the black box of the state. Doing so permits inquiry into the processes by which preferences and identities are formed. Indeed, Keohane argues that the field has gone overboard and moved too far in the direction of focusing almost exclusively on the domestic determinants of preferences and interests. He pleads for bringing the 'international' back into IPE (Keohane, 2009: 38–9, this issue).

In contrast to this earlier period, at a lower level of intellectual aggregation OEP scholarship has resisted the urge to open up for further analysis processes of preference and interest formation. What Lake regards here as the most exciting progressive research paradigm in the field IPE, starts with sets of individuals 'that can be reasonably assumed to share (nearly) identical interests… Deducing interests from economic theory was the essential innovation of OEP' (Lake, 2009: 50). In this formulation individual (not social) interests are stipulated to exist (not inquired into). Determined by the position of individuals in the international economy, interests are stipulated to be largely identical and then 'aggregated' institutionally (the conceptual language chosen here is very similar to structural functional theory of the 1960s) and 'translated' (in the metaphorical language of Eastonian systems theory) via institutions into policy outputs and outcomes. In Lake's formulation the great innovation of OEP was to import wholesale theories of politics from the field of economics. Since I am not partial to the often extreme forms of reductionism that pass as powerful theory among economists, this is an innovation that is often of dubious value for political analysis. The economic theories that OEP relies on are falsifiable and empirically robust for explaining economic outcomes. Whether they offer insights into significant political outcomes is a matter of considerable dispute. I grant readily that on this score the proof of the pudding should lie in the eating. Are the behavioral implications deduced from reductionist economic theories politically illuminating or not?

Despite the similarity in some of the key concepts, OEP's conceptualization differs from and improves on 1960s-style pluralist theory. Individual interests get refracted through and altered by institutions. OEP's recognition of the relative autonomy of institutions is a significant step forward. Lake is correct in highlighting the importance of institutions, compared, for example, to macro approaches to OEP which bypass them altogether, as in the original formulations of Jeffrey Frieden and Ron Rogowski's important work (Lake, 2009: 51, this issue). Yet the non-institutional strain of OEP also differs from pluralist theory 1960s-style. Pluralism regarded the making of sausages – with inputs, throughputs and outputs – as a good analogy for politics. Macro approaches to OEP recognize that it makes a big difference who is made into sausages and who gets to turn the crank.

But Lake's incorporation of institutional analysis is cautious and partial. He is content to bracket interests and preferences by taking them as given and to subscribe to a truncated view of what institutions are and do. The institutional theory (in the singular) that OEP relies on is rationalist institutional theory, one among a number of competing variants of institutionalist analyses (in the plural) fully articulated during the last two decades. OEP focuses exclusively on the regulative power of institutions and neglects altogether the constitutive powers of institutions that shape actor preferences and interests through identities. This remains an important, under-attended topic in IPE. Robert Wade's example, in this issue, of the low level of corruption in Japanese companies induced by peer group moral constraints rather than external controls, serves as a nice illustration (Wade, 2009: 115, this issue). Actor identity and the preferences and interests which follow from them are of paramount political importance. I am not questioning the importance of the insights gained by scholarship in the OEP tradition. What I question here is the assumption that OEP is now the consensually agreed understanding of what it means to do research on questions of IPE.[2] Variety is the spice of life. It also is an insurance against the risks of mono-crop agriculture, as McNamara argues in this issue (McNamara, 2009: 81, this issue). Lake, for one, concedes that, at best, disjointed and irregular bridges will be built between his favored partial equilibrium approach and a holistic alternative (Lake, 2009: 53). If the data provided by Maliniak and Tierney are valid, such bridges are apparently becoming ever more rickety in the top American IPE journals.

This discussion suggests that OEP and IPE pay a potentially very steep price in the questions that they consider interesting and the approaches they deem relevant by: making preferences and interests exogenous, assuming that interests can be derived only from a rationalist model of human behavior, excluding from analysis the constitutive aspects of institutional life, committing to an exclusively materialist conception of preferences and interests, and importing reductionist economic theories of politics.[3] Rather than acknowledging potential sources of weakness and looking for complementary or alternative conceptualizations, as is now quite common in the general IR literature, OEP and with it much of IPE is running the risk of cutting itself off from important insights offered by analytical alternatives which have a more capacious understanding of the concept of institution and are willing to inquire into processes of preference formation. The ironic twist of this episode is that some of the scholars (and their students) who succeeded in endogenizing preferences and interests in the analysis of IPE and IR a couple of decades ago, are now adhering firmly to the opposite intellectual position by making preferences and interests once again exogenous. What was right for the goose of international political theory apparently is not right for the gander of domestic economic theory.

Professional power and the Harvard mafia?

Let me turn to a second important issue in this symposium. In different ways Henry Farrell and Martha Finnemore, Kate McNamara, Nicola Phillips and Randall Germain are all seeking to explain Maliniak's and Tierney's data by focusing on professional power as manifested in our publishing, teaching and institutional affiliation. Based on my personal experience as editor of *International Organization* between 1980 and 1986, journal editors have less power to shape a field than authors would like to believe. Editors are largely hostages of the quantity, quality and diversity of submitted manuscripts. The overriding interest of any editor is to publish the best papers and to have reviewers competent to evaluate the manuscripts that are being submitted. The first requires intellectual judgment across different domains or inquiry, which, stipulated here simply for sake of argument, most editors of high-quality journals possess. The second requires an editorial board or a pool of reviewers that can cope with the broad array of manuscripts that are submitted for review. For sure, an editor's intellectual predilection for or empathy with the problem and approach of particular papers matters, as do editorial judgments about the selection of reviewers, especially of third reviewers for manuscripts, which may or may not be accepted. But in my personal experience these factors are much less important than the manuscript flow.

Through the training of graduate students, on the other hand, many of us have a more direct effect on the field of IPE. The data that Farrell and Finnemore report on methods training and McNamara on graduate IPE syllabi do give food for thought. Now that the qualitative methods section in the American Political Science Association is larger than the quantitative methods section, I remain hopeful that the great imbalance between quantitative and qualitative methods courses being offered in leading graduate programs will begin to change as younger political scientists enter the job market trained to teach qualitative research methods. The elimination of pluralistic approaches to the subject of IPE in the seminars taught in the leading graduate programs is a more serious matter that bodes ill for the IPE field. When important intellectual issues touching on ontology, epistemology and theory are simply no longer taught, the next generation of scholar will no longer be aware of the choices and trade-offs we all confront in our research. And that makes reorientation and fresh starts more difficult in any field of scholarship.[4]

Nuance and niceties aside, institutional affiliation offers a third power argument that purports to explain the monocultural turn in IPE that Maliniak and Tierney report. Randall Germain (this issue) has identified the real culprit not as America but as 'the "Harvard" school' which, for reasons of dramatic effect, I would like to dub here simply the Harvard Mafia. Being an Avis man myself, I took a certain pleasure when reading Germain's abstract. Although not publicly advertized, a certain amount of Hertz bashing is considered good sport among us Avis types. Were not the striking differences between Rawi Abdelal (constructivist *extraordinaire* teaching at the Harvard Business School), Jeff Frieden (most recently author of a fat book on the history of the world economy), Lisa Martin (now at Wisconsin), and Beth Simmons (with her forthcoming work on human rights) simply epiphenomenal? Would not the unmasking of the Harvard Mafia be a powerful indictment of the liberal–rationalist–quantitative monoculture that is bedeviling the IPE field? Alas, when reading the paper I discovered that Germain bypassed all of the young(er) Turks while training his gun sight on the old Dons of the Harvard Mafia.

Germain (2009: 98, n. 6, this issue) is correct in reminding us that before the current team of Emanuel Adler and Lou Pauly took over, the string of Harvard affiliated editors of *International Organization* included, in chronological order, Robert Keohane, myself, Stephen Krasner, John Odell, Peter Gourevitch and Lisa Martin. Poor David Lake, a Cornellian and co-editor with Peter Gourevitch, is for those focused on the Harvard Mafia probably an Avis runt in a Hertz litter. Susceptibility of 'group think and herd behavior' is what Germain (2009: 100) argues is the trademark of the Harvard Mafia. Its powerful reach accounts for the 'frankly bizarre herding' of many American scholars 'into and out of debates that might fairly be described as narrow, myopic and almost narcissistic' (Germain, 2009: 100). In sharp contrast Robert Keohane, at the beginning of his paper, reminisces about the Mafia quite differently. 'We were young, exuberant, and friends with one another, neither expecting nor wanting general agreement' (Keohane, 2009: 36). Who is right? The young lion roaring his powerful message down from up north or the old man rowing his canoe quietly across Golden Pond?

In my recollection it all happened a bit differently. Power there was for sure, mostly of the grey-matter kind, since junior faculty members and graduate students were not sitting, then or now, at the apex of the Harvard hierarchy of power and prestige. They were, however, sitting, in the early 1970s, in considerable numbers around the luncheon table – our very own Camelot. King Arthur was played by the intellectually indomitable and admirably argumentative James Kurth. Grouped around him were the regular knights as I recall them now: Peter Gourevitch, Robert Jervis, Robert Keohane, Stephen Krasner, Martin Shefter (then all assistant professors), and irregulars like myself (a lowly graduate student, but smart enough to realize that this was where the intellectual action was at Harvard, and where I could get a better education than in any graduate seminar).

One major debate at this roundtable centered on the liberal perspective reflected in the work of Keohane and Nye and realist arguments most forcefully put forth by Gilpin and Krasner. Rather than consensus on the big intellectual questions, there was disagreement. Over chowder and salad in the decrepit cafeteria of the old Center for International Affairs another of the knights' favorite sports was making up alternative explanations and grappling with questions of over- and under-determination in political analysis. This was an intellectual meeting place that surely created 'scholarly networks that grew around Harvard from the late 1960s onwards' as Germain accurately observes. And those networks, institutionalized in a seminar on 'State and Capitalism' convened for many years at the Center for European Studies, did have a lasting impact on development in the field of IPE.

Yet Germain's argument simply does not hold water. Although he is correct in pointing to the Mafia's impact on developments in the 1980s, he is plainly wrong to link it to the substantial shifts that Maliniak and Tierney have detected in the publication data since the mid-1990s. The debates at Harvard in the 1970s had the effect of pushing the agendas of comparative political economy, state theory, and historical institutionalism. Arguments in these fields helped in the 1980s to undermine the short-circuiting of processes of interest formation in IPE and IR that Keohane mentions in his contribution. To connect those intellectual networks and the ideas in which they trafficked to the monocultural turn in IPE after the mid-1990s is at least for me, hit man of the Mafia or bit player in Camelot, too much of a stretch. By then most of the Dons had moved to other forms of racketeering and were much less central in defining the intellectual currents in the field of IPE. Attractive as it may be for reasons of parsimony, Germain's argument simply does not get the timing right. Furthermore, serving in very different crime families, I suspect that Joseph Nye (a member of the Carter and Clinton administrations) and Stephen Krasner (who served under George W. Bush), hitched by Germain to the same wagon, will probably agree with Robert Wade when he writes: 'I see your bridle, but where is your horse?' (Wade, 2009: 117, this issue).

A plea for pragmatic pluralism in the geography of our thoughts

Germain's Canadian perspective offers no plausible solution for the meandering geography of our thoughts. It is true that the Canadian school of political economy (or is it schools?) offers an intellectually tolerant place for innovation and reflection. Germain is spot on when, in full agreement with Nicola Phillips, he argues that American IPE leads to too narrow an approach and too restricted a focus on only a few questions in the field. But after all is said and done, Canada remains caught between America and Europe, fire and ice, as Michael Adams (2004) argues in his bestseller.

This symposium is a particular instance of a general quandary of the social sciences. A decade ago Hunter Rawlings, then Cornell's incoming President, appointed three taskforces to report to him on the state of the natural sciences, the humanities and the social sciences. The taskforces went to great lengths to assess the accomplishments and failures of the past, evaluate trends, and assess future needs. At the final plenary, the natural sciences and humanities delivered their report in compelling fashions. Then it was the turn of the chair of the social science taskforce to summarize his report. Even before finishing, he encountered various challenges from the floor by fellow social scientists, who made telling criticisms on both substantive and procedural grounds. Rawlings looked a bit perplexed as he presided over this spectacle and then brought the proceedings to a premature end. Later he asked several members of the faculty what had gone wrong. Nothing had gone wrong. Rawlings had simply witnessed social science in action.

While the natural sciences and humanities face their own and distinctive quarrels, basic division is what constitutes the social sciences. Economic and sociological geographies of thought are too different and too powerful to lay low without a fight. There are of course times when that division is swept under the rug. One or the other side to the argument does at times succeed to establish a temporary, and all-too-often myopic, intellectual hegemony. But when and where that happens, often under particular labels (such as positivism, post-positivism, and post-modernism) or particular names (such as Popper, Kuhn, Lakatos, Laudan, Derrida, Foucault or Lacan), the fact remains that disagreement on fundamentals has simply migrated from one field of scholarship or discipline to another. 'Economic imperialism' in the field of IPE, for example, coincides with a historical institutionalism in the field of comparative political economy and with a broad range of substantive and methodological innovations in the field of economic sociology. Such disagreements were articulated paradigmatically in the late nineteenth century, in what came to be known as the *Methodenstreit* or battle of the methods (Swedberg, 1990). They lasted throughout the twentieth century. And there is no reason to believe that they will disappear in the twenty-first century. This symposium is welcome for many reasons. One of them is the reminder it offers us of many a fight fought during the good old days when the air was clean, cows gave hormone-free milk, and intellectual giants bestrode the earth.

We cannot help but live our disagreements in cacophonous debates, hopefully informed by a healthy dose of intellectual modesty and pragmatic tolerance. Where modesty and tolerance are in short supply, North-American social science departments no longer offer the institutional place in which intellectual divides are lived, productively and painfully. Disciplinary divides and the pressure of work make it difficult for more than the occasional member of the faculty to engage in cross-departmental discussions. And within departments intellectual divides often suffuse our research. Intellectual diversity in hiring and joint teaching that expose students to different intellectual perspectives of a field of scholarship remain in my opinion the only and the most effective barrier against the institutionalization of intellectual parochialism. Only through intensive intellectual engagement with perspectives and predilections that are not our own can we as teachers and researchers actually broaden in our outlook and mature in our judgment. If this avenue of scholarly recovery and renovation is as badly damaged as McNamara's paper suggests, then IPE may indeed be settling into what David Lake calls a kind of 'Kuhnian normalcy' (Lake, 2009: 49, this issue) and that Kate McNamara calls the 'desiccation of a field of study' in an increasingly arid intellectual 'monoculture' (McNamara, 2009: 79, this issue).

While we reflect on, engage and navigate between our disagreements, I see no reason why we would want to choose between either side of the Atlantic. After all, hybrids can combine ice and fire. Differences in approach and method are best debated not dogmatically, in the abstract, but pragmatically and eclectically, in the context of specific research questions. Rudra Sil and I have argued for precisely this alternative: pragmatism as a philosophical foundation and analytical eclecticism as a style of analysis (Katzenstein and Sil, 2008). The inclinations of different research traditions to either declare their inherent superiority or to practice flexibility in deploying strategies of intellectual subsumption may be productive at a certain stage in their evolution. But the publication statistics from leading journals that Maliniak and Tierney have assembled suggest that IPE in the United States has passed that point. Over time such strategies run the risk of diminishing intellectual returns for an entire field of scholarship. There is no need for dismantling existing research traditions. But those working within these traditions should be a bit more tolerant of those engaging in admittedly more risky eclectic scholarship.

This alternative invites us to follow the road of problem-driven rather than paradigm-driven research. These days it is a simple mantra that everybody is engaged in problem-driven rather than approach-driven research. However, our professional rankings (as indicated in Maliniak and Tierney's survey), reveal the great distance that separates ritualistic invocation of problem focus and paradigmatic diversity from scholarly practice. For most contributors to this symposium, therefore, the concept of paradigm connotes the institutionalization of intellectual blinkers. There is truth in this view as just under two-thirds of the IPE articles published in top journals do not take seriously any paradigm other than their chosen one.

Yet, paradigmatic thinking should not be met by outright condemnation. I tell my undergraduate students that paradigms (such as liberalism, realism and Marxism) are more powerful intellectual constructs than analytical perspectives that offer a conceptual language (such as rationalism and constructivism). The former have a normative dimension and offer insights that impel us to action; the latter do not. This is not to denigrate the importance of diverse analytical perspectives. Graduate research papers and dissertations that succeed in drawing on more than one paradigm or perspective are likely to have a larger audience and more impact than those which remain restricted to a single paradigm or perspective. Understood in the plural, paradigms and analytical perspectives are vitally important to maintain diversity of outlook on what constitutes an important question and what a satisfactory answer. Yet, I have always harbored admiration for my colleagues who were willing to march under some flag, both for the courage of their convictions and for the companionship that they so evidently enjoy. It is a quirk in my biography (I was born in Germany at the end of World War II) that makes me detest marching and dislike flags. Within limits, paradigmatic thinking is in my way of thinking a good rather than a bad thing.

Those limits are defined by two things. I agree with Robert Wade that common sense suggests that we should do all we can to avoid the bleak prospects of entering the long and dark tunnel from which our sister discipline of economics, beholden for too long to a dogmatic adherence to neo-classical theory, is just beginning to emerge. And it suggests also that scholars should be generous in their acknowledgement of the relevance of arguments advanced in different discourse communities. Quite simply, this requires doing no more in our various roles – as researchers, readers, reviewers and teachers – than to have enough intellectual humility, human decency, and professional wisdom to give a hearing to dissenting voices.

Under the best of circumstances scholars forego metatheoretical and methodological battles and, among thriving, multiple paradigms and perspectives, explore their interfaces looking for problematics and puzzles and developing analyses that draw on seemingly incommensurable research traditions. Trespassing (Hirschmann, 1981) would become a standard operating rather than exotic research procedure. Put differently, analytical eclecticism isolates specific features of theories initially embedded in distinct research traditions, separates them from their foundations, philosophical and otherwise, translates them meaningfully, and recombines them as part of an original amalgam of concepts and methods, analytics and empirics. Problem-driven research understood in this way would not, as Robert Keohane (2009: 42, this issue) correctly insists, sideline questions simply because they are not amenable to a certain set of methodological standards or because they lack ready-made or relatively easily produced statistical data.

As is true of other parts of the elusive geography of our thoughts, the British and American schools of IPE are intellectual resources in our search for understanding and making the world a better place. That search is not grounded in philosophical incoherence but, as Farrell and Finnemore suggest, in a pragmatism that sidesteps metatheoretical debates and encourages instead scholarly practices which aim to generate new insights drawing from disparate sources of knowledge (Farrell and Finnemore, 2009: 66–7, this issue). Eschewing the cozy cocoon of the like-minded and conducted in the stiff breeze of our imagined mid-Atlantic, we do some of our best scholarship and teaching while sitting on the knife's sharp edge.

Acknowledgements

I am very grateful for the critical comments and suggestions that I received from Rawi Abdelal, Peter Gourevitch, Mary Katzenstein, Suzanne Katzenstein, Robert Keohane, Stephen Krasner, Jonathan Kirshner, David Lake, Tom Pepinsky, Rudra Sil, and Chris Way. Kate Weaver provided superb editorial guidance. All of them are of course exempted from the shortcomings this opinionated paper undoubtedly has.

Notes

1 I would like to thank David Lake for extended correspondence on the treatment of preferences and interests in OEP and readily acknowledge that I surely did not understand the full import of everything he was telling me, and that there are more variants of OEP than the two that I mention in the following paragraphs.
2 For an important statement to this effect see Frieden and Martin (2002).
3 I am bypassing here the issue of methods that Farrell and Finnemore discuss in their paper in this special issue.
4 Even in this grim setting, the size of the American university system provides some insurance against excessive monoculturalism. As Kate McNamara (this issue: note 4) reports, 'the sole highly ranked program that continues to offer a pluralistic IPE field seminar is Cornell University'.

Part II

Perspectives on the 'British school' of IPE

10 The 'British school' in the global context

Robert Cox

R. Cox (2009) 'The "British School" in the global context', *New Political Economy* 14(3): 315–328, published by Taylor & Francis Ltd, http://www.informaworld.com. Permission has been granted by the publisher.

In his intellectual history of IPE, which discusses works in the English language since the early 1960s, Benjamin Jerry Cohen discerned a dichotomy between two principal schools of thought.

One school is preoccupied by analysis of ongoing economic processes that impinge upon politics (and *vice versa*) and perceives them as converging upon or instigated by states. Its aim is practical: to develop a series of hypotheses about political-economic behaviour that can be established by a rigorously applied empirical positivistic methodology as guidelines for public policy. In order to achieve this result, the range of factors that enter into the analysis must be limited – the principle of *ceteris paribus* must apply – and the parameters of the inquiry must be stable. This is the route taken by what Cohen designates as the 'American school'.

The other school is more concerned with what Cohen calls 'the Really Big Question' (RBQ): where is the world going and how can we influence its direction? Its aim is less practical than strategic. It is not how can the state best manage trade policy or monetary policy given the conditions prevailing at the moment. Rather, it is what are the stresses and conflicts within the whole complex of societies and states that could lead to a transformation of existing structures in directions that might be either disastrously divisive and conflictual or, alternatively, more equitable and more peaceful. To answer the RBQ a much broader range of factors must be taken into account, everything that can influence the movement of large masses of people and the political structures that govern them over considerable periods of time. A positivistic methodology is useless because the parameters are changing and all relevant factors must be embraced. The synchronic perspective of positivism has to be displaced by a diachronic historical perspective. Those who have taken this route are designated by Cohen as the 'British school'.

I do not think Cohen intended the geographical identifications of the two schools – American and British – to be in any way exclusive. He would, I think, recognise that some American scholars are concerned more with the transformation of society than with the management of current political-economic affairs. Indeed, at least two of the five American scholars he cites as inspiration for the American school – Robert Gilpin and Peter Katzenstein – have not been so entranced by rational choice theory as to abandon their sense of historical transformation. Conversely, there are surely non-Americans who are attracted not only by the policy oriented thrust of the 'American school', but also by its aim to develop a positivistic 'scientific' approach to political economy. The great usefulness and the challenge of Cohen's book is to have distinguished clearly between two different approaches to IPE and raised the question of their compatibility. Beyond compatibility, he has expressed a hope for reconciliation. For this finding of a separation between the two schools he has been severely criticised, mainly, it seems, on the grounds that pointing to the dichotomy in approaches might tend to favour one school over the other, to harden positions and build antipathy among scholars on different sides of the Atlantic.[1]

Some time ago, I pointed to the difference between problem-solving theory, which takes the structural characteristic of the present as given in order to be able to deal effectively with problems arising within it, and critical theory, which is concerned with how those structures emerged and how their existing forms may be liable to change (Cox 1981).[2] I think this distinction explains a lot about the coexistence of the two schools. My point was, as stated at the time, that theory always has a purpose and the purposes of the two approaches are different. It was not to say that one was better than the other, although my own interests lay in the critical theory approach because I am concerned with the kind of future that might be latent within the present. I clearly recognised the usefulness of problemsolving theory as a guide towards managing the present. Perhaps the possibility of reconciliation between two kinds of theory lies in a mutual recognition that their purposes are different but not necessarily opposed.

Although Cohen's survey is limited to the English-speaking world, the tendencies he links to the 'British school' are much broader in their origins and evolution.[3] That is why quotation marks around the term are necessary. The basic contradiction between the two approaches can be traced at least to the eighteenth-century European cleavage between the teaching of Descartes, the forerunner of nineteenth-century modern scientific thinking, and that of Giambattista Vico, the challenger of the northern European Enlightenment who lived in Naples. Vico was concerned with the origins and transformations of what he called 'nations', a term he used in the etymological sense of the birth and development of a system of institutions including language. Today we might say cultures or civilisations.

Vico pointed to the incompatibility of the method useful for the study of physical nature with that needed for the study of people and their history. He called the latter philology since evolution in the meanings of words was his primary research tool for studying the rise, transformation and decline of the social and political structures people created. Through language he traced the evolution of minds in their relation to changing realities and to the transformation of societies.

For the Enlightenment, by contrast, history was nothing but imprecise mythological stories. In the optimistic view of the Enlightenment, modern science would advance man's power over nature. The scientific method, not the historical method, was the path towards understanding the world. The idea of progress that emerged in the nineteenth-century expansion of Europe around the world was implicit in the eighteenth-century Enlightenment. Vico was more pessimistic; he was concerned not only with the birth and rise of civilisations, but also with their decline through the 'barbarism of reflection' and with the possibilities of 'recourse' through new creative beginnings. The physical world, in Vico's theology, was made by God and could not be understood *from within* by human beings. People could only attain to an approximate knowledge of nature as external observers by noting regularities in its processes. But history is made by human beings pursuing their purposes and can therefore be understood by human minds capable of reproducing and understanding the thoughts of its makers.

This distinction between knowledge of nature and knowledge of history became common in the thinking of nineteenth-century German historians with a philosophical bent. Wilhelm Dilthey, in the late nineteenth century, straddled the two traditions, one of Anglo-French empiricism which led to the positivism of Auguste Comte, the other of German idealism and romanticism which led to an understanding of history as something made by human minds and consequently intelligible to such minds. Positivism and historical understanding were both valid for their own purposes, and, for Dilthey, their purposes were different. Positivism was the avenue towards developing a 'scientific' technique for the study of phenomena – i.e. things observed *from without*. Historical knowledge is acquired *from within* through the possibility that the historian's mind can assimilate the substance of the minds that become 'objective' in the making of history.

In Italy, about the same time, Benedetto Croce, building upon the same German current of thought, reflected upon why an historian's mind becomes oriented towards specific problems for enquiry. Each unfolding era in the history of human development looks to the past in the light of the problems encountered in its own present. Each new era has a fresh perspective on the past and so requires a new history as a means towards understanding the present. In that sense, Croce thought, all history is contemporary history. This is the way in which history has *meaning*, as Dilthey would have put it. There is an almost personal relationship between the individual who is situated in a specific social and temporal context and the past understood by that individual as history. That is very different from the impersonal findings of positivistic logic.

In England, these currents of thought on the European continent were critically appraised and refined by the historian and philosopher R.G. Collingwood. Collingwood may be considered the philosophical founder of the 'British school'. Fundamental to 'British school' thinking is the distinction, rarely made in social science enquiry, between fact and datum. Referring to the Latin origins of these words, a datum is a given, a fact is a 'made'. That distinction explains the epistemological difference between the two concepts. Data are just externally observable items, there to be collected and classified. A fact presumes a maker and has to be understood through the mind that made it. Data are for positive science. Facts are for history and for those activities of the human mind that can be assimilated to historical thinking – problems of social organisation and development.

If Collingwood laid the philosophical foundation for the 'British school', E. H. Carr, his contemporary, gave practical expression to its approach to understanding transformations in world political economy. Carr is often just classified as a 'realist' in the narrow sense of someone who reduces everything to state power and interests. He looked at state politics but also at the economic changes and the transformation of societies which explain state politics and the reflection of all that in people's minds. He wrote about international political economy in the broadest sense without ever giving it that name.

During World War II, Carr was particularly concerned with the transformations going on in societies that would condition the possibilities of future peaceful relationships among the major states. He sketched out his thinking initially in a short essay *Nationalism and After* published in 1945 (Carr 1945) that might well be considered a founding text of today's international political economy. He looked at the way in which societies had been reshaped through economic changes that altered the conditions in which states could pursue their role. States, for their part, had also become instruments in the transformation of society. Implicitly, the entities engaged in international relations were not just states but the complex interactive relationship between states and societies – the state/society complex. Changing economic structures and ideological movements were both causes and effects of the changing nature of international relations. This whole process of social, economic, ideological and political transformation conditioned the kind of world order that would emerge out of World War II.

The 'democratisation' of nationalism in the early nineteenth century generated intense emotional fervor, but nationalisms, in transforming countries from within, did not combat each other. Rather, they fostered a new kind of internationalism – an internationalism supportive of national revolutions which turned out to be bourgeois revolutions. An internationalism of peoples displaced the international relations of governing monarchs, and the peaceful quality of this internationalism of peoples was sustained economically by a world economy very largely managed by Britain. The peaceful nineteenth-century world order, according to Carr, was based upon two illusions. The first was that 'the international character of the world economic system rested on the conviction that it was not an artificial creation of man but part of an order of nature' (Carr 1945: 13, 16). The second was the illusion of 'the formal divorce between political and economic power' (Carr 1945: 13, 16).

By the end of the nineteenth century, however, new social strata, the working classes, emerged within the European nations, bringing politics into economic affairs. Economic policy could no longer be regarded as functioning according to a law of nature but had to be adjusted to meet the political demands of newly articulate social forces. The period leading up to World War I was characterised by state rivalries driven by economic nationalism. The peaceful order of the earlier nineteenth century was disrupted by the changing social composition of the nations. The 'socialisation' of the nation resulted in uncertainty in the observance of obligations under international law and agreements. National governments could not and would not observe international rules or treaties that would be detrimental to the welfare or security of the nation.

The proliferation of sovereignties through the nationalisms that broke out with the disruption of empires in World War II would, Carr thought, create chaos and confusion in international relations unless the multiplicity of sovereignties could be grouped under the aegis of a few responsible centres of power. He also thought that the socially destructive consequences of *laissez faire* capitalism would lead to the adoption of various forms of planning both at the national and the international level. Politics would be subordinate to social and economic goals. The international order would, in effect, have to become a social order.

Karl Polanyi should also be included among the thinkers who shaped the thinking of the 'British school'. Raised and educated in Vienna, he took an early stand in opposition to the Vienna school of liberal economics. He criticised its efforts to construct an abstract theory of the economy as a sphere distinct from politics and society. He advanced his own concept of the economy as something that emerged out of and was embedded in culture and society. A refugee from fascism in London in the 1930s, Polanyi researched the emergence of capitalism in Britain in the eighteenth century and its transformation along with the transformation of society and politics in the nineteenth and early twentieth centuries. His magnum opus, *The Great Transformation*, was written ultimately in the United States and published in 1944 (Polanyi 1957). It signaled an open breach between the historical 'substantive' view of the economy and the dominant tendency in economic thinking towards the construction of a more formal and more mathematical science of economics.

It was this breach between historically oriented political studies and a more formally constructed economics that troubled Susan Strange. As an experienced journalist accustomed to considering all aspects of a problem, she recoiled from the tendency for academic disciplines to build boundaries around their areas of enquiry. Some 25 years after the publication of *The Great Transformation* she issued her manifesto about 'mutual neglect' of economists and international relations scholars for each other's spheres of study (Strange 1970). Cohen cites Susan Strange's manifesto as a starting point for IPE as it is today.

For Polanyi there was an implicit conflict between the abstract theory of the market and the substantive reality of society. The, to him utopian, theory of the self-regulating market, in its practical effects, had ripped apart the substantive bonds of the old society leaving a multitude of individuals helpless without the support of pre-existing social relations. This was the first phase of the 'double movement' which Polanyi perceived in his history of the Industrial Revolution. The second phase was an instinctive reaction to the social void: society attempting to reassert itself by reestablishing its supremacy over the economy. Forces in society used the state to regulate the economy and to provide protection to social groups that became victims of the market. Thus these social forces became a central concern in the study of political economy. They included the labour movement and peasant movements.

The illusion that politics and the economy were distinct and separate spheres had, according to Polanyi, been sustained through the nineteenth and early twentieth centuries by the operations of *haute finance*, a substantially covert interface between governments and international money managers. It was the collapse of international finance in the 1930s that finally demolished the illusion that politics and economics were two separate spheres. This collapse, in Polanyi's analysis, and its dramatic consequences for national politics in the Great Depression, opened the way for fascism.

Carr and Polanyi wrote in their publications of the early 1940s about a world centred in Europe. A decade later Geoffrey Barraclough, in *History in a Changing World* (1955), signaled the eclipse of a Eurocentric view of the world. '[I]t was only a pardonable exaggeration to say that, for me, it was the Russian victory at Stalingrad in 1943 that made a total revision of European history imperative' (Barraclough 1955: 9). Like Croce before him, Barraclough was affirming that every age needs its own view of the past.

Barraclough, because of his sense that the world was facing an entirely new situation in the aftermath of World War II, was interested in studying turning points in history. Continuity might be a common theme in historiography, but continuity is disrupted by crises and turning points when societies 'swing upwards, out of their existing course, on to a new plane'. The focus on Europe, he argued, had to be displaced by the perspective of a new age of global politics and coexisting civilisations. A decade later he proclaimed 'the revolt against the West' to be the central factor requiring a revision of thinking and a new view of the past (Barraclough 1967).

French historians, some of them like Fernand Braudel emerging from German prisoner of war camps, similarly experienced the need for a new approach to history. The approach had to be new not only in an extension of the historian's perspective from the local and national to the whole world, but also in an understanding of the nature of historical knowledge. In the peaceful and seemingly stable world of late nineteenth-century Europe, historians, Braudel thought, had been slipping into an illusory 'objectivity', focusing on the acts of individuals and thinking of themselves as external observers of events much as natural scientists observed the natural world. He wrote:

> In the living world there are no individuals entirely sealed off by themselves; all individual enterprise is rooted in a more complex reality... [H]istory...makes men and fashions their destiny – anonymous history, working in the depths and most often in silence, whose domain, immense and uncertain as it is, we must now approach.
>
> (Braudel 1950a [1980]: 10)

As against the natural scientist's need for fixed parameters within which to observe change, Braudel (1950a: 15) wrote: '(T)here is no problem which does not become increasingly complex when actively investigated, growing in scope and depth, endlessly opening up new vistas of work to be done'. Later he wrote about 'a general crisis in the human sciences' and of a 'necessary convergence' among them – a convergence of geography, sociology, economics and linguistics with history, world history and the history of civilisations (Braudel 1950b).

So the 'British school' was not so exclusively British after all. You might well call it the European school. It was shaped by history, especially by the history of the twentieth century and the personal experience of that history by its proponents. Economics had become an abstract mathematical analytic tool for the study of economic phenomena. *Political* economy would develop as a self-consciously philosophical approach to understanding the interactive relationships of social change, movements of ideas, and shifting political structures.

One of the schools identified by Cohen – the 'British' – took the diachronic approach considering change over time. The other – the 'American' – took the synchronic approach, studying interactions in the present. Assuming that each was valid for its own purposes, the question is what were the purposes for which scholars would opt for one or the other? Why do some scholars focus on changing structures while others are primarily concerned with analysing problems immediately facing them? This leads us into the more speculative field of the sociology of knowledge: what are the factors that orient a scholar's hierarchy of concerns?

The first is place. You look upon the world from a certain place in it. Of course, the good scholar is a nomad, accustomed to being in different places. But is there one place that becomes more prominent than others, determining the scholar's perspective on the world? Perhaps the sense of being in and belonging to the most powerful nation in the world fixes the mind on preserving that place of eminence, especially if you tell yourself it is for the good of all mankind. This feeling challenges the mind to perfect the methods or techniques of preserving that situation – building a science that, while objectively open to all, will facilitate dealing with problems in such a manner as to sustain the *status quo* and thus a situation of dominance or hegemony.[4]

An American scholar, especially one in the more prestigious institutions of learning, may naturally feel a responsibility, even perhaps a fervent desire, to be identified with the nation's position in the world and to be helpful in preserving a *status quo* that can easily be seen as beneficial to the world as a whole. It is not uncommon for an American scholar to alternate between academic life and service in government (when their political party is in power). A salient case is that of Joseph Nye, collaborator with Robert Keohane, the foremost exponent of the 'American school' according to Cohen, and alternately academic and senior official in Democratic administrations. Stephen Krasner, another of Cohen's representatives of the 'American school' also served in Democratic administrations. Condoleeza Rice, President George W. Bush's Secretary of State, is another academic-turned-government official. This to and fro between academia and government is far less common in other countries. Hegemonic world power has surely something to do with it.

There are, of course, American academics who shun proximity to government, some for fear it would tarnish their academic independence, others because they frankly oppose what they perceive to be US imperialism. But these scholars would not be assimilated to the 'American school' as depicted by Cohen. Critics of globalisation, which they would perceive as the hegemonic form of a new imperialism, or of a masculinist view of political economy, are among them. I am thinking of individual scholars like David Harvey, James Mittelman, V. Spike Peterson, William Robinson, Mark Rupert, and J. Ann Tickner.[5]

It is much easier for the scholars of a *former* empire to adopt the historical perspective of the rise and decline of empires, than it is for the scientifically tuned minds of citizens at the centre of the day's hegemony to think about anything other than the means of dealing with hegemony's current problems. The 'scientific' fix-it approach comes naturally to them. The past glories of the British Empire may cling in memory for a few British people and some British scholars do mutate this memory into a feeling for the 'special relationship' of the English-speaking peoples; but many serious scholars have shed the illusion of participating in hegemony and are able to take a more distant, critical and reflective view of the historical ebb and flow in world power. By and large the European mind is attuned like Vico's to the idea of transformations in societies and in power relations – in the problematic of rise, decline and creative revival (or what Vico called *ricorso*) – rather than to a fixation on maintenance of the status quo. America has known only a rise to overwhelming world power and responsibility, framed by John Winthrop's (1630) myth of the bright shining city on a hill, a light for the world.

Cold-War ideologies had a powerful impact upon scholarship. Any suspicion of Marxism is anathema to many American and to a few British scholars. Elsewhere, Marxism can be looked upon with more equanimity, accepted as a form of analysis which may or may not be attractive or useful but which can coexist intellectually with other modes of enquiry. In America, more generally than elsewhere, Marxism appears to thinkers in the mainstream as a manifestation of dissidence, obstinate ignorance, even treachery.

Another factor in the formation of 'British' and 'American' schools has been trends in graduate education. The doctoral degree in Britain and in its educational offshoots used to be primarily a research degree. The candidate worked on a problem by discovering all the factors that might be relevant and by determining what methods might be useful in investigating them. There were no *prima facie* exclusions or imperatives. The knowledge available in demography, sociology, linguistics, economics and any other relevant field of enquiry could be called upon. The researcher would use heuristic hypotheses as tools of enquiry, structural models drawn from other historical studies and various fields of social science. Braudel drew the analogy between structural models of social relations (and by social he would include economic and political) and a ship: 'I have sometimes compared models to ships. What interests me, once the boat is built, is to put it in the water to see if it will float, and then to make it ascend and descent the waters of time, at my will. The significant moment is when it can keep no longer afloat, and sinks' (Braudel 1950b: 45). This is a quite different kind of hypothesis from that subjected to the positivist test of falsifiability, because the point is to discover under what conditions the hypothesis works, not to establish its timeless validity. The historical thinker does not deal in timeless truths and knows that truths are always relative to concrete temporal situations.

Latterly, especially in American institutions of higher learning, graduate education has put the emphasis rather more on training teachers than on really independent and wide-ranging research. The training of teachers circumscribes fields of enquiry, often quite narrowly in sub-fields of disciplines, providing a canon of literature to form the basis for educating the next generation of teachers; and providing also the parameters within which an acceptable research topic can be selected. New research is to take the form of a dialogue with 'the field', building upon the work of others in the field, demonstrating a linkage to the existing canon and adding incrementally to it. Three years of reading and discussing prescribed texts gives the candidate a sense of what kind of subjects qualify for research and what methods should be used for the enquiry. Indeed, it would be difficult to evaluate any candidate's work that had the originality of laying outside the canon, just as it is difficult for keepers of the canon to admit outsiders into it. Cohen implicitly endorsed this judgement when he observed that the two representatives of the 'British school' he includes among his seven initiators of IPE – Susan Strange and me – while often respected as scholars in America, have not made much impact on graduate reading lists. You can read them if you like but their approach is not likely to help you get a job.

There does exist in America an undercurrent of scholarship which is critical of the dominant positivist tendency but it remains marginalised. The 'American school' as represented by Cohen is the expression of an elite group of thinkers, but there is no denying their effective influence. For all of the reasons mentioned above, junior scholars are under some pressure to be accepted by this group as the opening opportunity for a career in IPE, although some may be critically resentful of the group's hegemonic status and prefer to take their chances in a dissident attitude.

Conformity is a problem for young scholars everywhere.[6] In America it is unavowedly but latently keyed to the survival of American supremacy in the world order. The 'American school' is oriented towards maintaining the *status quo* of American supremacy by addressing the problems inherent in the world capitalist system. Critics of that system find the 'British school' approach more congenial because it directs attention to the crises and contradictions that could be indications of transformations in social, economic and political structures. The 'British school' contemplates the possibility of change in world order rather than being primarily preoccupied with the maintenance of the *status quo*.

There is also the matter of what we mean by 'school'. In the broadest sense, a number of scholars who feel a collegial bond in pursuing work in a field of knowledge could be thought of as constituting a 'school'. In a narrower sense, the word could imply a shared way of thinking, an interactive relationship in discussing and building upon each other's contributions to the field. The 'British school' is more like the former. It approximates the 'open range' Susan Strange called for (Strange 1991) – open to a variety of different approaches and disciplines. The 'American school' as depicted by Cohen is more like the latter. It is closer knit, more integrated in object and method, more of an organic phenomenon than the chaotic interplay of ideas and approaches to be found in the 'British school'.

This discussion has remained within the confines of Euro-American thought. It is, however, now more than ever obvious that Geoffrey Barraclough's injunction to look at the world as a whole is imperative. Fareed Zakaria, an American author of Indian origin, writes about a post-American world, a world in which the United States remains powerful but will have to adjust to the existence of some other major centres of power, including China in particular (Zakaria 2008).[7] The G8 is currently examining how to morph into a broader grouping of major powers. China, India and Russia realistically are being brought into the picture along with Europe and America. The United States, with the demise of the George W. Bush administration, may revert to a more multilateral and less unilateral approach to world affairs. Just as the development of IPE was influenced by the turning point of World War II, so IPE will be bound to reflect the reordering of world power now going on as a 'self-organising' process, in the manner in which physicists and biologists now understand 'self-organisation' in nature. The best chance is that major centres of world power will recognise each other and continue to negotiate together in building a consensual structure of relationships.

That will require that people, especially scholars, in the West be able to enter into the mind sets of people in the other major emerging centres of world power. The 'American' and 'British' schools of IPE will likely find that there is nothing universal in their respective assumptions about the world. They may be joined by divergent perspectives from China, Russia and India, and also from the South – Brazil, Mexico and South Africa – and from the parties to the inextricable dilemma of the Middle East.

Since theory always reflects the time and place of its origins, it would be an exercise in misplaced hegemony to expect that a reconciliation of contemporary British and American schools would form a universally acceptable IPE. Unlike economics, IPE cannot be an abstract science. Of its nature, IPE incorporates human concerns and intentions for social transformation and ethical values, and cultures and civilisations differ about these things. These aims and values are framed by people's innate sense of how the world works – a sense that has been shaped by a people's history. The impact of the *longue durée* in shaping mentalities provides the framework for thinking about policy.

Different approaches to IPE have to be understood historically. The English speaking world, long hegemonic in the dissemination of thought about global affairs, will need to listen more carefully to the other voices in a global dialogue. It is only when scholars are confronted with the full variety of perspectives that the work of intellectual bridge building can seriously begin.[8]

Just under a century ago Oswald Spengler (1928) wrote about the decline of the West. His verdict may have been premature but his mode of analysis and the questions he asked are still of interest. Today, if the West is not irrevocably in decline, the East is certainly on the rise, and the balance of world power is shifting. Spengler saw a world of cultures and civilisations coexisting in space and linked through time. Though his focus was upon problems of the West, he sought also to capture the inner essence of other civilisations. He observed that the culture of China, like that of the West, was profoundly historical, while the culture of India, like that of Classical Greece, was non-historical, the culture of an eternal present. Spengler was trying to grasp the ways in which people in different cultures and civilisations constructed their views of the world. He certainly did not have the final word on that; but his admonition to move from what he called a Ptolemaic to a Copernican concept of history – from the West being the centre around which all else revolves to an understanding of the individuality of coexisting cultures and civilisations revolving in space and time together – is particularly apposite to the present.

For people in the West, it is now particularly important to understand how the leaders and people of China look upon the world. Wang Gungwu, a historian of China who has lived and worked outside of China,[9] is well placed to represent the inside view of Chinese history to those outsiders who seek to grasp something of a Chinese perspective on the world. In 1972 he wrote: '[An] extraordinary historical event is taking place before us – a gigantic struggle between world history on the outside and Chinese history on the inside which began about a hundred years ago and which now appears to have reached its climax' (Wang 2002a: 67).

The Chinese word for revolution, *geming*, Wang points out, denotes a 'total comprehensive change that has been swiftly, often violently, achieved' (Wang 2002a: 6). It was used over 2500 years ago to describe the founding of the Shang dynasty (1600–1100 BCE) and its replacement by the Zhou dynasty (1100–221 BCE). The same word is used for the Communist takeover of power in 1949. It carries the meaning that the existing order has lost the Mandate of Heaven. In modern terms that would mean replacing a system of governance that was no longer viable and which has lost its legitimacy. The idea of reform, *gaige*, assumes that the political structure will survive but that it needs to change in some respects in order to retain its legitimacy – its mandate. *Geming* and *gaige* fit well with China's recent history of violent revolution followed by internal struggles within the Party leadership to find the reform policies that will sustain the regime by serving the people's needs.

One vital distinction between Chinese and Western traditions of thought is that in China there have never been religion-endorsed absolute truths. The terms good and evil applying to various forms of government that slide easily from the lips of American leaders, along with their invocations of God, are quite inconsistent with the Chinese tradition. In this regard, the totalitarian thought pattern of Mao's Cultural Revolution and the Gang of Four was an aberration. Wang (2002a: 88) writes that in the Chinese tradition 'people have been encouraged to react and respond to the relative merits of actions and events or to the relative goodness or badness of people'.

The Western idea of progress, derived from the eighteenth-century European Enlightenment – and residually from the Christian eschatological concept of a divinely inspired history leading to the City of God – is meaningless in Chinese thought. Chinese history through the ages has been thought of in cyclical rather than linear progressive terms. The analogy is to the biological cycle of birth, growth, maturity, decline and death. In political terms it becomes cycles of dynasties – of revolution, decline, reform, fall and replacement by a new dynasty (Wang 2002a: 89). The attempt under Mao to make Chinese history fit into the Marxist stage theory of history was a pathetic failure.[10]

If the cyclical pattern fits with the political history of China through the millennia, social history has been one of relative continuity up to recent times. China has been an agrarian society through the past two to three thousand years. Sometimes it has been a model of agrarian success, as during the eighteenth century when the European Jesuits reported back on China's achievements and the French physiocrats took China as the basis for their economic theory. Yet in other times the agrarian economy has been a miserable failure with drought, famine and suffering in overpopulation.

Perhaps the mentality and practices built up around the centrality of peasant agriculture were a deterrent to a broader kind of development. Perhaps that contained the answer to the question that troubled Joseph Needham, the historian of science and civilisation in China: why did the flowering scientific knowledge in China, which far outdistanced the West in earlier times, up to about the sixteenth or seventeenth centuries, not develop into a dynamic science-inspired economy preceding that which developed through the Industrial Revolution in the West? (see Winchester 2008).

In the Confucian empire the peasant was the central figure. The merchant lacked status and was in many ways restricted in his activities. This prejudice against commercial and entrepreneurial activity continued under Communist rule. The Chinese entrepreneurial spirit flourished then only in the diaspora. It is only in the post-Mao reform era that commerce and business initiative have gained high prestige and a burgeoning urban middle class has come to centre stage in Chinese society.

Today's governing elite is urban but the revolution that brought the Communist Party to power was based on the mobilisation of a peasant army. Yet the peasantry and rural China generally has been marginalised in the recent economic growth pattern of the country. The leadership now calls upon its innate Chinese pragmatism to reach a modus vivendi that will allow rural China to benefit equitably along with the new urban social forces which are behind the rapid economic growth of recent years. This social revolution as it works itself out through radical *gaige* will surely modify the hierarchy of Chinese values and perceptions of the world in a way that previous *geming* did not. A Chinese perspective on the world may now be in a state of mutation. Some of the key elements which will come to compose it will doubtless still derive from China's past, just like those relics of a European past which continue to govern European thought about world history and the making of the future.

A counterpoint to a Chinese perspective on the world can be found in Russia. The characteristic Russian view of the world had some analogies with the

Chinese but more significantly some very marked contrasts. Russian thought has shown an almost mystical attachment to the land and to the ideal of the peasant community as a myth of origin. But by contrast to the more pragmatic Chinese tradition of thought, Russians have been torn between the absolutism of eschatology, whether of religious or secular inspiration – the building of a New Jerusalem – and nihilistic anarchism. Russian literature has given expression to the most psychologically penetrating representations of individual personality in Dostoyevsky's novels, and at the same time has shown a strong feeling for impersonal collectivism. The historical experience of the Russian mind is bipolar: sometimes comfortably submissive to autocracy and sometimes violent in a struggle for an ethical transformation of society. There is an historical oscillation between the pursuit of Westernisation and the Slavophile sense of a distinctive moral mission for Russia in the world. Among the dissident exiles from the Soviet Union the Westernised Sakharov had little in common with the Slavophile Solzhenitsyn. The messianic quality of what some have called the *Russian idea* (Berdyaev 1949; McDaniel 1996), with its rejection of a cyclical view of history and its aspiration to the absolute, separates it both from a pragmatic and cyclical Chinese perspective and from the kind of Western perspective exemplified by the 'British' school.

The future of IPE on the global scale will require a fuller understanding of these and other different perspectives on history and on the future. IPE looks at the rarefied abstract and mathematical world of economics and confronts it with the messy unpredictable world of politics and society and with the ideas through which different peoples understand themselves and others. IPE looks to see the *inside* of events – evaluations and intentions – where economic analysis observes only the *outside*. IPE asks Cohen's Really Big Question about the making of the future. A diachronic historical approach along the lines of the 'British' school makes sense of this. But a 'British' school will turn out to be too narrow in the emerging world (dis)order. Susan Strange's appeal for an 'open range' now requires an openness to and understanding of the perspectives of all the civilisations that encounter each other in every world crisis.

Notes

1 For example, in a small symposium in RIPE: 'Review of International Political Economy', 15 (1) (February 2008) with articles by Richard Higgott and Mathew Watson, and by John Ravenhill, with a response by Benjamin J. Cohen.

2 This is reproduced in Cox and Sinclair 1996. Higgott and Watson in their critique of Cohen referred to this as 'Cox's (1981) initially useful but now limited and overworked analytical dichotomy…'.

3 The article by Geoffrey Underhill in this special issue of NPE stresses the contribution of European thinkers to both 'British' and 'American' schools. He also mentions contributions from Latin Americanists.

4 It was in this sense that Stanley Hoffman in 1977 proclaimed international relations to be an 'American' social science. It evolved as a collective effort to develop knowledge essential to managing America's new role as the centre of Western leadership in the making of the post-war world. See Hoffmann 1977.

5 These and others fall into the 'Left out' category discussed in the article by Craig Murphy in this issue.

6 The article by Catherine Weaver in this issue discusses the influence of graduate education in America and the positivist approach it tends to promote.

7 Former French foreign minister Hubert Vedrine (in *Le Monde dilomatique*, August 2008) welcomed this indication of a potential shift in US foreign policy.

8 Sindjoun (1999) discusses Africa as the 'object' of study in the perspectives of different, European and Western centred world views; and also the geographic and ethnic determinants of African self-perception. He writes: 'C'est le temps de la rencontre entre la science des relations internationales d'un monde étrange et la science des relations internationales d'un monde nouveau'. He suggests an anthropological approach to the understanding of international relations. I am indepted to Hélène Pellerin for drawing this article to my attention.

9 Wang Gungwu was until recently Director of the East Asian Institute, National University of Singapore. He has held academic posts in Malaysia, Hong Kong and Australia as well. His publications include *To Act is to Know: Chinese Dilemmas* (2002a), *Bind Us in Time: Nation and Civilisation in Asia* (2002b), *Anglo-Chinese Encounters since 1800: War, Trade, Science & Governance* (2003a), and *Ideas Won't Keep. The Struggle for China's Future* (2003b).

10 See Wang (2003b: 120) '... all the attempts to fit Marxist historical stages to the Chinese past led only to more disputes and disagreements – the difficulties also easily led to absurdities that must have had a subversive effect on Chinese confidence in Marxist historiography itself'.

11 Torn between two lovers?

Caught in the middle of British and American IPE[1]

Mark Blyth

M. Blyth (2009) 'Torn between two lovers? Caught in the middle of British and American IPE', *New Political Economy* 14(3): 329–336, published by Taylor & Francis Ltd, http://www.informaworld.com. Permission has been granted by the publisher.

I approach this topic much as a man without a country approaches international travel: with trepidation. I am a British subject who was educated at Strathclyde University in the 1980s. I left for the US to do my PhD in 1991 because I wanted to study international relations, a field which hardly existed in the UK at that time.[2] I have lived 'over there' for nearly two decades. Despite being both an admirer and consumer of a great deal of the work that British IPE scholars produce and being Scottish by birth, I am by training and temperament an American scholar. Little wonder then that I get some of my best writing done on BA 228/229 half way across the Atlantic.

If identity theory has taught us anything it's that the self is always defined against 'the other', and British IPE's 'other' is very much 'American IPE'. But despite spending my working life (to date) in the USA, I am still not sure what this thing called 'American IPE' actually is, and thus, what the British 'other' really is. Three scholars that have recently tried to answer this question are Benjamin J. Cohen (2007, 2008), on the one hand, and Daniel Maliniak and Michael Tierney (2009), on the other. Cohen set himself the project of writing an intellectual history of IPE as a discipline that has rightly garnered considerable attention on both sides of the Atlantic. Maliniak and Tierney set out to map statistically what this thing called 'American IPE' actually looks like by crunching the US publication data. Cohen built a biography based around key individuals who seized the moment in the 1970s to wrestle the study of the IPE away from economics towards political science. Maliniak and Tierney tell a story of the original methodological pluralism of US IPE at the time of Cohen's founding giving way to a disciplinary monotheism of quantitative and formal analysis today.

To a certain extent both stories are true. As Cohen puts it, it's hard to imagine US IPE without the likes of Robert Keohane and Peter Katzenstein, but is it fair to reduce all of British IPE to the presence or absence of Susan Strange (Langley 2009)? Similarly, it is true that much of US IPE has become extremely quantitative. If, for example, one attends the annual meeting of the International Political Economy Society (IPES) in the US, as I did recently (more on this below), it really is 75 scholars doing 'my cross-sectional time series analysis of X'. Yet is it fair to define US IPE by reference to the perhaps 100 scholars who attend the IPES as opposed to the thousands who attend the International Studies Association (ISA) meetings? To what extent then is there really such a thing as a homogenous American IPE for the equally homogenous British IPE to be constructed against? For if American IPE is far more plural than is generally acknowledged, then to what extent does it make sense to talk about a distinct British school that is constituted in opposition and that is supposedly 'more pluralist'?

Bridges over troubled waters?

Angus Cameron and Ronen Palan put it beautifully when they describe the distance between American and British IPE as being 'caught between two untenable positions ... one (the American) is that data and observation are so unproblematic we can accept them as real; the other (the un-rigorous British) that data and observation are so problematic that we must dispense with them altogether' (Cameron and Palan 2009: 123). Truth and beauty are supposed to go together, but being a skeptic I wanted to see to what extent this was true even if their line was beautiful, and so my American side wanted data to figure this out. So I poured over a decade of *International Studies Quarterly* (*ISQ*) (1997 Vol 41 (1) to 2008 Vol 52 (3)) and *New Political Economy* (*NPE*) (1997 Vol 2 (1) to 2008 Vol 13 (3)) to figure out what broad categories the research in each journal fell into.[3] Simply at the level of descriptive statistics, I wanted a data-picture of both of these so-called schools.

Doing this for *ISQ* was a breeze. Breaking it down by theoretical persuasion, of 372 articles published in ISQ over this period, 31 per cent were identifiable as 'liberal approaches', 17 per cent were 'realist', 9 per cent were 'mixed', with the rest, some 27 per cent, being scattered across the categories of constructivism, feminism, post-structuralism and neo-Marxism, which hardly suggests a disciplinary monotheism.[4] The data on methodological orientation is equally surprising. Of the same 372 articles, 30 per cent were identifiable as quantitative in their orientation, 30 per cent were qualitative, 24 per cent were mixed methods, and the rest, some 16 per cent, were not categorisable. In terms of country of origin, 75 per cent of the authors came from the US. Given this, it seems there is further diversity within the supposed homology. When one delves deeper into the data however the story gets even more interesting.

When faced with hundreds of discrete objects the natural temptation is to try and sort them into categories.[5] When one does this with *ISQ* the categories that emerge from the articles are depicted in Table 11.1. What this points to is something telling that has already been commented upon by Cohen (2008) and Clift and Rosamond (2009) but is worth repeating. In the US, IPE exists as part of a field called international relations (IR) once famously described by Stanley Hoffman (1987) as 'an American Social Science'. When you learn IPE in the US that learning takes place within departments of political science, and the authors of IPE dissertations are usually trained by international relations scholars. Given this, it is not really surprising then that the biggest single category that emerges from the *ISQ* sample is 'questions directly related to existing debates in IR theory', while the second is 'security studies', the twin cores of US international relations theory. Given this, while US IPE seems to appear more diverse than is often noticed, especially by methods, it also belongs within and is restricted to political science, particularly its IR subfield.

Doing the same for *New Political Economy* (*NPE*) was more problematic as *NPE* does not provide abstracts. However, repeating the categorisation for *NPE* as best I could yields radically different results, as depicted in Table 11.2.[6]

New Political Economy gives us a rather different picture of what IPE is. Practically none of the contributions to *NPE* speak to what might be termed core issues of IR theory as defined by the US literature and existing debates therein. Nods to 'liberalism and realism' are conspicuous by their absence. Instead, they cluster around three topic areas: the evolution of advanced capitalist states, the (lack of) development of the rest of the world, and globalisation. When *NPE* publishes theory it is general, not specific, and is far more likely to be about Deleuze than De Mesquita. Unfortunately, I was not able to get systematic data on author's country of origin and methods in time for this essay, but eyeballing

Table 11.1 International Studies Quarterly: breakdown by theme

International Studies Quarterly	
Categories	*Proportion (%)*
IR Theory	27
Security	15
Foreign Policy	6
Trade	6
Finance	5
Theory (general)	5

Table 11.2 New Political Economy: breakdown by theme

New Political Economy	
Categories	*Proportion (%)*
Capitalism	17
Development	17
Globalisation	14
Theory (general)	12
Finance	9

the data suggests a majority of UK-based authors and very few, almost no, quantitative contributions. So what can we take from this?

The lack of a link to International Relations theory among the articles is telling. Indeed, many of *NPE*'s articles would sit well in development studies journals or what US scholars would consider 'comparative politics' journals such as *Comparative Political Studies*. Moreover, given how scholars from multiple disciplines contribute to British IPE (the contributions of the Geography department at Durham University spring to mind immediately here) the comparison to an American 'other' that is self-consciously part of a defined field called IR, which exists inside a further defined field called political science, couldn't be more stark. They are just not the same things. So can they, and should they, be compared?[7]

Although I agree in principle with both Cohen and Maliniak and Tierney that there is a distinct American school and a distinct British school, I am beginning to doubt that we really can presume a divide between the two. For to be so divided presupposes a potential unity, that they are two parts of the same whole that were somehow separated. Reinforcing this image Cohen and his interlocutors often use the metaphor of a transatlantic divide and the need for a bridge between them (Cohen 2008; Higgot and Watson 2008; Cerny 2009), but looking at these two journals I wonder if a bridge can, or indeed should be built between such radically different things? To put it bluntly, when faced with two similar geographies separated by a river building a bridge makes sense, but to build one between a river bank and a cliff edge seems less compelling.

Be careful what you ask for …

What pushes me further in this direction, away from data (my American side?) and towards practice (my British side?), are three recent professional experiences: editing *The Routledge Handbook of IPE* (Blyth 2009); being a discussant at the Philadelphia meeting of the IPES in November 2008; and performing the same role at the meeting of the European Critical Political Economy (ECPE) Group at Oxford Brookes University two months earlier in September 2008. The first experience makes me see these two bodies of scholarship as different but complementary, that we can and should recognise both of these things as IPE while acknowledging their different roots. The second and third experiences make me doubt that desire can be realised.

Turning first to the experience of editing *The Handbook*, back in 2006 I asked four Americans and four British scholars (out of 16 global contributions) to write about what IPE looks like from their place in the world, based upon the not unreasonable assumption that where one sits in the world may shape how one thinks about it. When I asked the Americans to do this (and I fully admit that I led them in this direction) three of them responded with pieces that detailed a particular perspective that had its roots in US IR theory (realism, rationalism and constructivism) while the other one did an overview of the field that took all three positions into account.

In contrast, when I asked the British scholars to do the same (and I admit leading them too) I received a genealogy of the field, a critique of the notion of empiricism, a discussion of power-knowledge and a theory of globalisation. All these contributions were excellent, but what is perhaps most interesting is how the results pretty much mirror the findings of the brief survey of the two journals. None of the British contributions had anything to do with 'IR theory', while none of the US contributions thought of IPE in terms other than it. Why was this?

Ben Clift and Ben Rosamond (2009) address this issue in their contribution to *The Handbook of IPE*. For them, three things set British IPE apart from the American vintage. First, British IPE has a far longer lineage than can be ascribed to Susan Strange and the economic dislocations of the early 1970s (Cohen 2008). Second, as argued here, there never has been a 'parent discipline' for British IPE; it has always been a multi-disciplinary exercise. Third, Marxist approaches have a long pedigree in UK scholarship that has allowed the development of understandings of the IPE far removed from the realist–liberal duopoly of the American school. Add to this the long tradition of scholarship dealing with the political economy of British imperialism, the post-war literature on decolonisation and the global role of sterling, and the enormous literature on the UK's (relative) economic decline, and the very nature and generation of British IPE stands quite apart from this supposedly similar thing that the Americans call IPE.

In short, lacking the concerns that animated American scholarship from within political science, British IPE has become more historically focused and more open to a variety of disciplines than its American counterpart. This different lineage enables British scholarship, as Cohen noted, to 'take on the big questions, especially the normative questions, lurking behind the ostensibly positivist ones' (Cohen 2007: 207–16). I consider this to be British IPE's core strength. After all, if the IPE is (as I think it is) a complex open entropic adaptive system with disequilibrium dynamics and non-linear feedbacks (that is, things are more random than you think and the world is not programmable to a theory of history), then you might as well be sometimes right about the big questions rather than precisely right about the minutiae that may be wrong next week anyway.[8] So I am a Brit after all? Maybe. But there is another side to both schools of IPE that puts the supposed 'hard-core' of the American school into relief into a very different (and to my mind) more positive light. That is, it's not just the Yanks that are, in some cases, monotheists.

The dilemmas of discussants – a cautionary tale

In November 2008 I was a conference discussant at the annual meeting of the IPES in Philadelphia. As noted above, it really is 75 back-to-back PowerPoint presentations of CSTS, hierarchical linear models and GARCH techniques: it is quant heaven. Being a more historically inclined political economist, when I took the podium for my commentary on all this, I suspected that many people in the room thought of me as a dodgy relativist-journalist with no standards who opposed their 'science'. And while no doubt there were some of those folks around, I found many of these supposed monolithic thinkers to have a very pragmatic understanding of their work. For example, if you want to figure out why private pensions diffuse across the world you might want to think about the interaction of gross domestic product (GDP), welfare coverage, debt and dependence on capital flows, and, if you do, you will come up with some surprising results (Brooks 2008). Similarly, if you are interested in shifts in global inequality, try doing that without resort to statistics. In short, beneath the hegemonic technique I found a lot of genuine intellectual curiosity about the way the world works. There were definitely unanswered questions out there, and using statistics and models was one way of finding those answers.

Two months earlier I was a discussant at the ECPE group at Oxford Brookes University. Although this group contains more than just British scholars, it was definitely a British IPE experience. After two days there, rather than being seen as a dodgy relativist-journalist devoid of standards, I felt typecast in the role of dangerous neoliberal American apologist. At this meeting, rather than unanswered questions, what I found here was a set of unquestioned answers. Those answers were historical materialism, neoliberalism, hegemony, Gramsci, historical blocs, social forces and resistance. Regardless of the question, these were the answers, and they were, by definition, the right answers. That these concepts may provide us with good answers some of the time is not in doubt. That they always provide the right answers by virtue of being the only admissible possible answers is beyond dubious.

This was truly eye-opening. Far from the celebrated pluralism and openness that non-American (qua British) scholarship is supposed to produce, I encountered a disciplinary monotheism that would make the US quants blush. There was no other admissible perspective, and not at the level of methods, but at the more fundamental level of ontology. To be critical was to be Marxist. To be not Marxist, as I found out, was to be uncritical, and therefore, wrong, bad, against the 'global south', for 'American imperialism', and all the rest.

Suddenly, and quite unexpectedly, the Americans looked not just more pluralistic, but more intellectually open than their 'critical' other. In the American world of IPE there might be surprises (if the data showed it). In this 'critical' world there were no surprises since all questions were already answered; the trick was to simply find the evidence to back it up.[9] In quantitative circles this is known as curve-fitting and is seen as illegitimate.[10] Here it was what IPE scholars should do to 'uncover' the (rather-obvious-given-the-right-theory) reality of the IPE.

This is not to say that 'all' British IPE succumbs to such authoritarian tendencies and that all American quants are misunderstood pluralists. Rather, the point of these anecdotes is to stress the difficulty of drawing boundaries around real disciplinary communities. The British school can be open and plural or closed and monotheistic depending on which part of it you encounter. The same is true for the Americans. Are there tendencies, styles, elective affinities and the like that enable us to talk about distinct schools? Certainly there are. But the danger surely lies, as Richard Higgott and Matthew Watson (2008) have pointed out, in taking the (self)-representation as real. If we do we risk driving scholarship ever further apart.

Conclusions: burning bridges when we come to them?

Reflecting on both of these experiences, and on the worlds created by *ISQ* and *NPE* discussed above, has left me more confused than ever about the British school and its American other. Yes, they exist, and yes, their attributes can be listed, but the devil is in the details. I have learned that American IPE has no monopoly on intellectual narrowness and claims to 'the truth', while the idea that British IPE is more open and pluralistic depends very much upon the particular British IPE one encounters. So what then are we left with?

Personally, I think that the biggest problem facing American IPE is redundancy, not methodological sterility nor the lack of 'critical' analysis. If American IPE's contribution is econometrics, then there are some people out there already called economists who can already do this really well. If all American IPE is doing is sticking a 'beta' called 'politics' in the model, then it is not much of a value added. I don't worry about American IPE's pluralism. The fact that I get published over there tells me its not as closed as British scholars sometimes see it. I worry about its identity and long-term viability, especially since its intellectual muse – neoclassical economics – is hardly distinguishing itself in this moment of crisis (Wade 2009).

As for British IPE, I worry about its politics getting in the way of its analysis. The commitment to uncovering the politics, questioning the ethics, exposing the hypocrisy, celebrating the resistance is fine and good, but does it always have to be in the paper? Do my personal politics actually have a bearing on the credit default swap market? Is there always a 'hidden hand of hegemony' story in every outcome in the IPE? This is not some plea for an untenable 'value free' social science, but a plea to remember what Arthur Okun (reportedly) once said to Milton Friedman: 'Milton, with you everything is money. Money causes this, money does that, money matters, money is everything. To me everything is sex and sex is everything. It's just that I leave it out of the paper'.

Over the past 15 years I have learned much from British IPE. John Hobson has made it impossible for me to think about European economic development in the same way again, Colin Hay has inexorably altered the way I think about globalisation and the state, Matthew Watson has made me think twice about almost everything. I could go on and on. But I also learn a lot from American IPE, from the quants as well as the constructivists. I close with an example of this.

There have been two recent outstanding books on the politics of pension reform. Paul Langley's very British-school *The Everyday Life of Global Finance* (2008) and Sarah Brooks very American-school *Social Protection and the Market in Latin America* (2008). The former is poststructuralist actor network theory, the latter is quantitative and formal. But both are also deeply historical and are asking similar questions. When read together, Langley's book adds much to the account of 'selling' private pensions that Brooks makes part of her argument. Likewise, Brooks discussion of global capital flows, coverage, replacement rates and the like are surely of relevance to a project such as Langley's. Building bridges works at the level that there can be productive engagement. Some scholars are up for this: those who have the courage to say 'I don't know' and go off and read someone different who might help them out. But for those on either side of the Atlantic who have no unanswered questions, only unquestioned answers, there are only bridges to be burned, not built.

Notes

1 With apologies to Mary MacGregor.
2 There were a few places doing IR in the UK to be sure, but New York versus Canterbury really isn't a contest when you are 23 years old.
3 I chose International Studies Quarterly (ISQ) over International Organization (IO) because doing IO as representative of all American IPE would have been, in a sense, too easy a target. The recent editorial boards of IO have exhibited a penchant for the formal and the quantitative to the exclusion of other work (by no means totally). However, that does not mean that there is no other American work. So I chose ISQ, a more general journal that takes an interest in IPE issues.
4 Some 16 per cent had no obvious theoretical proclivity. All numbers are rounded up.
5 Any category scoring less than 5 per cent has been left off along with those that defy categorisation (36 per cent of the total).
6 Again, any category scoring less than 5 per cent has been eliminated.
7 A similar point is made by Nicola Phillips (2009: 89–91).
8 If you want an example of this, think about the huge literature on 'independent' central banks and how important they are for stability. Not looking too independent at the moment now are they?
9 Geoffrey Underhill, in this issue, seems to have had a very similar experience at BISA. Cameron and Palan (2009) report a similar story.
10 When I pointed this out at the conference I was told that such criticisms (curve fitting, data mining, confirmation bias etc.) are wide of the mark since this work is 'post-positivist'.

12 IPE's split brain

Catherine E. Weaver

C. Weaver (2009) 'IPE's split brain', *New Political Economy* 14(3): 337–346, published by Taylor & Francis Ltd, http://www.informaworld.com. Permission has been granted by the publisher.

> 'All right, brain, I don't like you and you don't like me – so let's just do this and I'll get back to killing you with beer.'
>
> Homer Simpson

I became aware of my scholarly schizophrenia nearly three years at the 2006 inaugural meeting of the International Political Economy Society. Benjamin J. Cohen provided the keynote address, in which he previewed his forthcoming intellectual history of the American and British schools of IPE. I remember sitting in the audience, one of the very few constructivist and qualitative-leaning scholars amidst a sea of quantitative rationalists. As Professor Cohen unveiled his vision of the discipline, I suddenly thought, 'I'm British?!'. A year later, in a smaller forum of mainly European, Canadian and Australian scholars in Copenhagen, I found myself describing my work in the very positivist terms of hypotheses and empirical testing, and had second thoughts. Similar to Mark Blyth's experiences, related in his essay here, my identity as either an American- or British-school IPE scholar depended not on the substance of my work as much the audience to whom I was presenting it. For an early-career American-born and trained scholar of the 'third generation' (as Eric Helleiner argues), this kind of identity crisis could be paralysing. But I instead find being stranded mid-Atlantic to be an enviable position, compelling me to be receptive to the insights and challenges of both schools of thought. As Oscar Levant once said, schizophrenia beats dining alone.

I have further reason to be encouraged by the current reflections on our discipline. At the beginning of this year, I started a new job at a policy school, which can best be described as uninterested in metatheoretical debates. I was told upon my hire that my task as a public intellectual would not be to change the way I conducted my work, but rather to make that work *relevant* beyond the ivory tower. This is not easy for the American side of my psyche. American IPE scholars of my generation, in our quest for the best testable model to prove the causal effect of X on Y, are not widely encouraged to ask the 'so what?' questions (Keohane 2009; Palan, this issue). The professional incentive structures we face seem to prize the science, not the significance. This certainly has merits, which I will explore later. But I also believe it makes us less imaginative, critical and problem-driven than our British cousins (though there are many exceptions to this rule on both sides). It even may, as Palan argues in this issue, have caused us to be more blindsided by the global financial crisis than scholars across the pond. Thus, when I was prompted by my new colleagues to become more 'useful' in my work, it seemed like an invitation to indulge my British sympathies and 'nomadic' tendencies (Cox, this issue). But how should a third generation American IPE scholar become more British? How can we learn from the British school to recapture our relevance without losing our rigour?

In posing these questions, I recognise that I am reifying a divide that I believe is more in our minds than in our practice. In doing this, I am implicitly agreeing with participants in this debate who critique the 'myth' of the divide between two orthodoxies (Murphy and Nelson 2001), the proffered stereotypes (Germain 2009; Blyth and Underhill, this issue), the wastefulness of such navel-gazing exercises (Lake 2009) or the dangers of reifying social constructs (Higgott and Watson 2008). We should not let our musings over an ethereal transatlantic divide soak up valuable journal space to the detriment of substantive research. Yet I think there is value added in taking time to reflect on how we pursue our craft, and categorisations can be useful analytical tools to this end. With such tools in hand, I believe we can tackle important questions, such as how we can best accumulate accurate and useful knowledge in our field. Should we in fact construct distinct camps, plant flags and competitively test one school of thought against the other in a Darwinian survival of the fittest? Or is progress here best achieved through an amalgamation of schools of thought, however incommensurable they appear on the surface?

Clearly I believe that the latter is the better approach. I thus seek in this essay not only to make the case for *why* we should seek better dialogue and collaboration between the American and British schools of IPE, but also *how* scholars might traverse the divide without trespassing upon the intellectual rights of those who seek progress within their chosen 'ologies' and paradigms. I envision, in the spirit of Susan Strange, a tolerant and diverse open range. I do not see this range defined by the unfettered intellectual eclecticism that Strange once called for, but rather a more pragmatic analytical eclecticism that her contemporary 'Magnificent Seven' partners have more recently articulated (Katzenstein 2009; Keohane 2009). I ultimately believe that it is through analytical eclecticism that we can build bridges while respecting different shores and engage in a hubris-free IPE that is more useful in addressing the pressing real-world problems of today.

The American- versus British-school: left brain, right brain?

In making the above case, I start with an observation: IPE today looks a lot like a split brain. The discipline (or at least our current perception of it) displays the characteristics of a patient whose corpus callosum – the mass of nerve fibres connecting the left and right sides of the cerebral cortex – has been severed. The two halves of the brain have started to function independently of one another. Each side is more or less perfectly capable of performing the basic functions of eating, talking and walking. However, the right and left brains see the world in different ways, and they can actually disagree on how they interpret their environment. Depending on which side of the brain receives input, the patient will display different cognitive abilities and behavioral characteristics. In colloquial terms, we understand this to produce 'right-brain' versus 'left-brain' personality types.[1]

Consider for a moment the popular categorisation of left- versus right-brain traits:

Table 12.1 Split brain personalities

Left Brain	*Right Brain*
Uses logic	Uses feeling
Detail-oriented	'Big picture'-oriented
Facts-ruled	Imagination-ruled
Words and language	Symbols and images
Present and past	Present and future
Math and science	Philosophy and religion
Can comprehend	Can 'get it' (i.e. meaning)
Knowing	Believes
Acknowledges	Appreciates
Order/pattern perception	Spatial perception
Knows object name	Know object function
Reality-based	Fantasy-based
Forms strategies	Presents possibilities
Practical	Impetuous
Safe	Risk-taking

Source: 'Right Brain v Left Brain,' *Herald Sun*, 9 October 2007. Available at www.news.com.au/heraldsun/story/0,21985,22556281–661,00. html. Accessed 16 January 2009

Now compare this to the features commonly ascribed to the American versus British schools of IPE (Table 12.2).

While I warn readers not to extend the metaphor too far (see the essays by Blyth and Underhill in this issue for critiques of these characterisations), it is easy to see how the recent literature suggests a simplified typology that prompts us to view the American and British schools as the left- and right-brain personalities of IPE. In a nutshell, the American school is deeply committed to the norms of science, carefully selecting and testing 'hard' data to provide persuasive causal explanations about the way the world *does* work. The British school is both more creative and risk-taking, aspiring to interpret political history and structures to say something powerful about the way the world *should* work. They appear to sharply diverge on questions of ontology, epistemology and methodology and even on the very purpose of inquiry. How did we come to such an impasse?

Table 12.2 IPE's split brain

American School	*British School*
Causal explanation (Farrell & Finnemore 2009)	Interpretative (Cohen 2007: 198–200; Cohen 2008: 44)
Reductionist epistemology (Cohen 2008: 41–43; Wade 2009); Partial equilibrium analysis (Lake 2009)	Rejection of reductionist epistemology (Cohen 2008; Cameron and Palan 2009) Holistic approach (Lake 2009: 52)
'Voracious for data' (Dickins 2006); controlled empirical tests (Lake 2009);'systemic collections and evaluation of empirical data' (Cohen 2008: 41–43)	'Attaching less importance to the systematic analysis of hard empirical evidence' (Cohen 2008: 44); 'weds together normative and empirical insights'* (Farrell & Finnemore 2009: 68)
Materialist & Neo-utilitarian rational choice/Less ideational (Dickins 2006, Cohen 2008: 174; Maliniak & Tierney 2009; Keohane 2009; Farrell & Finnemore 2009; Wade 2009)	Skeptical of rational choice/More ideational (Cohen 2008: 173–175; Cerny 2009; Hay 2004)
Emulation of neoclassical economics and 'hard science' (Murphy and Nelson 2001; Cohen 2008: 41–43; Lake 2009; Wade 2009)	Strong philosophical and historical roots, less valued attached to scientific method (Cohen 2008: 44; Clift and Rosamond 2009)
Paradigmatically-oriented (Maliniak & Tierney 2009: 14), 'shackled to IR' (Phillips 2009); monocultural (McNamara 2009; Wade 2009)	Multidisciplinary; pluralistic; IPE as broader than IR discipline (Murphy & Nelson 2001: 395; Phillips 2009; Clift and Rosamond 2009)
Neglect of critical theory; less reflective in theoretical work (Murphy & Nelson 2001)	Critical theory, concerned with '*cui bono*'? (Cox 1981; Strange 1984; Murphy and Nelson 2001; Ravenhill 2008; Cohen 2008)
Strongly favors quantitative methods/formal modelling (Cohen 2008; Maliniak & Tierney 2009; Farrell & Finnemore 2009; McNamara 2009)	Oriented towards qualitative methods (Cohen 2008: 44; Hay 2002)
Overwhelmingly positivist (Cohen 2007: 198–200; Maliniak & Tierney 2009: 25)	Inclined towards non/post-positivism (Cohen 2008: 176–77); rejection of norms of science (Murphy & Nelson 2001: 404; Wight 2006)
'Objective' questions of efficiency, competition, cooperation and collaboration (Dickins 2006; Cohen 2008)	Normative questions of equity, justice, morality and ethics (Murphy and Tooze 1991; Dickins 2006; Cohen 2008)
Studies reify hegemonic structures (Dickins 2006)	Critiques hidden workings of hegemony (Murphy & Nelson 2001; Dickins 2006; Bieler and Morton 2003; Langley 2008)
Problem solving (Dickins 2006)	Problem posing (Dickins 2006; Blyth, this issue)
Middle-range theorizing (Murphy and Nelson 2001: 394; Cohen 2008: 176)	'Ambition … to address the totality of human experience' (Cohen 2008: 177)

Source: Own Summary.

Note
* One exception here is Ravenhill (2008, 22) who describes the British school as strongly committed to empirical work.

I will leave it to others in this issue to speculate on the emergence of a right brain personality in the British school. I am swayed, however, by a few recent commentaries that try to explain the emergence of a left-brain personality in the American school. This 'monoculture' of American IPE (McNamara 2009), based upon a tripartite adherence to paradigm-driven research, positivism and quantitative methods (Maliniak & Tierney 2009), is the possible result of two social processes: the way in which US institutions now train and socialise graduate students (Farrell and Finnemore 2009; McNamara 2009; and Cox this issue); and the control over the field exercised by the editors of the leading international relations journals. I am not wholly convinced by the latter explanation (see Phillips 2009; Germain 2009). As a journal editor myself, I find little opportunity to exert influence over the direction of the discipline. Instead, as Peter Katzenstein (2009, 127) notes from his own experiences with *International Organization*, editors are held captive to the submission flow and there is thus a strong self-selection effect that drive journals into certain niches. Our ability to rig the review process is really a myth.[2]

In my experience, the more persuasive explanation for the current left-brain personality of the American school of IPE stems from observations of the training and professional socialisation of graduate students. From the early 1990s on, as evident in recent surveys of graduate IPE syllabi (Farrell & Finnemore 2009; McNamara 2009), there has been a tremendous emphasis on quantitative methods and formal modeling and a corresponding reliance upon paradigmatic work that utilises these techniques. To return to the split-brain metaphor, it almost seems as if those directing graduate training in the US chose an elective hemispherectomy – the willful removal of the entire right brain in order to devote energy towards sharpening the specialised functions of the left brain (and perhaps to prevent the kind of cognitive dissonance that might provoke epileptic intellectual behavior in their graduate students). Indeed, the increasing number of statistical course requirements and the neglect of systematic training in advanced qualitative methods contributed to the well-known *Perestroika* movement in the US and the establishment of qualitative methods sections in professional associations and programs such as the Institute for Qualitative Research Methods (IQRM). So while the tide now appears to be shifting back towards more pluralism, with a clear market preference for those demonstrating mixed methods skills, there is an implicit understanding amongst early career US IPE scholars that, to get a job in a mainstream political science department, to get published in the leading journals and to get tenure, you must demonstrate your quantitative chops. This particular mathematically oriented left-brain characteristic, I think, is not going to change any time in the near future. I suspect that a similar demonstration of interpretative methods and 'critical theory' chops might be a thinly veiled requirement for success in the British system.

This may help to explain why IPE's brain split over the past two or three decades, but it does not necessarily indicate why this is *dangerous* for the discipline. On some level, it may produce distinct comparative advantages. It is the rare scholar who can 'do it all' and do it well, and so a division of labour seems quite appropriate and desirable. Why not encourage the divide (Lake 2009)?

Yet, as good IPE scholars, we also know that the purpose of comparative advantage is to enhance trade. Is this what we observe in the IPE discipline today? Here is where I find perceptions of a widening divide between the American and British schools worrisome. Higgott & Watson (2008) are right to point out that, in creating the idea of a schism (and continuously talking about it), we compel scholars to 'socialise themselves in terms of the inherently oppositional categories that Cohen constructs' (Higgott & Watson 2008: 16). We have allowed ourselves to become so entrenched in our imagined communities or defensive of our respective identities that we fail to utilise emerging comparative strengths and exchange ideas across the divide in a constructive or even competitive manner.

The growth of the field is partially to blame for this collapse of dialogue and learning. It is becoming increasingly difficult to keep up with the proliferation of IPE journals and book series, particularly in the British school, which takes a much broader, multidisciplinary view of IPE (Phillips 2009). Parallel to this is the emergence of new professional conferences that, given the paucity of most academic travel budgets, compel scholars to carefully pick and choose forums. The natural tendency of bounded rational humans is to allow this specialisation, to retreat to our comfortable corners and preach to our own chosen choirs. Conscious dialogue across the Atlantic, despite the facilities of the internet and cheap air travel, is difficult.

On dichotomania, bridging divides and being useful

If there is any consolation in above metaphor, it is that the left-brain/right-brain personality split depicted in Table 12.1 is largely a scientific myth. Neuropsychologists are quick to point out that popular notions of right- versus left-brain personalities ('dichotomania') are social constructions with very little basis in scientific evidence (David 1989; Hampson 1994). The classification further breaks down when we recognise that distinct right- and left-brain personality traits are only evident in individuals who have had their corpus callosum surgically cut (usually due to epilepsy-related disorders) or who are participants in tightly controlled experimental settings.[3] 'In normal people, the corpus callosum is usually abuzz with communications being transmitted between the two hemispheres' (Hampson 1994: 2). The right- or left-brain personalities we see in people are usually the result not of nature, but nurture. As social constructs, personality types can be de- and re-constructed.

Therein lies my hope, insofar as I see the transatlantic divide not so much as two shores divided by an enormous ocean as much as two river banks separated by a mildly raging creek that only appears deep at first glance. The mirage, I feel, is fueled by the 'empirics' we use to substantiate the divide. Yet, like others, I find it difficult to draw such stark generalisations about the American versus British schools based upon a single journal, *International Organization*

(Murphy and Nelson 2001; Germain 2009) or the 'Magnificent Seven' (Cohen 2008). Maliniak and Tierney's (2009) data, based upon a survey of over 4,000 US and Canadian scholars plus a systemic coding of the twelve leading IR journals, is more persuasive, but perhaps that's just the left side of my brain speaking. Nonetheless, when we start to look beyond these problematic proxies, our vision of the field blurs. If the extremes of IPE are divided by a metaphorical or literal ocean, there sure seem to be a lot of islands (and Canada, Germany, France, China, Brazil ...) in between.

Yet even if we concede that the transatlantic divide in IPE is mostly based upon a collective delusion of difference, we also know that social constructs have real effects. As mentioned above, the more we think and write about ourselves in terms of competing schools of thought, the more we make the divide real. This divide, I believe, destroys the potential of the discipline to realise its broader relevance. This concerns me, and not just for the personal reason that I now face pressure to be 'useful' in order to get tenure at my new institution. It matters more than ever because we are in the midst of the worst financial crisis since the Great Depression of the 1920s and we need to find a way out. Frankly, I'll be damned if we leave this task to the economists.

I thus return to my uncomfortable question of how to make the third generation of American IPE more 'relevant'. As previously mentioned, we are simply not trained or encouraged to ask the 'should' questions. American IPE is obsessed with studying utility, but it rarely questions the utility of what it studies.[4] Despite its emulation of orthodox economists, who seem to have no problem dabbling in policy, the objective of IPE in the American tradition is to simply explain and (on occasion) predict why things happen, using the most rigorous and replicable techniques and data available (Cohen 2008: 171). Adhering a bit too blindly to the aim of a value-free social science, American IPE scholars rarely pontificate the normative implications of their work or make policy recommendations. This is perhaps the greatest deficit of the American school, and its greatest opportunity to learn from the British school. Cohen (2008: 164) is right when he argues that 'IPE ought to be about more than formal modelling or hypothesis testing. It should also be about *evaluating* behavior and its consequences – about normative analysis'. If the American school is so good at providing causal explanations, why are we not harnessing that explanatory power to proffer solutions to real-world problems? Why is the American school, well equipped with fine-tuned econometric models that possess such predictive power, apparently so apprehensive to offer speculation on Ronen Plan's million-dollar question, 'when will the market bottom out'?

I ultimately agree with Palan (in his essay here) that the British school's proclivity to be more descriptive, observational and seemingly un-beholden to any particular set of ontological presuppositions or methodological restraints may leave it more open to asking the kinds of big questions that enable its members to predict dramatic changes in the world economy, such as the current financial crisis. This is certainly the first step to becoming more relevant, and I believe we Americans should lose our inhibitions on this front. On the other hand, I do not believe that this foresight implies that the British school will be better able or willing to provide the answers we need to resolve the crisis. Amanda Dickins put it best when she argued that the British species *Querimonia* was better at 'problem posing' than 'problem answering' (Dickins 2006: 280), rooted perhaps in the British tradition of conscious normative engagement and a commitment to identifying and resolving social injustices. While noble in intent, there seems to me to be a kind of hubris here wrapped up in persistently problematising the *status quo* while stopping short of offering alternatives that are not only morally persuasive, but also *politically* viable. I thus agree with Mark Blyth's argument in his essay that the key challenge for the British school will be to resist the urge to proclaim that they already know the answers (neglecting the need to provide evidence to substantiate the evils of neoliberalism) and to try to explain these solutions to policy makers in Gramscian terms. The kind of theoretical and methodological pragmatism Palan attributes to British school's 'predisposition to the idea of historical epochal change' is not necessarily well suited to the hard-headed pragmatism demanded of real-world policy solutions.

Many IPE scholars quite reasonably believe it is futile to try to merge such different traditions (Blyth 2009) or to try to combine schools with such incompatible ontologies and epistemologies (Higgott & Watson 2008). I believe, however, that it is both possible and desirable to extract the best of both worlds: the causal and even constitutive explanatory rigour of the American school and the normative drive and unfettered (read: paradigmatic-free) intellectual curiosity, interdisciplinarity and creativity of the British school. To the Americans, the British school offers the inspiration to ask the big questions for which no readily available data may exist. To the British school, the American tradition encourages an openness to disconfirming evidence when it does arise. To be truly useful to an audience beyond our closed academic circles, we need this risk taking tempered by disciplined humility. We need better causal analysis of problems accompanied by a willingness to then use our persuasive explanations of events to make tough moral judgments and to offer solutions.

As a first step to mending the divide, I agree with the many others who have recently argued for a 'pragmatic' compromise between the two schools (Katzenstein 2009, Keohane 2009, Farrell & Finnemore 2009; Blyth 2009). The first step, as Dickins argues, is to simply establish a common language. If we are to talk to one another, we must 'be prepared to translate [our] work into a common vernacular and to reduce technical language of all sorts, both mathematical and philosophical, to a bare minimum' (Dickins 2006: 491). Bourdieu and Bayes, take a back seat.

The second and more ambitious step is to overcome the temptation to entrench ourselves in the task of trying to resolve the fundamental 'ology' disputes. I have slightly more faith that I'll see a resolution to the Israeli–Palestinian conflict in my lifetime than a general consensus among IPE scholars about ontology, epistemology, methodology and how to define progress in our field. To the end of dispensing with such first principle spats and getting down to the 'business of explaining, understanding, and possibly improving the world we inhabit and, in part, create' (Lake 2009, 48), I see great promise in the idea of analytical eclecticism, an approach recently articulated and advocated by Peter Katzenstein and Rudra Sil (2008). In short, 'features of analyses in theories initially embedded in separate research traditions can be separated from their respective foundations, translated meaningfully, and recombined as part of an original permutation of concepts, methods, analytics and empirics' (Katzenstein & Sil 2008, 111). Those adopting an analytically eclectic approach are motivated by problem-driven, rather than paradigm- or method-driven research. They willingly 'trespass' across seemingly incompatible research traditions to 'make better use of the innovative and creative scholarship produced within these traditions in the process of recognising socially important problems and building interpretations and hypotheses that, even if not especially parsimonious, can be analytically coherent, intellectual interesting, and responsive to normative concerns and policy debates surrounding these problems' (Katzenstein & Sil 2008: 111).

Analytical eclecticism need not imply 'intellectual incoherence' (Phillips 2005: 10) or the 'inability to adjudicate among competing claims' (Cohen 2008: 167). To the contrary, it represents to my mind an honesty and a willingness to take the reputational risks inherent in stepping beyond conventional disciplinary boundaries. These are the scholarly values that we should be imparting to the next generation of IPE scholars. And if others out there in the world of IPE also suffer from scholarly schizophrenia in the midst of this grand debate over the transatlantic divide, the invitation to eclecticism should warmly welcomed.

Notes

1 My apologies to Roger Sperry, Nobel-prize winning neuropsychologist and founder of the split-brain theory, for this grossly oversimplified explanation. For better explanations of the split-brain theory in neuropsychology, see David (1989).

2 There was a general consensus on these issues at the roundtables for IPE journal editors at ISA 2008 and 2009. Participants included editors from *International Organization, Review of International Political Economy, New Political Economy, Global Governance, International Studies Quarterly, Critical Perspectives on International Business*, and *Journal of International Business Studies*.

3 I thank Joseph Steinmetz, Dean of the College of Liberal Arts & Sciences at the University of Kansas and leading scholar in the field of behavioural neuroscience for this insight. See also David 1989 and Hampson 1994.

4 Thanks to Mark Blyth for this line.

13 Political economy, the 'US School', and the manifest destiny of everyone else

Geoffrey R.D. Underhill

G.R.D. Underhill (2009) 'Political economy, the "US School", and the manifest destiny of everyone else', *New Political Economy* 14(3): 347–356, published by Taylor & Francis Ltd, http://www.informaworld.com. Permission has been granted by the publisher.

The take-off growth phase of political economy (PE) as a discipline,[1] which began in the early 1980s, is over, and a 'crisis of maturity' involving opposing US and UK schools has been stylised by Benjamin J. Cohen in his thoughtful book. It is now incumbent upon scholars in the discipline on both sides of the Atlantic and elsewhere to ponder how the differences might be bridged and how the discipline might recapture the benefits of both the theoretical and disciplinary cross-fertilisation identified with the 'Magnificent Seven' and other pioneers. This essay addresses the future of the 'British school' first by observing an implicit Anglo-American centrism to Cohen's UK/US-school analysis and demonstrating the very oecumenical and *European* origins of both, a debt which Cohen recognises but underplays. A second section analyses the UK school in the same critical and European light, arguing that it has apparently abandoned historical moorings of sound, case-based *empirical* analysis which was (to a fault) rather disinterested in theory. These moorings have been replaced in the worst cases by 'template theorising' which pays insufficient attention to the high evidentiary standards required of theoretical claims. This feature is not fully explored by Cohen, and is a problem which the UK 'school' can and must address, because the key to bridging Cohen's divide lies in the UK/European tradition in the first place. The final section will develop a number of arguments as to why Cohen is perhaps overly pessimistic, pointing to how the divide between rationalist and cognitive modes of analysis might be bridged.

If these arguments are at all convincing, Professor Cohen would most likely welcome such a conclusion. These arguments are presented in the context of a scholarly career of over two decades of research and writing on the political economy of trade, money and finance across levels of analysis, a career firmly anchored in what Cohen labels as 'second-generation scholarship' and by a scholar who is neither British nor from the US, but from Canada, and whose appointment is at the University of Amsterdam in Europe. The work of the first generation and the giants on whose shoulders they stood was the bread and butter here. Their scholarship did not have such a national flavour (though provenance was not unimportant) and it also crossed *language* barriers in a relatively easy way because of the language skills of a number of scholars involved, and Cohen's competing styles were not yet definitively set. This perspective is important for section three in particular. I argue that the second generation and some key figures of the third remain well placed to build the necessary bridges.

A (yet more) oecumenical story: the US–UK schools of IPE (and everyone else)

As Cohen argues, the US–UK distinctions have emerged and settled over time, yielding a US 'school' characterised by the methodological rigour of Galbraith's 'imitative scientism', and largely a branch-plant enterprise of state-centric international relations (IR). This is in contrast to a British school which is wide open in terms of actors and levels of analysis, makes broad and often normative claims in terms of social constructivism and 'critical theory', is at best eclectic in terms of methodology, and often emphasises historical relativism. Yet Cohen's analysis also reveals the highly heterodox origins of each, including the interaction of the early and take-off phases.

The central point here is briefly to remind ourselves of the highly oecumenical origins of the contemporary US–UK schools of (I)PE. To Cohen's account should be added the influence of European social science and access to language skills on *both*. The methodological rigour and attention to systematic empiricism of the US school is surely a legacy of German and other European immigrant scholars as much as an inheritance of British utilitarian traditions (which were widely adopted in Europe), and the German historical school is surely the major influence behind the US focus on realism, balance of power and state-centric analysis. Hans Morgenthau, father of US post-war realism, was German to say the least, and the post-war realism of Raymond Aron (France) and Stanley Hoffman (US citizen, born in Vienna and educated in France) was likewise influential. Neither Karl Deutsch (Czech-Austrian) nor Albert Hirschmann (born in Berlin, with degrees from Paris, London and Trieste), who influenced so many US political economists, were American by birth; nor was Peter Katzenstein, one of Cohen's 'Magnificent Seven'. The tide of European political economists emigrating to the US, from Joseph Schumpeter on down, was enormous. The influence on US social science traditions of the functionalist and structuralist cross-currents (*and* the latter's eventual refutation via post-modernism/social constructivism) associated with such figures as Émile Durkheim, Max Weber, Bronislaw Malinowski and Claude Levi-Strauss was considerable. Johan Olsen of 'new institutionalism' and path-dependency fame was Norwegian. The utilitarianism of the Scottish enlightenment and English philosophers is a prime source of rationalist analytical rigour, which was clearly imported into the US as much by immigrant Europeans as by British scholars.

As Robert Cox also emphasises in this issue, the influences on the 'British' school were of similarly eclectic and heterodox origins, and would include all of the above in different proportions, as well as interaction with the US. Extremism and persecution in Europe lay behind much of the emigration: Europe's loss, UK and US (and, incidentally, Canada and Australia's) gain and one of the most important reasons why the intellectual traditions of each are historically so rich and varied. In terms of direct influences on (I)PE, Karl Polanyi was Hungarian, educated in Vienna, and he emigrated briefly to the US and eventually to Canada. Much of the British school's encounter with post-war and earlier Marxism came via Europe: Louis Althusser, Nicos Poulantzas, the Frankfurt School and off-shoots, the French 'Regulation School' led by Michel Aglietta and Robert Boyer, and of course Antonio Gramsci and Fernand Braudel, who, combined with Polanyi, eventually yielded Robert Cox's 'neo-Gramscian' synthesis. Post-modernism came out of the 'post-structuralist' intellectual ferment of France, with Michel Foucault and Pierre Bourdieu as founding figures. To round off this highly global picture and to emphasise a point raised by Craig Murphy in this issue, let us not forget Latin American influences such as Raúl Prebisch or Fernando Henrique Cardoso and Enzo Faletto, who also had an impact on US and UK thinking about underdevelopment. Finally, not yet mentioned is the tremendous influence of the study of European integration on both the US and UK traditions in (I)PE, and in this field the Europe–US–UK debates about functionalism, (social) constructivism and institutionalism appear to have remained perhaps more interlinked than in the case of (I)PE, despite 'national' trends. This was accompanied by considerable attention to the comparative political economy of welfare (-state) provision and economic openness which characterised much earlier work of Peter Katzenstein, one of Cohen's 'Magnificent Seven', and this focus still forms (as Helge Hveem also points out in this volume) a bridge of sorts between the two schools.[2]

If one accepts this 'more oecumenical origins and linkages' story, three points are at stake. Firstly, the British 'school' is in fact part of something much larger, historically embedded and shared. There is a broader shared world in Europe (Scandinavia, the Low Countries, Berlin), Latin America, parts of Asia. It is only in the US where these linkages and broader concerns have become so constrained. European, Asian, Canadian, Antipodean and UK scholars readily relate to each others' work and often and necessarily refer to US scholarship. So really it is the US school versus everyone else, a point echoed by Eric Helleiner in this issue. Secondly, many European and UK scholars always have aspired to methodological rigour and soundness (having invented the idea in the first place), while still asking the broader questions. Thirdly, the origins of *both* of Cohen's schools are heterodox and, as European scholarship migrated to the UK/US over time, much was always shared, and this process of cross-fertilisation has not entirely stopped. (I)PE is still part of a broad European political economy tradition in which the distinction between the national/comparative and the international of (I)PE was more a question of empirical focus than importance. These historical linkages are arguably more durable than is perhaps apparent, embedded transatlantically through scholars who cut across the two approaches.

But Cohen's claim is still essentially correct: there *has* emerged a dialogue of the deaf between US scholars and the rest. The next section looks critically at contemporary UK scholarship in IPE as it has emerged and how the weaknesses identified by Cohen might be shored up by a better combination of the historical strengths of the British empirical tradition tempered by versions of European–US–UK–utilitarian analytical and theoretical rigour.

The UK school: what it lost and may yet regain

If the US school is hostage to a parsimonious economism and state-centrism, shaped by a 'methodological nationalism' and which reduces enquiry to neat and testable hypotheses, I concur with Cohen's assessment that the UK school has become increasingly focused on the wide-open question of systemic globalisation in a sometimes rather undisciplined way (see also Blyth in this issue). But I am far less convinced that this agenda is overly broad and that, implicitly, one should abandon the notion of political economy as the study of wider social whole (Cohen 2008: 168). That would be to abandon Adam Smith, David Ricardo, Karl Marx, Karl Polanyi and the whole grand tradition of European political economy, from its origins as a study of the difficult social, political, and ethical questions related to the social whole, about how governance, economic transactions and social constituencies interact over time (See Krätke and Underhill 2006). If these scholars could do it, we are all capable of seeing further by standing on their giant shoulders. We should of course welcome sectoral, area/regional and other forms of empirical specialisation, but that does not diminish the possibility of a holistic approach to theory.

There is nevertheless a growing problem in the British school which affects the capacity of scholars to address the questions being posed. Some of course have joined the 'other side' (along with colleagues in Europe as well) by demonstrating a rather slavish devotion to the US-school preference for economistic data analysis and the testing of narrow and unoriginal hypotheses. On the other hand, in Cohen's British school the lack of analytical rigour is if anything becoming worse, deteriorating into declaratory theoretical posturing essentially devoid of empirical underpinnings and operating at a high level of systemic abstraction. Uncomfortably close to the quality median, especially among some of Cohen's 'third-generation' British-school scholars heavily shaped by postmodernism and a sloppy understanding of neo-Gramscian approaches, an increasingly postured adherence to 'critical theory' does little more than revive an inchoate range of concepts taken from more traditional Marxism, often mixed uneasily with post-modern relativism. This deteriorates into a sort of template oppositionalism to global capitalism, the *scholarly* content of which is difficult to discern. The critical 'attitude', opposition to established 'neoliberal' order and the identification of the pressures on the vulnerable and the inequities which are undoubtedly an ongoing part of global market integration become virtually an indulgent end in themselves.

Too little attention is then paid to demonstrating that the claims of this 'template theorising' are justified in terms of the emerging (mix of) available data and a rigorous analysis thereof, or that the theoretical template provides a better explanation than alternative approaches. Template theorising 'discovers' stylised facts, just like worst of the 'enemy' economists. To repeat a prescient quote employed by Mark Blyth in this issue: '[the US school understands] that data and observation are so unproblematic we can accept them as real ... the British that data and observation are so problematic that we must dispense with them altogether' (Cameron and Palan 2009: 123).

This is a new departure relative to the long-standing intellectual traditions of British political science and international relations scholarship. British scholars were once almost irritatingly content to lay out the facts in an orderly and largely chronological fashion. The story told itself, prompting Roger Tooze to comment in 1985 that 'the British "historical" approach could benefit from a more coherent, comprehensive, and articulated conceptual basis' (cited in Cohen 2008: 141). Quite so, and Cohen rightly complains that Susan Strange never fully developed her theoretical ideas, being not terribly interested in theory as such, despite her valuable contribution thereto. But there was great virtue in this unstructured British historical empiricism: it set the facts straight and often turned up a range of counter-intuitive truths which then found their way to supporting theoretical musings. This virtue is sadly absent from the postured template theorising of too much contemporary 'Global PE'.

Indeed, Strange's observations of the decline of sterling and of international monetary relations under the Bretton Woods 'system' lay behind her core theoretical insights. The short-lived (1959–71) Bretton Woods system never functioned as it was supposed to, and the IMF never played its designated central role; instead, central bank cooperation based in Basle did the job, yielding a dollar-centric structure featuring the US economy as the world's banker where the US government and private actors could get away with what the others could only hope for. This led to *instability*, not the stability usually attributed to Bretton Woods. The rise of the Eurodollar markets and the role played by international bankers was the key to understanding its collapse, not (just or even most importantly) the US payments deficit.[3] While states were important, nonstate actors were as well. Structural power was a crucial concept in (I)PE, this structural power was exercised by a variety of actors, and the theory of hegemonic stability was a nonsense because it was a state-centric version of affairs which is not how US power worked and, anyway, the period of most obvious US hegemony did not correspond to a period of monetary stability as the theory predicted.

Many British-school scholars likewise came to theory via expert case knowledge, coupled with posing innovative and even 'grand' questions. This concern with history was as true of UK (versus, for example, French) 'mainstream' Marxists, whatever that came to be,[4] in considerable contrast to the contemporary UK school propensity to prioritise theory. Asking grand questions is a virtue, but a weak command of the empirical terrain (which takes time and is not an instant gratification exercise like 'theoretical correctness') is inexcusable. So is a failure to explore appropriate methodologies for the different aspects of the analysis (wherein methodology is a *means* at the service of the questions we pose; using a *variety* of means is nearly always better than remaining limited because it will deliver *more* and *different sorts* of data), and a failure to demonstrate empirically if/how a broader model plays out in a case-specific context. The British tradition has lost its empirical moorings and jumped from a rather unstructured focus on the finer details of the story to a rather unstructured preoccupation with 'correct' theorising at its worst combined with a disdain for data.

Additionally, too much the British school claim to 'critical thinking' is little more than declaratory posture. The best scholars in this tradition do come up with new questions and responses thereto, but 'critical' has come to mean 'correct', some variant of radical posture which links tired and familiar questions to equally tired template answers. My last two visits to the annual conference of the British International Studies Association provided anecdotal evidence of the general predicament, and an experience which is reflected in Blyth's parallel conference experience related in this issue. Too many papers demonstrated a severe allergy to the basic findings of economics and other empirical literature outside the template theory approach. Effort was being poorly expended to collect and stylise what had already been well done elsewhere if one bothered to look. The reply to questioning was essentially that the correct 'critical' and/or 'financialisation' spin was missing from the 'other' literature and thus the latter was not relevant. Knowing one's (basic) economic concepts and statistics was apparently unnecessary. I was informed (after two decades of my own writing on power and conflict in the political economy of trade and finance) that it was all about power (in a particular way of course) and that the discipline was not about these 'technical' questions. How on earth would I have known this had I not happened on this happy gathering with such unique insights into the mysterious workings of the world?

Furthermore, the idea that economists or number-crunchers might actually *disagree* with each other in the literature, and sometimes viciously, was apparently lost, and the idea that there are economists with interesting and important ideas about institutions and their role in society as a whole was un*thought* of. Interacting with scholarship outside a defined theoretical terrain was loudly ruled out in favour of template theoretical correctness, perhaps illustrating that the UK third generation is less interdisciplinary than Cohen's account implies: the questions may be broad, the approach not always so.

In my view, critical thinking involves questioning *tous azimuths*, in particular questioning what makes *ourselves* as individual or 'clubs' of scholars feel most comfortable. The whole point about scholarship is that one's sentiment and intuition is dangerous to the truth and is *bound* to be for something, for someone (as Cox famously argued), indeed for oneself and one's sympathisers and no one else. This form of disciple assemblage, which has its unfortunate functional equivalent in the US school or for that matter in Europe, is antithetical to the scholarly enterprise. If economic 'science' makes political economists uncomfortable, then at least one should find out what it is about and what has been written. And one is also acutely aware that there are economists pushing at the bounds of their own discipline and who appreciate the fresh air which can be brought in by (I)PE and the other disciplines.

Clearly, the best scholars of the British school need to reclaim the 'critical' ground in terms of theory and data analysis. A disdain for the limitations of positivism untempered by neither empirically grounded analysis nor genuinely critical enquiry does not a school make. Yet Cohen's observations concerning analytical lassitude need not be true of a 'British' (I)PE tradition which rightly aspires to responding to grand questions. Section one established that there is plenty in the broad European/UK intellectual traditions that have to do with theoretical, analytical and methodological rigour in combination with an understanding of political economy as being about the social whole. A properly critical approach and openness must certainly be preserved, but attention to evidentiary standards and systematically establishing the explanatory 'value-added' of specific theoretical claims, however ambitious and 'world-order' oriented, must be reclaimed by rediscovering the UK historical tradition itself. Given UK school origins, this is certainly no concession to the US school, if that is what the worry might be. This would also partially restore a certain balance to the long-run complementarity of the British and US approaches. To bridge the gap, however, something also needs to happen on the US-school side of the equation, but the common European-British origins of both leaves room for optimism here too, though the process may take time.

By way of example: from complementarity to bridging the gap?

Arguably, Cohen's book and the above analysis indicate that the US school may be in bigger trouble than its 'British' equivalent. The British school may have lost its cautious empirical moorings, but it remains well integrated with its broader shared European and transatlantic- (which includes Canada and Latin America) plus antipodean-oecumenical heritage and with contemporary scholarship across a range of national and regional traditions in Asia, Europe and elsewhere. Repairing the damage only concerns the worst, not the best, of British-school scholarship. On the other hand, the isolation of the US school relative to (I)PE scholarship in Europe, the UK and Asia may be splendid and may represent the best of what the US approach has to offer, but like so much else in the US which has developed over the past two decades or so, it is isolation nonetheless. There are of course reasons why there remains (limited) interaction between the schools, but the reign of overly abstract rationalist modelling based on quantitative methodologies testing narrow, micro hypotheses will be difficult to break in US (I)PE.[5] The fact that the quality is as high as it is observed to be is part of the problem.

Yet this section is dedicated to arguing that Cohen is overly pessimistic in terms of the prospects of bridging the gap. The key lies in the British school and its European and other cousins. As argued above, a range of UK and European scholars have enthusiastically and perhaps slavishly embraced the US-school obsession with methodology. Already there is potential if insufficient condition for interaction. Still too many qualitative-methods British-school scholars remain highly sceptical about the net worth of employing quantitative methodologies *tout court*, and at its worst this has become an ideological stumbling block antithetical to a critical scholarly concern for discovery. While Cohen's own principled objections concerning the limitations of rational choice and quantitative methods clearly hold water, this is certainly no argument in favour of ignoring these altogether and Cohen never meant it as such. I strongly suspect that the postured and allergic opposition to quantity lies as much in self-interest as principle: in a weak capacity of many scholars to employ quantitative methodologies at a competitive level. This derives from a long-run blindness in the training of undergraduates and postgraduates combined with a failure to explore the economics and (I)PE literature which uses such methods – a point echoed by Cox and Weaver in this issue. Those who 'cannot', so to speak, have defended their incapacity as a principled objection. I do not mind admitting that I was too old to have received the required methodological training at the undergraduate level (that came at the MA stage in the 1970s in many universities in both the US and Canada), and then I went to Oxford where at the time there was combined an absence of postgraduate attention to methodology with a too-frequent, proud if misplaced opposition to standards of theoretical and analytical rigour in general. Thus to complete my thesis I of necessity gave myself a self-taught crash-course in industrial economics, international trade, the use of and problems of aggregate comparative national accounts and other statistics, and in the cost structures and the terms of competition among developed and developing country business enterprises in various sectors. If most of the literature available was in economics, my questions were very much associated with political economy. These various excursions have in the eyes of referees over the years neither hurt my ability to infuse my very qualitative methodological approach with a serious discussion of quantity, nor to focus on issues of sociopolitical conflict and power, nor to deal with theory and ask the 'big' questions, including the normative ones.

An important point is that while a high-level mastery of multivariate statistical analysis requires considerable devotion and specialisation, the basics are not overly difficult. They should simply be learned and students should be exposed to the range of methods available and their possible uses as means to varied sorts of enquiry. Method does *indeed* constrain what questions might be either asked or answered, but that is a particularly elementary point and it applies to *all* methodologies, not just rational choice or quantitative approaches. This implies flexibly deploying a range of methodologies appropriate to the theoretical and empirical context involved, including the availability of different sorts of data. This of course implies that US-school methods teaching should commensurately be broadened so as to alert students to the appropriate role of both qualitative and quantitative approaches, and in a number of places this has always been the case anyway. The British tradition of pragmatism could nonetheless show the way here. US-school methodological die-hards would have a lot less to be smug about if British-school scholars more consistently demonstrated the requisite attention to evidentiary and methodological standards. It is worth finding out why the 'others' think the way they do, and it can only add to, not detract from, one's own scholarly and *critical* capacity, a point echoed by Catherine Weaver in this issue. If political economy is by nature interdisciplinary, as Strange and other pioneers correctly argued, then an interdisciplinary and inter-methodological capacity can only prove positive.

There are additional reasons to resist Cohenian pessimism. The first is the very deep roots of the shared European heritage and the 'complex interdependence' of ongoing transatlantic intellectual traffic which cuts across social science disciplines. These roots have not yet been pulled up in the US school. The very nature of (I)PE as a discipline tends to yield such a situation. Secondly, and no doubt as a result, there *is* frustration in the US and there is an audience for Cohen's argument about the costs to be born the more the US school pursues the current track. There are also institutional economists, as argued above, who are pushing at the bounds of their discipline by asking political economy questions, particularly in development economics. The emphasis of research funding councils on interdisciplinarity certainly helps and this should be pushed yet harder. Financial crisis has also helped discredit market fundamentalism and the methodologies which accompanied its rise, and has clearly opened the book on normative issues of the legitimacy and sustainability of market-driven processes and their governance at national and global levels. Most important is the ongoing presence of transatlantic 'bridging scholars' of the first, second and even third generations who are strongly rooted in the grand tradition of political economy yet care greatly for intellectual rigour (Cerny, Murphy, Katzenstein, Gourevitch, Pauly, Hiscox, Stasavage, Boix, Burgoon, Scharpf … the list could go on and Cohen's does). The current gulf identified by Cohen is unlikely to remain static.

Conclusion

One might conclude here by pointing out that Cohen's analysis also points to a certain relationship between the questions asked in (I)PE scholarship, and the state of global affairs (for example the differences during and post-Cold War). Scholars are naturally and rightly drawn to what is going on around them. If this is the case, then one might note that the financial crisis and seismic shifts in the global economy which have gone with it have once more placed us in 'interesting' times. These are world order questions. Just as the United States itself will likely be drawn by dramatic world events out of its current phase of unilateralist introspection, so American scholarship in political economy will need to reconnect with its broader heritage. If US scholars fail to ask the larger order questions, then this time around others may provide answers for them. The rest of the world can show them how this might be done.

Notes

1 As Cohen demonstrates, the levels of analysis distinction became crucial for the US 'school', yet this was and remains much less the case for the UK school. Part of the argument in this piece is that 'PE' is the appropriate label to build the necessary bridges. This article recognises the levels of analysis tension within the discipline by employing the abbreviation '(I)PE' in place of Cohen's (and the more typical) 'IPE' formula.

2 See, for example, the (sometimes co-authored) work of (Australian) Michael Hiscox at Harvard and (American) Brian Burgoon at the University of Amsterdam, who have published frequently in the pages of *International Organization* and the *Review of International Political Economy*, among other outlets.

3 Few bother to read Strange's longest and best work, *International Monetary Relations* (1976).

4 See, for example, the avowedly Marxist but essentially empirical works by Peter Burnham (1990, 2003).

5 As Cox and Weaver argue separately in this volume, this may have a deal to do with the nature of US postgraduate training programmes.

14 Do the Left-Out matter?

Craig N. Murphy

C.N. Murphy (2009) 'Do the Left-Out matter?', *New Political Economy* 14(3): 357–365, published by Taylor & Francis Ltd, http://www.informaworld.com. Permission has been granted by the publisher.

Benjamin J. Cohen's *International Political Economy: An Intellectual History* is a remarkably admirable book. Its organisation around the intellectual biographies of seven of the field's indisputable leaders succeeds in making what could have been a very dry story unusually engaging. The clarity, perceptivity and graciousness of each of these biographies prepare the reader to be well-disposed to Cohen's summary of what IPE has learned and his own conclusions about what the field should do next. Moreover, Cohen's argument for those, largely methodological, conclusions is convincing in and of itself. It is an argument that most readers would accept even without Cohen's demonstrated goodwill toward all of his 'Magnificent Seven' and his acute understanding of each of their contributions: 'American' IPE has much to learn 'from the British side's broad multidisciplinarity' and its greater scope, something needed 'to combat [the American field's] shrinkage of horizons that has been so noticeable in recent years'. The 'British', on the other hand, have something to learn from the Americans' more steadfast attempt to 'bring consistency and replicability to theoretical analysis'.

Yet, for all its strengths, Cohen's book does not provide the definitive history of the field. Since 1989, the International Studies Association's IPE Section (the second-oldest professional organisation in the field[1]) has awarded a prize to a 'distinguished scholar' in the field. The list of those 21 awardees, and the content of the annual roundtables that have honoured them, tell a different story than the one recounted in Cohen's *History*.

All but one of Cohen's 'Magnificent Seven' are here. The late Charles Kindleberger died in 2003, two years before the last of the Seven was honoured, but there are 11 other scholars who were also honoured before the last of the Seven. There are some patterns and perhaps some ready explanations for those that Cohen does not include. He himself is on the ISA list and the graciousness and modesty that Cohen displays throughout the book explains that oversight.

Perhaps less immediately explicable is the fact that, among the remaining 10, there are two sociologists, Wallerstein and Cardoso, although none is included among Cohen's Seven.[2] Similarly, there are four economists among the early ISA awardees (Frank, Hirschmann Amin and Vernon) and only one among the Seven.[3]

More noticeably, while the research of only one of the Seven (Krasner) has focused on the developing world, and then only in the context of North-South relations, the early ISA awardees include two Africanists (Amin and Wallerstein) and three Latin Americanists (Frank, Hirschmann and Cardoso).[4] Perhaps most noticeably, four of these scholars who focus on the global South (Frank, Amin, Wallerstein and Cardoso) are among the most widely recognised and most widely cited social scientists on the political left,[5] a characteristic that they may share with only one of the Seven, Robert Cox.[6]

This group might be called the 'Left-Out': scholars politically on the left who are left out of Cohen's history of IPE. Amin and Cardoso do not appear. Wallerstein appears only as an influence on Cox, Frank as an example of economists on the left who, in the 1960s tried (apparently unsuccessfully) to engage questions of political economy (Cohen 2008: 90, 38). The political position of these scholars appears to be critically important to Cohen's decision to leave them out of the history of the field. After all, Cohen's clear support of multidisciplinarity would make him sympathetic to including some sociologists and more economists among the founding figures of the field, if indeed these scholars have continued to have impact – if their work has let us learn something significant about the global political economy and if it has generated new questions. Moreover,

Table 14.1 ISA-IPE section distinguished scholars

1989	André Gunder Frank
1990	Albert O. Hirschmann
1991	Samir Amin
1992	Susan Strange*
1993	Robert Cox*
1994	Raymond Vernon
1995	Robert Keohane*
1996	Robert Gilpin*
1997	Peter Katzenstein*
1998	Immanuel Wallerstein
1999	John G. Ruggie
2000	Benjamin Cohen
2001	David Baldwin
2002	Peter Gourevitch
2003	James Caporaso
2004	Fernando Henrique Cardoso
2005	Stephen Krasner*
2006	Stephen Gill
2007	Sylvia Ostry
2008	Jeffrey Frieden
2009	Christopher Chase-Dunn

Source: www.indiana.edu/~ipe/ipesection/IPE% 20Distinguished%20Senior%20Scholar.html

Note

* One of the 'Magnificent Seven'.

Cohen's distress over the 'shrinkage of horizons', at least of 'American' scholars, would make him sympathetic to IPE that includes the problems of the global South as a central object of inquiry. Finally, Amin, Cardoso, Frank, Wallerstein and many of the ISA awardees with whom they share close connections (especially Hirschmann, Caporaso, Gill and Chase-Dunn) are, like Cohen, deeply committed to evidence-based research.

In evaluating Cohen's contribution to the intellectual history of IPE, scholars in the field need to take very seriously his implicit argument that the Left-Out scholars really have dropped from the story of the progressive research programmes that link together the field of IPE. Do the *questions* raised by these scholars still matter? What about the *answers* that they have offered? The rest of this essay argues that, on balance, both the questions and the answers still *do* matter, but there certainly is a great deal of *prima facie* evidence that they do *not*. Recent surveys of international relations scholars in the United States suggest that the 'Marxist' perspective that was once considered central to teaching and research in the field has all but dropped from the syllabi at US universities (Maliniak *et al.* 2007). ('Marxist' is the researchers' catch-all for a wide array of theorising on the left including the dependency and world system's perspectives.)[7]

One possible explanation for this shift in teaching preferences may be the ineffectiveness of the policy prescriptions provided by the theories of the left. Cardoso's personal journey, from sociologist of the left in the 1970s to champion of neoliberalism as Brazil's president in the 1990s, exemplifies this argument. '[T]he people', Cardoso writes, 'are not concerned with whether the political left or the political right delivers the services as long as those demanded services are delivered', and he adds, somewhat smugly, that his more popular successor, 'Lula espouses a leftist ideology … but pragmatism and realism prevail in his economic policy (Cardoso 2006).' More broadly, a survey of global economic policy prescriptions written for this journal a decade ago noted that even mildly social-democratic international economic policy proposals were much rarer in 1999 than they had been in 1979, suggesting, perhaps, that experience had proved the left's analysis to be wanting (Murphy 1999).

The Left-Out may indeed have been left out with good reason, but to be sure that that is the case it may be worth recalling some of the events in the past of IPE suggested by the sequence of ISA-IPE Distinguished Scholars.

The early days of IPE through the lens of the ISA-IPE Section

The ISA's IPE research section was formed in the early 1980s largely on the initiative of Ladd Hollist, a political scientist at Brigham Young University who had been introduced to problems of Latin American poverty and to the dependency perspective as a young Mormon missionary in Brazil. Hollist was a friend of Susan Strange, had been hosted by her in London, and was familiar with the International Political Economy Group (IPEG) that she had started in 1971. A few years before establishing the IPE section, Hollist had worked with Jim Rosenau, already one of the most distinguished scholars in the field of international relations as whole, to publish a critical anthology of *competing* perspectives on the world system, including those of Wallerstein, Amin, Frank and Cardoso (Hollist and Rosenau 1981).

The membership of the IPE Section grew quickly, largely because a popular *teaching* field of International Political Economy had existed in the United States since the mid-1970s. The first textbook had been published in 1976 (Blake and Waters 1976). Not surprisingly, only one of the Magnificent Seven, Susan Strange, appears in its index. Six years later, when the ISA's section formed, few of the Seven (unlike the Left-Out) had completed what would become their most influential works. Kindleberger's *Power and Money* had appeared in 1970 and Gilpin's *War and Change* was published in 1981. That year, Susan Strange published *The International Politics of Surplus Capacity* with Roger Tooze. A little earlier, Peter Katzenstein had edited a book that compared the foreign economic policies of wealthy and powerful states (Katzenstein 1978). The others had published seminal papers that anticipated later, larger works (Cox 1981; Keohane 1980; Krasner 1978). Since the early teaching field of IPE began before the seminal works of the Seven were published, much of what the field covered was about what the textbook called 'Radical Thought,' the work of the Left-Out, the dependency theorists and sociologists and economists of imperialism.

A few other things about the intellectual milieu of the late 1970s and early 1980s are worth remembering. The world system's scholars who now appear to be so far to the left of today's IPE were, at the time, confronting academic critics who accused Amin, Frank, Wallerstein and their colleagues of accepting aspects of the global status quo. The Spring 1977 issue of *The Insurgent Sociologist* (whose editorial board included Chase-Dunn as well as Fred Block, author of one of the books most frequently included in early IPE syllabi (Block 1977)) took Amin and Wallerstein to task for their 'rather mechanical' models and their lack of attention to global class struggle (Gerstein 1977).

At the same time, the debates about the structure and consequences of the global political economy that engaged British and American Scholars at the time were much more multinational than many of today's debates that Cohen outlines so well in the penultimate chapter of his book. Quite typically, the economist's equivalent of *The Insurgent Sociologist, The Review of Radical Political Economics,* devoted the whole of one of its 1977 issues to a rapidly commissioned abridgement and translation of a study of multinational enterprise and the self-expansion of capitalism on a global scale by a French economist, Christian Palloix (Palloix 1977). The sense of urgency that existed a generation ago – the desire to find and learn as quickly as possible from all the scholarship in the world that could shed light on what was happening in a rapidly transforming global economy – is no longer characteristic of academic IPE, especially within the shrinking horizons of Cohen's 'American School'.

This brings us to the final characteristic of the early IPE in which the Left-Out played such a role: early IPE was a social science that grew in response to fundamental, difficult-to-understand change, in response to the breakdown of the post-war Bretton Woods system and the successful application of the 'oil weapon' by the Arab members of the Organization of Petroleum-Exporting Countries (OPEC), to stagflation and the unexpected assertion of Third World power. The title of economic historian Michael Hudson's 1977 academic best-seller, *Global Fracture: The New International Economic Order*, encapsulated the era's sense of crisis.

Otherwise unexamined questions and answers that still matter

Recently, in 2005, Pluto Press and its US partner – the once staidly orthodox University of Michigan Press-released an updated edition of Hudson's book, a sign that the questions raised by the early generation of IPE scholars still can sell books. But is that enough reason to include the Left-Out in the history of IPE? Well, here is one set of questions that otherwise would not be included in the field, and the answers currently offered by IPE scholars on the left – and by those in other fields who have learned from them – that does provide a case for keeping the left in: what are the origins of today's global patterns of inequality and what are the political and economic consequences of that history?

These are the fundamental questions that Amin, Cardoso, Frank and Wallerstein were addressing in the 1970s, the questions that generated the vast, multi-disciplinary dialogue that still responds to the early arguments of dependency and world systems scholars. In André Gunder Frank's last years, he devoted much of his time to attempting to translate back into the field of IPE empirical insights gained by economic historians, especially ecological historians and regional specialists, who rejected the relatively simple global narratives that he and others had provided (Frank 1998). The same work on industrialisation outside of Europe before the English industrial revolution, and on the critical role of the 'ecological' conquest of the Americas and of the African slave trade in that 'revolution', has been taken up by a younger generation of IPE scholars, including John M. Hobson (2004), who have continued the progressive research programme.

Hobson's careful demonstration that earlier, exclusively materialist accounts of the European conquest and of the slave trade underestimate the power of changing 'Western' ideas about European superiority intersects with, and reinforces, scholarship in a host of other fields (including law) that cautions Western policy analysts to be much more humble about the policy prescriptions that they wish to offer (or impose on) governments in the poorer parts of the world (Hobson 2004; Kennedy 2009). 'Development' theory, and even much of IPE, bears many of the same characteristics of the earlier authoritative sciences that once provided justifications for actions that led to deeper global inequalities.

Finally, the resulting critical perspective on development theory, combined with an engagement with the most recent research (and research methods) in economic history has helped give rise to a host of regionally based studies that have helped to identify specific historical impediments to economic change in many of the less industrialised regions of the world, including studies on the impact of the African slave trade on current economic and political conditions throughout the continent (Nunn 2008; Nunn and Wantchekon 2008). This is fundamentally significant research conducted outside the field of IPE, but informed by the research traditions of the Left-Out. As Robert Cox notes in this issue, 'The future of IPE on the global scale will require a fuller understanding of … perspectives on history and on the future' that grow out the experience of people in all parts of the world. That has always been the great strength of the Left-Out scholars and it is one of the main reasons for bringing them back in.

Yet, while these open questions about global inequalities may be the most significant ones that would be left out of IPE if we were to leave the left out of the field, they are not the only questions. IPE scholars on the left have also continued to study the historical, and current, characteristics of the internationalisation of capitalist industrial economies. These scholars have provided a major bridge between international relations and the communities of scholars investigating globalisation in economic history, geography, politics and sociology.[9] Left IPE scholars have also remained deeply concerned with the sources of political globalisation, the emergence of global elites and of a global capitalist class, and the prospects for the democratisation of global governance, all questions of fundamental significance (Boswell and Chase-Dunn 2000; Robinson 2004; Wallerstein 1998). In each of these cases, scholars on the left continue to engage in rigorous, empirical research aimed at much larger questions than those that, Cohen argues, have come to occupy the equally rigorous 'American School'.

Why are the Left-Out left out? (take two)

If the Left-Out – the older generation that grew up alongside the Magnificent Seven as well as that generation's successors – continue to answer critically important questions, find significant answers to them, and even inspire and engage researchers from other fields, why did Cohen leave them out of his account? There is certainly no evidence of intentional malice, of a deliberate attempt to overlook the contributions of the left in Cohen's *Intellectual History*. After all, he paints a wonderfully sympathetic portrait of one scholar of the left (Robert W. Cox) and a second, equally compelling portrait of another scholar who inspired so many scholars on the left (Susan Strange).

Yet, as would be the case with any scholar who writes the history of his own field, Cohen is more familiar with the work of some of the founding figures than with others. He needed a conceptual device to help him identify the entire range of scholarship that deserved consideration. He found that device in the distinction between the 'British' and 'American' schools. This is a somewhat inadequate categorisation, but one that other (at least partially competent) scholars had already used to map the field.[10] Yet, many of the distinctions that Cohen (and others before him) make between the 'British' and the 'American' schools, or between 'critical' and 'mainstream' IPE, are simply the current version of the much older distinction between left and right, between, as Alain Noël and Jean-Philippe Thérien (2008) put it, those who are 'satisfied' with the global political economy as it is and those who are critical of its failures.

The list of IPE distinguished scholars reminds us that the field began with the work of scholars who were deeply dissatisfied with global political economy of the 1970s, people who wanted to discover knowledge that could help ameliorate the conditions that gave rise to the contemporary outrage in the Third World. As time went on, the field attracted other scholars, people who were more satisfied with the *status quo*, including Cohen, but people were by no means apologists for the world as it was. Nonetheless, the scholars who came to IPE from places of greater satisfaction with the world were, understandably, not particularly interested in questions about the origins of global inequality and its consequences, or in the nature of the new forms of elite governance that have developed along with economic globalisation, or in the prospects for democratic global governance, a question of critical interest to world's poorer majority.

Many of the satisfied scholars may indeed be 'American', but that is probably not the reason that many of them might not initially think of an intellectual history of IPE that embraces a set of questions that speaks to the world's majority. At the end of a groundbreaking 1999 study on global patterns of economic inequality, World Bank economist Branko Milanovic wondered how it was possible for humanity to accept the apparent injustice of the global status quo. 'Such a high inequality', he says, 'is sustainable precisely because the world is not unified, and rich people do not mingle, meet, or even know about the existence of the poor other than in the most abstract way' (Milanovic 1999: 51). It takes a great deal of effort for an international relations scholar in the richer parts of the world to develop more than that abstract knowledge. Those scholars that do develop an ability to mingle, meet, and know the world's poor most often have spent years developing linguistic skills and ethnographic methods that are even more difficult to master than the mathematical models and econometric methods that now seem so central to 'American' IPE. It should not be surprising that those who make that additional effort often confronted some of the injustice of the global *status quo*, and became dissatisfied, when they were young. Ladd Hollist's experience as a young missionary is far from atypical of a larger group of ethnographically sensitive international relations who, nonetheless remain a very small fraction of the field, a very small fraction that is especially valuable if we want to achieve Cox's vision of a truly global IPE.

Prospects and the role of the 'English' school

Of course, given the global economic conditions of early 2009, many of the IPE scholars a decade, or even a year, ago may be quite dissatisfied today, and much more ready to embrace questions and colleagues who once were to their left. This is one reason why Cohen's history of the field is unlikely to remain completely definitive, but it is not the primary reason. The primary reason has to do with commitment to rational analysis and to evidence-based conclusions that links the 'American' school to the Left-Out. The situation is similar to the one that Peter Singer highlights when pointing out an obvious inadequacy of John Rawls's masterwork. Singer writes, 'When I first read *A Theory of Justice* I was astonished that a book of nearly 600 pages could fail even to tackle the injustice of unequal wealth between societies'. However, if Rawls followed his own principles his would become 'an argument for maximizing the prospects of the worst-off people in the world' a conclusion 'in direct and deep conflict with our settled institutions about what we owe people from other countries' (Singer 2004: 25). Given Rawls's philosophical commitments, the problem continued to gnaw and led, many years later, to a reformulation in his *The Law of Peoples* (albeit a reformulation that Singer still considers inadequate).

Similarly, the commitments to rigour, consistency and evidence of Cohen's 'American' colleagues should lead to more inclusive reformulations of the history of the field-reformulations that do not diminish what Cohen has included, but that do bring the left back in.

In the meantime, one thing would worry me if the 'American-British' distinction were uncritically accepted, that is, if it were accepted without also remembering the 'right-left' distinction that it obscures. It may become all too easy for British scholars to identify themselves with 'progress', and with the left, simply because they are, in some way, distinctively different from their American colleagues. I suspect that this is a bit of what worries Geoffrey Underhill when he thinks back on some BISA presentations and what worries Mark Blyth when he summarises the lessons he was taught at the European Critical Political Economy Conference: 'To be critical was to be Marxist. To be not Marxist, as I found out, was to be uncritical, and therefore, wrong, bad, against the "global south," for "American imperialism," and all the rest'. That is really all too easy – all too easy to use such group norms as a way to feel self-satisfied without really being able to reflect and understand some part of the disadvantaged world, and all to easy to avoid critical reflection on the record of IPE (of any sort) to ameliorate the conditions that make some of us critics of the *status quo*.

That critical reflection is also the job of historians of the field. It may be the most important job that Cohen has left for his successors.

Notes

1 Founded in 1982. The International Political Economy Group (IPEG), now part of the British International Studies Association, was founded in 1971. *Ibid.*, p. 48.

2 From the more recent period, Stephen Gill and Christopher Chase-Dunn also trained as sociologists.

3 Sylvia Ostry is also an economist.

4 Ruggie, like Krasner, has done important work on North-South relations. Caporaso's work includes one of the first introductions of Latin American-based dependency theory to a largerly US audience. Chase-Dunn has also done a great deal of work in Latin America.

5 Two of the later awardees, Gill and Chase-Dunn, are also scholars of the Left.

6 Should Susan Strange also be considered a scholar of the left? Strange's own discomfort with such a characterisation should count for something. In *States and Markets* she insisted that what she offered was 'a way to think about the politics of the world economy … It will leave you free to be an arch conservative or a radical Marxist' (Strange 1988: 8).

7 A similar shift is not as apparent among Canadian faculty.

8 Frank is deeply influenced by Alfred Crosby and other ecological historians who highlight the role of 'Old World' diseases in the European conquest, and by Kenneth Pomeranz and others who have investigated the development of liberal economies and industrialisation in China before the English industrial revolution (See Crosby 1986; Pomeranz 2000).

9 Consider the empirical studies cited throughout David Held and Anthony McGrew 2007 and a work that Cohen correct cites as exemplary (Cameron and Palan 2004).

10 *Mea culpa*, especially because Cohen (see, for example, 2008, pp. 32, 40) credits Douglas Nelson and me with the first publication that tried to make some analytical use of what was once a commonplace distinction made by scholars on both sides of the Atlantic.

15 Pluralist IPE

A view from outside the 'schools'

Helge Hveem

H. Hveem (2009) 'Pluralist IPE: A view from outside the "schools"', *New Political Economy* 14(3): 367–376, published by Taylor & Francis Ltd, http://www.informaworld.com. Permission has been granted by the publisher.

Benjamin J. Cohen's book is a well-written and interesting set of biographies by a scholar who has come to IPE from economics and contributed much to it (Cohen 2008). It made me confirm that I am not a full member of either of the two 'schools'. A 'school' is characterised by high internal consistency and marked difference with other 'schools'. After having reflected further, I concluded that the dichotomy he proposes is not very useful; in fact I question whether the idea of constructing 'schools' in IPE is a good one. As a field IPE *is* diverse and it should continue to be. Pluralism is our comparative advantage, not a nuisance. Unlike neoclassical economics, it makes us able to view the real world as it is: varied, complex, dynamic and changing, producing disequilibria as much as equilibria. And, if after all we were to construct 'schools', doing it along geographical lines is absolutely not a good idea.

Although he offers a fairly generous account of alternative approaches, Cohen basically reduces the criteria he applies for constructing the two schools down to methodological difference. At the same time an informal additional criterion emerges from his text, that of methodological sophistication. This criterion makes him observe that the *International Organization* (*IO*) represents 'the American school'. I suggest that the problems and themes we address, the analytical perspectives we apply, *and* the normative aspects and policy implications we address all represent key criteria for establishing what IPE is. According to these criteria, to which I return below, *IO* used to be one of my preferred readings. Its turn towards economism and 'scientism' has made me less enthusiastic, although I sometimes find something useful there.[1] But long before *IO* turning became monocultural, I had turned with interest to Susan Strange and other non-American scholars of a pluralist tradition.

I have come to see IPE not as a subset of international relations (IR) but a multidisciplinary field with an anchor in political science and a considerable overlap with IR. My own training as a political scientist in the 1960s was certainly strongly influenced by the kind of American scholarship that emphasised rationalist theory and methodological positivism. But what particularly influenced me was the 'blend' of European and American backgrounds which Deutsch, Morgenthau and others of the so-called '*emigré* generation' represent. Later on Hirschman and Polanyi would contribute much to moving me into IPE. Among those in my own generation with that kind of background Katzenstein, one of Cohen's Magnificant Seven, has been a source of inspiration. These 'European-American' scholars have been vital in laying the foundation for American IPE, but also pillars in what still remains a shaky cross-Atlantic bridge. Their impact has declined over the years (Waever 1998), and it probably continues to. And for reasons that are not so obvious the continental European migrants have not had much of an impact in Britain. I therefore not only question whether there actually is an Atlantic divide; it is more obvious to me that the Channel is as deep as the Atlantic is wide (a point also made by Underhill in this issue). Because it could not possibly be the language barrier that isolates the Continent from the British?

I shall argue that the pluralism in British IPE offers it a huge potential to contribute to the core of IPE, the study of global governance of the creation and distribution of wealth. But in order for it to exploit that potential it has to make better use of IPE history and let sources of insight outside the Anglo-American academic environment influence it.

The core of (I)PE

Meta-theoretical issues represent a priority theme for many if not most IPE colleagues. They are the root cause for observations about an 'Atlantic divide'; they also explain why few IPE scholars have attempted to define what the core of it is.[2] But the core is not found at the level of meta-theory, in either rationalist or constructivist theory. To me, that is only the third question in the logical sequence of questions to address when research is designed. It should be answered only after we have first determined: what is the *problem*? An obvious, common-sense question, but one which is often neglected. Too many skip it and go directly to applying *a priori* their preferred theory, uncritically and exclusively, no matter which research problem they address and often with consequences such as those described by Blyth in this issue. But research must be problem-driven (see also Katzenstein 2009). The question that then follows is: how do I go about addressing the problem I have identified? Again a simple answer lies in quoting a founding father in political science: our focus is the power/distribution relationship, or 'Who gets what, when and how?' (Lasswell 1936)[3] Within the 'family tree' that is political science and IR no 'branch' can answer this question better than IPE – provided we are able to agree on its core. And that is where lack of agreement in the field is most challenging. Gilpin's perspective of politics and the economy being two interrelated but separate spheres (Gilpin 1987) did not help much, although his most recent textbook did better in that respect (Gilpin 2001).[4] The contributions that in my mind helped most were the ones identified by Cohen as landmarks: Keohane and Nye's *Power and Interdependence* (1977), Katzenstein's edited *Power and Plenty* and his works on the small open European economies (Katzenstein 1985) and Susan Strange's work (1970), from her call to integrate IR and economics, repeated in her presidential address to the International Studies Association (ISA) in 1995, to a series of later works, well summarised and commented in the posthumous tribute to her (Lawton, Rosenau and Verdun 2000).

The works of these three of Cohen's Magnificent Seven, although clearly different in some important respects, all helped to develop the analytical core which I define as *governance* of the creation and distribution of wealth through linking (in different ways) the international systemic, the national state, and the sector and societal levels. They also laid the ground for sound decisions in the third step of the logical design sequence – making the choice between broad analytical perspectives, or whether to combine them. The reason why I got interested in Strange and other British researchers is that I pretty soon discovered that this decision is not as straightforward as my training in realism and structuralism would have it. While I included cognitive factors, including cognitive psychology, early in my own research, I have been rather slow, that is sceptical, to include the newer and varied approaches known as constructivism.

I could identify myself, though, with the introduction to the IO anniversary issue on this point (Katzenstein, Keohane and Krasner 1998). A major reason is John Ruggie. My own initial use of cognitive theory was based on the assumption that perceptions are a function of position in the international structure. Open economy politics (OEP) theory (Hveem 1972) makes a somewhat similar assumption about preference formation (Lake 2009). It was only well after I had collaborated with Ruggie that I realised that my view was too structuralist.[5] Cohen refers to Ruggie, but could have made him the Magnificent Eight. The relevance of using Polanyi to introduce 'embedded liberalism', and of much of his later work on the place of ideas in IPE (Ruggie 1998), are repeatedly illustrated in the dynamics of the real world such as in the turn from Keynes to neoliberal economics, in the opening up of former socialist space to the market economy (that is in initiating globalisation) and in the current return to Keynesianism.

The core problem and British IPE

System stability, Cohen's 'Really Big Question', is obviously a research problem for IPE. But so is *The Other Big Question* of asymmetric distribution of power and of wealth, and its consequences. American IPE has been much more concerned with the former than the latter; with some reservations I observe that British IPE has been doing both. American IPE is not only more inclined towards reductionist theory; it is also more selective in treating the core research problem than British IPE. The challenge for the British is to continue to face both questions without becoming excessively eclectic.

As for the stability issue there are obviously competing perspectives in the neo-Marxist world systems (see Murphy in this issue) and the realist-liberal Hegemonic Stability Theory (HST) approaches. The current financial crisis should be an occasion for those who still stick to HST to reconsider the merits of not only Keohane's *After Hegemony* (1984), but also the 'radical' view of the sources and implications of systemic (in)stability. Few would disagree that the crisis represents a blow to HST assumptions about the role of the hegemon. There are good critical analyses of the financial system by North American political economists, including Cohen.[6] But to me nobody has offered a more convincing theoretical and empirical analysis than Susan Strange. It is not difficult to imagine – or perhaps read out of *Casino Capitalism* (1986) what she would have said about the current crisis. Rather than 'hard' scientism, 'soft' approaches emphasising cognitive, reflexive factors showing up as trust, fear and herd mentality are much better prospects for understanding, not to mention explaining. And they *are* slowly entering economics. But read also an insider like George Soros for his critique of rationalist (neoclassical, equilibrium) theory's account of the workings of the financial system and his alternative, reflexivist perspective (Soros 2008). It certainly challenges the partial equilibrium assumption of the OEP model and its assumption that preferences are exogenous (Lake 2009; Palan, this issue).

The analytical perspective offered by 'complex interdependence' (CI) is still relevant for the study of crisis governance. When it appeared it was a whole new research agenda that I found more nuanced and useful than the view on hegemonic dominance that I presented in my first publication on IPE, using the term 'global political economy', in 1973 (Hveem 1973). CI should be able to tell us something interesting about prospects for the China–US relationship as the former's role as a financer of the US economy is analysed in relation to the latter's role as a market for and an investor in China. But again Strange comes to mind with her insistence that structural power (of the United States) may be used against whatever resources for bilateral power China may think of applying in that relationship. Moreover, Keohane and Nye's proposition that complex interdependence may be asymmetrical has not been followed up to the extent and in the way it should. Nor has their insistence that non-state, transnational actors should be included in the analysis, something I had been trying to do myself when working with the UN at the time *Power and Interdependence* was produced,[7] and something Keohane and Nye admitted they did not follow up sufficiently themselves (Keohane and Nye 1987). The solid grip that a state centric model has on American IPE apparently keep most others from doing it.

Have the British done better? Since their IPE contributions are too many, diverse and widely dispersed, I cannot possibly be the jury on that. Besides I do not think it is appropriate to speak of a 'British school'. The comments I make in the following are therefore necessarily based on selective reading, occasional participant observation and for the rest on impressions. My main point is that British IPE has great *potential* because it is pluralist and because the total of its various research environments represent a critical mass. The lack of a commanding figure (Strange) may be a weakness, but also a strength. For one thing Strange's view of the state as retreating was not convincing, although it may have been intended to have us see other agents. On the contemporary British IPE scene I see first-class work on the role of regional institutions in global governance, on non-state transnational agency, on the European welfare state in globalisation and on a few more issues of particular interest to myself.

One is to study international *market power*. In view of American corporate dominance it is a paradox that American IPE hardly researches transnational corporations (TNCs) but rather leaves the issue to business economics. Strangely enough, for all its eclecticism British IPE has not done better, with Julius (1990) representing an excellent exception. As states differ in international strategy and power, so do corporations, a fact most IPE scholars have blackboxed. Some have shown though that corporate differences are broadly following differences in national business culture, but there are even differences among corporations from one and the same nation-state (Doremus *et al.* 1998).

What Cohen largely misses with his emphasis on trade is market power exercised through foreign direct investments, networking, alliances and cartels formed and value chains organised by transnational corporations. In order not to get completely lost in actors and factors the analytical model should build on a restricted view of who exercises power over outcomes, how and under which conditions. The method may be process tracing or studying power exercise along the value chain. But above all the contribution that IPE may make, is to show how corporate and civil society agents interact with state actors to produce policy outcomes. Rather than asking whether either state or non-state agency is primary, the question is when, where and why one, or an alliance of two or several, take precedence. British IPE scarcely followed up Strange's not entirely successful attempt to collaborate with business economics to study state corporate bargaining (Stopford and Strange 1991).

Like Blyth and Underhill in this issue, I have also spotted tendencies in British IPE moving towards teleological, out-of-this-world positions. Rather than constructivists insulating themselves from, or being insulated by, the Others, they should join forces to exploit the comparative advantage that pluralism represents and develop combinations of rationalist and constructivist approaches that offer new insight into the core problem of governance. I doubt, however, that this can be achieved without making two important improvements: making better use of IPE history and letting sources of insight outside the Anglo–American academic environment influence ontology and epistemology.

Contemporary IPE's lack of reflection of its *long* history is striking; here Robert Cox is a model to follow (see his essay in this issue). Every serious IR scholar goes at least back to Machiavelli. I follow Cox back to the Enlightenment but even further back in time. About 100 years after *The Prince*, another Florentine intellectual, Antonio Serra, wrote what is maybe the first solid introduction to industrial policy. He described (and explained) how Florence, with no natural resources but with innovative entrepreneurs, an export orientation and a relatively strong state, had managed to become a growing industrial economy while Naples with natural resources declined (Serra 1623; Reinert 2007). I am not sure that Serra is IPE's Machiavelli. My point is the one that Cox and Underhill are making (this issue): we stand on the shoulder of giants but tend to forget them. Other good examples of scholars who recognise giants are Herman Schwartz in his rediscovery of Johann von Thünen and Ha-joon Chang in his adaptation of Alexander Hamilton (surprisingly overlooked by Cohen) and Friedrich List to the contemporary world (Schwartz 1994; Chang 2002).

Crossing the Channel and globalising IPE

There are many excellent IPE scholars on both the American and British side. My argument this far does not exclude the obvious – that they continue to work closely together. So why can they not do without others?

I am the only contributor to the issue whose mother tongue is not English. I have grown up and live in Scandinavia whose security and wealth is highly dependent on the outside world, for security (still) the United States, for wealth (mainly) the European Union (EU) – of which my home country Norway happens *not* to be a member. I graduated in Oslo, spent four years working abroad in Congo (for the United Nations), Uganda, France and Switzerland and have visited the United States as often as I have crossed the North Sea. No surprise perhaps that I see variety and complexity in the subject matter we study and prefer pluralist, eclectic theorising to reductionist, single-cause theory – provided the type of problem to be addressed does not make the latter an obvious choice. Nor that my English is not as elegant as that of my peers.

At the risk of excessive generalisation, British IPE for the most part has overlooked continental institutional theories and industrial policy ideas, and the French macrosociology 'school'. If British IPE is subject to the 'unconscious tunnel vision' that Cohen sees in contemporary IPE (Cohen 2008: 172), it may use The Tunnel to leave it. While Weber and Bordieu are recognised, Durkheim hardly is. His followers in French IR, from Raymond Aron on, have made useful epistemological contributions on power that are only partly and rarely showing up in the Anglo-American academe. Lack of space prevents elaboration, but the distinction the French made between resources, *puissance* and *pouvoir* is useful. In 1974 Marcel Merle published *Sociologie des Relations Internationales* that emphasised a multiple actor set, agency, multilevel analysis, the importance of non-military channels and means of power, including ideological propaganda and a systems view of the world influenced by geopolitics and economic geography. Similarities with American (Keohane/Nye) and British (Strange) texts that appeared later are obvious. But Merle had original arguments on cooperation versus power contests in state-company relations and on the role of transnational civil society. And about the time Strange deflated the state, he argued that there was no retreat of the territorial state generally speaking, but a disintegration between state and nation (Merle 1996).

And there is more across the Channel. German Karl Kaiser was an innovator on transnational relations. Cohen mentions the French Regulation school, but economist Francois Perroux is as relevant. Since the 1950s he and his colleagues contributed several texts on power and dominance in the economy, national *and* international, analysing the role of hegemony, variety in political systems and 'interterritorial units' (firms). He even used 'interdependence' well before *Power and Interdependence* appeared.[8] He followed closely neo-classical economics and criticised it with terms well known to contemporary IPE scholars. And he made use of historical Anglo-American sources of insight on market power strangely forgotten in the Anglo-American academes and was one of the first and few to apply these theories to the international level. Yet another interesting French sociologist is Michel Callon.

As a young researcher doing work on Africa I was never able to conceptualise what I learned the way Gourevitch did some years later (Gourevitch 1978). But I certainly learned that studying African politics, foreign policy and regional integration necessarily ends up with the 'reversed image', with how the international system shapes and often dominates national politics. That lesson directed me to North-South, imperialism and *dependencia* theories and later to apply it to Norway (Hveem 1994). Cardoso and Katzenstein are clearly different, but their works on Latin America and Europe respectively offer a solid basis to study how states of different levels of socioeconomic development and forms of political institutionalisation may organise themselves nationally to cope with systemic influences. The research task now is to further develop a multi-level theory of governance that captures variance on both the state–market, power–society and national–international system dimensions.

A big question in 2009 that links Cohen's 'Really Big Question' to my 'Another Big Question' is which institutions and what sort of power structure offer the most stable *and legitimate* governance system. Democratising nation-states and establishing a global human rights system are demanding, many would say unrealistic, but they are issues that will stay with us and probably become more, not less important. So will the associated issue of what governance compromise between efficiency-seeking supporters of hierarchy and legitimacy-seeking defenders of equal representation may be established in the post Bretton Woods and postcrisis multilateral system. And issues of business' social responsibility that have been accentuated by the raw capitalism that the climate and financial crises have uncovered.

These issues cannot possibly be dealt with without an opening up of IPE to perspectives not only outside of the Anglo-American world, but outside of Europe.[9] A call for this has already been made by 'critical BS' scholars (Phillips 2005; see also Murphy and Cox, this issue), and colleagues have also done excellent comparative research that includes careful representation of 'non-Western' views.[10] More recently such comparative research addresses the level of international regions in the same manner.[11] The time is certain to come soon, however, when Asian and African scholars will present much more innovative new perspectives like Latin American *dependendistas* once did, and on the basis of which we will be challenged. These perspectives are likely to be paralleled by a similar move in the political world to question systemic rules, or regimes, set by Western states.[12] I expect British IPE to contribute considerably.

Conclusion

There is no American or British 'school' in IPE. Nor is there a Continental European school. Even the *dependencia* tradition did not form one school, but several positions. And obviously there is no 'Scandinavian school' in IPE.

In terms of size the Nordic IR community is one of the largest in the world, but strangely enough not represented in Maliniak *et al.* (2009). Nordic IPE contributions are mostly to be found in the study of North–South relations and of national governance, in particular of developing countries and the European welfare states. In pursuing these issues Nordic IPE has been deliberately networking with research environments abroad including British IPE; they have included contributions on varieties of capitalism theory, regionalisation and the European welfare state.

Why do I conclude on a note about a marginal part of the IPE world? Simply in order to make another point that goes back to Cohen. The names he profiles have made some magnificent contributions. But so have many others, and I am not sure that they always get the recognition that they deserve. One reason may be the increasing emphasis on celebrity. Rankings like the one the TRIPs survey offers some interesting information, but may also reflect the bias that comes with size, language and the choice of indicators. Katzenstein (2009) makes a point about one such bias: his institution concentrates on books whereas the citation indices are constructed on the basis of journals. But what about those in the research community who do not publish in English – and even write books? What about those who take their responsibility to maintain and develop their mother language and thus spend time producing textbooks rather than articles to be cited English language journals with a high impact factor?

Good ideas should always get around language barriers, and maybe they do eventually. But it would be nice to be convinced. American and British IPE are producing truly excellent work. But they get an extra 'bonus' in the academic world because of the language factor.[13] The next major TRIP-like survey should therefore study what I propose could be called 'citation networks', patterned relationships among researchers that emerge from their citing each other. Maybe such networks, if they show distinct patterns of repeated references, are the closest we come to a 'school'?

Notes

1 I do hope, as John Ravenhill does (see Ravenhill, 2008), that the new editors will take the IO back towards where it used to be.
2 See Verbeek 2000 for an interesting, but somewhat different argument.
3 Drawing on a historical survey of political economy thinking Stilwell extended the phrase to say, in textbook language, that (I)PE is about 'What is happening? Why? Who gains, who loses? Does it matter? If so, what can be done and by whom? (Stilwell 2006: 4).
4 It lost some of the value of the 1987 text by leaving mercantilism and Marxism at the margins to give most of the space to liberalism.
5 I was invited to produce an article on North-South dependency relations in a book edited by Ruggie and with Katzenstein and Keohane in the team (see Ruggie 1983).

6 Given Cohen's solid background in that issue area it is surprising that the book makes so few illustrations from it, using recent historical examples such at the near-bankruptcy of Long Term Capital Management in 1998.
7 See Hveem 1978. I was asked to analyse whether OPEC could be copied in other primary commodities. My peers in UNCTAD decided not to publish the report as a UN report probably because it was a 'political' economy text and not economics, and because it treated transnational corporations and their market power, a politically sensitive topic then more than now.
8 See Perroux's most comphrehensive statement is *l'Economie du Xxieme Siècle*; see also *Independence d'economie nationale et interdépendence des nations* (Paris, 10/18).
9 Canada and Oceania included in the former.
10 I am referring to Peter Evans on dependency and development states, Katzenstein's work on Asian identity, and TJ Pempel, Shaun Breslin and John Ravenhill on Asia's political economy.
11 A major effort is the GARNET network directed by Richard Higgott.
12 Contrary to what is assumed by John Ikenberry (2008).
13 Seglen 1992 demonstrates the bias for the medical sciences.

16 Division and dialogue in Anglo-American IPE

A reluctant Canadian view

Eric Helleiner

E. Helleiner (2009) 'Division and dialogue in Anglo-American IPE: a reluctant Canadian view', *New Political Economy* 14(3): 377–383, published by Taylor & Francis Ltd, http://www.informaworld.com. Permission has been granted by the publisher.

I must confess that I agreed to contribute to this volume somewhat reluctantly. I enjoyed reading Benjamin Cohen's recent book, but found myself wondering when I saw the subsequent commentaries whether the field might be about to plunge into a long phase of navel gazing. Self-reflection is an important activity, but it can be overdone. I have also sometimes worried that discussions about 'the state of IPE' attempt to draw much stricter boundaries around the field and impose a greater degree of order on it than is compatible with the rather open-ended and eclectic intellectual enterprise that actually exists under this banner. All the same, Benjamin Cohen's book raises some interesting issues on which I have some views. And since he has cast me in the book as one of the Canadians playing a bridge-building role between the 'British' and 'American' schools, I feel compelled to share some reactions in the spirit of Canadian compromise.

A similar vision at the creation

To begin with, I was struck by Cohen's observation near the start of the book that the distinction between the British and US schools was not terribly pronounced in the early years of the field. In their approach, the pioneers that Cohen identifies with the British school (Susan Strange and Robert Cox) and those of the American school (Robert Gilpin, Peter Katzenstein, Robert Keohane, Charles Kindleberger and Stephen Krasner) were not terribly far apart. To be sure, these 'Magnificent Seven' (to which Cohen could have added himself as an eighth member) had many intellectual disagreements, but Cohen (2008a: 7) observes that 'on a deeper, more personal level, it is as if they all came from the same mold'. In addition to a 'contrarian cast of mind', Cohen notes two key traits that united these pioneers.

One was that 'these were people who preferred to build bridges across disciplinary barriers' (Cohen 2008a: 8). They were, in other words, all thinkers who saw IPE as an inter-disciplinary field of inquiry, one that brought together insights from political science and economics, with a strong dose of history thrown in. In so doing, all of these pioneers, in different ways, built explicitly upon, and were inspired by, an older tradition of political economy scholarship which had addressed international issues. This scholarship included the work of people such as Albert Hirschman, John Maynard Keynes, Karl Polanyi and Jacob Viner, as well as older thinkers ranging from Adam Smith and Richard Cobden through Friedrich List and Alexander Hamilton to Karl Marx and the various Marxist theorists of imperialism.

Second, Cohen (2008a: 8) notes that they all had 'an acute sensitivity to experience, which inspired them to question ideas and theories that seemed at variance with the evidence before their own eyes'. 'For them', Cohen continues, 'the value of scholarship could be measured not by the sophistication of a model or the elegance of a technique but rather by how much it added to the understanding of the real world'. And what was this real world focus? In their conception, IPE was a field united by the questions it asked (Cohen 2008a: 142). What was the relationship between politics and economics in world affairs? In what ways do power and wealth, or states and markets, interact at the international and global level? These questions formed the common focus for the empirical intellectual inquiries in which they were engaged.

In short, the founders of the American and British schools shared a fairly similar view of the field's nature and purpose. Indeed, Cohen's observations about this correspond with my own memories of the mid-1980s when I was first introduced to the study of IPE as a Masters student in the 'Politics of the World Economy' program that Susan Strange had established at the LSE. I quickly learned of the various disagreements between the Magnificent Seven and others, but I don't recall having a sense that there was a profound division between a British and American school at that time. Instead, I was attracted to the underlying unity in the vision of this work as an inter-disciplinary enterprise driven by the questions above.

Division emerges: the 'third generation' of the US school

If a sharp division has emerged in the field, then it has come more recently. In his final chapter, Cohen describes the emergence of a 'Third Generation' of IPE scholars in the American school who received their graduate degrees after 1990 or so and whose work was quite different from the first two generations. His description of the difference is worth quoting at length:

> ... whereas the Second Generation was largely content to work with the same kind of prosy epistemology as had Keohane and the other pioneers of the American school (indeed, many had trained with one or another of the pioneers), the Third Generation has tilted far more in favor of what Galbraith called imitative scientism. Second-Generation scholars did not entirely eschew formal modeling or systematic empirical analysis; but

> neither were these elements central to their research efforts. Among Third-Generation scholars, by contrast, the reductionist methodology of neoclassical economics – with all its emphasis on parsimony and numeracy – has come to be the defining characteristic of the US approach to IPE.
>
> (Cohen 2008a: 171)

Cohen is certainly right to describe this contrast between the Third Generation and earlier IPE scholarship as 'profound'. The new generation's penchant for formal modelling and abstract deductive theory based on rationalist assumptions is a far cry from the Magnificent Seven's 'real-world' focus and their skepticism of 'the elegance of the technique'. No longer is IPE to be defined merely by the questions it asked. Instead, this group sees the field moving towards a single standardised formal method and epistemology: that of neoclassical economics. There is even an IPE textbook now that puts forward this view of the field for undergraduates (Sobel 2006).

The economism of the Third Generation leads it to conceive of 'politics' in a narrower way than the Magnificent Seven. While the former focus on rational wealth-maximising behaviour of individuals, the latter were much more open to the idea that actors – including not just individuals but also groups – might be driven by non-material goals such as those relating to power, security, prestige, justice or various identities. For many of the pioneers of IPE, these non-material goals were in fact assumed to be much more important drivers of human behaviour. Indeed, the pursuit of wealth was even seen often to be simply a means to these broader ends. The Third-Generation scholarship is built on a more restrictive view of politics derived from its materialist and individualist assumptions.[1]

Scholars working in this new tradition have also increasingly turned their back on the other feature that had united the founders of the field: their embrace of a wide concept of inter-disciplinarity. To be sure, this new work is inter-disciplinary in its application of the methods of neoclassical economics to the study of political phenomena. But Cohen notes how scholars working in this school have come to see IPE simply as subfield of international relations (IR) rather than a kind of 'inter-discipline' that brings together economists, political scientists, historians and others. As Mark Blyth notes in this issue, their theorectical debates often revolve primarily around questions of IR theory and their engagement with scholars outside of IR has become more limited. I might add that I have also noticed that students trained in this new tradition often have much less knowledge of the history of the global economy and of classical political economy than earlier generations of IPE students.

Some future intellectual historian may provide us with a detailed explanation for the emergence of this Third Generation of the US school. Cohen (2008a: 42) himself suggests briefly that it may have been a product of 'the deceptive accessibility of a reductionist style' as well as 'an element of envy' of the status of economists. Whatever its source, this recent trend has provided, in my view, the main basis for the distinction that Cohen draws between the American and British school. And he is right that the trend has not been followed by most scholars from the British school. Indeed, Cohen accurately notes that many of them have moved in recent years in an even more inter-disciplinary direction which has been characterised by increasing methodological pluralism.

But he also notes that the path blazed by this Third Generation is not one than any of the pioneers of the original US school have followed (Cohen 2008a: 144; Katzenstein 2009; Keohane 2009; Ravenhill 2008: 25). And neither have many of the followers of these pioneers in the US school. Many of the latter have increasingly identified themselves with a 'constructivist' approach to IPE whose openness to inter-disciplinary work and skepticism of abstract modelling leaves it closer to the approach followed by the first two generations of US IPE scholars. For this reason, I find myself wondering (along with Mark Blyth in this issue and Ravenhill 2008: 24) whether it makes sense to speak of the 'US school' as such a homogeneous group. While one branch of this school has recently moved to formal rationalist modelling, others have remained closer to the vision of the Magnificent Seven. This suggests a slightly different framing of the 'division' question. Instead of seeing a split between an American and British school, it may be more accurate to describe the key divide as between what Cohen's 'Third Generation' of the American school and everyone else (including much IPE scholarship outside the English-speaking world, as Robert Cox and Craig Murphy also note in their contributions to this symposium).

Is there a British school?

With this mind, it remains an interesting question to ask whether there is a 'British' school. Cohen identifies a number of core distinguishing features of the school. At an ontological level, he suggests that the British school 'treats the state as just one agent among many' whereas the American school remains 'determinedly state-centric'. In terms of their conceptions of the field, the British school is said to see IPE more as an inter-discipline than as a subfield of IR. And finally, at a more epistemological level, the British school 'embraces approaches that are more institutional and historical in nature, and more interpretative in tone' while the American school 'remains wedded to the principles of positivism and empiricism' (Cohen 2008a: 175–6).

How helpful are these distinctions? As someone who studied and taught both at York University with Robert Cox and in the LSE program that Susan Strange established, I suppose I should have some familiarity with this 'British school'. From this experience, I am not sure that I see it in exactly the same light as Cohen does. To begin with, I am not really persuaded that the ontological issue of challenging state-centrism should be seen as a defining feature of the British school. After all, there are students of Cox and Strange who have embraced state-centric approaches of analysis just as many followers of the pioneers of the American school are very critical of state-centrism. This ontological question, it seems to me, has been the subject of heated scholarly debate in both schools from the start rather than a defining feature of either of them.

I find much more convincing Cohen's observation that the 'British school' conceives IPE as an inter-discipline. This is indeed a core belief of those working in the tradition of Strange and Cox. But as we have seen, it was also an important part of the approach embraced by the pioneers of the American school in the 1970s. It is only more recently that some members of the US school have moved towards a more narrow conception of the field as a subfield of IR. I am not sure, then, that I can agree that the conception of IPE as an 'inter-discipline' is a defining feature of a 'British school' vis-à-vis the US school as a whole.

Still, I think Cohen is right that the 'British school' has been more ambitious in its embrace of inter-disciplinarity. The US pioneers of IPE were concerned primarily with integrating insights from economics, political science and history. But for both Strange and Cox, the disciplinary horizons of IPE were always much wider, including insights from such diverse fields as sociology, business studies, law, philosophy, geography and environmental studies. And their followers have continued in this wider tradition that Strange (1991: 33) so memorably summed up with her metaphor of IPE as an 'open range, like the old Wild West, accessible – as the classical study of political economy had been – to literate people of all walks of life, from all the professions and all political proclivities'. As scholars in those various fields have become increasingly interested in the politics of the global economy, they have been embraced by members of the British school as full participants in the intellectual field of IPE. From a British school perspective, IPE is a big tent. For this reason, the recent efforts to examine trends in the field of IPE by studying the content of IR journals miss the point that scholars in the British school tradition are just as inclined to read and publish in journals of comparative politics, history, economics, law, business studies and the other fields mentioned above.

What about the epistemological distinction that Cohen draws? It is certainly true that Cox and Strange, as well as many of their followers, have been very sympathetic to more institutional, historical and interpretative approaches to scholarship. But couldn't this also describe some of the pioneering IPE work of Gilpin, Kindleberger, Katzenstein, Keohane and Krasner (as well as some of Cohen's own work)? Like Ravenhill (2008: 22), I was also initially rather baffled by Cohen's suggestion that the British school is less committed to 'empiricism' or that it has less emphasis on 'formal empirical inquiry' (Cohen 2008a: 54). Susan Strange was famous for lecturing students to get their hands dirty with detailed empirical work examining how specific sectors of the world economy actually worked. And many of Strange's followers have kept up this longstanding British empiricist tradition with very detailed sectoral studies, often drawing on painstaking archival and interview-based research. Indeed, as Underhill notes in this issue, the overly empiricist orientation of British scholarship was often the target of criticism in the past. In a recent response to critics, Cohen (2008b: 32) clarifies that he was using the term 'empiricism' as a synonym for the more quantitative approach of the more recent Third-Generation work of US scholars. While I don't see why qualitative research is any less empiricist than quantitative research, Cohen is certainly right that the followers of Strange and Cox have been much less inclined to embrace the kind of statistical testing that has become so prominent in US journals in recent years. Again, however, this tendency does not seem so different from the standards set by the five pioneers of the American school.

In sum, I think Cohen is right that there is such a thing as a British school. But the defining features of the school that resonate with my experience – its commitment to inter-disciplinarity and to institutional-historical-interpretative work – do not seem all that distinctive from work of the pioneers of the American school in the 1970s. To be sure, there are some differences at the margin, particularly the British school's embrace of a wider conception of inter-disciplinarity from the start. But to draw too sharp a distinction between the British and US schools risks overlooking the diversity within each. In addition to the distinct groups among followers of the US pioneers already mentioned above, there is the diversity among British IPE scholars that Ravenhill (2008) notes, including many who seem to fall in a kind of 'missing middle' category between two alternatives presented in Cohen's typology.

The need for dialogue

What is the future of IPE as a field in the Anglo-American world? Cohen suggests that the field would be greatly strengthened by more dialogue between the British and American schools. I have suggested, however, that the pioneers of these two schools in fact shared a broadly similar vision of the field from the start. The more serious division that has emerged is between the Third Generation of the American school and everyone else (including many in the US school who remain inspired by its pioneers' vision of the field). Cohen's plea, it seems to me, is really for a dialogue between these two groups. This is a plea that I fully endorse.

Some of those in the 'everyone else' category can be too dismissive of the contributions of this new Third-Generation work. The latter is sometimes portrayed as either too removed from the 'real world' or simply a temporary fad which is unlikely to produce scholarship with the same kind of shelf-life of the weighty classic texts in IPE. These attitudes are unfortunate in my view. This new scholarship is demonstrating new and interesting ways to integrate insights from the economics discipline into the study of IPE. Underlying the dismissal of Third-Generation work often seems to be a view that the only useful insights economics has to offer IPE will come from the more institutionalism, development-oriented or historical branches of that field rather than from its contemporary neoclassical core. I think this view is difficult to defend by those who claim a commitment to a genuinely inclusive inter-disciplinarity.

Equally important, some members of the Third Generation of the American school can be too quick to assume that their approach to the field is the only legitimate one. This assumption may stem from a trend that Cohen and others have noted in which US IPE literature increasingly references primarily only other US scholarship (Cohen 2008a: 64–5; Ravenhill 2008: 19; Paul 2006). Not surprisingly, the assumption generates fierce resistance in the rest of the field since it implies an effort to cast the future of IPE on the Third Generation's terms as a more narrow enterprise both in terms of its disciplinary base and its methodology. These Third-Generation scholars would benefit from a little more humility and open-mindedness. They must recognise that their view of the field is but one among many. There are, and will continue to be, a great number of scholars who associate themselves with a field called 'IPE' and whose work is different from that of the Third Generation. These scholars can be found not just in IR but also in other parts of political science and many other disciplines as well. For them, the field remains defined by the parameters outlined by the first generation of IPE scholars of both the British and American schools: an interdisciplinary field united not by any single method but simply by certain core questions exploring the relationship between economic and politics in world affairs. Nothing more precise than that.

It is not only impossible to rein in the field on a more narrow basis, but also undesirable in my view. The field has benefited a great deal from the broad foundations that were laid by the Magnificent Seven. These foundations, in turn, built upon a productive tradition of political economy that dates back well before the 1970s. The field is more likely to attract the next generation of creative thinkers by retaining this intellectual inclusiveness. And this inclusiveness needs to be extended much more actively to scholarship outside the Anglo-American and English-speaking worlds in ways that create a more genuinely global dialogue, as other contributors to this volume also suggest.

Note

I am grateful to Derek Hall, Jonathan Kirshner and the editors of NPE for their comments.

1 I am grateful to Jonathan Kirshner for the ideas in this paragraph.

17 The proof of the pudding is in the eating

IPE in light of the crisis of 2007/8

Ronen Palan

R. Palan (2009) 'The proof of the pudding is in the eating: IPE in light of the crisis of 2007/8', *New Political Economy* 14(3): 385–394, published by Taylor & Francis Ltd, http://www.informaworld.com. Permission has been granted by the publisher.

This special issue of NPE aims to discuss the recent anthology of our discipline as described by Benjamin J. Cohen (2008). Like all attempts at characterising a fluid situation, it is easy to poke holes in Cohen's argument. Let me say from the outset, therefore, that I accept two of his central tenets. First, I agree with the proposition that there are different traditions of IPE. Terms such as 'British' and 'American' are problematic for obvious reasons. Many members of the 'British' school are, of course, not really British, in terms of neither nationality nor residence. In fact, not only do many Europeans and Australians adopt the 'British' school's approach, but a considerable number of prominent North American scholars may have greater affinities with the type of research that Cohen brands 'British' than with American-style IPE. At the same time, American IPE is far more influential in the UK, particularly among the UK's version of the ivy league universities, than Cohen acknowledges. The division lines that Cohen refers to, therefore, have less to do with geography or an academic discipline, and more with well-rehearsed debates in the social sciences between orthodoxy and heterodoxy, rationalism and the 'continental tradition', and so on.[1]

Second, and more controversially, I accept Cohen's characterisation of the two approaches to the extent that I believe he managed to distil successfully a characterisation that combines each of these schools' rather charitable view of their own aims and goals, with a somewhat less charitable view others have of them. Predictably, the resulting portrayal of the two schools delights no one, but the controversy that has followed the publication of Cohen's book suggests that he may have touched a raw nerve. In fact, I believe that our American colleagues view of the 'British' school's combined efforts in the past 30 years far less sympathetically than Cohen presents it (and *vice versa*). Privately, 'American' perception of the British school is of a group of fuzzy thinkers and navel gazers – big on statements, weak on empirics.

Cohen wrote his book during the good times. Meanwhile, a crisis of global proportion has erupted–a 'meltdown', as Bloomberg now calls it. Might it not be interesting to revisit some of views that have shaped the two traditions of IPE in light of the crisis? For however grandiose, esoteric or rational our theories may appear to us, however rigorous or comprehensive our methods of theory of construction might be, are they not judged at some point in the context of real historical events?

Theory and historical evidence

The American IPE school's answers these question with a resounding 'yes'. An excellent summary of the American position on theory and methodology was produced in a collaborative effort of three of the seven giants of IPE in Cohen's description, Peter Katzenstein, Robert Keohane and Stephen Krasner, all previous editors of the journal *International Organization*. 'Confrontation with evidence', they declare, is key to any theoretical development (Katzenstein *et al.*, 1998: 647).

Katzenstein *et al.* (1998: 646–7) point out, correctly in my view, that theory is used in IPE in two ways. First, as *general theoretical orientations* that 'provide heuristics – they suggest relevant variables and causal patterns that provide guidelines for developing specific research programs'. General theoretical orientations are closely linked to a second level theorising, or 'specific research programs [which] link explanatory variables to a set of outcomes, or dependent variables'. The former produce 'many research tasks and clusters of testable hypotheses'. The latter consist of 'specific tasks and hypotheses'. There must be some connection between the two – although Katzenstein *et al.* are wise enough, and experienced enough, to know that empirical verification and real world situations may have a limited impact on the development of general theoretical orientation. Nonetheless, '[T]he connection between generic orientations and research programs means that the intellectual standing of generic orientations is affected, though not entirely determined, by empirical evidence'. As a result, they conclude, of 'confrontation with evidence, and also due to shifts in world politics itself, some hypotheses, and the research programs in which they are embedded, have received more support than others'. I would surmise from this that the American school's notion of theory construction is founded on the belief that, to use an old English proverb, 'the proof of the pudding is in the eating': theories must be tested by real events.

I cannot think of an equivalent statement written with such clarity and precision on the relationship between theory and empirics emanating from the British school. Susan Strange made repeated references to eclecticism and empiricism, but her notion of theory construction was somewhat elusive, illustrated with the aid of analogies or metaphors (cooking an omelette, etc.). Like Eric Helleiner in his contribution to this issue, I believe that the British school never really perceived the American version of IPE to be 'empirical', or nearly as in tune with historical developments as it likes to think of itself. With my colleague Angus

Cameron (Cameron and Palan 2009), I have argued that the 'British' school in fact has greater claims to empiricism than the American school – a point to which I will return later in this essay. In typically forceful fashion, Strange (1994) expressed the same idea in a commissioned article celebrating the arrival of the journal *Review of International Political Economy*: 'Wake Up Krasner! The World Has Changed'. In that article, Strange had no intention of attacking her good friend Stephen Krasner personally: he was simply the unlucky representative of the American school of IPE to be invited to contribute to a theme discussion. Strange's article could equally be titled 'Wake up American IPE! The World Has Changed!' If truth is to be told, Strange and other contributors to the British IPE consider the American variant to be nonempirical, ideologically driven and politically uncritical.

British IPE and mad money

Considering that the 'British' school is weak on theory construction and apparently lacks methodological rigour, an important question needs to be raised: how did members of this school handle the developments in world political economy that have unfolded in the past three decades? Actually, rather well. During the 1980s – a period that saw great debates in American IPE on the merits of regime theory, hegemonic stability theory and two-level game theory – Strange wrote her seminal contribution, *Casino Capitalism* (1986). *Casino Capitalism* was a trenchant critique of the post-Bretton Woods American dominated global economy, cantering on what Strange considered the most serious flaw in the fledgling global economic system, namely, unregulated finance prone to bouts of speculation. In retrospect, it appears she had a point. If anyone thinks this was a fluke, then let us remember that when she learned of her terminal illness, she decided to write her last testament, *Mad Money* (1998). Nearly everything she wrote about in these two prophetic works is applicable to the crisis that we are experiencing today.

Strange, of course, was not alone. The British school has developed what many of our American friends have seen as rather odd, if not unhealthy, obsession with finance. Louis Pauly (yes, we, the 'Brits', claim him as one of our own) wrote *Who Elected the Bankers?* (1997), Eric Helleiner *States and the Re-emergence of Global Finance* (1994), Randall Germain *The International Organization of Credit* (1997), Paul Langley *World Financial Orders* (2002) and I add to this list my own *The Offshore World* (Palan 2003). More recently, Anastasia Nesvetailova published *Fragile Finance: Debt, Speculation and Crisis in the Age of Global Credit* (2007), predicting that the subprime market in the US may trigger a global financial crisis. I should add to the list of those working on finance the names of Timothy Sinclair, Adam Harmes, Gary Burn, Philip Cerny, Jaqueline Best, Christopher May, Johnna Montgomerie, Duncan Wigan, Richard Bryan and Mike Rafferty. As per Mark Blyth's complaints in this symposium about Marxist monotheism, I would argue that an important – possibly the leading – strand of British IPE, the one obsessed throughout with finance, is neither Marxist nor Marxian, but oriented around post-Keynesian perspectives and evolutionary economics. Philip Cerny captured well that distinction when asked once if he was by any chance a Marxist: his answer was yes, but more of the Graucho type (sic!). There are, however, significant Marxist works as well which centred broadly on finance, including those of Peter Gowan, Neil Brenner and Gerard Dúmenil and Dominique Lévy.

The attitude of British IPE has been extremely critical; much of the work tends to reach for apocalyptic tones, somewhat conspiratorial and with a strong sense of a looming crisis of global proportion. A concept was even invented to describe the key trend of our time, 'financialisation', the idea that globalisation is unhealthily dominated by an unregulated financial sector (Froud *et al.* 2000; Epstein 2005).

The contrast with American IPE could not be greater. Here, the financial sector has generated its own share of specialists, and I would not like in any way to belittle the contribution of our American colleagues working on the subject. Nevertheless, I have tried to think in vain of major studies conducted in the past thirty years that may be considered at the cutting edge of American IPE. Charles Kindleberger, Benjmain Cohen, Ethan Kapstein and Jonathan Kirshner stand out as great contributors to study of finance. But, as all the contributions to this issue suggest, finance and financial crisis was never a core interest of American IPE. Interestingly, Kindelberger proved to be very influential on both traditions of IPE, but only in British circles is Kindleberger (1973; 1996) read as the great critique of a liberalised financial system. For American IPE, Kindleberger is – erroneously in my view, and as far as I can tell, in his as well (Kindleberger 1988) – the progenitor of hegemonic stability theory.

Having failed to recall great many significant contributions on finance within the American IPE, I revisited the journal Cohen associates most closely with American IPE, namely, *International Organization*. I scanned some recent volumes of the journal to learn what exactly occupied our American colleagues in the period leading to this great crisis. There is evidence of considerable interest in questions of peace and war, and in trade volatility, extensive sophisticated work of constructivist/institutionalism nature, and indeed, from time to time, if not very often, we do come across some work in the broad area of finance. Let me cite a few titles of published articles in *IO* between 2003 and early 2007, which I think are indicative of a trend: 'Capital Rules: The Domestic Politics of International Regulatory Harmonization' (Singer 2004), 'Reviving Leviathan: Fiscal Federalism and the Growth of Government' (Rodden 2003), and 'Money Talks: Supplementary Financiers and International Monetary Fund Conditionality' (Gould 2003).

Now, this is by no means a scientific sample, but it does represent, I submit, what we, the 'Brits', believe is shaping the agenda of American IPE. This sort of academic work chimes well with Cohen's characterisation of the school. The articles are rigorous within the very narrow confines of the question they chose to address; they exhibit strong preference for modelling behaviour; they are largely methodologically individualist in character, leaving little doubt about the authors' chosen methodology; they draw explicitly or implicitly on mainstream economic thinking – and I use the term judiciously because I do not believe that modern economics is still neoclassical in any meaningful way; and they are certainly not asking any of the 'big' or, indeed, uncomfortable questions of our time. Meanwhile, British IPE was verging on the hysterical in its critique of what it perceived was an American-led 'neoliberalism', failing to note in the hype that (a) neoliberalism may not have been an American invention and (b) it was no longer the dominant political movement from at least the beginning of the new century (Chavagneux 2007). American IPE, in turn, apparently saw little reason to be concerned with the international financial system as such. Indeed, the two traditions seem to have inhabited parallel worlds. In one, the British, finance was considered an all-conquering, all-encompassing, speculative and highly volatile. In fact, finance is often used as a metaphor for the entire capitalist system. British IPE's critique of finance was a critique of globalisation. In the other, the American, finance was a secondary sphere of activity, and by itself was not problematised.

Orthodox and heterodox political economy

Now, Cohen calls – as, indeed, does everyone else writing in this issue – for greater conversation between the two strands of IPE. I would not like to spoil the party. However, real conversation will take place if, and only if, both sides perceive some value-added in the conversation. The value-added may be personal – in my case, for instance, I have tried consistently to publish in American journals because I believe that American editors and referees have forced me to reflect the best I can on my terminology, concepts and methodology. I will therefore continue pursuing what felt on many occasions like a Sisyphean task. The value-added could also be conceptual or theoretical – and there, I am afraid, I detect problems.

The perceived theoretical and methodological weaknesses of the British school (as seen from an American perspective) notwithstanding, the British school somehow managed to hone in on some of the critical developments of our time. It also appears that despite the supposedly far greater sophistication and methodological rigour of the American school, the American school failed to appreciate these developments. Was it an accident? I do not think so. And because I do not think so, I am afraid that we might need to insist that before we walk joyfully and lovingly down the aisle, we negotiate the terms of a prenuptial agreement.

Why, then, the differences in attitude to the impending catastrophe of the current crisis by the two schools? The differences are due, first and foremost, to the general theoretical orientations of the two schools. Katzentstein *et al.* (1998) correctly point out that IPE draws heavily on economics, but conveniently forget (like most economists) that there are a few different schools of economics. American IPE draws heavily on the ideas, methods and concepts of mainstream economics; British IPE draws on a number of traditions that make up the heterodoxy in political economy and, admittedly, has never developed a consensus as to how to relate one to the other.

That theory explains best the differences in approach between American and British IPE can be seen in two related developments. First, there had been similar debates in economics. Mainstream economists certainly raised concerns about growing American federal and private debt, but elevated the belief in actor rationality and market equilibrium to the status of undisputed facts. 'Post-Keynesian' financial economists, largely banished from the 'Ivy League' universities in the US, often not even considered as economists by their peers, took a dim view of developments in finance. I am referring, for instance, to colleagues working at the Levy institute, such as Jan Kregel, Gary Dimski, Jan Toporowski and Nouriel Roubini. Each one of these has established a name for himself as an eternal pessimist and an unreconstructed moaner. Second, those North American IPE financial specialists who have never abandoned Keynesianism, such as Cohen, Pauly or Kirshner, were extremely critical throughout the past 30 years of developments in the financial system and were able to take a far broader, political-economic perspective on events.

Diverging general theoretical orientations were important, but not the sole causes for the differences in approaches. In fact, there is little about the causes of the current crisis that cannot be explained within an orthodox framework, or even predicted by orthodox economics. Yet, with one or two rare exceptions, orthodox economists have failed to see the writings on the wall, while the majority of heterodox economists have not. I suspect that orthodox economists have failed to appreciate the problems brewing in the 'markets' for two related reasons. First, economic orthodoxy is not only a theory or an approach, but, as its critiques argue, an ideology. It had become, for all intents and purposes, the ideology of the market. The 'big debates' in economics were settled long ago – or so it was thought. As a result (and this is the second and probably the principal reason for the failure of mainstream economics to appreciate the growing problems in the global markets) the specific research programs in the field have focused on very narrow set of questions and, indeed, an ever narrower one – the sort of questions that the *IO* articles cited above tend to address.

This brings me to the second reason why I believe British IPE was able to grasp the significance of finance, while the American has not, and it has to do with methodology. American IPE is resolutely methodologically individualist in orientation, and increasingly so. British IPE, on the other hand, is less interested in 'actors', actors' preferences and behavioural patterns, and more concerned with structural and historical change.

Until not so long ago the prevalent view in American IPE was that economics *is* neoclassical economics, that is, a combination of methodological individualism and rational choice (Blyth & Varghese 1999). As Bruce Russett (1968: 5) explains: 'Economic theory is at heart a set of assumptions and deductions about rational choice on the part of individuals and organizations. It is relevant whenever actors have determinate goals but limited means of achieving those goals, and hence must allocate scarce resources.' Granted, mainstream economics has changed considerably since Russett wrote these unfortunate words. But it takes time for new thinking in economics, sociology or comparative politics to filter through to international relations – where interesting forms of synthesis between rationalism and 'constructivism' are emerging now. Nevertheless, until fairly recently American IPE was rooted in the sort of neoclassical economics that Russett thought was the only economics available.

The appeal to economics had served to legitimise the narrowing of American IPE in the direction of rational choice theory. 'Rational choice theory has three advantages', Helen Milner (1997: 5) writes eloquently. 'It pushes one to specify explicitly the assumptions of the model used, to derive one's conclusions logically, and to examine systematically the effects of changes in any variable used in the analysis'. I agree. But there are equally great disadvantages to rational choice theory, if and when it is treated, as it is often the case, as the *only* theory. While it pushes us to be far more explicit about our assumptions, it provides little indication as to how to select these assumptions or models in the first place. When it is taken as the only theory available, the unfortunate results are that assumptions are often treated as observational facts.

As a result, it is often the case with American IPE, methodology has replaced theory, and the resulting narrow concern of this type of methodology-turned theory with actors, rationality, behaviour and actor preferences has created blind spots hiding most, if not all, the important structural developments of our day. The preferred methodology of American IPE precludes serious discussion of finance as a generalised system, or even a term that captures the fundamental trends of our time and is linked to the deeper forms of power and wealth. From a narrow methodologically individualist perspective, it was difficult to see that finance has become, as Cerny (1994) dubbed it, 'the infrastructure of the infrastructure' of the global economy. Finance is not an 'actor' in a methodologically individualist sense and, not being an actor, its behaviour cannot be modelled. Hence, within the framework of American IPE, Cerny's notion of finance as an infrastructure is assumed (if it was ever noticed in the first place) to be little more than confused dribble. The attitude of the British school to the growth of speculative finance at the heart of globalisation, which distinguishes IPE from heterodox economics, was that politics was key to understanding these developments. Strange pointed to a series of political decisions and, equally important, nondecisions that have created spaces of possibilities that were taken advantage of by well-positioned vested interests. In Strange's depiction, outcomes are rarely traced directly to intent, but rather arose from a combination of factors, many of which apparently have little to do with the subject at hand and often are fuelled by inter-state competition. Rational choice theory can, in principle, accommodate such complex set of circumstances; in reality, it rarely does.

The third reason why British IPE was able to grasp the significance of the changes in the world economy has to do with its strong empirical bent. Any theoretical approach that begins with generalised formula about the nature of agency, the state or, indeed, a system – such as rational choice theory or classical realism – is inherently non-empirical. This is for the obvious reason that it is founded on theoretical assumptions rather than on observation. The British school, on the other hand, begins not with a general assumption but with an observation. So when Cerny identifies finance as the new infrastructure of power in the world, his thesis was not generated in some rigorous specific research programme rooted in a general theoretical orientation. His thesis is rooted in an observation, naturally open to challenges, and theory is then used to analyse, explain or present this observation in a more generalised discussion.

Observation takes precedence in the British school for two good reasons. First, general theoretical orientations are not settled yet on this side of the intellectual Atlantic – if they will ever be. The 'British', or continental, tradition consists of a mixture of at least three perspectives, two of which, interestingly enough, are entirely missing in Katzenstein *et al.*'s presentation of IPE. They include Marxism (curiously, contrary to the perception on the other side of the Atlantic, British Marxists on the whole do not consider neo-Gramscians such as Robert Cox to be Marxists), and those left out, as Murphy in this issue shows, such as evolutionary economists (which include Schumpeter, Polanyi and the post-Keynesian tradition) and post-structuralists (or, as I prefer to think of them, libidinal economists). Lacking common theoretical ground, or an agreed 'ontology' as some like to call it, British IPE had little choice but remain more pragmatic, descriptive and observational. Second, British IPE is strongly historical, by which I mean not only that it pays greater attention to history, but also that it is far better predisposed to the idea of historical epochal change. Hence the idea that theory, any theory, is largely time-specific.

That is certainly not the way things are done in American IPE. There, 'theory' is more or less settled, at least on the rationalist side of the equation, and the rest, as they say, is history.

Conclusion

Cohen ends his book with a call for reconciliation between the two schools of IPE. Doesn't the crisis present us with the moment of such reconciliation? We can point to few positive signs. There are clear indications that leading American journals like *IO*, *World Politics* and *International Studies Quarterly* are far more receptive these days to scholars of the British tradition. They remain, however, decidedly a minority. If truth is to be told, the more creative leading scholars from the two schools were always interested in the other school's work.

But are we to expect a greater degree of conversation between the two schools? Perhaps even a fundamental reorientation of either British or American IPE in light of the crisis and deep historical changes that are likely to take place as a result? I remain doubtful. I strongly suspect, as Roubini argues, that the crisis was not painful enough. It failed to shake the economists' and policy makers' belief in economic orthodoxy, and I would imagine that it will fail to shake American IPE's belief in its preferred theoretical orientation and methodologies.

If anything, the crisis is likely to strengthen British IPE's belief in itself. The British school appears to be better equipped to reflect on an emerging post-crisis world economy. I have a fairly good idea of the current and likely discussions among members of the British school about future trends. I would be interested, indeed, intrigued, to learn how current debates in American IPE can help us understand the near future. The British school has deep roots in those historical sociological and institutional traditions which saw the rise of the New Deal or 'Fordism' as social and political responses to mass society, or the post-1970s 'Washington consensus' and rise of the 'competition state', as a class-based project that was aimed at resolving the crisis of Fordism.

Following this line of thinking, the current debate in the British IPE circles is centred less on the shift of power or hegemony, and certainly not on what is currently a million-dollar question: when will the market bottom out? Rather, the debate focuses on perceived structural juncture, the acceleration of the trend in which an Asian type of capitalism may either replace, or supplant Anglo-Saxon capitalism. The British school seeks to understand the linkages between the changes in the state and possible transformation of the capitalist system itself – assuming, as it normally does, that the solutions themselves are riddled with contradictions, unintended consequences and unexpected system dynamics. They are likely, however, to serve the material interests of the few, to the detriment of the many.

Notes

I would like to thank the editors of NPE, Mark Blyth, Anastasia Nesvetailova and Lou Pauly for the comments and support.

1 For an excellent discussion, see Ross (1991).

Part III

The future of IPE

18 Mantras, bridges and benchmarks

Assessing the future of IPE

J.C. Sharman

In their contributions to this volume, Benjamin Cohen and Robert Keohane in particular have offered some masterful and compelling suggestions as to productive future directions for International Political Economy (IPE) research. Given the unlikelihood of being able to improve on these agendas, the much more modest contribution offered in this chapter is to pose a paradox, and provide some rough benchmarks against which future progress towards the seemingly shared aim of bridge-building and greater dialogue between the American and British schools of IPE might be judged. Nearly every contributor has endorsed Cohen's (2008) call for greater dialogue, respect for diversity and bridge-building between different intellectual communities (albeit with some strong reservations in some cases). Thus as the standard-bearer for the American liberal school, David Lake notes in his contribution that explanations which synthesize elements of both traditions 'are undoubtedly more insightful and complete than either alone'. At the other end of the spectrum, although Robert Cox sees the preferred arrangement more in terms of complementary strengths, the shared desire for a more co-operative relationship is clear. And there are indeed some modest, positive signs of enhanced engagement between the two schools, beyond that represented by the exchange contained in this volume.

The mystery or paradox, however, is that if everyone is so much in favour of exchange, cross-fertilization, tolerance of diversity and so on, why do we have the sort of problems of intellectual isolationism and uninformed mutual disdain that most contributors identify? Given the combined intellectual and institutional heft of the contributors to the volume, the near-consensus in favour of exchange should have prevented the very problem that motivated Cohen to write his very insightful book in the first place (a point echoed by Kathleen McNamara). How can we explain this situation? The notion of mantras included in Peter Katzenstein's incisive and good-humoured chapter provides one answer, while another (possibly complementary) factor might be the influence of structures of power within the discipline acting to entrench and widen the transatlantic scholarly divide. In either case, the repeated public protestations of the desire to bridge the gap between American and British-school IPE scholars might not amount to much. This chapter is not so much an exercise in predicting whether the gap will widen or close in future years, but more an attempt to identify some relevant current trends, and to suggest a couple of rough-and-ready benchmarks against which progress in narrowing any transatlantic divide might be gauged.

First, however, it is necessary to briefly situate this contribution. To follow Ronen Palan's lead, Cohen's characterization of the field as roughly divided into American and British camps seems very convincing. No doubt critics are correct when they point out exceptions, simplifications and omissions. But Cohen's careful prior disclaimers to this effect mean that they are largely kicking against an open door. Alternative ways of drawing the divide either seem to have empirical problems (the 'Harvard school'), or depend on idiosyncratic neologisms ('Open Economy Politics'). Any effort to capture the field in one volume will of course be incomplete and open to challenge. But it is difficult to imagine a more sensitive, even-handed or generous treatment than it receives in Cohen's book. The impression that there is something more to the division than just intellectual artifice is further bolstered by the data collected by the TRIP project, reported by Daniel Maliniak and Michael Tierney. By 2006 this provided powerful testimony that the commanding heights of the discipline (or sub-discipline, depending on one's taste) in the United States had seen a rapid and dramatic homogenization around a shared research programme of rationalism and quantitative or related formal methods. The contributors to the original issues did not have access to the 2008 ten-country TRIP survey released in February 2009. This brief chapter does not have space to do justice to its intriguing findings, but in important instances the results reinforce the notion that there is something to the divide. The divide seems to extend far beyond the geographical confines of the Atlantic. With interesting exceptions (Israel and Hong Kong), International Relations (IR) scholars in the United States are far more positivist and quantitative than those in the United Kingdom, Canada, New Zealand and Australia (the last-mentioned being more British school than the British themselves on this and other measures) (TRIP 2009: 38). Those of the British-school persuasion might be quick to respond that extrapolating from a survey of IR scholars to draw conclusions about IPE is to commit the typically American mistake of assuming that the latter is a subset of the former – a point made by Nicola Phillips in her contribution. But although an outsider is not really qualified to judge, Chris Brown's critique of IR theory as 'the new black' in the United Kingdom (Brown 2006) does seem to echo many of the themes raised by contributors to Part II of this volume, and most of the British IPE contributors do seem to hail from what are recognizably politics or IR departments.

Whence the disconnect? Mantras and structural power

Why, then, does there seem to be such a conspicuous disconnect between the widely expressed desire for a more ecumenical IPE, and the almost equally widespread concern about monocultures and inward-looking rival camps (for a carefully argued critique of this portrayal, see Ravenhill 2008)? In this sense, there might be not one but in fact two disconnects to be explained: the disconnect between American and British-school scholarship, and the disconnect between the way members of the IPE community say they want their discipline to be, and the way they say it is. Perhaps akin to politicians resorting to valence issues, Katzenstein notes that repeated commitments to intellectual diversity and problem-driven research together constitute 'a simple mantra ... our professional rankings ... reveal the great distance that separates ritualistic invocation of problem focus and paradigmatic diversity from scholarly practice'. These mantras may be a result of professing one view in public and another in private, as Henry Farrell and Martha Finnemore suggest. But their origins may also lie in the near-universal tendency whereby in all sincerity one can only find intellectual narrow-mindedness in other people's work, never in one's own (given Katzenstein's entirely admirable tendency to put his research programme where his mouth is, he is clearly an exception to the problem).

The second explanation might be the sort of structural power in the discipline as a social institution that some of the American contributors refer to. These could include the sociological pressures of conforming to national priorities. Or it might be due to unintended self-reinforcing effects: a journal is increasingly associated with one school of thought, leading those outside the school to stop submitting to that journal. In this case, everyone in the field could be genuinely and sincerely in favour of rapprochement, but nevertheless constrained by forces outside their individual control. The British scholars, despite being the aficionados of structural explanations in the world at large, are strangely silent about any institutional biases in their camp (with the partial exception of Mark Blyth and Geoffrey Underhill in their comments about political-theoretical correctness). Possibly this does indeed represent the greater openness that is said to characterize this school. Or there might be one more 'hidden hand' for critical theorists to discover. It is a little surprising that the government-mandated Research Assessment Exercise and the resulting changes in the way publication outlets are valued, as well as the associated labour market effects, do not seem rate much mention in discussing IPE in the United Kingdom. Whether it is mantras or structural power that has led to the coincidence of an overwhelming number of scholars publicly in favour of cross-fertilization or a division of labour, and the failure to discern much progress in this direction, we must use other benchmarks. We cannot rely on high-minded declarations.

Reconciliation prospects and benchmarks

Cohen and others list several areas that might be the source of the problem of intellectual isolationism, but also the breeding ground of some solutions. The first of these is graduate training. Here there is both some reason to believe that the divide is even deeper than some may realize, but also some modest though significant recent signs that the gap may be narrowing. To begin with, it is important to stress more strongly an issue raised by Underhill relating to quantitative skills, the significance of which might have been missed by American readers. In the United Kingdom and its Antipodean intellectual offshoots, with rare exceptions there has been little if any graduate training (this has just begun to change, as discussed below). The doctoral degree is a three- or four-year exercise solely comprising of a dissertation, as opposed to the 6–7 year programme of course work, exams and the dissertation that is standard in the United States. During the three- or four-year Anglo undergraduate degree there are no general education requirements, and most students opt not to take mathematics. The result is that most of those graduate students going through a British, Australian or New Zealand IR or IPE doctoral programme will have no ability to understand quantitative methods. Now consider the fact that, according to the 2006 TRIP count, 90 per cent of IPE articles in the leading journals employed quantitative methods, and the scale of the problem becomes clear. For a majority of the IPE scholars in the British school, the bulk of the work done by US scholars is completely incomprehensible, literally all Greek to them. It is not so much a field divided by a common language, as a field divided by a two different languages, quantitative methods and English. To make matters worse, it is reasonably common to hear senior British-school figures dismiss all quantitative work out of hand, using the logic that since they know this work is no good, there is no need to acquire the skills necessary to understand it (often these sentiments are followed by a critique of Americans for their narrow intellectual horizons and lack of tolerance).

Happily, there are signs of change in the United Kingdom (though not yet Australia or New Zealand), which is instituting a year of compulsory methods training before embarking on the dissertation, perhaps emulating the Canadian model. This leaves room for passing on at least as much knowledge of quantitative methods as is necessary for students to comprehend the literature that uses such techniques, not to mention a whole range of very valuable qualitative methods. Although it is early days, this development shows good potential to begin to bridge the gap with the American school. Even more encouraging is the growing interest in qualitative methods on the other shore of the intellectual Atlantic. Here great credit is due to those like Colin Ellman, Andrew Bennett and David Collier who have done so much to rehabilitate qualitative methods through the excellent Institute for Qualitative Research Methods summer programme, and the qualitative methods section of the American Political Science Association.

Again, none of this contradicts or obviates the current dominance of quantitative methods shown by the TRIP publication data, or the job pressures to invest huge amounts of time mastering quantitative methods that McNamara, Weaver and Cohen remark on in their chapters. The overwhelmingly American-dominated Intellectual Political Economy Society (with 80 of 95 participants in the 2008 conference from US institutions, according to the author's rough count) is likely to be 'quant heaven' for some time to come. But if, as some direct experience and anecdotal evidence suggests, the most common sentence among American applications for entry-level academic jobs is 'The dissertation uses a mix of quantitative and qualitative methods', this represents progress. Indeed, given the huge numbers of applications for IPE jobs in the United States, up to 300 for individual positions, the cover letters alone must comprise a useful snap-shot of the exercise of structural power in the discipline. They show in starkest terms what those at the bottom of the pyramid believe that those at the top wish to hear.

Lest the comments about the lack of quantitative skills in much of the British camp be seen as the kind of 'lazy fist-waving' that Phillips very properly cautions against, the countervailing example is from first-hand experience as the sole non-economist among precisely the sort of economists that appear to be the inspiration for US liberal IPE scholars. Over the course of the three-day workshop, the most striking feature from an outsider's point of view was precisely the unscientific character of many presentations, very much in the manner critiqued in Donald Green and Ian Shapiro's excellent *Pathologies of Rational Choice Theory*. These hurriedly glossed over heroic assumptions bolstering mushy data in the first few minutes, before then spending the bulk of the time lovingly dwelling on the methods employed to reach fairly contrived conclusions. From the perspective of the uninitiated (or perhaps just ignorant), explanations seemed to be judged more in line with prevailing aesthetic expectations, rather than the goodness of fit with evidence. To the extent that significant sections of the field in the United States seem to be socializing their graduate students to conduct exactly this sort of research in IPE, it is easy to appreciate the worries expressed on this score by a wide variety of both American and British critics, from Keohane to Cox. The extent that the move towards formal coursework in Britain includes a move towards quantitative literacy provides an important benchmark of future convergence. Similarly, if qualitative methods training in the United States continues to gain respectability (and facilitate employment), and can counter-balance the often dominant liberal triumphalism, this will likewise constitute an important yardstick of progress.

Another place where Cohen enjoins us to bring down barriers is, of course, in our research. Publications constitute another benchmark against which to test the mantras of diversity, tolerance and bridge-building. Here the TRIP data are again valuable, though, as Maliniak and Tierney readily admit, incomplete. Especially important, many worry about the exclusion of books from the TRIP project, and the skewed impression of the field this omission might have created. In particular, McNamara speculates that the 'ideational turn' IPE work missing from the leading journals is to be found in books. There are moves afoot to include books in a broader TRIP project, but there are also major challenges to be overcome before such a project is feasible. And even if such an exercise is feasible in principle, the pay-off may simply be too low to justify the time and effort required.

If such a survey of books were attempted, there are a number of crucial issues to be resolved.[1] The first is to perform some equivalent of selecting the 'dirty dozen' journals in terms of book presses. Judging from the results of the ten-country TRIP 2008 survey, eight presses suggest themselves for an initial list: Cambridge, Princeton, Cornell, Oxford, Routledge, Columbia, Palgrave and Harvard (see TRIP 2009: Question 44). Again, of course, any such effort to restrict the publishers considered would put some offside. But while the issue of selecting which book publishers to include maps fairly closely onto the journal selection process, the much more difficult (possibly insurmountable) problem is deciding where to draw the line between

IPE (or IR) books, and those outside the field. While some publishers have series that are clearly IPE (the Cornell and Routledge series in political economy, for instance), others simply bundle together all books on 'politics' broadly defined in their catalogues. Surprisingly, preliminary investigations reveal that publishers' catalogues themselves do not include the full range of the books the publisher has produced. Then there is the question about series or individual titles on 'globalization', 'development' or other cognate terms. But even leaving the thorny issue of books to one side, journal publications will continue to give a compelling, if partial, picture of the field. If prestigious journals that claim to represent the field as a whole are in future dominated by work from one narrow perspective, then declarations of pluralism and tolerance will ring hollow.

Conclusion

We cannot take the protestations of tolerance and the commitments to pluralism and exchange between different schools at face value. If such sweet reasonableness were indeed the norm, then there would be no division between American and British-school IPE scholarship. Instead, future progress towards the ostensibly shared goal of rapprochement (or at least more dialogue) should be judged not by what scholars say in volumes such as this, but by benchmarks like the way they design their graduate syllabi, and by the results of the decisions they make as journal referees and editors, as well as on job committees.

To raise a slightly discordant note, the idea of IPE as the 'open range … still unfenced and open to all comers' sounds like a rather quaint and naive self-portrait by which the field flatters to deceive itself regarding its boundaries, gate-keepers and hierarchies. Certainly in one sense there may be more people thinking, talking and writing about the intersection of politics and economics in the international arena than ever before, from bloggers to journalists, NGOs and government officials, without any need or thought of sanction by IPE academics. But presumably this is not what Strange and those quoting this formula have in mind. Finally, a number of the other contributors express some disquiet with the attention devoted to internecine squabbles at the expense of studying the world. Catherine Weaver notes that she hopes the debate doesn't take up too much valuable journal space that could be devoted to other concerns; 20 articles later, perhaps that worry has been confirmed. As a contributor, there is a limit to the extent this line can be pushed; the principled response to this concern would be not to contribute at all. But there does seem something slightly untoward in the context of so much economically induced human suffering, both because of the crisis of 2007 and the 'normal' kind that Murphy quite properly emphasizes, that we look out into the world and the find that the most interesting object of attention is … ourselves.

Note

1 The author would welcome feedback on whether such an exercise would be useful, and if so how it might be carried out.

19 The second crisis in IPE theory

Jonathan Kirshner[1]

'We have nothing to say', a dissenting lion of the discipline once lectured, about matters that 'above all others' occupy 'the minds of the people whom [we are] supposed to enlighten'. Joan Robinson (1972: 9, 10) was addressing her fellow economists, expressing a concern about 'the evident bankruptcy of economic theory which for the second time has nothing to say on the questions that, to everyone except economists, appear to be most in need of an answer'.[2]

Reviewing the collection of essays in this volume reinforces my view that mainstream scholarship in International Political Economy (IPE), as practiced in the United States, is facing its own, similar, second crisis, which, like Robinson's, 'is related to the first crisis'. In IPE, both crises are rooted in treatment of *politics*. The first crisis of IPE was the challenge of its formation as a sub-field: during the first decades of the Cold War, with regard to the study of economic relations, politics was the factor about which only the scandalous dared to speak. In those decades characterized by fantastic abundance (the golden age of capitalism) and the satisfactions of hegemony (from an American perspective, at least), who but a radical dissident would pollute the pristine waters of economic analysis with cynical, even subversive, political bilgewater?

Robert Gilpin used to tell his students that when he first gave talks on what we would now call IPE, he was routinely labeled a Marxist, because that was the only perspective around that considered politics a formative or motivating engine of economic affairs. 'But I was a philosophy major in college', Gilpin continued, pausing for the punch-line, 'and I was pretty sure that I wasn't a Marxist.' Nevertheless, he held the view that political factors – things like the anarchic nature of world politics, the power of states, and the social purpose of action – shaped the contours, content, and consequence of international economic interactions. Susan Strange was another early advocate for the need to bring high politics to the international economic table (see Strange 1970, 1970–1; Gilpin 1971).

The political-economic upheavals of the late 1960s and early 1970s – increasing macroeconomic disquiet and then especially the naked politics associated with the collapse of the Bretton Woods international monetary system and the oil shocks – provided the hard shove of reality that encouraged and perhaps even demanded that scholars attend to the international political foundations of economic relations. And so the first crisis of IPE ended well, stimulating the bubbling cauldron (what Robert Keohane in this volume calls the period of 'joyous contestation') that produced a fertile wave of books and articles that came to define IPE as a subfield.[3]

Today, we face a second crisis, and it again relates to the absence, or, in this case, the atrophy, of politics. Keohane, in his contribution, is 'disheartened by the suppression of I in IPE', with the field substituting instead a 'C' (for comparative), leaving us with CPE, or possibly even just PE; he also laments that no one is asking the 'big questions' any more. Keohane is exactly right on the second point, but the cause is rooted in what has happened to IPE, which he misdiagnoses. The problem is not that we have gone from IPE to CPE or PE, the problem is that we've gone from IPE to IpE – that is, a subfield with a vanishingly small and narrow conception of politics – which, in many ways, points to a recreation of conditions associated with the first crisis. IPE as a subfield was essentially founded by bringing IR to IE; that is, by integrating sensitivity to both political power and market forces. Another way of conceptualizing this is that the initial contribution of IPE was to bring some (very broadly varying) degree of realism to liberalism.

This is no longer the case, as the data reported by Daniel Maliniak and Michael Tierney in this collection make clear. We now have liberalism – individuals, markets, egoistic material interests, with a hint, as subtext (not theory), of Marxism – that is, the definition of politics as distributional economic conflict. John Maynard Keynes recognized this implicit, if counter-intuitive, affinity in his own critique of styles of analyses that depended on an 'over-valuation of the economic criterion', which he argued resulted in 'the final reductio ad absurdum of Benthamism known as Marxism' (Keynes 1972: 445).

What has been lost in this shift in the intellectual center of gravity? Of necessity, raising the volume on individuals, markets, and material interests requires that other factors are drowned out in the mix, and what has been muted is much Politics: first and foremost, international politics – how the concern for war and the pursuit of power and national interest by states shape the international economy – but also the role and influence of collective goals over individual pursuits, and the influence of the pursuit of non-economic goals (by individuals or groups or states).

This vanishing conception of politics is related to and reinforced by an inward-looking fascination with methodological specialization. In IpE, technique is no longer (as it should be) the handmaiden of inquiry; rather, inquiry is increasingly shaped to serve a rather severe methodological mistress. This has contributed, crucially, to Keohane's 'gnawing sense of dissatisfaction' about the field. There is, however, something incongruous about his unease; Keohane, a generous and accomplished scholar, is accurately reported by Maliniak and Tierney to be the most influential figure in IPE. As such, in his dismay at the field's renunciation of the 'big questions' that matter, personally I can't help but hear echoes of Claude Rains' shock at discovering that there was gambling going on at Rick's place in *Casablanca* – Keohane, after all, is the biggest shareholder in our casino. And as Benjamin J. Cohen (2009: 141) notes, this 'loss of ambition … is hardly an accident'; it is instead a consequence of limiting inquiry to research of a certain style and technique.

Living with HIM

Contemporary IpE is characterized by Hyper-rationalism, Individualism, and Materialism (which I will now dub HIM for short) – three foundational attributes which are either empirically wrong (in the case of hyper-rationalism) or profoundly and consequentially narrowing in terms of the questions that can be asked or answered (in the cases of individualism and materialism).

The hyper-rationalist turn in IpE was inspired by the Rational Expectations revolution in macroeconomic theory. In an (oversimplified) nutshell, the rational expectations approach holds that actors process information quickly, efficiently, and correctly, and, crucially, that they share knowledge of the correct underlying model of the economy (see Miller 1994). This did indeed bring about a revolution in macroeconomics, generated a vast literature, and established a number of empirically testable implications. But rational expectations did not test well; even leading conservative monetarists concluded that 'the strong rational expectations hypothesis cannot be accepted as a serious empirical hypothesis'. Other mainstream economists concluded that 'the weight of the empirical evidence is sufficiently strong to compel us to suspend belief in the hypothesis of rational expectations'; most attributed the empirical failure of rational expectations to the flawed underlying assumptions of the approach (Brunner and Meltzer 1993: 42; Lovell 1986: 122; Friedman 1979: 26–7).

But it is an analog of rational expectations that informs the hyper-rationalist approach; in particular, the view that rational actors must know and share the same, correct, model of international politics. A central tenet of IpE, for example, is that if rational actors have access to the same information, they will reach the same conclusions about expected outcomes. This is why the 'rationalist explanations for war' literature puts so much emphasis on asymmetric information as a source of war between rational actors. But, as with rational expectations in economics, empirically, this claim is rather easily falsified. Thoughtful, dispassionate experts looking at the same information can and commonly do reach different conclusions about expectations for the future, even in the best possible (richest and most complete) information environments (Kirshner 2000).

In economics, mistakes in the treatment of expectations and rationality come at a high cost, and the limits to the deductive logic and empirical applications of mainstream theories were exposed by the global financial crisis of 2007–8, which is better understood through a more Keynesian approach to uncertainty and the modeling of expectations (see Keynes 1937). IpE's embrace of hyper-rationalism will likely lead to similar blunders; an old-fashioned IPE approach, on the other hand, would be to assume that actors have what could be called 'realistic expectations' – that is, that actors aim to advance relatively stable, ordered preferences by drawing thoughtfully and logically on implicit models of how the world works, models which they update in the light of new information.

HIM is individualist in that the unit of analysis is the maximizing individual; the interests, for example, of families, clans, groups, regions, ethnicities, nations, and states from this perspective are reducible to the sum of individual interests of their constituent members. This is not as much wrong (though personally I doubt it) as it is limiting: much international relations theory (and typically in the more realist tradition) assumes that states pursue distinct, general interests and with some degree of autonomy. IPE puts more of an emphasis on this type of international politics in explaining the nature and pattern of international economic relations, which disappears from IpE.

Finally, HIM is materialist, in that its individual maximizers are interested in maximizing their command over material possessions – they are single-minded in their pursuit of more stuff. Thus the pursuit of status, prestige, power, security, or the costly commitment to an ideology, can only be understood as indirect means to material ends. To give an extreme and perhaps even caricatured example of this (but one which I heard expressed by a distinguished scholar working in this tradition), from this perspective a rational actor would prefer to be governed by foreigners if his personal income were marginally higher as a colonial subject than as the citizen of an independent country. This also points to the more general and perhaps less controversial point that IpE cannot account for the influence of nationalism as an independent variable (whereas IPE can – see Abdelal 2001; Helleiner and Pickel 2005).

Exclusive materialism pulls IpE away not just from politics, but further away still from sociology, history, and cultural studies. Certainly, these may be disciplines that many scholars of IpE are happy to leave behind. But, again, IPE as exemplified by the work of many of its founders was eagerly and voraciously interdisciplinary. To limit actors solely to materialist motives is again to narrow the range of questions that can be answered (or, worse, that can even be asked).

Into the monoculture

On the other hand, embracing HIM does make it easier to engage in formal modeling and large-scale statistical analysis. That is fine. The problem with HIM is *not* that it privileges studies of distributional conflict, or that inquiries in the HIM tradition tend to favor statistical analysis. This crucial point is easily misunderstood, so I will underscore it with a few examples from my own intellectual history. I spent a fair amount of time, for example, arguing that IPE scholars have been *underestimating* the role of distributional conflict in some macroeconomic policy choices (Kirshner 1998, 2001). I also greatly appreciate the use of statistical analysis for hypothesis testing. Indeed, my first, tentative scholarly effort – a senior honors thesis called 'Open Versus Closed Strategies of Development' (I was an economics major) – included two statistical tests. In my most recent book, I had a hypothesis that I saw could be evaluated quantitatively. I constructed two novel data sets, and was pleased to be able to find that the statistical analysis provided support for my argument (Kirshner 2007: 196–7).

To be sure, I have some reservations about the contemporary use of statistical analysis in political science (but I have some reservations about most things). I am quite enthusiastic about the use of quantitative tests, when appropriate, to test (that is, to provide evidence which supports or raises doubts about) a given hypothesis. However, with the amount of data around these days, and, crucially, with the speed and power of computers, I am concerned that it is too easy to trawl through vast pools of data and then come up with explanations based on what happens to show up in the net. (The most commonly heard answer at a political science job talk: 'I ran it that way.') I have also been greatly influenced by McCloskey, who, speaking to fellow economists, has for decades warned that econometrics encourages an emphasis on statistical significance at the expense of what could be called 'economic significance' (McCloskey 1985; McCloskey and Ziliak 1996). Similarly, I wonder if at times quantitative work in political science has chased statistical significance at the expense of what could be called 'political significance'. And especially with large data sets and the proliferation of increasingly specialized techniques, I am concerned that it has become easier to establish 'statistically significant' findings (that is, some deviation from randomness), even in the context of diminishing 'political significance'.

But these are qualifying reservations, and I would have some about any style of inquiry. No, the fundamental problem with HIM is not that it overemphasizes distributional conflict or certain methods; the problem, as Kathleen McNamara so convincingly explains in this collection, is with monocultures – a point echoed by Peter Katzenstein. In the United States at least, HIM has become hegemonic, and we are living in a monoculture with strict and narrow limits on the definition of legitimate inquiry. McNamara (and Katzenstein also) observes that things are more promising in book publishing (as opposed to the journals), where series at Cornell and Princeton University Presses (and elsewhere) still provide outlets for IPE scholarship outside the monoculture. But they also understand that the real action, where HIM has its foot on the jugular of the discipline, is in graduate training. Even Katzenstein, who, characteristically, 'remain(s) hopeful', nevertheless is forced to conclude that 'the elimination of pluralistic approaches to the subject of IPE in the seminars taught in the leading graduate programs is a more serious matter that bodes ill for the IPE field'.

Concerns for the future of the field loom ever larger when one considers three ironies associated with the rise of HIM. First, as good students of the international economics literature, IPE scholars certainly grasp the concept of comparative advantage. But this suggests that, as political scientists, our comparative advantage lies in our understanding of *politics*. Many IpE scholars, on the other hand, act as if (and sometimes say) that they wish to be as much like economists as possible. Second, often and increasingly (though not exclusively), 'political economy', especially at the level of graduate training, is *not* a synonym for 'a strong and rich command of economic theory', but rather is used as shorthand for 'using the types of methods that economists typically use in their work'. Thus IpE scholars are not only devaluing politics; they are, ironically as econophiles, drifting away from economic theory as well.

Finally, there is the mother of all ironies: the hyper-rationalists have successfully established a monoculture for reasons that can only be explained by constructivists: they have established an epistemic community that shares a set of self-fulfilling, aesthetic criteria as to what is considered 'good work'. David Lake, for example, has previously written that 'some of the best new research employs very large time series data-sets and powerful econometric tools' (Lake 2006: 772); in this collection, Lake refers to his preferred approach to the study of IPE, Open Economy Politics, as 'the most important paradigm in American IPE scholarship'. The key words in these two sentences are 'best' and 'important'. Lake attributes the triumph of HIM to its emergence as the winner in scientific struggle between competing approaches, but by what criteria of evaluation does he conclude which work is 'the best' and 'the most important'? The logic is circular, the tastes shared, the outcome the result of a positive feedback loop.[4]

Albert, Charlie, and John

As McNamara and Katzenstein observed, the hegemony of the HIM monoculture in graduate training matters. It is the mechanism by which the transformation of IPE to IpE will be reinforced, and, if unchecked, eventually locked in. It is visible not simply on graduate syllabi, but at that anxiety-filled moment of choosing a dissertation topic. This used to provoke an existential crisis: 'why did I go to graduate school?', 'what will I become?'. Nowadays, many if not most graduate students approach this instead by thinking first 'I must construct a big, novel data set', by thinking second 'I must then manipulate that data set in a way that shows I am proficient in techniques valued by the profession', and then finally asking 'what kind of question can I come up with that will satisfy the first two needs?'. It is as if it is 1974 and we are music teachers, saying to our students

> you can make any kind of music you want – Bach, Verdi, Reggae, Country, Salsa, Dylan, Blues, Zydeco, Disco – but you all have to play it on Moog synthesizers. Everyone knows, after all, that the new Moog Sonic 6 is the most sophisticated and advanced piece of musical equipment ever produced.

No doubt this approach would have produced some enormously talented musicians playing fine music. But it probably would have left us with a lot of disco (even if it was some of the best and most important disco ever produced), and it would have meant that many gifted musicians who didn't want to be synthesizer players would have left the field.

It is often overheard at political science meetings, usually over drinks, that 'people like John Maynard Keynes, Albert Hirschman, and Charles Kindleberger – all economists, no less! – could not get jobs today in Political Science departments', because their work would not meet the standards of the monoculture. But this is not right – it's actually much more tragic than that. A quick look at their intellectual histories would lead to the conclusion that Albert, Charlie, and

John could have easily taken, and aced, four or five semesters of statistics and two of game theory, and that they would have been capable of producing successful and celebrated work within the traditions of the monoculture. But chances are they wouldn't have wanted to, and they would have walked away and done something else. It's not that they couldn't get jobs today; it's that they wouldn't seek them. That is the monoculture in action.

What would we have lost? From Hirschman, for openers, no *Exit Voice and Loyalty*; no *National Power and the Structure of Foreign Trade* (which showed how important patterns of trade were determined by states pursuing power, not by individuals maximizing material interests); from Keynes, no *General Theory* (of course), and no *Economic Consequences of the Peace* (which was not just a brilliant polemic against the Versailles Treaty, but also a prescient, careful analysis of underappreciated economic fragilities in Europe and the world economy before and after the Great War); from Kindleberger, no *World in Depression*, no *Manias, Panics and Crashes*. This last book, published in 1978, presents a model that is not 'sophisticated' in the slightest by the standards of the gatekeepers of HIM IpE. Yet, written over 30 years ago, it is hard to imagine a more cogent explication of (or vital resource for understanding) the financial crisis of 2007–8.

'Monocultures', McNamara warns us in her chapter, 'are never healthy.' Like agricultural monocultures, intellectual monocultures are vulnerable to 'catastrophic failure'. But this second crisis of IPE theory may have a less successful resolution than the first, because, even in failure, a Nash Equilibrium is visible: the field will have less and less to say to anyone outside the monoculture, but inside the bubble, nothing will be heard but the sound of its own applause.

Notes

1 I thank Rawi Abdelal, Eric Helliener, Peter Katzenstein, and Karl Mueller for comments on earlier versions of this chapter.

2 Robinson located a similar 'first crisis' during the Great Depression.

3 Leading the charge were Richard Cooper (1968), Charles Kindleberger (1970), and Robert Keohane and Joseph Nye (1972); quickly on the heels of these followed the classic contributions of the 1970s.

4 See also the critiques raised by Cohen (2009: 140).

20 The gift of skepticism and the future of IPE

Louis W. Pauly

One fine morning in the fall of 1988, the telephone rang on my desk at the International Monetary Fund. 'Strange here. I'm calling from the lobby.' Recognizing her distinctive voice, I replied, 'Susan Strange?' 'Yes, of course. Listen, I understand that you studied at the LSE a few years ago.' 'Yes, indeed. In the mid-1970s. I even attended your oversubscribed lectures on "The politics of international business" when you were a part-time instructor.' 'Can we meet?' came the response from the now-distinguished professor. 'When?' 'How about now?' A few minutes later, my new mentor in international political economy (IPE) began her work by asking me question after question about what I was learning, whom I was meeting, and what we were all thinking.

Between my first distant meeting with Susan Strange and this surprising second one, I had worked in the banking industry in Montreal, New York, and Toronto but then left to pursue doctoral studies in government at Cornell. It was there that I was re-introduced to Susan's work and to that of the seven pioneers profiled in Benjamin J. Cohen's (2008b) *International Political Economy: An Intellectual History*, all of whom I soon came to know personally. I also encountered the stimulating work of the other pioneer who would have earned an honored place in the pantheon of IPE if someone else had written the book, namely, Cohen himself.

Many years later, my dissertation supervisor, Peter Katzenstein, distilled the summary lesson from all of these encounters in the term 'analytical eclecticism' – the pragmatic embrace of ontological and epistemological pluralism. Like others in this volume, with the exception of Bastiaan van Apeldoorn, Ian Bruff, and Magnus Ryner, I believe analytical eclecticism captures the essence of IPE and provides the key to the intellectual excitement that will attract the next generation of fine scholars to the field's 'Big Questions', like the ones Robert Keohane highlights in this volume. In her own idiosyncratic way, Strange foreshadowed the idea of disciplined open-mindedness and modeled it in her own professional life. Borrowing Cohen's organizing principle, one might discern the 'magnificent seven' tenets of Strange's scholarly philosophy. First and foremost, focus on real-world problems and puzzles. Second, seek useful theories that are as elegant and parsimonious as possible. Third, use whatever methods seem appropriate to examine them – including time-tested techniques of good economists, sociologists, historians, and (although only Susan would say it out loud) good journalists. Fourth, subject theoretical hunches to ruthless skeptical scrutiny. Fifth, consider plausible alternatives. Sixth, draw out implications for future theory and, in order to stay grounded, for future policy. Seventh, write and speak about this entire process of discernment clearly and accessibly.

The controversies spurred by Cohen's book well exemplify the notion that analytical eclecticism of the kind Strange championed is far more prevalent in our field than many might believe. Unlike others in this volume, this leaves me quite optimistic about the future. The IPE tent is a large one, and most of us inside want to keep it that way.

Toward fundamental consensus?

The emergence of an unhealthy monoculture in our field would certainly be worth worrying about, but my sense is that any such worry is still premature. Perhaps some fields can establish and maintain ideological or methodological conformity, but IPE is not among them. Three reasons leap to mind. First, those attracted to the study of international politics have an especially low tolerance for boredom. Although they can see the value of incremental 'knowledge production', testing, re-testing, and replication, they put a much higher value on innovation and novelty. This tendency may in fact be widely shared across the human sciences, but it seems especially prevalent in fields like IPE and International Relations. Big questions attracted us, and little answers can't sustain our interest.

The second reason for the failure of hegemonic bids in IPE, I suspect, has to do with the generally unsatisfying conclusions many participants see coming out of periodic waves of methodological specialization in some corners of the field, conclusions that endure only until a surprise confronts them. Robert Wade's contribution to this volume makes a similar point. By way of analogy, consider for a moment the shock to mainstream economics posed by the financial crisis that began in the summer of 2007. Alan Greenspan captured it well in a famous confession one year into the crisis.

> Yes, I found a flaw [in my thinking about free markets] and that is precisely the reason I was shocked because I'd been going for 40 years or more with very considerable evidence that it was working exceptionally well.... Those of us who have looked to the self-interest of lending institutions to protect shareholders' equity were in a state of shocked disbelief.
>
> (Greenspan 2008)

It is not hard to find similar moments of disquiet in the literatures of any of our own major schools of thought within IPE. If anything joins us together today, it is skepticism concerning the word 'end', as in the end of ideology, the end of history, or the end of capitalism.

The third reason for the continued openness of IPE has to do with the fact that participants have absorbed basic political lessons from their own studies. Inside the field, they know how to behave like realists or Gramscians, whether those are their stated scholarly faith-commitments or not. In short, they know all about the importance of balancing power, both material and ideational. Let me illustrate this point with another analogy. A friend of mine is a faculty member at a prominent Catholic university in the United States. A few years ago, the Vatican, worried about the weakening Catholic character of such universities, backed a preferential option for Catholics in the selection process for all new faculty members. The intervention likely achieved some of its intended effect in theology departments, but my friend tells me that it often backfired elsewhere. Given the sense among colleagues that any Catholic hired would be likely to win future favors unfairly from university administrators, some departments began quietly and informally to discriminate against Catholic candidates. Obviously, my friend only shared an ironic anecdote, but it certainly resonates with my own observation of reactions to hierarchical signaling in both IPE and IR. We distrust attempts to dominate turf within the discipline, and we enjoy undermining them.

Current fears of the abuse of professional power leading to intellectual monopolies are therefore overblown. Emanuel Adler and I have seen much to reinforce such a view during our three years as editors of *International Organization*. Indeed, it has been fascinating to observe the practice of anonymous peer review. Like our predecessors, we have taken the principle of fairness to define our own primary editorial obligation. We therefore always try to send papers to referees whom we hope will both understand them and provide useful criticism. We also need good advice if we are to make good decisions, so, for example, it would make no sense whatsoever to send a paper with a highly technical formal model or set of advanced quantitative tests to a critical constructivist allergic to mathematics, or vice versa. Beyond observing the fact that fellow-travelers – from both sides of the so-called transatlantic divide – are usually very tough critics, two noteworthy trends stand out from among reviews that do not summarily recommend that papers be rejected. Referees who might commonly be considered rationalists often conclude reviews of papers that might commonly be considered rationalist with a sentence like the following: ‘Although the analysis in this paper is sound and I can find little fault with it, the theoretical payoff is very modest and not likely to interest many readers.’ At the same time, rigorous constructivists reviewing solid constructivist papers not infrequently conclude with a phrase like this one: ‘The basic argument made in this paper is good and interesting, but its plausibility is insufficiently examined in the light of relevant empirical evidence, and reasonable alternative interpretations are not examined.’

My conclusion? Common sense still rules, and the idea that the peer-review process in our neck of the academic woods masks an ideological or methodological struggle that will eventually succeed in eliminating dissidents is much exaggerated. To be sure, that process is naturally conservative. When it works well, peer review is guided by some basic standards concerning what qualifies as good work. Although they are dynamic and constantly evolving, such standards define a scholarly community. In IPE at the present moment, these include clarity of thought, thematic significance, and a preference for counter-intuitive claims within a specific analytical framework. It is a rare reviewer who is fully prepared to say, ‘Although I do not share this author’s intellectual priors and I disagree with her argument, on its own terms the article contributes to important debates in the field and deserves to be published.’ But such reviewers do exist, and editors seeking such advice are not rare.

It must nevertheless be admitted that community standards at any given moment can occasionally lead reviewers and editors to miss brilliant flashes of original, even seminal thought. To be sure, all aggrieved authors feel that their misunderstood work falls into this category, but real errors of judgment, happily, are easy to correct. Sufficient is a little persistence on the part of authors convinced of their originality, regular turnover among journal editors (every five years in the case of *IO*), and the proliferation of new journals aspiring to rise rapidly in the league tables. In IPE, we have all heard about famous articles initially dismissed as ‘Marxist claptrap’, ‘realist story-telling’, or ‘semiotic mumbo-jumbo’. But we also know that they were eventually published anyway. More generally, our collective antennae are quite sensitive to contradictions, for example, when labels like ‘free markets’ and ‘open economy’ are deployed to undercut free and open debates. If we truly valued epistemological, methodological, or paradigmatic closure, perhaps so that we could be more useful to policy practitioners, we would have become economists-without-adjectives.

Finally, most scholars attracted to IPE continue to recognize hubris when they see it. On this point, Ronen Palan is on to something important in his chapter above when he bids us not to see the Atlantic Ocean as signifying the most important divide in contemporary IPE. If there are stylistic differences between American and British scholarship in IPE, there are plenty of US-style scholars in the United Kingdom and plenty of UK-style scholars in the United States and Canada. Moreover, if such distinctions were once strong, they began weakening a while ago. Both styles are now widely diffused, and article submissions to *IO* influenced by either or both traditions are now frequently coming in from Germany, France, the Netherlands, Switzerland, and the Scandinavian countries. To be sure, guiding promising papers from outside the Anglosphere through the vagaries of peer review remains a challenge, but the widest remaining gap concerns the rest of the world.

As Mark Blyth and Jason Sharman both note in this volume, good scholarship is now developing quite rapidly around the world, especially in Asia and South America. Little of it, however, yet makes it into leading IPE journals or scholarly presses in the Anglosphere. This divide renders the putative transatlantic one minor, really just a longstanding difference in academic tastes between cousins who actually understand one another all too well and who travel frequently across an already quite solid bridge. My guess is that it is financial constraint, and not simply linguistic and cultural divisions, that curtail broader participation in contemporary IPE (see Weaver’s chapter in this volume). A paramount challenge before us therefore is to build and strengthen new bridges by, for example, seeking and funding new research partnerships around the world, experimenting with new measures to open and expand the reach of our journals, investing in two-way translation efforts, providing more conference travel subventions to young scholars around the world, opening post-doctoral programs to candidates with degrees from outside the Anglosphere, and generally encouraging much greater faculty and student mobility. The challenge is beginning to get more attention from our leading scholarly associations. It deserves our time, energy, and financial resources.

An enduring legacy

My last meeting with Susan Strange came in Washington, DC at a scholarly convention in the year before her death. She was obviously unwell. Still, she insisted on joining a few old and new friends for dinner. She didn't eat much, but her appetite for knowing what was happening in the United States and in the minds of her companions was as healthy as ever. As usual, she gave voice to her frustrations, both with the direction of US foreign policy and with what she considered the narrowness of vision among those studying it, including many international political economists. We all knew that disappointment had long since driven her to put much personal energy behind potential counter-balancing forces in the British International Studies Association and the UK-based International Political Economy Group. But she still wanted to stay connected.

If she were with us today, Susan would surely be enjoying a brief 'I told you so' moment by reminding us of her prescient books, *Casino Capitalism* (1986) and *Mad Money* (1998). She might be reminding us of her famous *apologia*:

> I am doubly lucky to have had [both students and children] – and both have taught me a great deal. In return, I have tried to teach [them] not to expect justice in life – but to try hard to get it; to work hard – but to question authority, whether political or academic; to distrust ideologies – but to respect evidence; to avoid following the crowd – but to trust [their] own judgment and to stand up for [their] own ideas. The freedom to do so is one of which, in free countries, the universities should be the most jealous guardians. That and not the service of the state is the true justification for their existence.
>
> (Strange 1989: 436)

If Susan had survived to contribute to this volume, she would likely have focused on the future, her critical gaze aimed less at the transatlantic divide than at another becoming more obvious by the day. She would be taking scholars of IPE to task for our self-absorption within the Anglosphere and for our confidence that scholars from elsewhere will necessarily gravitate toward us and toward our way of thinking. She would be prodding us to leave our analytical comfort zones and to immerse ourselves as deeply as we possibly could outside them (for a step in this direction, see Blyth 2009b). She would herself most likely be wandering around Xi'an, Bangalore, Rio de Janeiro, Moscow, Teheran, Nairobi, and Jakarta, seeking out former students and new insights. Back home, she would be on the lookout for new dragons seeking to control the neighborhood.

21 The richness and diversity of critical IPE perspectives

Moving beyond the debate on the 'British school'

Bastiaan van Apeldoorn, Ian Bruff and Magnus Ryner

This chapter seeks to highlight the richness and diversity of 'critical IPE'. This should be viewed not as a singular but a collective and thus plural term, for although broadly committed to certain modes of inquiring into the world in which we live, critical IPE is defined by open and reflexive research. Therefore, this chapter seeks to outline what we feel has been unduly neglected in the debates which take place in the opening two parts of this volume – that is, the remit of political economy as classically conceived. As Smith, List and Marx at least implicitly agreed, political economy should be concerned with the co-constitution of production and power in order to ascertain the material conditions of existence of human civilizations. Indeed, this means that '[p]roduction creates the material basis for all forms of social existence, and the ways in which human efforts are combined in productive processes affect all other aspects of social life' (Cox 1987: 1).

We hope to demonstrate that this foundational starting point does not lead us into the 'grand theory' trap of deterministic and universal explanations, but rather orients us towards a complex world which requires conceptual reflection upon it in order to conduct research of any kind. For this reason (and inevitably), numerous 'critical IPE' perspectives exist, and indeed there have been many debates within and across them. Therefore, it is a body of scholarship that is both thriving and producing excellent journal articles and monographs. Moreover, as illustrated by the membership of a network that the three of us are part of – the Critical Political Economy Research Network (CPERN) of the European Sociological Association – such work extends well beyond that of the Anglo-Saxon world that is normally taken to be home to the discipline of IPE.

As such, it is inevitable that there will be more than merely two (national!) flavours in IPE and, more specifically, even if the 'critical' label is sometimes used too easily or even gratuitously, there is a growing community of European scholars that cannot be reduced to, or seen as merely a part of, 'British' IPE (however it is defined). Rather, steeped in the cultural milieux that once spawned continental philosophy, critical theory, or for that matter the mercantilist-historical school, these scholars do not recognize as theirs much of the current debates on the state of the discipline. This is particularly the case when one considers the first two parts of this volume, where most interventions did not transcend the rather narrow discourse in which the breadth of IPE is reduced to a dichotomy of 'American' rationalist-institutionalist approaches versus 'British' constructivist-institutionalist perspectives.

In addition, some serious misrepresentations of what critical IPE brings to the table were articulated during the course of these debates. For example, Mark Blyth believes that if one adheres to a Marxist perspective then the result is a closed and monotheistic approach to the world, and Geoffrey Underhill is critical of 'template theorizing' that cloaks an allergy to empirical work in radical posturing. Moreover, Benjamin Cohen (2007) has referred before now to 'leftist doctrines', and Helge Hveem in his contribution is unhappy with what he views as teleological, out-of-this-world positions which ignore the potential of combining rationalism and constructivism. While there are certainly examples that one could cite in support of these claims – and we have criticized such work in our own writings – this is hardly a trait peculiar to critical IPE. Poor research exists everywhere in IPE, and indeed in the social sciences as a whole.

Critical IPE: evolving, open-ended, progressive research

The issue, therefore, is what might constitute high-quality research and what this entails. In our view, and in contrast to the above assertions, critical IPE is a valuable and distinctive enterprise precisely because it is problem-driven. However, we depart from the chapters collected in the first two parts of this volume – where Katzenstein's notion of 'analytical eclecticism', which was advocated by many, appears sometimes to be nothing more than 'add perspective/factor x, perhaps y and maybe z, and stir' – by contending that '[e]ven what is in principle a holistic perspective cannot say everything and must necessarily prioritise' (Dunn 2009: 318). The complexity of the world in which we live means that research has to be undertaken in myriad overlapping and interconnected social relations. Hence to ascertain constituent determinants and their effects requires abstraction and therefore concept formation at every stage of the research process (Sayer 1992).

In other words, IPE, and social science in general, would not be possible without foundational assumptions. That is, *all* research is *necessarily* underpinned by a conceptual asymmetry; the scholar has chosen (implicitly or explicitly) to privilege certain ways of viewing the world over others (see Dunn 2009: 81–6). Hence the need for careful, reflexive research which seeks to make judgements without collapsing into an 'anything goes' stance which frequently leaves intact unacknowledged assumptions about how the world 'works' (Dunn 2009: 45). Different meta-theoretical foundations are thus part of what makes up the diversity of research within IPE – see, for example, Robert Gilpin's (2001: 15) comments on realism as a 'philosophic position' – that goes far beyond the misleading dichotomy of 'American' versus 'British' IPE. But this is not to assert that being critical is dependent upon or follows naturally from any particular social ontology, even if it might be incompatible with some. Nor does being critical imply a fixed commitment to a certain political programme; indeed, such dogmatism would be quite alien to critical thought. What critical approaches do share is the preoccupation with 'asking how orders [which may be of various nature] came about ... and how and whether they may be in the process of changing' (Cox 1986: 208), and an analytical commitment that relates detailed and local developments to the totality that they in part constitute (Wolf 1982). In other words, they advance a broadly 'global' perspective.

To further specify what it means to be critical one can do worse than consult Paul Connerton's (1976) review of the Frankfurt school. 'Critique' in this sense has its etymological root in the Reformation and refers to the art of informed judgement appropriate to the study of ancient texts. In the transition to the Enlightenment this method obtained a status separate from Church and Scripture, and the appeal of critique gradually displaced truth from revelation, from which it henceforth was distinguished. From this vantage point, Kant and Hegel advanced two distinct but related meanings of critique. From Kant we get critique in the sense of 'rational reconstruction' (Connerton 1976: 18). It concerns the conditions of possible knowledge and the potential abilities of human beings possessing the faculties of knowing, and indeed speaking and acting. The starting point of critique is via the senses only, for we need to order (through the way we perceive them) the incoherent profusion of impressions we receive into something comprehensible – that is, from arbitrary perception to systematic logical conception. Rational reconstruction is thus all about asking questions about our perceptions, their subjective limitations and the possible transcendence of these.

This brings us to critique in the second sense, developed by Hegel in his discussions of the Master and the Slave in the *Philosophy of Spirit*. Here critique denotes reflections 'on a system of *constraints*, which are humanly produced: distorting pressures to which individuals, or a group of individuals or the human race as a whole succumb in their process in self-formation' (Connerton 1976: 18; original emphasis). Critique in this sense entails revealing these constraints as humanly produced and thus dispelling their sense of inevitability and objectivity. As such, the adequacy of the given critical theory is rooted in the extent to which it both perceives the constraints that a given social subject faces and reconstructs the way(s) in which the world is conceptualized in order to help overcome such constraints.

This can be related to Underhill's complaint that critical IPE tends to reduce all matters to power. While not wishing to say that power relations are all that matter, it is clear to us that the representation of humanly produced constraints as natural and objective is intimately bound up in power relations in a broad sense. As the likes of Gramsci, Lukes and Foucault have taught us, some of the most profound aspects of power are difficult to observe without some conceptual apparatus. The claim of being able to observe these does not hinge on a privileged access to them as such; it has to do with deploying conceptual frameworks that are geared exactly towards analysis of such aspects. To cite Gilpin again (2001: 31), 'what you seek is what you find'.

Given what we have said above, it is clear that we make no apologies for considering it legitimate to make a mainly 'interpretative' contribution by reconceptualizing and recasting well-known 'facts' by putting them in a new context. Nevertheless, this does not mean that critical IPE shuns hard empirical work; on the contrary, this is a necessity. Although conceptual reflection is an essential part of research inasmuch as it is concepts that allow us to make sense of – that is, to interpret and re-interpret – social reality in the first place, empirical analysis is an equally integral part as it enables us to see whether our concepts and theories themselves make sense. It is the latter that also ensures that our scholarly practices are 'realist' in the broadest sense of the word. From a critical (theoretical) perspective, this 'realism' is indispensable. If the purpose of our knowledge is to further human freedom by raising awareness of what constrains it, we need to make sure that we actually get a grasp of those structures and are able to distinguish the necessary from the contingent. This is clearly preferable to either positing the existence of structures that are not there in reality or, in an idealist move, just defining out of existence whatever you do not wish to see.

Drawing on Lakatos, Michael Burawoy (1998: 5) has usefully understood this to entail a 'dialogue' between theory and empirics, where falsification cannot result in the all-out abandonment of a theory (because that rests on unrealistic assumptions about the independence of observation from conception), but should rather result in the 'parsimonious reconstruction of theory to accommodate anomalies'. If there is a strong dissonance between empirics and theory, the most parsimonious accommodation that is possible may result in the abandonment, or at least a radical reformulation, of the theory. And to build on an earlier point, this calls for a conceptual asymmetry that is both explicit – for we must decide what to study and write about – and built into methodologies and research design. As is suggested by the meaning of the word, the commitment to such asymmetry entails remaining on the uncertain but entirely appropriate terrain which positions us between slavishly adhering to a particular perspective and abandoning informed reflexivity about how we conduct research.

Burawoy's modified falsification principle is, in our view, a good one for IPE of all stripes and certainly one to which critical IPE should submit as well. At the same time, as Burawoy also makes clear, what counts as 'facts' is a deeply problematic question. Statistical categories are not conceptually – and hence politically – innocent, as revealed, for example, by Isabella Bakker's (1994) feminist work on the 'strategic silences' in national accounts with regard to reproductive work. Cynthia Enloe (1996: 186–202) has also demonstrated with great effect that International Relations, because of a narrow definition of what are considered to be legitimate 'facts' to draw upon (and discounting ethnography), totally missed the causes of the Chiapas crisis in Mexico, although 'the evidence' was there for the perceptive and conceptually astute to see. In a similar vein, Jeffrey Harrod (2006) has shown that what he calls 'conceptual dustbins' – such as overly stylized categories like 'the informal sector' – result in international organizations collecting population statistics of limited use for understanding the multiple unequal power relations experienced by 'the poor' (viewed merely as varieties of poverty by these institutions). He contends that this constrains strongly our ability to understand and inquire into the varied forms of alienation and antagonism that generate oppositional movements – and prospects for (counter) hegemonic strategies – in the capitalist periphery. Therefore, consideration of 'the facts' in IPE must entail a much more (dare we say) critical attitude towards the categories that are handed down to us by the dominant agents of the global political economy than what the debate suggests. Part of the problem for critical scholarship is that it often depends on data that is not systematically collected, and that it has limited resources in generating such data itself.

For this reason, we would argue – in contrast to Catherine Weaver's and Craig Murphy's assertions – that merely to measure the success of critical scholarship by the impact it has on policy is naive inasmuch as it rests on an assumption that governments would listen readily to such a position. (Murphy is remarkably sanguine as to why 'Left' policy prescriptions 'failed', as if they were simply not as good as 'Right' recommendations.) Indeed, Weaver's claim that we should put Pierre Bourdieu's work in 'the back seat' flies in the face of the detailed (quantitative and qualitative) empirical research he conducted throughout his career *and* the significant impact he made on French and also more broadly European political debates in the 1990s on socio-economic reform and globalization (although perhaps less so in the United Kingdom and the United States). Therefore, there is more than one path to high-quality research and to interventions in political and social debates. That being said, critical theory makes no apologies for relating its knowledge production to normative commitments through a broad conception of social praxis. It may be the case that most critical scholarship is broadly commensurate with 'the Left', but if this is so, it is a well motivated antidote to the knowledge production that systematically has favoured 'the Right' (one example being the growing emphasis by UK funding agencies on descriptors such as 'esteem' and 'impact').

As such, we believe that in critical IPE we can find progressive research programmes that are also critical in their emancipatory commitments. In keeping with what we have outlined above, such programmes are distinct from much of the IPE that has been represented in the debate thus far, above all with respect to the kind of questions that are being asked. These questions relate to interrogating hegemonic discourses and practices – whether within the social sciences or within society, and often pointing out the inner connections between the two – and thereby seeking to reveal the power structures within the global political economy that limit the realization of human freedom. Most emphatically, this does not prevent but rather requires the production of high-quality empirical research.

Although critical political economy in this sense has a long history, within IPE there is also a new and growing generation of scholars producing excellent empirical research within this tradition – research that is testimony to a thriving intellectual enterprise that transcends the narrow terms of the current debate. This work is neither 'American' nor 'British', and it does not fit either Cohen's or anyone else's canon, but it is definitely part of the 'discipline' of IPE.

Examples just from CPERN members include Jan Drahokoupil's research on the differential but connected transitions to capitalism among the Visegrád Four countries in central and eastern Europe (Drahokoupil 2008), Martijn Konings' sustained interrogation of the nature of American financial power since the end of the Bretton Woods system and the implications for our understanding of the present economic crisis (Konings 2009), and Susanne Soederberg's critical inquiries into the nature of global governance in relation to neoliberal economic strategies in developing countries (Soederberg 2006), as well as the work of many others.

Critical IPE and the evolving global political economy

In sum, critical IPE perspectives are characterized by a richness and diversity that extends well beyond the academic nationalism that the US/UK dichotomy encourages. Furthermore, being self-consciously critical by definition implies being reflexive and open to new interpretations and perspectives. For this reason, we are keen to stress that we do not believe that we have found the philosopher's stone which enables us to enjoy an inherent advantage over all other approaches. For instance, despite the above recognition of the work of feminist scholars, the question of social reproduction has often been a blind spot. 'Public' notions of production that are prevalent across IPE, critical or otherwise, have tended to marginalize the constitutive role of unequal gender relations in the emergence and ongoing reproduction of capitalism (Steans and Tepe 2010). Moreover, the recent upsurge of contributions aimed at reorienting IPE towards everyday life as means of correcting its (and IR's) perceived excessive bias towards the macro level is another challenge to be taken up (Hobson and Seabrooke 2007).

It is clear to us that the approach outlined above is more than capable of engaging with these issues and developments, and indeed a closer scrutiny of the critical IPE literatures will reveal that some such work already exists. Consider, for example, Teresa Healy's (2006) analysis of the integral dialectics of gender and class in Mexico's post-NAFTA restructuring. This work is revealing not just because of how it addresses social reproduction as well as more 'public' notions of production; it is also because of the particular manner in which it explores the internal relations between high politics and the everyday. Healy achieves this via a more comprehensive exploration of the potential contained in Cox's paradigmatic work and his neglected, disaggregated conception of 'modes of social relations of production'. Hence, her contribution is also an excellent illustration of how future research ought to engage in a less selective reading of previous works in order to better realize their potential when considering contemporary issues and debates. Nevertheless, the number of examples in this respect is still small, and more needs to be done in order to substantiate the confidence we have (although see Bruff 2010).

A critical analysis of the (gendered) politics of everyday life and the global political economy should not only help us to better understand the constitution of extant social structures and their reproduction, but also their potential for transformation – given that what we study are humanly produced and thus amenable to change. Indeed, we need to be more open to the possibility – and thus take the inherently relational nature of the micro–macro connection more seriously than has sometimes been the case – that some of the structures and processes within the global political economy that we have been studying over the past decades are subject to shifts and transformations that raise new questions for research. This calls not just for new conceptual imaginations, but also for a rediscovery of older insights within the rich tradition of critical political economy. This seems to be especially pertinent in light of the current global and financial crisis, and of what some see as an interrelated (hegemonic) shift towards East Asia within the global political economy.

Although it is too early to fully assess the consequences of the crisis within global capitalism, it is clear that it has deepened what was arguably *already* a multifaceted crisis of the neoliberal globalization process that has been driving the restructuring of the global political economy for some years, diverse aspects of which have been studied by many of us within 'critical IPE'. In turn, this necessitates a reflexive and open-ended approach to processes at a range of levels that are in the midst of potentially transformative change. While on the one hand we observe social forces in both the core and the periphery increasingly resisting the neoliberal discipline of commodification, we on the other hand see a tendency towards increasingly illiberal state practices partly in response to these pressures, and growing sympathy to calls for a strong (even authoritarian) state to prop up a disintegrating social order. This raises the question of whether the current crisis may lead to the neoliberal order morphing into a new, similarly unequal form, rather than anything more progressive (cf. Kannankulam 2008).

Similarly, the rise of what is arguably a 'statist' capitalism in the erstwhile periphery (China in particular) implies not just a challenge to 'Western' liberal capitalism but also to our established understandings of the current world order. This suggests that – in addition to the above suggestions – we need to become more attentive again to geopolitics, as this has made something of a comeback since the turn of the millennium in the context of the aforementioned power shifts as well as in response to, and as an expression of, a new variety of US imperialism. Although the tradition of critical political economy provides a rich and diverse source of insights into the geopolitical, some seemed to be placed on the backburner while many of us focused on the apparently inexorable deterritorialization logic of globalization. However, lest we retreat from arguably too strong a globalism perspective into an unwarranted state-centrism, it is crucial that rather than taking geopolitical dynamics as a separate and autonomous realm, we – reconnecting to the traditions alluded to above – analyse how these dynamics are internally related to those of capitalist accumulation and to capitalist social relations in general (cf. Callinicos and Rosenberg 2008).

In light of the above developments, and with a view to continuing the thriving research programmes within critical IPE, we thus need to do two things. One, we need to recognize the rising contradictions to and limits of global neoliberalism, and the concomitant growing contestation of and resistance to it at multiple levels (e.g. van Apeldoorn *et al.* 2009). Two, we need to engage with the question of what may come after neoliberalism (e.g. Brenner *et al.* 2010), and what this might imply for our understanding of the opportunities for and constraints on human emancipation, whether conceived at the micro or macro level, or indeed both.

Conclusion

The above discussion indicates the continued potential of critical IPE perspectives, and reminds us of the redundancy of subjective assertions that, intentionally or not, limit dialogue to notions of academic nationalism. Therefore, although the debates in the chapters collected here have been superficially beneficial as an exercise in stock-taking, we need to move beyond them. The fact that, as Palan argues, many IPE scholars failed to foresee the current crisis – even in the minimal sense that trouble was brewing through the 2000s – is a stark warning against intellectual navel-gazing and an indication of the need to engage critically with the complex world in which we live. Whether this is achieved via a systematic examination of the current economic crisis through historical reflection (McNally 2009), a study of the conflict-ridden relationship between Latin America and global capitalism (Robinson 2008), a focus on the gendered and racialized nature of liberalization and development in Southeast Asia (Elias 2010) or indeed whatever else, is in some ways less important than the continued existence of spaces for such scholarship to thrive and flourish.

22 The global financial crisis

Lessons and opportunities for international political economy

Layna Mosley and David A. Singer

L. Mosley and D.A. Singer (2009) 'The Global Financial Crisis: Lessons and Opportunities for International Political Economy', *International Interactions* Vol. 35, No. 4, pp 420–429.

The global financial crisis that began in 2007 is a once-in-a-lifetime event with wide-ranging consequences for government policy-making. The crisis has prompted much soul-searching among economists and financial experts who failed to anticipate it, or whose warnings were not taken seriously by regulators and investors. Scholars of international political economy (IPE), however, are generally not in the business of predicting financial crises or recessions, and so the field is unlikely to see the crisis as a manifestation of scholarly failure. Yet the crisis may have an appreciable impact on the trajectory of IPE, just as the downfall of the Soviet Union shaped subsequent scholarship on international relations and great-power conflict and prompted a movement away from grand, and toward mid-range, theories.

We discuss three categories of inquiry – or puzzles within the realm of global finance – that have received relatively little attention within the field of IPE, but which should receive greater scrutiny as a result of the crisis: the determinants of cross-national variation in financial regulation; patterns of cooperation and discord within global regulatory bodies and the involvement of emerging-market countries in these bodies; and the interplay between individual firms-as-political-actors and public policy outcomes.

Domestic financial regulation

There is considerable cross-national and temporal variation in the manner in which national governments regulate their financial sectors. Some aspects of this variation are particularly striking. Government ownership of banks is still prevalent in certain countries of the Organisation for Economic Cooperation and Development (OECD), including Greece, Italy, Portugal, and Switzerland, and is relatively common in the developing world. The dynamics of regulation in these countries – in particular, the relationships between regulators and regulated firms – almost certainly differ from countries in which there is a clear public–private divide.

Regulators themselves also differ across countries, in their ties to other government bureaucrats and elected leaders. Some regulators are relatively independent from political pressures and from the entities they regulate, while others are highly susceptible to partisan pressures or regulatory capture. In some nations, central banks are responsible for bank supervision, while other countries have separate – and sometimes multiple – agencies for bank supervision (Copelovitch and Singer 2008). Perhaps most importantly, there are substantial cross-national differences in the content of regulation, including capital requirements, financial transparency, holding company supervision, and portfolio limitations. These regulatory differences are of interest for scholars of comparative politics as well as international relations, because disparate national policy requirements are potential drivers of international systemic risk. Given the diversity of national regulatory structures, multinational firms' incentives for forum shopping and regulatory arbitrage are significant. And given contemporary global financial interdependence, the system as a whole is vulnerable to financial instability within any individual country.

To date, the study of domestic financial regulation has received relatively little attention from political scientists in the International Relations subfield. Existing studies often focus on individual countries or regions rather than taking a broader cross-national approach.[1] The field of IPE has generally not appreciated the fact that cross-national differences in domestic financial regulation can have international repercussions. While the open-economy implications of domestic policy areas such as central banking, taxation, and even welfare spending have garnered substantial attention, the political economy of domestic financial regulation has remained curiously outside the traditional confines of the IPE field.[2]

Today's financial crisis highlights the international salience of domestic regulation. Countries with relatively lax banking supervision, such as Belgium and the United Kingdom, were more vulnerable to the contagious effects of the bursting of the housing bubble in the United States than were countries with more conservative banking restrictions, such as Australia and Spain. To be sure, assessing the effects of regulatory laxity or stringency is no easy matter. Canada, for example, employs a principles-based approach to regulation, which is ostensibly less stringent than the rigid rules-based (or 'checklist') approach of US regulators. However, the Canadian banking sector has been remarkably resilient during this financial crisis, whereas US banks are faltering as a result of imprudent decisions, such as shifting risky investments off their balance sheets, that were technically in compliance with regulators' dictates. Future empirical analyses of domestic regulatory variation, then, would need to consider not only the formal procedures in place, but their application in practice (e.g., Quillin 2008).

Will scholars of IPE take an interest in domestic financial regulation? The macroeconomic developments of the 1970s and 1980s provide a clue. After the fall of the Bretton Woods monetary system, scholars began to pay more attention to the inflation that wreaked havoc on the industrial world, from the first oil shocks and into the 1980s. Economists noted the importance, in a rational expectations setting, of institutional mechanisms that addressed policy-makers' time-inconsistency problems. Empirically, they began to assess the political independence of central banks and the relationship between these institutional structures and inflation outcomes. At the same time, political scientists began to explore the range of reforms that countries undertook to manage their economies in the absence of a dollar- and gold-based currency standard. Over time, the field of IPE came to embrace the study of exchange rate regimes, the politics of currency crises, the structures and mandates of central banks, and the liberalization of capital controls.

Some of these topics – especially central bank independence – were ostensibly domestic in nature, and yet the steady increase in capital mobility and economic integration made their international implications clear. For example, countries that chose to grant independence to their central banks could expect lower borrowing costs on international capital markets (Maxfield 1997); those that fixed their exchange rates could potentially benefit from increased international trade (Klein and Shambaugh 2006); and governments that altered their provision of welfare-state programs could expect a corresponding change in public perceptions of globalization and political support for economic openness (Baker 2005; Hays *et al.* 2005; Scheve and Slaughter 2004).

The incorporation of these topics into IPE scholarship offers a clue as to the trajectory of future scholarship. The global financial crisis has laid bare the international consequences of domestic regulatory policies. Several areas are ripe for exploration, including the determinants of domestic financial regulation, the measurement of the political independence of regulatory agencies, and more generally, the relative impact of domestic and international influences on national regulatory outcomes. However, barriers to entry for IPE scholars are relatively high. Graduate students often perceive financial regulation as a topic too arcane to understand, especially in the context of also needing to master a variety of methodological tools and existing theoretical literatures. While this may be an unfair stereotype, financial regulation is indeed a complex phenomenon, and not only because of the dizzying array of financial instruments and domestic and international regulatory bodies.

The complexity of regulation also results from the ways in which regulatory institutions emerge. Today's regulatory regimes, especially the configuration of regulatory agencies and the varying responsibilities of central banks, are likely to reflect a path-dependent process of piecemeal legislative decisions, historical accidents, and possibly international diffusion of policy innovations over the course of many decades (see Bach and Newman 2007; Copelovitch and Singer 2008; Levi-Faur 2005; Posner 2005). This makes large-N statistical analysis of the determinants and effects of financial regulation extremely challenging: regulatory structures are unlikely to stem from current interest-group configurations, partisan biases, electoral institutions, or epistemic communities. This is not to say that single-country or small-N studies are the only resort for studies of regulation: some regulations (such as capital adequacy requirements) exist in a variety of institutional contexts, and governments are able to modify such rules without necessarily reforming their regulatory structures writ large. In such cases, large-N analyses can reveal important patterns. In others, however, a more historically sensitive, qualitatively focused approach is necessary to tease out causal relationships. Whereas students tend to perceive the study of finance as one that largely involves econometric and formal work, the study of its regulation is one in which interview, archival, and process-tracing techniques also may be particularly important.

Global governance

There are early signs that the crisis has prompted the greater inclusion of emerging-market countries in global financial governance. Whereas the Group of Seven (G7) was the common negotiating forum for macroeconomic policy as well as for global efforts at financial standards and codes throughout the 1990s, the Group of Twenty (G20) has emerged as the locus of international cooperation in the aftermath of today's financial crisis. To date there have been two high-profile meetings of the G20. The first, in November 2008, resulted in a fairly detailed communiqué in which member states committed to pursuing regulatory and financial reforms in areas such as capital adequacy, liquidity management, and the expansion of regulation to previously unregulated financial institutions (Helleiner and Pagliari 2008). The second meeting, in April 2009, resulted in a communiqué that reaffirmed the commitments from the November meeting but also emphasized international cooperation on fiscal and monetary policy, and pledged to triple the resources of the International Monetary Fund (IMF) and support a new $250 billion allocation of Special Drawing Rights (SDRs). G20 governments also agreed to dismantle the rich-country Financial Stability Forum (a main locus of global regulatory efforts during the last decade; see Drezner 2007) and establish a more inclusive Financial Stability Board, which would give voice to all G20 members (G20 2009).

The increasing prominence of the G20, and of emerging-market countries in general, could signal a move away from a Bretton Woods-era distribution of global financial power, in which sizeable economies such as Brazil's and India's have been given short shrift in international governing bodies. Of particular importance is China, whose previous exclusion from the international bargaining table was particularly striking in light of its enormous economy – currently behind only the European Union and the United States – and its substantial holdings of dollar-denominated reserve assets. China was an active participant in the G20 summits and even pushed (unsuccessfully) its own agenda of supplanting the dollar with an alternative global currency, possibly based on the International Monetary Fund (IMF)'s SDRs or some other construction.[3] An expanded role for major emerging-market countries may suggest that, within the context of individual institutions, scholars will need to consider the extent to which shifts in formal governance structures (including IMF quotas) generate changes in institutional behavior. For example, will an increased quota for China lead to appreciable changes in the IMF's lending behavior, or will the preferences of the G7 – shaped by post-colonial ties, security considerations, and cross-border financial relationships – continue to shape the IMF's decisions? (Copelovitch forthcoming; Dreher *et al.* 2009; Pop-Eleches 2008; Stone 2008).

Beyond the participation of China, though, the efforts to expand the number and type of countries involved in global governance may fall short. The marked public pressure for inclusion suggests that the G20 will indeed be the locus of many future discussions of regulation and governance. But the sheer size of the group, as well as its diversity of interests, domestic political environments, and development levels, will render agreements difficult. Relying on the G20 could alter the distributional nature of negotiated outcomes (leading to different locations along the Pareto frontier), but it also makes such outcomes harder to achieve (so that reaching the Pareto frontier becomes less likely). This may, however, be perfectly acceptable to some current G7 members, particularly the United States: given the ambivalence of the United States toward past global regulatory efforts, the US government may correctly anticipate that the G20 forum will lead to gridlock. And indeed, the ostensible success of the first two G20 meetings might reflect the consonance of the group's proposals with the reform agenda of the Financial Stability Forum, rather than a significant shift beyond the G7's preferred outcomes (Helleiner and Pagliari 2008).

The financial crisis, then, poses a test not only of the efficacy of existing global governance institutions, but also of existing theories of international cooperation. A breakdown in negotiations within the G20 could open a window of opportunity for national and regional governance initiatives – such as the creation of an Asian banking standard, or the development of disparate national regulatory standards – as well as bilateral discussions between key players such as the United States and China (in a so-called G2 forum). If the complex labyrinth of transgovernmental regulatory networks fails to promote international cooperation in the midst of a truly global crisis, then scholars of IPE will have to re-evaluate whether the structures of global financial governance have an independent impact on state behavior (e.g., Slaughter 2004). Scholars also will need to consider whether a proliferation of trans- and intergovernmental institutions leads to higher levels of cooperation, or to increased opportunities for 'forum shopping', especially by powerful countries. More research is required to understand the conditions under which the multiplication of institutions, including the various 'G' groupings, the Basel Committee, the International Organization of Securities Commissions, and a host of others, fosters regulatory convergence, and the circumstances under which this proliferation generates centrifugal pressures that lead to regulatory fragmentation.

Public–private interactions

A third way in which the current crisis may alter the face of IPE scholarship concerns the treatment of private actors, particularly financial firms, as key players in the policy-making process. In the wake of the Asian financial crisis, efforts to govern global finance – to improve the transparency of economic policy-making, or to standardize accounting rules – often were located in the private sector. In some cases, public-sector initiatives were backed by private-sector enforcement, with the hopes that such private-market pressures would improve compliance. In other cases, private actors sat alongside finance ministry officials and central bank personnel, helping to craft new rules. And in still other circumstances, industry self-regulation was the norm (Mosley 2009). Although the rise of private actors as direct regulators occurred in some realms of finance as well as in areas such as human and labor rights (Bartley 2005; Vogel 1995), scholars paid very little attention to this phenomenon.[4] Thus far, relatively little research has explored the conditions under which delegation to the private sector occurs or the extent to which it is effective.

The participation of private financial actors in the governance of various elements of finance reminds us of the more general importance of firms as political, as well as economic, actors. In the case of delegation to private actors, firms play a direct role in the creation and/or enforcement of global and national standards, such as accounting and auditing rules (Büthe and Mattli 2005). In other instances, multinational corporations have created their own codes of conduct for labor and environmental practices, which may supplement or substitute for existing national laws. In still other instances, private-sector assessments – such as corporate and sovereign credit ratings, or indices of government corruption – are used as part of public regulatory efforts (Sinclair 2005). Even when firms are not directly involved as creators of regulatory structures, they often play an important, albeit indirect, role. In a wide range of issue areas, they respond to political institutions, lobby elected officials for policy changes, and implement (or refuse to implement) a wide range of national laws.

In the area of finance, the current crisis has cast an ominous shadow over the concept of industry self-regulation and the involvement of private firms in shaping their own regulatory environments. Willem Buiter (2009) recently quipped that 'self-regulation stands to regulation as self-importance stands to importance'. Legislators have accused financial regulators of being too cozy with the firms under their jurisdictions, and the regulators themselves are now scrambling for new authority to supervise previously unregulated firms such as hedge funds and some financial holding companies. The backlash against industry involvement in regulation could be a double-edged sword. The crisis might prompt regulators to expand their jurisdictions to non-bank financial institutions and complex financial instruments like derivatives, and to shift toward a more adversarial relationship with their regulated constituents. On the other hand, the lack of buy-in from regulated firms could hinder the implementation phase of new regulations (Mosley 2003) and foster new forms of regulatory arbitrage, revealing again the importance of domestic regulatory structures for global financial stability.

From the point of view of IPE scholarship, direct and indirect firm participation in the making and enforcement of regulations highlights the empirical and theoretical importance of micro-level (or firm-level) analyses. While many theories of IPE are based on firm-level behaviors – for instance, on the preference of import-competing firms for protection, or on the desire of multinational corporations to invest in locales with stable property rights – very few empirical analyses occur at the firm level.[5] Rather, much scholarship employs aggregate national (or sectoral) data to test firm-level propositions. While such analyses allow for relatively large samples in the context of limited (sub-national) data availability, they also obscure much of the variation within sectors and countries. As such, they may fail to illuminate the precise causal mechanisms by which firms influence public policy outcomes. What are the sources of firm preferences over public policies? Under what conditions do firms pressure governments for regulatory changes? And what determines governments' responsiveness to such demands, beyond select firms' perceived status – as we might think about in the recent cases of AIG, Citigroup, or even General Motors – as 'too big to fail'? Analyzing the policy preferences and political activities of firms in a range of sectors and countries should be of considerable interest to scholars of IPE, particularly in light of the current crisis.

Conclusion

This chapter identifies three areas of study within IPE that should receive greater attention in the coming years. Financial regulation is certain to receive increased scrutiny; indeed, concepts such as capital adequacy and mark-to-market accounting – previously considered arcane – have already received substantial coverage in the press. Political scientists should have more to say about the political determinants and economic consequences of these regulations, especially as they relate to global financial stability. The financial crisis also highlights, and perhaps promotes, shifting patterns of global governance, including the greater inclusion of developing countries in international standard-setting bodies and the resulting difficulties in reaching meaningful agreements. These shifts, coupled with the increasing financial clout of China, should trigger a re-evaluation of the efficacy of transgovernmental networks, soft law, epistemic communities, and international cooperation more generally. And finally, the extraordinary prominence of a handful of large firms as instigators and victims of the financial crisis should prompt a closer look at the linkages between government policy-makers and specific firms, especially those with the dubious honor of being 'too big to fail'.

Beyond these key issues, the crisis also points to a much larger question: is global finance is entering a new era, one that eventually will be seen as the successor to the Bretton Woods system and the three decades of muddling through that followed it? Will the current financial crisis mark the emergence of a distinctive set of global rules for currencies, capital flows, financial regulation, and transparency? IPE scholars, just like everyone else, will have to wait and see.

Notes

1 Notable examples of national or regional treatments of financial regulation by political scientists include Amyx (2006), Huang *et al.* (2005), Moran (1991), Rosas (2007), Rosenbluth (1989), Underhill (1997), and Vogel (1996). Braithwaite and Drahos (2006) and Rosenbluth and Schaap (2003) take a cross-national approach. See Kapstein (1994) and Wood (2005) on international banking regulation and Singer (2004, 2007) on the domestic origins of international financial regulation.

2 Recent work by economists highlights the cross-national variation in bank supervision and analyzes its effect on macroeconomic outcomes. See, for example, Barth *et al.* (2006).

3 Market size alone is an imperfect indicator of regulatory influence; see Bach and Newman (2007).

4 Exceptions include Büthe and Mattli (2005), Cutler (2003), Haufler (2000), and Mattli and Woods (2009).

5 Notable exceptions include Bauer *et al.* (1963), Jensen (2007), Mares (2003), Martin and Swank (2001), Milner (1988) and Murphy (2004).

23 Toward a new consensus

From denial to acceptance

Benjamin J. Cohen[1]

Little did I anticipate, when I first undertook to write an intellectual history of International Political Economy (IPE) (Cohen 2008b), that I might trigger a debate as rich and extensive as that represented in the pages of this collection. My purpose in highlighting what I described as a transatlantic divide – first in an essay in the *Review of International Political Economy* (Cohen 2007) and then in my book, *International Political Economy: An Intellectual History* (Cohen 2008b) – was of course not innocent. Long distressed by the lack of communication between different factions within IPE's 'invisible college', I had modestly hoped to stir up at least a bit of interest in renewed exchange and dialogue. The impact, however, has gone well beyond my expectations. Evidently my discontent with the state of the field was shared by many. The tinder was there; all that was needed was a spark.

My main premise was straightforward. Within the English-speaking world, the study of IPE had become divided between two broad 'schools': one, an 'American' school, hewing close to the norms of conventional social science, emphasizing the twin principles of positivism and empiricism; the other, a 'British' school, more inclusive and multidisciplinary in nature and more critical and normative in tone. Catherine Weaver captures the comparison well in her left brain, right brain metaphor. The American school is rationalist, practical, and prizes objectivity above all. Analysis is all about the logics of causation and consequence. The British school, by contrast, is interpretive, skeptical about rational choice, and rejects a positivist epistemology. Analysis focuses more on institutions and history and aspires to say something powerful about broad questions of equity and social justice.

Worse, the two schools had become increasingly isolated and insular, largely deaf to what the other had to offer. Some four decades ago, back when the modern field of IPE was just getting started, Susan Strange (1970) wrote of the regrettable 'case of mutual neglect' that had long persisted between students of international economics and international relations (IR). The triumph of Strange and the other pioneering scholars that I wrote about in my *Intellectual History* was that they succeeded, quite remarkably, in overcoming that historical dialogue of the deaf. The sad irony, I suggested, was that in time a new case of mutual neglect had developed, between the American and British schools. Today a new effort was needed to 'build bridges' between disparate intellectual traditions.

Reactions to my argument, not surprisingly, have been mixed, as the chapters in this volume testify. Commentary on the transatlantic divide, in effect, has traced all four of the classic stages of grief: denial, anger, bargaining, and – finally – acceptance. Some sources have questioned whether a problem even exists; others have denounced any effort to talk about it; yet others have sought to redefine or refine the issues involved. In the end, however, a broad consensus does seem to have been forged. The field of IPE is fractured, and something ought to be done about it. Collectively, the chapters in this volume help us to see what our future priorities should be.

Denial and anger

The first two stages of grief are said to be denial and anger. Each is a natural, reflexive mode of response to an unwelcome surprise. Both could be found in initial reactions to the issues I raised.

Some sources, for example, acknowledged that a divide may exist but denied there was any point to discussing it. On the American side of the pond, a sense of self-satisfaction prevailed. Little value could be added, I was told, by an attempt to promote transatlantic dialogue. British IPE 'is not positivist social science', wrote one senior US colleague in private correspondence. So 'there really is not much room for discussion … There is simply not enough common language, or enough common understanding … Conversations across this barrier are essentially fruitless'. On the British side, responses were more defensive. One scholar in the United Kingdom insisted that in calling for more bridges between the two schools, my intention could only have been 'to prolong the reach and the hegemony of US IPE by absorbing British IPE into its project'. Another described my approach as 'smelling of US intellectual imperialism'. Responses like these might be thought risible were they not also indicative of a truly grave malaise in the field.

Others reacted angrily, contending that any talk of distinct schools would only serve to polarize the field. Scholars would feel the need to declare their allegiance to one side or the other, hardening positions. So why not just let sleeping dogs lie? Representative is Catherine Weaver in this volume, who confesses to some concern that 'the more we think and write about ourselves in terms of competing schools of thought, the more we make the divide real'. Similarly, Eric Helleiner worries that we 'might be about to plunge into a long phase of navel gazing'. But as scholars, can we really afford the luxury of avoiding debate just because, as Helleiner puts it, 'it can be overdone'? Divisions over matters of ontology and epistemology are integral to all the social sciences. Argument is essential if we are to avoid intellectual complacency. If we do not occasionally rouse the sleeping dogs, testing hidden assumptions, how can we ever have confidence in the foundations of our research?

Besides, no one can claim to have a monopoly on truth. We all can learn from one other, as both Weaver and Helleiner ultimately concede. Even as they fret about the risk of deepening the transatlantic divide, they acknowledge the costs of the status quo. In Weaver's words: 'We have allowed ourselves to become so entrenched in our imagined communities or defensive of our respective identities that we fail to utilize emerging comparative strengths and exchange ideas across the divide in a constructive or even competitive manner.' Helleiner pleas eloquently for 'a little more humility'. Both recognize the value of building bridges across factional lines.

Bargaining

After denial and anger came bargaining – attempts to come to terms with the unwelcome surprise in one way or another. For many of the contributors to this volume, this has meant negotiating over where the lines in IPE are drawn. A divide may exist, but I have mischaracterized it. Variously, I have been accused of: distortion; over-emphasis on geography; incompleteness; drawing the line in the wrong place; political bias; and cultural bias. The list of alleged sins is long.

Not that any of this is surprising, of course. After all, as Ronen Palan wryly remarks, 'it is easy to poke holes' in any attempt at social classification. But there is no denying the value of the discussion. Though the litany of criticisms may seem dizzying, it is clear that out of this polyphonous chorus a much richer understanding has been attained about the current state of our field of study.

Distortion

One charge is that my characterization of a transatlantic divide was a distortion. Typical was an early commentary by John Ravenhill (2008), who contended that my description of the British version of IPE was 'ambiguous' while my characterization of the American school was 'narrow'. In a parallel comment Richard Higgott and Matthew Watson (2008) went further, accusing me of nothing less than outright caricature. Is there truth to such suggestions?

Personally, I find it hard to deny that a deep gap persists between the versions of IPE that predominate on either side of the pond. Studies of article citations in representative journals or course syllabi in US and British universities show relatively little overlap in what is read or taught. For the most part, scholars in each faction meet separately, in their own respective conferences and professional associations, and even in an age of electronic communications talk largely to one another rather than across the ocean. Jason Sharman is right when he speaks of the 'problems of intellectual isolationalism and uninformed mutual disdain' across the Atlantic. What he calls a 'conspicuous disconnect' is real.

As evidence I can offer my own version of Mark Blyth's 'cautionary tale'. In the autumn of 2009 I happened to attend two academic conferences in rapid succession: first a meeting of International Political Economy Society, a new group that is rapidly becoming the principal venue for presentation of IPE research in the United States; and then, just four weeks later, the annual meeting of the British International Studies Association, a traditional showcase for British IPE. The disconnect between the two events could not have been greater. Not only was there no overlap between the scholars in attendance, there was also no communication at all between the bodies of research on display. On neither side did presenters show even the slightest awareness of, or interest in, work produced on the other side. It was as if they occupied two parallel worlds.

Admittedly, my characterization of the divide is a broad, stylized generalization – and therefore, like all generalizations, something of an over-simplification. Not every detail is likely to conform to the generalization; exceptions can always be found if one is inclined to look for them. But that is nitpicking, which risks losing sight of the forest for the trees. Like it or not, there is a serious communications problem in IPE – a true dialogue of the deaf – however we characterize it. On that point just about all of the contributors to this volume concur.

Over-emphasis on geography

A second charge is that I over-emphasize geography. The gap is not 'between Brits and Yanks', as Kathleen McNamara puts it, but between competing ontologies – basic differences over what constitutes valid explanation of social phenomena. At issue is really a fundamental distinction between two sharply varying traditions in social research, one aspiring to scientific positivism, the other to historical understanding. The dichotomy is of long standing. Robert Cox traces it back to at least the eighteenth century, contrasting what he calls 'problem-solving' theory (which takes the structural characteristics of the present as given in order to be able to deal effectively with problems arising within it) with 'critical' theory (which is concerned with how those structures emerged and how their existing forms may be liable to change). Similarly, David Lake sees it as a contest between rigorously objective social science, with its formal models and statistical tests, and looser, more 'holistic' epistemologies.

The point is valid, of course. The question is indeed one of contrasting scholarly standards. But it is also true that the contrast corresponds accurately to a basic difference of intellectual cultures on the two sides of the Atlantic – broadly, to the way international studies traditionally have been approached in British universities as compared with the United States. On the American side, links with political science have always dominated. International studies grew up in an environment framed by the norms of conventional social science, with a particular emphasis on training in quantitative methods. Once IPE was born, it seemed natural for US scholars to channel the infant field's development along similar lines. In Britain, by contrast, international studies had roots that were spread much more widely into a variety of other disciplines such as sociology, history, religion, and law. Direct links with political science were weaker, with most universities maintaining a strong institutional separation between IR faculty and others. British academics are much more conditioned to think about the international realm in multidisciplinary and normative terms. In terms of underlying modal tendencies, therefore, the geographic appellations do not seem unreasonable. Brits and Yanks, by and large, simply see the world differently.

Incompleteness

A third charge is that my characterization of the divide is incomplete, particularly on the American side. Based on their analysis of the top 12 English-language journals in political science and international relations plus their survey of over a 1,000 US and Canadian IR specialists, Daniel Maliniak and Michael Tierney conclude that I got it right. In their words: 'The picture that Cohen paints of an American school of IPE is largely consistent with our findings.' The predominant version of IPE in the United States, their data attest, appears to have become increasingly homogeneous in terms of both paradigmatic orientation and research methodology. Versions of liberalism trump other theoretical traditions; states and interstate relations form the principal focus of analysis; and scientific method – a pure or hard science model – has come to be viewed as the only valid basis for a cumulation of knowledge. Nicola Phillips describes it as 'the slow death of pluralism'. McNamara, Peter Katzenstein, Jonathan Kirshner, and Robert Wade all use the word 'monoculture'.

Not everyone agrees, however, that this characterization is wholly accurate. Randall Germain, as well as Katzenstein, McNamara, and Phillips, all dissent, rightly drawing attention to anomalies in Maliniak and Tierney's methodology that would appear to bias their results. By limiting themselves to just a small handful of political science journals – the 'dirty dozen', Germain calls them – Maliniak and Tierney effectively exclude a wide range of research that is published elsewhere, in more specialized journals, in book form, or in cognate disciplines. Katzenstein seems especially sensitive on this point, decrying the failure of his home department at Cornell to make Maliniak and Tierney's top ten simply because it is a 'book' department. Likewise, by limiting their survey only to IR specialists, Maliniak and Tierney effectively reinforce the close association of the American school with the state-centric ontology of conventional political science. Excluded, as Phillips points out, are an array of colleagues with training or affiliations in other disciplines, such as sociology, geography, or business. What we are served is, in Germain's words, 'a narrow slice of IPE that cannot be considered to be the field as a whole.... a pinched portrayal of IPE in America'.

This point, too, is valid. But as both Germain and McNamara acknowledge, there is also a high degree of hierarchy in US IPE in terms of both publications and training. Some publishing venues – journals or university presses – clearly carry more prestige than others. Likewise, department rankings plainly distinguish elite institutions from all the rest. Maliniak and Tierney's methodology may not capture the full *breadth* of the field as it actually exists in the United States. But it arguably does succeed in capturing what is done at the *peak* of the field, where standards are established and aspirations are defined. Germain may not like the 'seeming concentration of academic influence within IPE in America', which he believes tends to promote 'group think and herd behavior'. McNamara may disapprove of the 'strikingly narrower view of IPE' that is typically taught at America's premier universities, which she fears circumscribes students' ambitions. But both acknowledge that the result is a high degree of consensus on the basic norms of the field – what is or is not to be considered 'good' scholarship. In terms of what is privileged as mainstream, the word 'monoculture' does not seem at all inaccurate as a way to describe the American school.

The wrong place

A fourth charge comes from Helleiner, who accepts that the divide is real but feels that I have drawn the line in the wrong place. The founders of both schools, Helleiner argues, shared a fairly similar view of the field's nature and purpose – a point emphasized by Cox and Geoffrey Underhill as well. Thus in Helleiner's view it was only with the emergence of what I have called the Third Generation of US scholars, with their penchant for the reductionist methodology of neoclassical economics, that a serious gap began to emerge. The key divide today, he concludes, is not between a British and an American school but rather between the Third Generation of US scholars and everyone else.

Helleiner's point is appealing, especially to those of us of an earlier generation who have watched the evolution of the American school with, in Robert Keohane's words, 'a gnawing sense of dissatisfaction'. But as with the previous charge of incompleteness, the argument discounts the degree of hierarchy in US IPE. There are, no doubt, many in the United States who would prefer the 'joyous contestation' and 'intellectual adventure' that Keohane recalls from the day when the field (and he) was young. Certainly it can be argued that with the ascendancy of the Third Generation has come a 'certain degree of aridity' in US scholarship, as Henry Farrell and Martha Finnemore suggest. In Keohane's words, 'a price has been paid'. Yet no one can deny that today it is the Third Generation, at the peak of the field, that sets the standards for most American scholarship. In Gramscian terms the Third Generation is 'hegemonic', setting the norms even for scholars in the United States whose intellectual preferences might differ.

Political bias

A fifth charge comes from Craig Murphy, who thinks my characterization of the American school is 'inadequate' since it omits a range of important scholars on the political left – the 'Left-Out', as he wittily puts it. For Murphy, the real divide is between those who, in his words, are 'satisfied' with the status quo and those who are not, which ultimately reduces to 'the much older distinction between left and right'. The implication is that my omission of the Left-Out may have been politically motivated. A similar argument is made in a recent commentary by Heikki Patomäki, who reminds us that throughout the post-World War II period 'political economy remained vibrant amongst Marxists, post-Keynesians, Gramscians and other branches of what has become known as heterodox economics'.

In reality, such criticisms once again discount the degree of hierarchy in US IPE. We know that there are a good number of heterodox scholars in the United States. But we also know that their impact on mainstream American scholarship is close to nil. In spirit, they are more Brit than Yank – more like their counterparts in British academia who share their dissatisfaction with the global political economy and who, like them, want to do something about it. Consistent with the divide between research traditions that underlies the transatlantic divide as I have described it, the Left-Out in the United States are probably better viewed not as part of the American school but rather, as Cox suggests, more or less an extraterritorial outpost of the British school.

Cultural bias

Finally, I have been charged with what amounts to a cultural bias for omitting scholars outside the transatlantic area – voices from Latin America, Asia, or elsewhere. In this volume the point is stressed explicitly by Cox and Helge Hveem and is implicit in the comments of Louis Pauly. Elsewhere, it has been made most forcefully by Anna Leander (2009), who emphasizes the need for 'linking the Anglo-Saxon Atlantic to the world beyond'. In her words: 'We need more than a dialogue across the Atlantic. . . . We need multiple stories.'

In response I can only plead *mea culpa*. My *Intellectual History* was limited to what Pauly calls the 'Anglosphere' for reasons of language alone, and I wholeheartedly agree that we could all benefit from a greater exposure to perspectives and traditions that have grown up elsewhere. Recently a start was made with a new *Routledge Handbook of International Political Economy*, edited by Mark Blyth (2009a), containing chapters on IPE in many parts of the world. One can only hope that more such initiatives will be forthcoming in the future.

The way forward

So what is the way forward? Can anything be done to build bridges between IPE's parallel worlds? Herein, arguably, lies the greatest value of this volume. All the contributors, in one way or another, make worthwhile suggestions about what might be done. Not surprising, opinions differ over who bears heavier responsibility. Blyth and Underhill appear to put most of the onus on British scholars, whom they accuse of curve-fitting and what Underhill calls 'template theorizing'. Others point an accusing finger at the arrogant Americans. For Palan, it is US scholars who are 'ideologically driven and uncritical', unaware or dismissive of 'blind spots' in their research. For Helleiner, it is specifically the Third Generation. For Murphy, it is scholars of the right. Opinions also differ over priorities – what is most essential and what should be done first. Collectively, however, a roadmap emerges to point the way forward. Efforts must be addressed in three key directions: toward ourselves, toward our students, and toward our research. All three are crucial.

First, ourselves. Scholarship, by definition, is supposed to be an exercise in inquiry. There is simply no excuse for arbitrarily excluding anything that does not happen to fall into our comfort zone. Several contributors speak of the desirability of greater personal openness. If we truly seek knowledge, each of us individually must commit to the fullest cultivation of Strange's open range: to be prepared to expose ourselves to what passes for knowledge in every part of the invisible college, no matter how much at variance with our own priors. In Cox's words, we must be willing to enter the 'mind sets' of others. We can all learn from work that proceeds from other theoretical paradigms, methodological approaches, or empirical interests.

Greater open-mindedness was precisely what I had in mind in writing my *Intellectual History*. Mainstream US scholars, it seemed to me, had become remarkably insular, ignoring just about anything originating outside North America. By counterposing the alternative of the British school, I hoped to heighten awareness of the American school's own self-imposed limitations. Other opportunities for raising consciousness are stressed by contributors to this volume. For Keohane it means daring to ask about big changes going on in the world political economy. For Mosley and Singer, it means addressing neglected puzzles in the realm of global finance. For Murphy it means paying more attention to global patterns of inequality, an issue long neglected by mainstream American IPE. For Underhill, it means overcoming a British phobia for the statistical techniques so popular among US scholars. For Palan, it means persuading US scholars to accept the validity of research that does *not* make use of such formal methodologies. For Cox and Hveem, it means listening to voices not just on either side of the Atlantic but from all corners of the world – a genuine 'globalization' of the field. To say that there is room for more genuine intellectual curiosity in IPE would be an understatement. The field is rich with diversity for those disposed to look for it.

Second, our students. Another motivation for my *Intellectual History* was my sense that our mutual insularity was doing a distinct disservice to our students. Too often, I wrote, students are exposed to just a single version of the field. Hence, all too frequently, they complete their training regrettably unaware of the full range of possibilities for research. Without consciously realizing it – and reinforced by pervasive patterns of professional socialization – they become members of a faction, spontaneously distancing themselves from traditions with which they are unacquainted. The theme is picked up on by several authors in this collection, including Farrell and Finnemore, Kirshner, and Sharman. Weaver is especially sharp about the American side, citing the disproportionate emphasis placed in US graduate programs on methodological skills. 'There is an implicit understanding amongst early career US IPE scholars', she rightly observes, 'that to get a job in a mainstream political science department, to get published in the leading journals and to get tenure, you demonstrate your quantitative chops.' I have, with regret, told the same thing to my own students. Both Cox and Underhill stress the need to widen our curricula to include more about the common intellectual origins of the field in European writings from the eighteenth century onward. Hveem calls for a greater emphasis on pluralism, which he sees as the key strength of the British school. IPE, he suggests, should be taught as a broad multidisciplinary field, understood to overlap integrally with other related specialties such as comparative politics, sociology, or history.

Finally, our research. As important as it is to open our own minds and those of our students, ultimately the real test will be the impact on our research. Several of this volume's contributors are skeptical that any fruitful dialogue can ever be promoted between the British and American schools. One might have thought, for instance, as Underhill suggests, that the current global crisis has been severe enough to shake the American school's faith in 'market fundamentalism and the methodologies which accompanied its rise'. Yet Palan finds no evidence of any change in US IPE's 'belief in its preferred theoretical orientation and methodologies'. Blyth is most adamant, wondering 'if a bridge can, or indeed should be built between such radically different things'. Respectfully, however, I dissent and remain optimistic about possibilities for future discourse (contrary to Underhill's unexpected characterization of me as a pessimist). The whole burden of the argument in my *Intellectual History*, summarized in the final pages, was that there are in fact real complementarities between the American and British traditions that could be productively exploited to the benefit of both. As Cox puts it succinctly: 'The possibility of reconciliation … lies in a mutual recognition that their purposes are different but not necessarily opposed.'

The key, it would seem, lies in what Peter Katzenstein calls 'analytical eclecticism' – a pragmatic research style that is willing to borrow concepts, theories, and methods from a variety of scholarly traditions as needed to address socially important problems. As summarized by Weaver, 'those adopting an analytically eclectic approach are motivated by problem-driven, rather than paradigm- or method-driven research'. The allegiance is to intellectual inquiry rather than to any particular school of thought. The aim is to use whatever tools may seem relevant to the task at hand, building bridges as we go along. In my *Intellectual History*, I offered several recent examples of published scholarship that might serve as models for that sort of approach, including Katzenstein's own recent study of *A World of Regions*, which quite explicitly borrowed from both the American and British traditions. The Canadians Helleiner and Underhill, in what Helleiner calls 'the spirit of Canadian compromise', offer additional examples. The way forward is clearly marked. All that is needed is the will.

Note

1 My thanks to the editors, Nicola Phillips and Catherine Weaver, for inviting me to contribute a final word to this volume. Thanks also to the authors for their many astute observations about my book. I am just sorry that my parents are not alive to see their more generous comments. My father would have enjoyed them. My mother would have believed them.

References

Abdelal, R. (2001) *National Purpose in the World Economy: Post-Soviet States in Comparative Perspective*, Ithaca, NY: Cornell University Press.

Abdelal, R. (2007) *Capital Rules: The Construction of Global Finance*, Cambridge, MA: Harvard University Press.

Abdelal, R., Blyth, M. and Parsons, C. (eds) (2010) *Constructivist Political Economy*, Ithaca, NY: Cornell University Press.

Adams, M. (2004) *Fire and Ice: The United States, Canada, and the Myth of Converging Values*, Toronto: Penguin Books.

Adler, E. (2002) 'Constructivism and International Relations', in W. Carlsnaes, T. Risse and B. Simmons (eds) *Handbook of International Relations*, London: Sage Publications.

Amyx, J. (2004) *Japan's Financial Crisis*, Princeton, NJ: Princeton University Press.

Bach, D. and Newman, A. (2007) 'The European Regulatory State and Global Public Policy: Micro-institutions, Macro-influence', *Journal of European Public Policy*, 14: 827–46.

Backhouse, R. (1998) 'The Transformation of U.S. Economics, 1920–1960, Viewed Through a Survey of Journal Articles', in M. Morgan and M. Rutherford (eds) *From Interwar Pluralism to Postwar Neoclassicism*, Durham, NC: Duke University Press.

Baker, A. (2005) 'Who Wants to Globalize? Consumer Tastes and Labor Markets in a Theory of Trade Policy Beliefs', *American Journal of Political Science*, 49: 924–38.

Bakker, I. (ed.) (1994) *The Strategic Silence: Gender and Economic Policy*, London: Zed Books.

Barraclough, G. (1955) *History in a Changing World Order*, Oxford: Basil Blackwell.

Barraclough, G. (1967) *An Introduction to Contemporary History*, Harmondsworth: Penguin Books.

Bartley, T. (2005) 'Corporate Accountability and the Privatization of Labor Standards: Struggles over Codes of Conduct in the Apparel Industry', *Research in Political Sociology*, 14: 211–44.

Bates, Robert H. (1997) *Open-Economy Politics: The Political Economy of the World Coffee Trade*, Princeton, NJ: Princeton University Press.

Bauer, R., de Sola Pool, I. and Dexter, L.A. (1963) *American Business and Public Policy: the Politics of Foreign Trade*, New York: Atherton Press.

Becker, G. (1976) *The Economic Approach to Human Behavior*, Chicago, IL: University of Chicago Press.

Bennett, A., Barth, A. and Rutherford, K.R. (2003) 'Do We Preach What We Practice? A Survey of Methods in Political Science Journals and Curricula', *PS: Political Science and Politics*, 36(3): 373–8.

Berdyaev, N. (1947) *The Russian Idea*, London: Geoffrey Bles.

Bergsten, C.F. and Krause, L.B. (eds) (1975) *World Politics and International Economics*, Washington DC: Brookings Institution.

Bernhard, W., Broz, J.L. and Clark, W.R. (eds) (2003) *The Political Economy of Monetary Institutions*, Cambridge, MA: MIT Press.

Best, J. (2005) *The Limits of Transparency: Ambiguity and the History of International Finance*, Ithaca, NY: Cornell University Press.

Best, J. and Paterson, M. (eds) *Cultural Political Economy*, unpublished manuscript.

Bieler, A. and Morton, A.D. (2003) 'Globalisation, the State and Class Struggle: A "Critical Economy" Engagement with Open Marxism', *British Journal of Politics and International Relations*, 5(4): 467–99.

Blake, D.H. and Walters, R.S. (1976) *The Politics of Global Economic Relations*, New York: Prentice-Hall.

Block, F.L. (1977) *The Origins of International Economic Disorder: A Study of United States International Monetary Policy from World War II to the Present*, Berkeley, CA: University of California Press.

Blyth, M. (2002) *Great Transformation: Economic Ideas and Institutional Change in the Twentieth Century*, Cambridge: Cambridge University Press.

Blyth, M. (ed.) (2009a) *The Routledge Handbook of IPE: IPE as a Global Conversation*, London and New York: Routledge.

Blyth, M. (2009b) 'Torn Between Two Lovers? Caught in the Middle of British and American IPE', *New Political Economy*, 14(3): 329–36.

Blyth, M. and Varghese, R. (1999) 'The State of the Discipline in American Political Science: Be Careful What You Wish For?' *British Journal of Politics and International Relations*, 1(3): 345–65.

Boswell, T. and Chase-Dunn, C. (2000) *The Spiral of Capitalism and Socialism: Toward Global Democracy*, Boulder, CO: Lynne Rienner.

Braithwaite, J. and Drahos, P. (2006) *Global Business Regulation*, Cambridge: Cambridge University Press.

Braudel, F. (1950a) 'The Situation of History in 1950', Inaugural lecture given to the Collège de France, 1 December. Trans. in F. Braudel (1980) *On History*, Chicago, IL: University of Chicago Press.

Braudel, F. (1950b) 'History and the Social Sciences. The Longue Durée', in F. Braudel (1980), *On History*, Chicago, IL: University of Chicago Press.

Braudel, F. (1992) *Civilization and Capitalism, 15th–18th Century*, vols 1–3, trans. Sian Reynolds, Berkeley, CA: University of California Press.

Brenner, N., Peck, J. and Theodore, N. (2010) 'After Neoliberalization?', *Globalizations*, forthcoming.

Brooks, S. (2005) *Producing Security: Multinational Corporations, Globalization, and the Changing Calculus of Conflict*, Princeton, NJ: Princeton University Press.

Brooks, S.M. (2008) *Social Protection and the Market in Latin America: The Transformation of Social Security Institutions*, Cambridge: Cambridge University Press.

Brown, C. (2006) 'International Relations Theory in Britain: The New Black?', *Review of International Studies*, 32(4): 677–87.

Bruff, I. (2010) 'The Case for a Foundational Materialism: Going Beyond Historical Materialist IPE in Order to Strengthen It', *Journal of International Relations and Development*, forthcoming.

Brunner, K. and Meltzer, A.H. (1993) *Money in the Economy: Issues in Monetary Analysis*, Cambridge: Cambridge University Press.

Buiter, W. (2007) 'Comment on Martin Wolf, "Why America Will Need Some Elements of a Welfare State"', *Financial Times*, 14 February: 15.

Buiter, W. (2009) 'Regulating the New Financial Sector', *Vox*, 9 March. Online: www.voxeu.org/index.php?q=node/3232 (accessed June 15 2009).

Burawoy, M. (1998) 'The Extended Case Method', *Sociological Theory*, 16(1): 4–33.

Burnham, P. (1990) *The Political Economy of Postwar Reconstruction*, London: Macmillan.

Burnham, P. (2003) *Remaking the Postwar World Economy: Robot and British Policy in the 1950s*, London: Palgrave Macmillan.

Büthe, T. and Mattli, W. (2005) 'Accountability in Accounting? The Politics of Private Rule-Making in the Public Interest', *Governance*, 18: 399–429.

Callinicos, A. and Rosenberg, J. (2008) 'Uneven and Combined Development: The Social-relational Substratum of "the International"? An Exchange of Letters', *Cambridge Review of International Affairs*, 21(1): 77–112.

Callon, M. (1988) *The Laws of Markets*, Oxford: Blackwell.

Cameron, A. and Palan, R. (2004) *The Imagined Economies of Globalization*, London: Sage Publications.

Cameron, A. and Palan, R. (2009) 'Empiricism and Objectivity: Reflexive Theory Construction in a Complex World', in M. Blyth (ed.) *The Routledge Handbook of IPE: IPE as a Global Conversation*, London and New York: Routledge, 112–25.

Cardoso, F.H. (2006) 'More than Ideology: The Conflation of Populism with the Left in Latin America', *Harvard International Review*, 28(2): 15–16.

Carr, E.H. (1945) *Nationalism*, London: Macmillan.

Cerny, P. (1994) 'The Infrastructure of the Infrastructure? Towards Embedded Financial Orthodoxy in the International Political Economy', in R.P. Palan and B. Gills (eds) *Transcending The State–Global Divide: A Neostructuralist Agenda in International Relations*, Boulder, CO: Lynne Reinner, 223–49.

Cerny, P. (2009) 'Bridging the Transatlantic Divide? Toward a Structurational Approach to International Political Economy', in Blyth, M. (ed.) *The Routledge Handbook of IPE: IPE as a Global Conversation*, London and New York: Routledge, 140–59.

Chang, C. (2002) *Kicking Away the Ladder: Development Strategy in Historical Perspective*, London: Anthem Press.

Chavagneux, C. (2007) *Les Dernieres Heures du Liberalisme. Mort d'une Idéologie*, Paris: Perrin.

Checkel, J. (1998) 'The Constructivist Turn in International Relations Theory', *World Politics*, 50: 324–48.

Chwieroth, J.M. (2007a) 'Testing and Measuring the Role of Ideas: The Case of Neoliberalism in the International Monetary Fund', *International Studies Quarterly*, 51(1): 5–30.

Chwieroth, J.M. (2007b) 'Neoliberal Economies and Capital Account Liberalization in Emerging Markets', *International Organization*, 61(2): 443–63.

Clift, B. and Rosamond, B. (2009) 'Lineages of a British International Political Economy', in M. Blyth (ed.) *The Routledge Handbook of IPE: IPE as a Global Conversation*, London and New York: Routledge, 95–111.

Cohen, B.J. (2007) 'The Transatlantic Divide: Why are American and British IPE So Different?' *Review of International Political Economy*, 14: 197–219.

Cohen, B.J. (2008a) 'The Transatlantic Divide: A Rejoinder', *Review of International Political Economy*, 15(1): 30–4.

Cohen, B.J. (2008b) *International Political Economy: An Intellectual History*, Princeton, NJ: Princeton University Press.

Colander, D. and Klamer, A. (1987) 'The Making of an Economist', *Journal of Economic Perspectives*, 1 (Fall).

Collier, D. and Elman, C. (2008) 'Qualitative and Multi-Method Research: Organizations, Publication, and Reflections on Integration', in J. Box-Steffensmeier, H.E. Brady and D. Collier (eds) *Oxford Handbook of Political Methodology*, Oxford: Oxford University Press.

Collier, P. (2007) *The Bottom Billion*, Oxford: Oxford University Press.

Collingwood, R.G. (1946) *The Idea of History*, Oxford: Clarendon Press.

Connerton, P. (1976) 'Introduction', in P. Connerton (ed.) *Critical Sociology*, Harmondsworth: Penguin, 11–39.

Cooper, R.N. (1968) *The Economics of Interdependence*, New York: McGraw-Hill.

Copelovitch, M.S. (forthcoming) 'Master or Servant? Common Agency and the Political Economy of IMF Lending', *International Studies Quarterly*.

Copelovitch, M.S. and Singer, D.A. (2008) 'Financial Regulation, Monetary Policy, and Inflation in the Industrialized World', *Journal of Politics*, 70(3): 663–80.

Cox, R.W. (1981) 'Social Forces, States and World Orders: Beyond International Relations Theory', *Millennium: Journal of International Studies*, 10(2): 126–55.

Cox, R.W. (1986) 'Social Forces, States and World Orders: Beyond International Relations Theory', in R.O. Keohane (ed.) *Neorealism and Its Critics*, New York: Columbia University Press, 204–54.

Cox, R.W. (1987) *Production, Power and World Order: Social Forces in the Making of History*, New York: Columbia University Press.

Cox, R.W., with Sinclair, T. (1996) *Approaches to World Order*, Cambridge: Cambridge University Press.

Crosby, A.W. (1986) *Ecological Imperialism: The Biological Expansion of Europe, 900–1900*, New York: Cambridge University Press.

Cutler, C.A. (2003) *Private Power and Global Authority: Transnational Merchant Law in the Global Political Economy*, Cambridge: Cambridge University Press.

David, A.S. (1989) 'The Split-Brain Syndrome', *British Journal of Psychiatry*, 154: 422–5.

Davies, M. (2005) 'World Financial Orders: An Historical International Political Economy', *Review of Radical Political Economics*, 37(3): 396–9.

Davis, G.F., Diekmann, K.A. and Tinsley, C.H. (1994) 'The Decline and Fall of the Conglomerate Firm in the 1980s: The Deinstitutionalization of an Organizational Form', *American Sociological Review*, 59(4): 547–70.

Dessler, D. (1989) 'What's at Stake in the Agent-Structure Debate?' *International Organization*, 43(3): 441–73.

Dickins, A. (2006) 'The Evolution of International Political Economy', *International Affairs*, 82(3): 479–92.

Dore, R. (2000) *Stock Market Capitalism: Welfare Capitalism*, New York: Oxford University Press.

Doremus, P.N., Keller, W.W., Pauly, L.W. and Reich, S. (1998). *The Myth of the Global Corporation*, Princeton, NJ: Princeton University Press.

Doyle, M.W. (1983a) 'Kant, Liberal Legacies, and Foreign Affairs, Part 1', *Philosophy and Public Affairs*, 12(3): 205–35

Doyle, M.W. (1983b) 'Kant, Liberal Legacies, and Foreign Affairs, Part 2', *Philosophy and Public Affairs*, 12(4): 323–53.

Doyle, M.W. (1997) *The Ways of War and Peace*, New York: W.W. Norton.

Drahokoupil, J. (2008) *Globalization and the State in Central and Eastern Europe: The Politics of Foreign Direct Investment*, London: Routledge.

Dreher, A., Sturm, J.-E. and Vreeland, J.R. (2009) 'Global Horse Trading: IMF Loans for Votes in the United Nations Security Council', *European Economic Review*, 53(7): 742–57.

Drezner, D. (2007) *All Politics is Global: Explaining International Regulatory Regimes*, Princeton, NJ: Princeton University Press.

Drori, G., Meyer, J.W. and Hwang, W. (eds) (2006) *Globalization and Organization: World Society and Organizational Change*, New York: Oxford University Press.

Dunn, B. (2009) *Global Political Economy: A Marxist Critique*, London: Pluto Press.

Elias, J. (2010) 'Gendered Political Economy and the Politics of Migrant Worker Rights: The View from Southeast Asia', *Australian Journal of International Affairs*, 64(1): 70–85.

Enloe, C. (1996) 'Margins, Silences and Bottom Rungs: How to Overcome the Underestimation of Power in the Study of International Relations', in S. Smith, K. Booth and M. Zalewski (eds) *International Theory: Positivism and Beyond*, Cambridge: Cambridge University Press, 186–202.

Epstein, G.A. (ed.) (2005) *Financialization and the World Economy*, London: Edward Elgar.

Farrell, H. (2003) 'Constructing the International Foundations of E-Commerce: The EU–US Safe Harbor Arrangement', *International Organization*, 57(2): 277–306.

Farrell, H. and Finnemore, M. (2009) 'Ontology, Methodology and Causation in the American School of International Political Economy', *Review of International Political Economy*, 16(1): 58–71.

Finnemore, M. (2003) *The Purpose of Intervention: Changing Beliefs About the Use of Force*, Ithaca, NY: Cornell University Press.

Fligstein, N. (1985) 'The Spread of the Multidivisional Form among Large Firms, 1919–1979', *American Sociological Review*, 50(3): 377–91.

Frank, A.G. (1988) *ReOrient: Global Economy in the Asian Age*, Berkeley, CA: University of California Press.

Frey, B., Pommerehne, W., Schneider, F. and Gilbert, G. (1984) 'Consensus and Dissensus among Economists: An Empirical Inquiry', *American Economic Review*, 74(5): 986–94.

Frieden, J.A. (1988) 'Capital Politics: Creditors and the International Political Economy', *Journal of Public Policy*, 8(3/4): 265–86.

Frieden, J.A. (1991a) *Debt, Development, and Democracy: Modern Political Economy and Latin America, 1965–1985*, Princeton, NJ: Princeton University Press.

Frieden, J.A. (1991b) 'Invested Interests: The Politics of National Economic Policies in a World of Global Finance', *International Organization*, 45(4): 425–51.

Frieden, J. and Lake, D. (1999) *International Political Economy: Perspectives on Global Power and Wealth*, London: Routledge.

Frieden, J. and Martin, L. (2002) 'International Political Economy: The State of the Subdiscipline', in I. Katznelson and H. Milner (eds) *Political Science: The State of the Discipline*, New York: Norton.

Frieden, J.A. and Rogowski, R. (1996) 'The Impact of the International Economy on National Politics: An Analytical Overview', in R.O. Keohane and H.V. Milner (eds) *Internationalization and Domestic Politics*, New York: Cambridge University Press, 25–47.

Friedman, B. (1979) 'Optimal Expectations and the Extreme Information Assumptions of "Rational Expectations" Macromodels', *Journal of Monetary Economics*, 5(1): 26–7.

Friedrichs, Jörg and Kratochwil, Friedrich (2009) 'On Acting and Knowing: How Pragmatism Can Advance International Relations Research and Methodology', *International Organization*, 63(4): 701–31.

Froud, J., Haslam, C., Johal, S. and Williams, K. (2000) 'Shareholder Value and Financialization: Consultancy Promises, Management Moves', *Economy and Society*, 29(1): 80–110.

G20 (2009) 'The Global Plan for Recovery and Reform', Leaders' Statement, London, 2 April. Online: www.g20.org/pub_communiques.aspx (accessed 15 September 2009).

Gamble, A., Payne, A., Hoogvelt, A., Kenny, M. and Dietrich, M. (1996) 'Editorial: New Political Economy', *New Political Economy*, 1(1): 5–11.

Garand, J. and Giles, M. (2003) 'Journals in the Discipline: A Report on a New Survey of American Political Scientists', *PS: Political Science and Politics*, 36(2) (April): 293–308.

Germain, R. (1997) *International Organization of Credit: States and Global Finance in the World Economy*, New York: Cambridge University Press.

Gerstein, I. (1977) 'Theories of the World Economy and Imperialism', *The Insurgent Sociologist*, 7(2): 9–22.

Giles, M.W. and Garand, J.C. (2007) 'Ranking Political Science Journals: Reputational and Citational Approaches', *PS: Political Science and Politics*, 40(4): 741–51.

Gilpin, R. (1971) 'The Politics of Transitional Economic Relations', *International Organization*, 25(3): 398–419.

Gilpin, R. (1975) *U.S. Power and the Multinational Corporation*, New York: Basic Books.

Gilpin, R. (1981) *War and Change in World Politics*, New York: Cambridge University Press.

Gilpin, R. (1987) *The Political Economy of International Relations*, Princeton, NJ: Princeton University Press.

Gilpin, R. (2001) *Global Political Economy*, Princeton, NJ: Princeton University Press.

Goff, P. (2006) *Limits to Liberalization: Local Culture in a Global Marketplace*, Ithaca, NY: Cornell University Press.

Goldstein, J. and Keohane, R.O. (eds) (1993) *Ideas and Foreign Policy*, Ithaca, NY: Cornell University Press.

Goodwin, C. (1998) 'The Patrons of Economics in a Time of Transformation', in M. Morgan and M. Rutherford (eds) *From Interwar Pluralism to Postwar Neoclassicism*, Durham, NC: Duke University Press.

Gould, E. (2003) 'Money Talks: Supplementary Financiers and International Monetary Fund Conditionality', *International Organization*, 57(3): 551–86.

Gourevitch, P.A. (1977) 'International Trade, Domestic Coalitions, and Liberty: Comparative Responses to the Crisis of 1873–1896', *Journal of Interdisciplinary History*, 8(2): 281–313.

Gourevitch, P.A. (1978) 'The Second Image Reversed', *International Organization*, 32(4): 882–912.

Gourevitch, P.A. (1986) *Politics in Hard Times: Comparative Responses to International Economic Crises*, Ithaca, NY: Cornell University Press.

Gourevitch, P.A. and Shinn, J. (2005) *Political Power and Corporate Control: The New Global Politics of Corporate Governance*, Princeton, NJ: Princeton University Press.

Green, D. and Shapiro, I. (1996) *Pathologies of Rational Choice Theory: A Critique of Applications in Political Science*, New Haven, CT: Yale University Press.

Greif, A. (2006) *Institutions and the Path of the Modern Economy: Lessons from Medieval Trade*, New York: Cambridge University Press.

Grewal, D.S. (2008) *Network Power*, Princeton, NJ: Princeton University Press.

Gruber, L. (2000) *Ruling the World*, Princeton, NJ: Princeton University Press.

Haas, E.B. (1958) *The Uniting of Europe*, Stanford, CA: Stanford University Press.

Hall, P. (2003) 'Aligning Ontology and Methodology in Comparative Research', in J. Mahoney and D. Rueschemeyer (eds) *Comparative Historical Analysis in the Social Sciences*, New York: Cambridge University Press, pp. 373–406.

Hall, P.A. and Soskice, D. (2001) *Varieties of Capitalism: The Institutional Foundations of Comparative Advantage*, New York: Oxford University Press.

Hall, R.B. (1999) *National Collective Identity: Social Constructs and International Systems*, New York: Columbia University Press.

Hampson, E. (1994) 'Left Brain, Right Brain: Fact and Fiction', *Organization for Quality Education Forum*, 3(3): 2.

Harrod, J. (2006) 'The Global Poor and Global Politics: Neomaterialism and the Sources of Political Action', in M. Davies and M. Ryner (eds) *Poverty and the Production of World Politics*, Basingstoke: Palgrave Macmillan, 89–112.

Haufler, V. (2000) *A Public Role for the Private Sector: Industry Self-Regulation in a Global Economy*, New York: Carnegie Endowment for International Peace.

Hay, C. (2002) *Political Analysis*, London: Palgrave.

Hays, J., Ehrlich, S. and Peinhardt, C. (2005) 'Government Spending and Public Support for Trade in the OECD: An Empirical Test of the Embedded Liberalism Thesis', *International Organization*, 59: 473–94.

Healy, T. (2006) 'The Condition of Hegemony and Labour Militancy: The Restructuring of Gender Relations and Production Patterns in Mexico', in M. Davies and M. Ryner (eds) *Poverty and the Production of World Politics*, Basingstoke: Palgrave Macmillan, 178–203.

Held, D. and McGrew, A. (2007) *Globalization/Anti-Globalization*, 2nd edn, London: Polity.

Helleiner, E. (1994) *States and the Reemergence of Global Finance*, Ithaca, NY: Cornell University Press.

Helleiner, E. and Pagliari, S. (2008) 'The G20 Leaders' Summit and the Regulation of Global Finance: What Was Accomplished?' *CIGI Policy Brief #11*, 1 December.

Helleiner, E. and Pickel, A. (eds) (2005) *Economic Nationalism in a Globalizing World*, Ithaca, NY: Cornell University Press.

Hicks, J. (1946) *Value and Capital*, 2nd edn, New York: Oxford University Press.

Higgott, R. and Watson, M. (2008) 'All at Sea in a Barbed Wire Canoe: Professor Cohen's Transatlantic Voyage in IPE', *Review of International Political Economy*, 15(1): 1–17.

Hirschman, A.O. (1981) *Essays in Trespassing: Economics to Politics and Beyond*, New York: Cambridge University Press.

Hiscox, M.J. (2002) *International Trade and Political Conflict: Commerce, Coalitions, and Mobility*, Princeton, NJ: Princeton University Press.

Hobson, J.M. (2004) *The Eastern Origins of Western Civilization*, New York: Cambridge University Press.

Hobson, J.M. and Seabrooke, L. (eds) (2007) *Everyday Politics of the World Economy*, Cambridge: Cambridge University Press.

Hoffmann, S. (1977) 'An American Social Science: International Relations', *Daedalus*, 106(3): 41–60.

Hollist, W.L. and Rosenau, J.N. (eds) (1981) *World System Structure: Continuity and Change*, London: Sage.

Holsti, K.J. (1985) *The Dividing Discipline: Hegemony and Diversity in International Theory*, London: Allen & Unwin.

Huang, Y., Saich, A. and Steinfeld, E.S. (eds) (2005) *Financial Sector Reform in China*, Cambridge, MA: Harvard University Asia Center.

Hudson, M. (2005) *Global Fracture: The New International Economic Order*, London: Pluto Press.

Hveem, H. (1972) *International Relations and World Images: A Study of Norwegian Foreign Policy Elites*, Oslo: Universitetsforlaget.

Hveem, H. (1973) 'The Global Dominance System; Notes on a Theory of Global Political Economy', *Journal of Peace Research*, 10(4): 319–40.

Hveem, H. (1978) *The Political Economy of Third World Producer Associations*, Oslo: Universitetsforlaget.

Hveem, H. (1994) *Internasjonalisering og Politikk*, Oslo: TANO.

Ikenberry, J.G. (2008) 'The Rise of China and the Future of the West: Can the Liberal System Survive?' *Foreign Affairs*, 87(1): 23–37.

Jabko, N. (2006) *Playing the Market: A Political Strategy for United Europe, 1985–2005*, Ithaca, NY: Cornell University Press.

Jennings, C. and Mclean, I. (2008) 'Political Economics and Normative Analysis', *New Political Economy*, 13(1): 61–76.

Jensen, N.M. (2006) *Nation-States and the Multinational Corporation: A Political Economy of Foreign Direct Investment*, Princeton, NJ: Princeton University Press.

Jensen, N.M. (2007) 'Firm-level Responses to Politics: Political Institutions and the Operations of U.S. Multinationals', Working Paper, Washington University, St. Louis.

Johnson, J. (2006) 'Consequences of Positivism: A Pragmatist Assessment', *Comparative Political Studies*, 39(2): 224–52.

Julius, D. (1990) *Global Companies and Public Policy*, London: Pinter.

Kahler, M. and Lake, D.A. (eds) (2003) *Governance in a Global Economy: Political Authority in Transition*, Princeton, NJ: Princeton University Press.

Kannankulam, J. (2008) *Autoritärer Etatismus in Neoliberalismus: Zur Staatstheory von Nicos Poulantzas*, Hamburg: VSA-Verlag.

Kapstein, E.B. (1994) *Governing the Global Economy: International Finance and the State*, Cambridge, MA: Harvard University Press.

Katzenstein, P.J. (ed.) (1978) *Between Power and Plenty: Foreign Economic Policies of Advanced Industrial States*, Madison: University of Wisconsin Press.

Katzenstein, P.J. (1985) *Small States in World Markets: Industrial Policy in Europe*, Ithaca, NY: Cornell University Press.

Katzenstein, P.J. (2009) 'Mid-Atlantic: Sitting on the Knife's Sharp Edge', *Review of International Political Economy*, 16(1): 122–34.

Katzenstein, P.J. and Sil, R. (2008) 'The Contributions of Eclectic Theorizing to the Study and Practice of International Relations', in C. Reus-Smit and D. Snidal (eds) *Oxford Handbook of International Relations*, Oxford: Oxford University Press.

Katzenstein, P.J., Keohane, R. and Krasner, S. (1998) 'International Organization and the Study of World Politics', *International Organization*, 52(4): 645–85.

Kennedy, D. (2009) *Economic Development: An Intellectual History*, Princeton, NJ: Princeton University Press.

Keohane, R.O. (1980) 'The Theory of Hegemonic Stability and Change in International Economic Regimes, 1967–1977', in O.R. Holsti *et al.* (eds) *Change in the International System*, Boulder, CO: Westview Press.

Keohane, R.O. (1984) *After Hegemony: Cooperation and Discord in the World Political Economy*, Princeton, NJ: Princeton University Press.

Keohane, R.O. (2009) 'The Old IPE and the New', *Review of International Political Economy*, 16(1): 34–46.

Keohane, R.O. and Milner, H.V. (eds) (1996) *Internationalization and Domestic Politics*, New York: Cambridge University Press.

Keohane, R.O. and Nye, J.S., Jr. (eds) (1972) *Transnational Relations and World Politics*, Cambridge, MA: Harvard University Press.

Keohane, R.O. and Nye, J.S., Jr. (1977) *Power and Interdependence*, Boston, MA: Little, Brown.

Keohane, R.O. and Nye, J.S., Jr. (1987) 'Complex Interdependence Revisited', *International Organization*, 41(4): 725–53.

Keynes, J.M. (1936) *The General Theory of Employment, Interest and Money*, New York: Macmillan.

Keynes, J.M. (1937) 'The General Theory of Employment', *Quarterly Journal of Economics*, 51(2): 209–223.

Keynes, J.M. (1972) 'My Early Beliefs', in *Two Memoirs* (1949) (Reprinted in *The Collected Writings of John Maynard Keynes*, vol. 10, Cambridge: Macmillan).

Kindleberger, C.P. (1970) *The International Corporation: A Symposium*, Cambridge, MA: MIT Press.

Kindleberger, C.P. (1970) *Power and Money: The Politics of International Economics and the Economics of International Politics*, New York: Basic Books.

Kindleberger, C.P. (1973) *The World in Depression, 1929–1939*, Berkeley, CA: University of California Press.

Kindleberger, C.P. (1988) *The International Economic Order: Essays on Financial Crisis and International Public Goods*, London: Harvester-Wheatsheaf.

Kindleberger, C.P. (1996) *History of Financial Crises: Mania, Panic and Crash*, London: John Wiley & Sons.

King, G., Keohane, R.O. and Verba, S. (1994) *Designing Social Inquiry*, Princeton, NJ: Princeton University Press.

Kingsbury, B. and Krisch, N. (eds) (2006) *Global Governance and Global Administrative Law in the International Legal Order*, Special issue of European *Journal of International Law*, 17(1).

Kingsbury, B., Krisch, N. and Stewart, R.B. (2005) 'The Emergence of Global Administrative Law', *Law and Contemporary Problems*, 68(3/4): 15–62.

Kirshner, J. (1998) 'Disinflation, Structural Change, and Distribution', *Review of Radical Political Economics*, 30(1): 53–89.

Kirshner, J. (2000) 'Rationalist Explanations for War?' *Security Studies*, 10(1): 143–50.

Kirshner, J. (2001) 'The Political Economy of Low Inflation', *Journal of Economic Surveys*, 15(1): 41–70.

Kirshner, J. (2007) *Appeasing Bankers: Financial Caution on the Road to War*, Princeton, NJ: Princeton University Press.

Klein, M.W. and Shambaugh, J.C. (2006) 'Fixed Exchange Rates and Trade', *Journal of International Economics*, 70(1): 359–83.

Knorr, K. and Rosenau, J.N. (eds) (1969) *Contending Approaches to International Politic*s, Princeton, NJ: Princeton University Press.

Konings, M. (2009) 'The Construction of US Financial Power', *Review of International Studies*, 35 (1): 69–94.

Krasner, S.D. (1976) 'State Power and the Structure of International Trade', *World Politics*, 28(3): 317–43.

Krasner, S.D. (1978) 'United States Commercial and Monetary Policy: Unraveling the Paradox of External Strength and Internal Weakness', in P.J. Katzenstein (ed.) *Between Power and Plenty*, Madison: University of Wisconsin Press, 51–87.

Krasner, S.D. (ed.) (1983) *International Regimes*, Ithaca, NY: Cornell University Press.

Krasner, S.D. (1985) *Structural Conflict: The Third World against Global Liberalism*, Berkeley, CA: University of California Press.

Krätke, M. and Underhill, G. (2006) 'Political Economy: The Revival of the "Interdiscipline"', in R. Stubbs and G. Underhill (eds) *Political Economy and the Changing Global Order*, 3rd edn, New York: Oxford University Press, 24–38.

Kuhn, T.S. (1970) *The Structure of Scientific Revolutions*, Chicago, IL: University of Chicago Press.

Lakatos, I. (1978) *The Methodology of Scientific Research Programmes: Philosophical Papers*, vol. 1, New York: Cambridge University Press.

Lake, D.A. (1988) *Power, Protection and Free Trade: The International Sources of American Commercial Strategy, 1887–1939*, Ithaca, NY: Cornell University Press.

Lake, D.A. (1999) *Entangling Relations: American Foreign Policy in Its Century*, Princeton, NJ: Princeton University Press.

Lake, D.A. (2006) 'International Political Economy: An Emerging Interdiscipline', in B. Weingast and D. Wittman (eds) *The Oxford Handbook of Political Economy*, New York: Oxford University Press, pp. 757–77.

Lake, D.A. (2009) 'TRIPs across the Atlantic: Theory and Epistemology in IPE', *Review of International Political Economy*, 16(1): 47–57.

Lake, D.A. and Powell, R. (eds) (1999) *Strategic Choice and International Relations*, Princeton, NJ: Princeton University Press.

Langley, P. (2008) *The Everyday Life of Global Finance: Saving and Borrowing in Anglo-America*, Oxford: Oxford University Press.

Langley, P. (2009) 'Power-knowledge Estranged: From Susan Strange to Poststructuralism in British IPE', in M. Blyth (ed.) *The Routledge Handbook of IPE: IPE as a Global Conversation*, London and New York: Routledge, pp. 126–39.

Lasswell, H. (1936) *Politics: Who Gets What, When, How*, New York: McGraw-Hill.

Lawton, T., Rosenau, J. and Veru, A. (eds) (2000) *Strange Power*, Aldershot: Ashgate.

Leander, A. (2009) 'Why We Need Multiple Stories about the Global Political Economy', *Review of International Political Economy*, 16(2): 321–8.

Leblang, D., Fitzgerard, J. and Teets, J. (2007) 'Defying the Law of Gravity: The Political Economy of International Migration', Department of Political Science, University of Colorado, Boulder.

Leontief, W. (1971) 'Theoretical Assumptions and Nonobservable Facts', *American Economic Review*, 61(1): 1–7.

Leontief, W. (1982) 'Academic Economics', Letters, *Science*, 217(4555): 104–7.

Levi-Faur, D. (2005) 'The Global Diffusion of Regulatory Capitalism', *Annals of the American Academy of Political and Social Science*, 598(12): 12–32.

Lipson, C. (1984) 'International Cooperation in Economic and Security Affairs', *World Politics*, 37(1): 1–23.

Lipson, M., Maliniak, D., Oakes, A., Peterson, S. and Tierney, M. (2007) 'Divided Discipline? Comparing Views of U.S. and Canadian IR Scholars', *International Journal*, 62(3): 327–43.

Little, D. (1998) *Microfoundations, Method, and Causation*, New Brunswick, NY: Transaction Press.

Little, D. (2008) 'Agents, Structures and Social Contingency: New Thinking about the Foundations of the Social Sciences', unpublished paper. Online: www-personal.umd.umich.edu/~delittle/PAPER%20FOR%20TSINGHUA%20DDM%20LECTURE%20delivered.htm (accessed 15 June 2008).

Long, D. (1995) 'The Harvard School of Liberal International Theory: A Case for Closure', *Millennium*, 24(3): 489–505.

Lovell, M.C. (1986) 'Tests of the Rational Expectations Hypothesis', *American Economic Review*, 76(1): 110–24.

McCloskey, D.N. (1985) 'The Loss Function Has Been Mislaid: The Rhetoric of Significance Tests', *American Economic Review*, 75(2): 201–5.

McCloskey, D.N. and Ziliak, S.T. (1996) 'The Standard Error of Regressions', *Journal of Economic Literature*, 34(1): 94–114.

McDaniel, T. (1996) *The Agony of the Russian Idea*, Princeton, NJ: Princeton University Press.

McNally, D. (2009) 'From Financial Crisis to World-slump: Accumulation, Financialisation, and the Global Slowdown', *Historical Materialism*, 17(2): 35–83.

McNamara, K. (1998) *The Currency of Ideas: Monetary Politics in the European Union*, Ithaca, NY: Cornell University Press.

McNamara, K. (2009) 'Of Intellectual Monocultures and the Study of IPE', *Review of International Political Economy*, 16(1): 72–84.

Mahoney, J. (2003) 'Tentative Answers to Questions about Causal Mechanisms', paper presented at the annual meetings of the American Political Science Association, Philadelphia, PA, August 28, 2003. Online: www.asu.edu/clas/polisci/cqrm/APSA2003/Mahoney_APSA_2003.pdf.

Maliniak, D. and Tierney, M.J. (2009) 'The American School of IPE', *Review of International Political Economy*, 16(1): 6–33.

Maliniak, D., Oakes, A., Peterson, S. and Tierney, M. (2007a) 'The International Relations Discipline: 1980–2007', paper presented at the American Political Science Association, Chicago, IL.

Maliniak, D., Oakes, A., Peterson, S. and Tierney, M. (2007b) 'Inside the Ivory Tower', *Foreign Policy*, March/April: 62–8.

Maliniak, D., Oakes, A., Peterson, S. and Tierney, M. (2007c) 'The View from the Ivory Tower: TRIP Survey of IR Faculty in the U.S. and Canada', Institute for the Theory and Practice of International Relations, College of William and Mary, Williamsburg, VA. Online: www.wm.edu/irtheoryandpractice/trip/surveyreport06-07.pdf

Maliniak, D., Oakes, A., Peterson, S. and Tierney, M. (2008) 'Women in International Relations', *Politics & Gender*, 4(1): 122–44.

Mares, I. (2003) *The Politics of Social Risk: Business and Welfare State Development*, Cambridge: Cambridge University Press.

Martin, C.J. and Swank, D. (2001) 'Employers and the Welfare State', *Comparative Political Studies*, 34(8): 889–923.

Mattli, W. and Woods, N. (eds) (2009) *The Politics of Global Regulation*, Princeton, NJ: Princeton University Press.

Maxfield, S. (1997) *Gatekeepers of Growth: The International Political Economy of Central Banking in Developing Countries*, Princeton, NJ: Princeton University Press.

Merle, M. (1996) 'Un Système International sans Territoire?' *Cultures & Conflicts*, 21(11): 289–309.

Meyer, J.W. and Hannan, M.T. (eds) (1979) *National Development and the World System: Educational, Economic, and Political Change, 1950–1970*, Chicago, IL: University of Chicago Press.

Milanovic, B. (1999) 'True World Income Distribution 1988 and 1993: First Calculation Based on Household Surveys Alone', World Bank Development Research Group Paper No. 2244, December 1999, 51.

Miller, P. (ed.) (1994) *The Rational Expectations Revolution*, Cambridge, MA: MIT Press.

Milner, H.V. (1988) *Resisting Protectionism: Global Industries and the Politics of International Trade*, Princeton, NJ: Princeton University Press.

Milner, H.V. (1997) *Interests, Institutions and Information*, Princeton, NJ: Princeton University Press.

Milner, H.V. (2006) 'Why Multilateralism? Foreign Aid and Domestic Principal–Agent Problems', in D. Hawkins *et al.* (eds) *Delegation and Agency in International Organizations*, New York: Cambridge University Press, 107–39.

Moran, M. (1991) *The Politics of the Financial Services Revolution*, New York: St. Martin's Press.

Moran, M. (2006) 'Interdisciplinarity and Political Science', *Politics*, 26(2): 73–83.

Moravcsik, A. (1997) 'Taking Preferences Seriously: A Liberal Theory of International Politics', *International Organization*, 51: 513–53.

Moravcsik, A. (1998) *The Choice for Europe*, Ithaca, NY: Cornell University Press.

Morgan, M. and Rutherford, M. (1998) 'American Economics: The Character of the Transformation', in M. Morgan and M. Rutherford (eds) *From Interwar Pluralism to Postwar Neoclassicism*, Durham, NC: Duke University Press.

Mosley, L. (2003) 'Attempting Global Standards: National Governments, International Finance, and the IMF's Data Regime', *Review of International Political Economy*, 10(2): 331–62.

Mosley, L. (2009) 'Private Governance for the Public Good? Exploring Private Sector Participation in Global Financial Regulation', in H.V. Milner and A. Moravcsik (eds) *Power, Interdependence and Non-State Actors in World Politics*, Princeton, NJ: Princeton University Press, 126–46.

Murphy, C. and Tooze, R. (1991) 'Getting Beyond the "Common Sense" of the IPE Orthodoxy', in C. Murphy and R. Tooze (eds) *New International Political Economy*, Boulder, CO: Lynne Rienner, 11–31.

Murphy, C.N. (1999) 'Inequality, Turmoil, and Democracy: Global Political-economic Visions at the End of the Century', *New Political Economy*, 4(2): 289–304.

Murphy, C. and Nelson, D. (2001) 'International Political Economy: A Tale of Two Heterodoxies', *British Journal of Politics and International Relations*, 3(3): 393–412.

Murphy, D.D. (2004) *The Structure of Regulatory Competition: Corporations and Public Policies in a Global Economy*, New York: Oxford University Press.

Nesvetailova, A. (2007) *Fragile Finance: Debt, Speculation and Crisis in the Age of Global Credit*, London and Basingstoke: Palgrave.

Nisbett, R.E. (2003) *The Geography of Thought: How Asians and Westerners Think Differently ... and Why*, New York: The Free Press.

Nitzan, J. (1998) 'Differential Accumulation: Toward a New Political Economy of Capital', *Review of International Political Economy*, 5(2): 169–216.

Noël, A. and Thérien, J.P. (2008) 'Two Tales of Globalization', in A. Noel and J.P. Therien (eds) *Left and Right in Global Politics*, Cambridge: Cambridge University Press, pp. 56–82.

North, D.C. (1990) *Institutions, Institutional Change and Economic Performance*, New York: Cambridge University Press.

Nunn, N. (2008) 'The Long-term Effects of Africa's Slave Trades', *Quarterly Journal of Economics*, 123(1): 139–76.

Nunn, N. and Wantchekon, L. (2008) 'The Trans-Atlantic Slave Trade and the Origins of Mistrust within Africa', Department of Economics, Harvard University.

Ornter, S. (2003) 'East Brain, West Brain: Do Ways of Thinking Cleave along Lines of Geography?' *New York Times Book Review*, 20 April: 17.

Oye, K.A. (ed.) (1986) *Cooperation under Anarchy*, Princeton, NJ: Princeton University Press.

Palan, R. (2003) *The Offshore World: Sovereign Markets, Virtual Places, and Nomad Millionaires*, Ithaca, NY: Cornell University Press.

Palan, R. (2004) 'Pragmatism and International Relations in the Age of Banker's Capitalism: Susan Strange's Vision for a Critical International Political Economy', in H. Bauer and E. Brighi (eds) *75 Years of International Relations at LSE: A History*, London: Millennium Publishing Group.

Palloix, C. (1977) 'The Self-expansion of Capitalism on a World Scale', *The Review of Radical Political Economics*, 9(2): 3–17.

Parsons, C. (2003) *A Certain Idea of Europe*, Ithaca, NY: Cornell University Press.

Patomäki, H. (2009) 'How to Tell Better Stories about the History and Future of Global Political Economy', *Review of International Political Economy*, 16(2): 309–20.

Paul, D. (2006) 'Teaching Political Economy in Political Science: A Review of International and Comparative Political Economy Syllabi', *Perspectives on Politics*, 4(4): 729–34.

Pauly, L. (1997) *Who Elected the Bankers? Surveillance and Control in the World Economy*, Ithaca, NY: Cornell University Press.

Perroux, F. (1969) *L'Economies du Xxieme Siècle*, Paris: PUF.

Perroux, F. (1969) *Indepenence de Economic Nationale et Interdependence des Nations*, Paris: Editions Aubier Montaigne.

Peterson, S. and Tierney, M. (2005a) 'Codebook and User's Guide for TRIP Journal Article Database', unpublished manual, Williamsburg, VA (revised May 2007).

Peterson, S. and Tierney, M., with Maliniak, D. (2005b) 'Teaching and Research Practices, Views on the Discipline, and Policy Attitudes of International Relations Faculty at U.S. Colleges and Universities', Reves Center for International Studies, College of William and Mary, Williamsburg, VA.

Peterson, S., Tierney, M. and Maliniak, D. (2005c) 'Inside the Ivory Tower', *Foreign Policy*, November/December: 58–64.

Phillips, N. (ed.) (2005) *Globalizing International Political Economy*, Basingstoke: Palgrave Macmillan.

Phillips, N. (2009) 'The Slow Death of Pluralism', *Review of International Political Economy*, 16(1): 85–94.

Pinto, P.M. and Pinto, S.M. (2008) 'The Politics of Investment: Partisanship and the Sectoral Allocation of Foreign Direct Investment', *Economics and Politics*, 20(2): 216–54.

Polyani, K. (1957) *The Great Transformation*, Boston, MA: Beacon Press.

Pomeranz, K. (2000) *The Great Divergence: China, Europe, and the Making of the Modern World Economy*, Princeton, NJ: Princeton University Press.

Pop-Eleches, G. (2008) *From Economic Crisis to Reform: IMF Programs in Latin America and Eastern Europe*, Princeton, NJ: Princeton University Press.

Posner, E. (2005) 'Sources of Institutional Change: The Supranational Origins of Europe's New Stock Markets', *World Politics*, 58(1): 1–40.

Quillin, B. (2008) *International Financial Cooperation: Political Economics of Compliance with the 1988 Basel Accord*, London: Routledge.

Ragin, C.C. (2000) *Fuzzy-set Social Science*, Chicago, IL: University of Chicago Press.

Ragin, C.C. *et al.* (2003) 'Complexity, Generality, and Qualitative Comparative Analysis', *Field Methods*, 15(4): 323–40.

Ravenhill, J. (2008) 'In Search of the Missing Middle', *Review of International Political Economy*, 15(1): 18–29.

Reinert, E. (2007) *How Rich Countries Got Rich … and How Poor Countries Stay Poor*, London: Constable & Robison.

Richards, J.E. (1999) 'Towards a Positive Theory of International Institutions: Regulating International Aviation Markets', *International Organization*, 53(1): 1–37.

Robbins, L. (1932) *An Essay on the Nature and Significance of Economic Science*, London: Macmillan.

Robinson, J. (1972) 'The Second Crisis of Economic Theory', *American Economic Review*, 61(1–2): 9–10.

Robinson, W.I. (2004) *A Theory of Global Capitalism: Production, Class, and State in a Transnational World*, Baltimore, MD: Johns Hopkins University Press.

Robinson, W.I. (2008) *Latin America and Global Capitalism: A Critical Globalization Perspective*, Baltimore, MD: Johns Hopkins University Press.

Rodden, J. (2003) 'Reviving Leviathan: Fiscal Federalism and the Growth of Government', *International Organization*, 57(4): 695–729.

Rodrik, D. (2007) *One Economics, Many Recipes*, Princeton, NJ: Princeton University Press.

Rogowski, R. (1989) *Commerce and Coalitions: How Trade Affects Domestic Political Alignments*, Princeton, NJ: Princeton University Press.

Rosas, G. (2006) 'Bagehot or Bailout? An Analysis of Government Responses to Banking Crises', *American Journal of Political Science*, 50(1): 175–91.

Rosenbluth, F. (1989) *Financial Politics in Contemporary Japan*, Ithaca, NY: Cornell University Press.

Rosenbluth, F. and Schaap, R. (2003) 'The Domestic Politics of Banking Regulation', *International Organization*, 57(2): 307–36.

Ross, D. (1991) *The Origins of American Social Science*, Cambridge: Cambridge University Press.

Ross, M. (2001) 'Does Oil Hinder Democracy?' *World Politics*, 53(3): 325–61.

Ruggie, J.G. (1975) 'International Responses to Technology: Concepts and Trends', *International Organization*, 29(3): 557–83.

Ruggie, J.G. (1982) 'International Regimes, Transactions, and Change: Embedded Liberalism in the Postwar Economic Order', *International Organization*, 36(2): 379–415.

Ruggie, J.G. (1983) *The Antimonies of Interdependence*, New York: Columbia University Press.

Ruggie, J.G. (1998) *Constructing the World Polity*, London: Routledge.

Ruggie, J.G. (2004) 'Reconstituting the Public Domain: Issues, Actors, and Practices', *European Journal of International Relations*, 10(4): 499–531.

Ruggie, J.G. and Kratochwil, F. (1986) 'International Organization: A State of the Art on an Art of the State', *International Organization*, 40(4): 753–75.

Rupert, M. (2000) *Ideologies of Globalization: Contending Visions of a New World Order*, London: Routledge.

Russett, B.M. (1968) *Economic Theories of International Politics*, Chicago, IL: Markham.

Sayer, A. (1992) *Method in Social Science: A Realist Approach*, 2nd edn, London: Routledge.

Scheve, K. and Slaughter, M.J. (2004) 'Economic Insecurity and the Globalization of Production', *American Journal of Political Science*, 48(4): 662–74.

Schmidt, B. (2008) 'International Relations Theory: Hegemony or Pluralism?', *Millennium*, 36(2): 295–304.

Schwartz, H. (1994) *States versus Markets: History, Geography, and the Development of the International Political Economy*, New York: St. Martin's Press.

Seabrooke, L. (2006) *The Social Sources of Financial Power: Domestic Legitimacy and International Financial Orders*, Ithaca, NY: Cornell University Press.

Seglen, P. (1997) 'Why the Impact Factor of Journals Should Not Be Used for Evaluating Research', *British Medical Journal*, February: 314–497.

Serra, A. (1623) *Breve trattato delle cause che possono far abbondare li regni d'oro, d'argento dove non sono miniere: Con appliczione al regno di Napoli*, Naples: Lazzaro Scorriggio.

Sharman, J. (2006) *Havens in a Storm: The Struggle for Global Tax Regulation*, Ithaca, NY: Cornell University Press.

Sinclair, T. (2005) *The New Masters of Capitalism: American Bond Rating Agencies and the Politics of Creditworthiness*, Ithaca, NY: Cornell University Press.

Sindjoun, L. (1999) 'L'Afrique dans la Science des Relations Internationales: Notes Introductive et Provisoires pour une Sociologie de la Connaissance Internationalist', *Revue Africaine de Sociologie*, 3(2): 142–67.

Singer, D.A. (2004) 'Capital Rules: The Domestic Politics of International Regulatory Harmonization', *International Organization*, 58(3): 531–65.

Singer, D.A. (2007) *Regulating Capital: Setting Standards for the International Financial System*, Ithaca, NY: Cornell University Press.

Singer, P. (2004) 'Outsiders: Our Obligations to Those Beyond Our Borders', in D.K. Chatterjee (ed.) *The Ethics of Assistance*, Cambridge: Cambridge University Press, 11–32.

Slaughter, A.-M. (2004) *A New World Order*, Princeton, NJ: Princeton University Press.

Sobel, A. (2006) *Political Economy and Global Affairs*, Washington, DC: CQ Press.

Soederberg, S. (2006) *Global Governance in Question: Empire, Class, and the New Common Sense in Managing North-South Relations*, London: Pluto Press.

Soros, G. (2008) *The New Paradigm for Financial Markets: The Credit Crisis of 2008 and What It Means*, New York: Public Affairs.

Spengler, O. (1928) *The Decline of the West*, New York: Knopf.

Steans, J. and Tepe, D. (forthcoming) 'What's "Critical" About Critical IPE? Critical Theory/Feminist Theory and the Crisis of Social Reproduction', *Journal of International Relations and Development.*

Stilwell, F. (2006) *Political Economy: The Contest of Economic Ideas*, Melbourne: Oxford University Press.

Stone, R.W. (2008) 'The Scope of IMF Conditionality', *International Organization*, 62(4): 589–620.

Stopford, J. and Strange, S. (1991) *Rival States, Rival Firms*, Oxford: Blackwell.

Strange, S. (1970) 'International Economics and International Relations: A Case of Mutual Neglect', *International Affairs*, 46(2): 304–15.

Strange, S. (1970) 'The Politics of International Currencies in World Politics', *World Politics*, 23(2): 215–31.

Strange, S. (1971) *Sterling and British Policy: A Political Study of an International Currency in Decline*, London and New York: Oxford University Press.

Strange, S. (1976) *International Monetary Relations*, vol. 2 of Andrew Shonfield (ed.) *International Economic Relations of the Western World 1959–1971*, Oxford: Oxford University Press.

Strange, S. (1984) *Paths to International Political Economy*, London: Unwin Press.

Strange, S. (1986) *Casino Capitalism*, Oxford: Blackwell.

Strange, S. (1988) *States and Markets*, London: Pinter.

Susan, S. (1989) 'I Never Meant to Be an Academic', in J. Kruzel and J.N. Rosenau (eds) *Journeys through World Politics*, Lexington, KY: Lexington Books.

Strange, S. (1991) 'An Eclectic Approach', in C.M. Murphy and R. Tooze (eds) *The New International Political Economy*, Basingstoke: Macmillan, pp. 33–49.

Strange, S. (1994) 'Wake Up, Krasner! The World Has Changed', *Review of International Political Economy*, 1(2): 209–20.

Strange, S. (1995) 'The Limits of Politics', *Government & Opposition*, 30(3): 291–311.

Strange, S. (1995) '1995 Presidential Election: ISA as a Microcosm', *International Studies Quarterly*, 39(3): 289–96.

Strange, S. (1998) *Mad Money*, Manchester: Manchester University Press.

Strange, S. and Tooze, R. (1981) *The International Politics of Surplus Capacity: Competition for Market Shares in the World Recession*, London: Allen & Unwin.

Summers, L. (2008a) 'America Needs to Make a New Case for Trade', *Financial Times*, 28 April: 9.

Summers, L. (2008b) 'A Strategy to Promote Healthy Globalization', *Financial Times*, 4 May.

Swedberg, R. (1990) 'The New "Battle of Methods"', *Challenge*, 33(1): 33–8.

Underhill, G.R.D. (ed.) (1997) *The New World Order in International Finance*, New York: St. Martin's Press.

Underhill, G.R.D. (2000) 'State, Market, and Global Political Economy: Genealogy of an (Inter-?) Discipline', *International Affairs*, 76(4): 805–24.

Underhill, G.R.D. (2009) 'Political Economy, the "US School," and the Manifest Destiny of Everyone Else', *New Political Economy*, 14(3): 347–56.

van Apeldoorn, B., Drahokoupil, J. and Horn, L. (eds) (2009) *The Contradictions and Limits of Neoliberal European Governance: From Lisbon to Lisbon*, London: Palgrave Macmillan.

Vasquez, J. (1998) *The Power of Power Politics: From Classical Realism to Neotraditionalism*, Cambridge: Cambridge University Press.

Verbeek, B. (2000) 'Criticizing US Method and Thought in International Relations: Why a Trans-Atlantic Divide Narrows IR's Research Subject', in T.C. Lawton, J.N. Rosenau and A.C. Verdun (eds) *Strange Power: Shaping the Parameters of International Relations and International Political Economy*, Aldershot: Ashgate, 139–57.

Vernon, R. (1971) *Sovereignty at Bay: The Multinational Spread of U.S. Enterprises*, New York: Basic Books.

Vogel, D. (1995) *Trading Up: Consumer and Environmental Regulation in a Global Economy*, Cambridge, MA: Harvard University Press.

Vogel, S. (1996) *Freer Markets, More Rules: Regulatory Reform in Advanced Industrial Societies*, Ithaca, NY: Cornell University Press.

Wade, R. (1992) 'East Asia's Economic Success', *World Politics*, 44(2): 270–320.

Wade, R. (2004) *Governing the Market*, 2nd edn, Princeton, NJ: Princeton University Press.

Wade, R. (2007a) "Globalization as the Institutionalization of Neoliberalism: Commodification, Financialization, and the Anchorless Economy', in W.R. Garside (ed.) *Institutions and Market Economies*, New York: Palgrave Macmillan.

Wade, R. (2007b). 'Should We Worry about Income Inequality?', in D. Held and A. Kaya (eds) *Global Inequality*, New York: Polity.

Wade, R. (2009) 'Be Careful What You Wish For: Lessons for International Political Economy from the Transformation of Economics', *Review of International Political Economy*, 16(1): 106–21.

Wade, R. and Goldstein, M. (2003) 'The Causes of Village Cooperation: Comment on Ragin et al.', *Field Methods*, 15(4): 341–50.

Waever, O. (1998) 'The Sociology of a Not So International Discipline', *International Organization*, 52(4): 687–728.

Wallerstein, I.M. (1988) *Utopistics: Or Historical Choices of the Twenty-First Century*, New York: The New Press.

Waltz, K. (1979) *Theory of International Politics*, New York: McGraw-Hill.

Wang, G. (2002a) *To Act is to Know: Chinese Dilemmas*, Singapore: Times Academic Press.

Wang, G. (2002b) *Bind Us in Time: Nation and Civilization in Asia*, Singapore: Times Academic Press.

Wang, G. (2003a) *Anglo-Chinese Encounters since 1800: War, Trade, Science & Governance*, Cambridge: Cambridge University Press.

Wang, G. (2003b) *Ideas Won't Keep: The Struggle for China's Future*, Singapore: Eastern University Press.

Watson, M. (2006) *Foundations of International Political Economy*, Basingstoke: Palgrave Macmillan.

Weaver, C. (2008) *Hypocrisy Trap: The World Bank and the Poverty of Reform*, Princeton, NJ: Princeton University Press.

Weingast, B. and Wittman, D.A. (eds) (2006) *The Oxford Handbook of Political Economy*, Oxford: Oxford University Press.

Wendt, A. (1987) 'The Agent–Structure Problem in International Relations Theory', *International Organization*, 41(3): 335–70.

Wendt, A. (1999) *Social Theory of International Politics*, New York: Cambridge University Press.

Wight, C. (2006) *Agents, Structures, and International Relations: Politics as Ontology*, Cambridge: Cambridge University Press.

Winchester, S. (2008) *The Man Who Loved China*, New York: HarperCollins.

Wolf, M. (2004) *Why Globalization Works*, New Haven, CT: Yale University Press.

Wood, D. (2005) *Governing Global Banking: The Basel Committee and the Politics of Financial Globalisation*, Aldershot: Ashgate.

Zacher, M. and Matthew, R. (1995) 'Liberal International Theory', in C. Kegley (ed.) *Controversies in International Relations Theory*, New York: St. Martin's Press.

Zakaria, F. (2008) *The Post-American World*, New York: W.W. Norton.

Index